The Ideal of the Practical

Colombia's Struggle to Form a Technical Elite

Latin American Monographs, No. 39

Sponsored by the Institute of Latin American Studies The University of Texas at Austin

Frank
Safford

The Ideal of
the Practical

Colombia's Struggle to
Form a Technical Elite

University of Texas Press
Austin & London

T95
.S2

Library of Congress Cataloging in Publication Data

Safford, Frank, 1935–
  The ideal of the practical.

  (Latin American monographs; no. 39)
  Bibliography: p.
  Includes index.
  1. Technical education—Colombia—History.
2. Colombia—Economic conditions. I. Title.
II. Series.
T95.S2   607'.861   75-16072
ISBN 0-292-73803-X

With Joan,

for my parents

Contents

Preface   xiii

Conventions Followed   xvii

Introduction   3

Part One. Colombia: Its Geography and Society   19
1. Opportunities and Incentives   21

Part Two. Moral and Industrial Education   47
2. Learning to Work   49

**Part Three. Academic Science for the Upper Class:
Bourbons and Neo-Bourbons**   81
3. The Enlightenment in New Granada   85
4. The Neo-Bourbons, 1821–1845   99
5. The Decline of Neo-Bourbonism   124

**Part Four. The Origins of a Colombian Engineering
Profession**   141
6. Study Abroad   147
7. The Colegio Militar   166
8. Stumbling Progress, 1863–1903   185
9. A Place for Engineers   209

Epilogue   227

Appendixes   243
1. Prominent Public Figures Who Promoted Technical
   Education, 1821–1864   244

2. Students in the Care of Gen. Pedro Alcántara Herrán,
   1848–1863   252

3. Careers of Prominent Alumni of Colegio Militar,
   1848–1854   264

Notes   271

Glossary   327

Bibliographic Note   331

Bibliography   333

Index   363

Tables and Maps

Tables

1. Primary Education: Statistical Comparison by Region   32
2. Representative Government Salaries, 1836–1839   36 & 37
3. Educational Investment, 1847   51
4. Total Enrollment in Public and Private Primary Schools, Selected Years, 1834–1852   54
5. Foundlings in the Casa de Refugio at Date of Annual Report   61
6. Chairs Authorized or Reauthorized by Congress, September, 1832–September, 1838   110
7. Enrollments in Public Institutions of Secondary and Higher Education, by Field   131
8. Students from the Hispanic World Who Attended Rensselaer Polytechnic Institute, 1850–1884   150
9. Provinces of Origin of Students Enrolled in the Colegio Militar   175
10. Students in the Escuelas Superiores of the National University, by Faculty   194
11. Engineering Students by Field, 1965   237

Maps

1. Physical Map of Colombia   22
2. Topographical Profile of Colombia   23
3. Political Map of Colombia   28

Preface

THIS volume is an outgrowth of earlier research into aspects of economic development in nineteenth-century Colombia. It deals with the problem of inculcating the technical skills and value orientations appropriate for economic development into an aristocratic society notably lacking in such skills and values. Both antieconomic values and lack of technical skill can be ascribed in part to economic isolation and a lack of compelling economic opportunities. This being the case, how in an isolated, relatively undynamic economy, can these remedial economic orientations be introduced? This particular study deals with the efforts of Colombian political leaders, primarily men of conservative hue, to carry on the Bourbon aim of introducing "useful knowledge" and an appreciation of the value of useful knowledge into their country during the years before 1900.

The study describes and analyzes the intentions, principal efforts, and achievements of the political leaders who attempted to implant scientific and technical education in Colombia. As until 1870 their efforts were largely failures, one must question why they failed. Were dominant cultural values solely responsible? Should one not look to other intractable problems for part of the answer? And if dominant cultural values played an important role in the retardation of technical education, in what ways did these values work to frustrate the aims of those who would have changed them?

This study argues that, while social structure and social values tended to retard the development of a Colombian technical elite, an extremely limited economy presented the more fundamental obstruction—for a static economy provided the context in which anti- or untechnical values were formed. Only when economic growth created a demand for technical skills could such values be modified effectively. Thus economic growth, at least in the nineteenth century, was a prerequisite for, more than a product of, successful technical training. It should be noted, however, that the relationships between an economy and technical training are not simple or singular. Although technical education proved unable to cut through the ties binding the stagnant economy of the nineteenth century, it doubtless is of greater relevance, indeed of strategic importance, in the more dynamic change of the twentieth century.

This study is not intended as a general survey of Colombian education in the nineteenth century. It does not deal with primary education, a major theme in itself. Nor does it pretend to present a thorough structural analysis of secondary or university education in all its ramifications. It covers various, though not all, aspects of scientific or technical education, including training in manual arts and crafts. In the area of academic science it focuses primarily on the engineering sciences. Medical science enters in only tangentially. Medicine was a socially approved profession, one that New Granadan youths did not hesitate to pursue at the beginning of the republican era. The development of medicine, therefore, met with no resistance from traditional social values.

The story of Colombia's nineteenth-century struggle toward the practical is presented in topical segments that overlap chronologically. Early efforts in industrial training (chap. 2) and academic science (chaps. 3–5) were made more or less contemporaneously (1760–1850). Industrial training is considered before academic science because the latter more closely relates to the subsequent development of engineering education and an engineering profession (1845–1900) (chaps. 6–9).

In this study the term *elites* refers to leading figures in some field of endeavor (politics, education, economic enterprise, etc.). The elites discussed here may be considered members of the upper class. But *elites* and *upper class* are not interchangeable terms; the former applies only to those members of the upper class who played a leadership role. When the term *elites* is used without a modifier, it refers to political leaders. Other kinds of elite are explicitly identified.

Research for this study was aided by support from the Research Committee of Northwestern University and the Spencer Foundation– Northwestern University Interdisciplinary Research in Education Program. I am indebted to several fellow laborers in the vineyard for their aid. John L. Young, whose dissertation "The University Reform in New Granada, 1820–1850" approaches some of the matter of this book from a different angle, has generously shared information with me and helped to enlighten me on various points. Prominent among those to whom I am indebted for access to essential research materials are J. Leon Helguera of Vanderbilt University; Fr. Alberto Lee López, archivist of the Academia de Historia, Bogotá; Dr. Jaime Duarte French, director of the Biblioteca Luis Angel Arango; and Marjorie Carpenter of the Northwestern University

Library. I am also indebted to a host of reference librarians—too many to name—in universities across the United States. In research I have benefited from leads suggested by Roger Brew, Malcolm Dees, Guillermo Hernández de Alba, Jaime Jaramillo Uribe, and Robert Bezucha. George H. Daniels and various participants in his symposium on nineteenth-century American science (Northwestern University, spring, 1970) helped me to develop a comparative reference point. Helpful suggestions on the manuscript have been offered by a number of friends and colleagues, most notably Woodrow Borah, David Bushnell, William Coleman, George H. Daniels, Richard Graham, Edward Malefakis, James J. Sheehan, and Robert Wiebe. My wife, Joan, has provided steady encouragement and indispensable editorial advice at every stage of the writing.

Conventions Followed

DURING the period covered in this volume the country now known as the Republic of Colombia went under a variety of names. In the colonial era it was known as el Nuevo Reino de Granada, and in the republican period it was called Colombia (including Venezuela and Ecuador, 1819[1822]–1830), Nueva Granada (1832–1857), the Confederación Granadina (1857–1863), Estados Unidos de Colombia (1863–1886), and, finally, Republic of Colombia (1886–present). In discussions of the colonial period the area's inhabitants are called New Granadans, and in discussions dealing with the years from 1819 to 1863 they are called either Colombians or New Granadans.

Another convention should be noted. Most of the political leaders with whom the first parts of this study deal formed part of a political group that became increasingly cohesive after 1830. Ultimately the group formed the backbone of the Conservative party. But this party was not so called until 1849. Before that time the group went under several names—*moderados* in the 1830s, *ministeriales* in the late 1830s and 1840s. In this study these men are usually referred to by the term appropriate to the period under discussion. But they are also sometimes designated as neo-Bourbons, conservatives, and, after 1849, Conservatives. Similarly, after 1849 liberals become Liberals.

The value of the Colombian peso varied during the period covered in this study. Until 1810 it was comparable to the dollar. In the republican era its relative value declined, and by the 1840s it was worth approximately 80 percent of the dollar. Efforts to reestablish the peso as more or less equivalent to the dollar (1847–1880) were not entirely successful. After 1880 paper inflation brought a rapid decline in the value of the peso, making it difficult to establish the value of the currency for the period as a whole. For the period 1820 to 1880 one may think of the peso as being worth roughly 80 to 100 percent of the dollar.

The Ideal of the Practical

Colombia's Struggle to Form a Technical Elite

". . . there is no country where more *doctores* are encountered than in Bogotá; and the story is told that a Spaniard recently arrived in this capital asked why the Granadans had changed the old title of *don*, which was used in Spain, for that of *doctor* . . ."

Counselheiro Miguel María Lisboa, 1853
(*Relaçao de uma viagem a Venezuela, Nova Granada e Equador*, p. 254)

Introduction

FOR years foreign observers and many Latin Americans have believed that the dominant social values in Latin America constitute fundamental obstructions to economic development. With a resounding unanimity, North American and other students of the region have declared that Latin Americans fall on what might be considered the "negative" side (from an American or positivistic-developmental perspective) of Talcott Parsons's pattern variables. Though a careful student of Latin America can perceive notable evidence of achievement orientation, it is nonetheless true that its society has been strongly laced with ascriptive values. To a greater degree than in the United States, work has been viewed by most sectors as a necessary evil rather than as a means of self-fulfillment. Those who have been able to do so have shied away from manual labor as destructive of status. Latin American societies in general, and the upper classes in particular, have been considered weak in those pursuits that North Americans consider practical, such as the assimilation, creation, and manipulation of technology and business enterprise in general. The Latin American upper classes have been noted for their devotion to the study of law, the humanities, and the arts and their lack of interest in the natural sciences and technology. In the hands of the upper classes, Latin America's educational systems, at least in times past, have been dedicated to forming and maintaining the political elite and have been only mildly effective in furthering such economically practical aims as the broad diffusion of literacy and technical capacities.[1]

In many respects Colombian society has exemplified these stereotypical conceptions of Latin American values and behavior. But it would be a mistake to consider the values of the Colombian upper classes or those of the upper classes of other Latin American countries as entirely homogeneous. In any society or social group as it really exists the attitudes and behavior of individuals do not correspond to the ideal types constructed by social theorists. Value systems are not absolutes but rather ways of depicting preponderant tendencies. Nevertheless, in practice, social scientists often take little notice of social tendencies running counter to the dominant ones. As a result, the unwary student (and perhaps also the social scientist himself) is led to confuse ideal types with reality. When the complexities, tensions, and struggles within a society are ignored, the picture painted is a rather static and two-dimensional caricature.

This study examines the efforts of a segment of the Colombian upper class to alter the dominant values of their society in the years between 1760 and 1900. Nineteenth-century Colombia was dominated by an upper class whose values were in many respects markedly aristocratic. Individuals with pretensions to social status shunned manual labor. And the upper sector tended to seek patents of social honor through the pursuit of legal, political, or literary careers. There were nonetheless countervailing tendencies. Leading upper-class politicians recognized the obstacles to economic development posed by many of the dominant patterns, and they worked to alter at least some of them. The development-oriented political elite tried to introduce various forms of technical education. Their purpose was not merely to provide their society with the mechanical tools for economic progress. They also hoped through technical training to instill new, more practical value orientations in the upper and lower classes alike. Most fondly they hoped that technical education would divert upper-sector youths from legal, literary, and political careers and toward more productive economic enterprise.

The development-sponsoring minority within the Colombian upper class was not a "deviant" group, at least in the sense that the term is usually applied in social science literature. Its members were not subordinate in the society but rather among its leading, most respected figures. This fact had important implications for the success or failure of their efforts. Colombia's nineteenth-century advocates of the technical were in an ambiguous situation. They were political leaders, in many cases trained in the law, who were attempting to steer succeeding generations away from the paths they had followed. As they were preeminent symbols of the prevailing legal-bureaucratic pattern, they were not in a good position to urge others to shun political careers. The development-sponsoring elite presented a confusing model in more than occupational terms. Some of its members who were politicians behaved in ways that contradicted their own doctrines. Not only were they devoted to politics, but also, in its practice, some of them displayed the kind of passion for honorifics that they decried as destructive features of their society. Thus, as models for Colombian youths, their own careers belied their preachments.

What follows is a dramatization of the competition of opposing values within the ranks of the Colombian elite and even, at different levels of consciousness, within single individuals. This study attempts to take into account not only how values affect economic, social, or political behavior, but also how the economic, social, and political contexts condition values. Do opportunities within the society reinforce the dominant values or subordinate competing ones? Do models of behavior exist that will encourage a shift in values, or do the most compelling social models tend to perpetuate currently dominant values? These are some of the questions that should be considered, at least in subordinate clauses, as we so confidently pronounce judgment on people of other cultures.

While recognizing the complexity and the reciprocal character of the relationships between economic and social structures and social values, I have been guided in my interpretation by the belief that values are more likely to be determined by structures than the other way around. My assumptions have been similar to those of Aldo Solari in his discussion of secondary education and elite development in the twentieth century:

> . . . the scale of values is deeply rooted in the real structure of occupational opportunities afforded in Latin America . . . the traditional scale of values encourages certain studies that lead to definite activities; experience shows that these are . . . the most open, the best compensated, and carry the greatest social prestige . . . It is not, therefore, the mere inheritance of certain values that maintains the structure in almost unchanged form. To a great extent, it is the structure that supports the traditional system of values. The scale of values is actually not as static as it is sometimes thought to be. Where there are structural changes favorable to certain activities, when these activities are in strong demand and their level of compensation rises, those activities, as is logical, rise rapidly in the scale of social prestige.[2]

Thus, while noting the operation of values as a deterrent to development, one must also look at the ways in which the economic and political context narrows choices and conditions behavior and values.

One problem frequently arising in this study is how seriously to take the statements and actions of the political elite. Upper-class leaders often confected grandiose plans, many if not most of which remained largely unfulfilled—*programas soñados* ("fantasy plans"), as one young Colombian recently called them. Anyone with experience in Latin America is familiar with the phenomenon of elaborate projects that exist only on paper (*quedan escritos*). What do they signify? Should one take the programs and the rhetoric at face value and look solely to external causes for the explanation of failure? Or should the pattern of repeated failure lead one to suspect that the speeches and projects were no more than professions of pious hopes to which not even their proponents were seriously committed? This study considers both possibilities. In some cases the evident internal contradictions in the attitudes of the elite seem to call for skepticism. Nevertheless, the consistency with which at least some Colombian leaders pursued their educational goals leads one to believe that they meant some of what they said. It is well to remember also that not all the plans of Latin Americans go awry. When their projects take hold and flourish, is it because the advocates of successful plans are purer of intention than those of failures, or is it because the external conditions happen to be more propitious? One may entertain the former possibility, but in this study the latter is considered to be more important.

The Cultural Heritage

The traditional indifference of Latin America's upper sectors to the technical and the economically productive has frequently been ascribed to cultural heritage. There is much to be said for this approach. As in the case of France, the upper sectors of Spanish society in the early modern period were dominated and molded by a military-bureaucratic culture. Among the aristocracy state power and service to the state played a more notable role and independent economic enterprise played a less important one than among the aristocracy in England. The Spanish military-bureaucratic culture is generally linked to the Iberian reconquista, in which chronic strife encouraged the dominance of a military aristocracy and its values over other groups in the society. A nobility built on privileges conceded for military services from the ninth to the thirteenth centuries found itself challenged from the thirteenth to the fifteenth centuries by new commercial groups. The nobility set itself apart from the emerging merchants, bolstering its claim to social superiority by adopting an essentially noncommercial code of honor—emphasizing liberality as well as the avoidance of some kinds of trade and manual labor. The nobility's special position was codified in the thirteenth-century *Siete Partidas*, which cautioned Spanish nobles against defilement in commerce. After the reconquista, military values were reinforced by Spain's elaborate efforts to defend its European empire and the Catholic faith. In the imperial period, the Spanish nobility increasingly based its claim to special privilege not merely on its military function but on administrative service to the Crown. During the sixteenth and seventeenth centuries, there developed a concept of honor, a rationale for noble privilege founded on an ideal of public service that rejected petty profit making. These idealized conceptions, which often failed to correspond completely to real behavior, were adopted more broadly in the society, most particularly by those who stood close enough to aristocratic status to be able to aspire to it.[3]

Public service as an ideal could in fact be appropriated by one nonnoble sector of Spanish society, the university-educated *letrados* who emerged to staff the Spanish royal (and later imperial) bureaucracy. Like their noble superiors, Spain's lawyer-bureaucrats could argue that as makers and executors of the law they performed a superior social function. The near nobility of the *letrado* was recognized by special privileges and honors conceded in the *Siete Partidas* and afterward. In the thirteenth-century law code, masters of civil law were granted the title of *caballero* or *señor de leyes*; and, at least in theory, doctors of law could retire as counts.[4] The university degree in law therefore represented a form of ennoblement. The Spanish word *título*, it may be noted, applies both to titles of nobility and to professional patents. University education for the Spanish bourgeoisie was a channel to, an approximation of, nobility. Thus, Spain brought to the New World not merely the ideal of the disinterested noble but also that of the *letrado* as a public servant of high status.

The Iberian patterns were confirmed by the Hispanic experience in the New World. In America the place of the subordinated Moslem population was taken by the even larger and more submissive and more exploitable Indian and African ones. From the very beginnings of Hispanic America there existed a socioeconomic base for constructing a new nobility patterned on the established ones in Spain and Portugal. The European conquest temporarily revived the governing roles of warrior and priest, and over the long run the lawyer-bureaucrat became a central figure in the colonial system. In the upper sectors of Hispanic American society, the association of work with servility, of leisure with honor, was reinforced. As in Iberia a university education in the law followed by a bureaucratic career in either the ecclesiastical or civil arms of the government was looked upon as a sure road to social honor. Even if it did not lead to royal service, a university education conferred status, for entering the university meant admission to a privileged and exclusive corporate group whose members were certified as "pure of blood" and enjoyed honors and dignities that placed them apart from the general population.

The values and institutional forms inherited from Spain and Portugal help to explain why Hispanic Americans were drawn toward literary-legal education and government service. To understand why economic enterprise and technical development were retarded, however, it is necessary to look not only at inherited institutions and values but also at the choices presented by Hispanic American economic contexts.

Economic and Social Structures

In the colonial period Hispanic upper-class control over a subservient labor population and a virtual upper-class monopoly of land and other economic resources created an economic structure that discouraged interest in technical development. Upper-class control of land and labor made it possible to hold down wages. Low pay meant that local markets lacked a broad base and were rather anemic. Because of the weakness of demand and the low cost of labor, the colonial economy provided no stimulus to labor-saving and other technical advances. Thus the upper class, which had the economic resources required to undertake innovations, had little interest in doing so. The lower classes, which to the end of the colonial period were almost entirely illiterate, were ignorant of possibilities for technical improvement, as well as too poor and vulnerable to risk significant innovations. In any case, they, too, were constrained by the limited possibilities of a poor market.

The concentration of economic resources in the hands of the upper class also perpetuated a social system that discouraged an interest in economic enterprise or in the technical. Oligopoly control of economic resources strictly limited opportunities for social mobility. Limited economic opportunities and a relatively static social structure provided a context in which ascriptive values rather than achievement orientations flourished. With few visible economic or social opportunities, the lower classes subsided into a state of depressed fatalism. Because manual labor was identified with a despised subservient class, the upper sector of society felt strong social prohibitions against close involvement with the process of production. The upper class was therefore not simply indolent but also largely abstracted from the techniques of production. Little hope of technical innovation could be hoped for from this quarter.

Thus the distribution of income and the social structure in colonial New Granada and republican Colombia limited both the market demand required to stimulate technical innovation and the proportion of the society that might have worked to introduce such innovations. This is markedly in contrast with the situation of such pioneers in the Industrial Revolution as

England and English America. In these countries somewhat better income distribution and relatively high wages for labor provided broad consumer bases, with demand particularly strong for inexpensive standardized goods that could be produced by mechanized factory methods.[5] Comparatively high lower-sector incomes provided the demand required for technical change to occur, and the relative social mobility and interpenetration of classes in these societies helped to supply innovators. Social mobility encouraged large segments of the English and English American societies to believe that achievement might be rewarded, while the interpenetration of classes enabled members of the upper classes to feel that commercial and industrial activity was not demeaning. More particularly, economic opportunity and social mobility promoted the emergence of ambitious, energetic, literate, skilled craftsmen. Dynamically growing demand in both England and English America fostered the development of numerous communities with what might be called a "shop culture," in which various machine builders competed to solve fairly clearly defined technical problems obstructing the advance of productivity.[6]

While the social structure played a major part in creating demand and making possible the supply of technical skills, it was not the only important factor distinguishing the technologically advanced nations from Colombia. Colombia's geographic structure also sharply limited technology-inducing demand. The industrial progress of both England and English America was greatly aided by topographies that permitted cheap internal transportation of raw materials and the integration of the domestic markets. In addition to easy integration of domestic markets, England and English America had populations and resources well located for early and expeditious involvement in maritime commerce, and foreign trade helped to supplement domestic demand. In Colombia, as in many parts of Latin America, however, the size of the domestic market was drastically limited by a difficult mountainous topography, which held most of its population in relatively small pockets. Further, most of these pockets were locked in the interior and could not easily engage in foreign trade. This problem of geographical structure may be thought of as the true foundation of Colombia's technical backwardness, for the social structure might be modified by an active economy, but the economy could be activitated only if some means could be found to break through the topographical obstructions to trade.

In addition to geography and social structure, a third element limiting Colombia's technological progress was the country's stock of scientific and technical knowledge. As bastions of the Counter-Reformation, Spain and her dominions resisted the new, un-Aristotelian scientific conceptions of the sixteenth and seventeenth centuries more tenaciously than other parts of the Atlantic world. In England the abolition of religious orders in 1530 freed the universities from scholastic dogmas and opened them to the eventual penetration of new intellectual currents. By the end of the seventeenth century British universities had embraced the Copernican and Cartesian systems; in the persons of William Harvey, Robert Boyle, Isaac Newton and others, England had already made substantial contributions to the European scientific revolution; and the Royal Society (1662) stood as a monument to the Baconian ideal of practically oriented, experimental scientific development. Recent research also indicates that much of the new science was being absorbed by British craftsmen, primarily clock and other instrument makers, who contributed importantly to the work of England's gentleman scientists.[7] In France, in a somewhat different manner, a parallel development occurred, at least in higher education and among gentleman scientists. In Spain, however, the new scientific ideas were not effectively introduced until the middle of the eighteenth century (with the works of Fray Benito Gerónimo Feijóo y Montenegro), and the academic monopoly of religious orders and medieval schools was not breached until the 1760s. Baconian societies of gentlemen interested in practical applications of science appeared almost a century after they had taken root in England and France. Though the Crown and a fraction of the upper sectors made a strenuous effort to catch up to England and France in the latter part of the eighteenth century, Spain and her progeny remained at the margin of European scientific activity; they were at best passive recipients of advances developed elsewhere.

Of the three problems noted here—a difficult geography, a rigid social structure, and the outdated stock of scientific and technical knowledge— the last was the least fundamental and, seemingly, the most easily remedied. Geography could be conquered only by radical improvements in overland transportation, which in the nineteenth century meant the railroad. But railroad construction was extremely expensive in tropical, mountainous countries. Changing the social structure was an even more painful proposition; indeed it was unlikely, if not impossible, in the absence of substantial economic movement. The stock of scientific and technical knowledge, on the other hand, seemed to nineteenth-century Colombian leaders at least susceptible of improvement at a cost that the country might sustain. In a certain superficial sense this was true. By importing a few foreign science teachers and by sending Colombian youths abroad for training, the upper class could be introduced to new scientific ideas at relatively little cost. At a somewhat greater cost, the lower classes might be introduced to new techniques if they could be made literate and taught elementary mathematics. On the other hand, the idea that scientific and technical learning might achieve a significant developmental breakthrough was something of an illusion. As long as economic demand remained limited by geography and social structure, neither the upper nor the lower classes could have much effective interest in the new scientific ideas or techniques.

Thus, the efforts of Colombia's political leaders to inculcate the practical were obstructed by factors beyond their control. Political and economic conditions in nineteenth-century Colombia did not provide a favorable environment for the kind of change they advocated. Colombia's poor and backward economy offered little opportunity for economic enterprise and even less demand for the services of the technically trained. Unfavorable economic circumstances were complicated by the country's unstable politics, which weakened government support for any kind of technical development and thwarted the plans of private entrepreneurs.

Lacking favorable economic conditions, the Colombian leaders placed excessive faith in formal education as an instrument for changing values. The instrument, of course, was inadequate to the purpose. Technical training alone, without the support and stimulus of a vigorously growing economy could not work the dramatic change in values that they sought. For a long time technical instruction was able to survive only in a vestigial form because the Colombian economy could neither provide the financial basis to sustain effective educational institutions nor offer attractive professional opportunities.

Ultimately, toward the end of the nineteenth century, the Colombian economy began to develop sufficiently to provide a base for a small native technical elite. Although some progress has been made during the twentieth century, Colombia continues to pay dearly for its nineteenth-century stagnation. While the country can now boast its own corps of engineers and technicians, Colombia, like other Latin American countries, remains a consumer rather than a creator of technology.

Though the endeavors of Colombia's nineteenth-century leaders were largely frustrated, their efforts indicate that value attachments in Latin American society have been more ambiguous than they generally are represented to be. The story of their largely unsuccessful efforts provides some insight into the problems of a traditional, yet modernizing, elite as it attempts to modify existing values and patterns of behavior, introducing newer, only partly desired, ones.

The Ideal of the Practical

The material in this study falls into three topical groupings—education in the manual arts, the natural sciences, and engineering. These topical groups also correspond very roughly to a chronological division in the book. The first two sections of this study encompass the first forty or fifty years of the republican era (to about 1865). It is a period marked by intense political strife and rather little economic progress. During the first three decades of the period some patterns of thought and institutions still strongly bore the marks of the late Bourbon colonial era, although the attitudes of the Anglo-American bourgeoisie were rapidly penetrating. An understanding of this period, therefore, requires some attention to its colonial roots. The latter part of the early republican era, particularly the decade of the 1850s, was one of struggle by political Liberals to demolish the remnants of Spanish institutional patterns and to substitute others based on Anglo-American models. The second broad period, to which the last chapters of the book are devoted, is that from the middle of the 1860s onward, a period during which the struggle over the colonial inheritance receded to the background and Bourbon models and attitudes were no longer so noticeable. In this period Colombia became more effectively engaged in the tasks of economic modernization—the founding of banks, the construction of railroads, the expansion of primary education, the incorporation of technical training into the university, and ultimately the establishment of manufacturing. Among Colombia's upper classes, at least formally, the Anglo-European bourgeois style had largely displaced the Spanish colonial one, though the Colombian upper class continued to use these new forms in accord with their inherited social tradition.

Most of the book deals with the activities of Colombian leaders prominent in the neo-Bourbon era, men who played important roles in governing the country and forming its policies, particularly between 1819 and 1850. Of those who took an interest in the advancement of technical training, almost all were firmly ensconced in the upper class. Indeed, in most cases they figured among the most honored of aristocratic families. Many were the descendants of Bourbon administrators. Most were the sons of substantial landowners and were themselves large landowners. Almost all passed their childhoods either in the leading colonial cities of New Granada (Bogotá, Cartagena, Popayán) or on their parents' haciendas. Almost all, no matter in what province they were born, received secondary or higher education in Bogotá, in most cases studying at one of the two seedbeds of the elite, the Colegio del Rosario or the Colegio San Bartolomé. Of a group of eighteen political leaders selected for their prominence in the cause of practical education, at least five studied with some of New Granada's scientists or science teachers of the late Bourbon period. Although all of them had some exposure to the natural sciences in their "philosophy" courses, only two had a background in what could be considered engineering. Most of them had taken the conventional course in the law (see Appendix 1).

The science-promoting political leaders of the first half of the nineteenth century were descended from Bourbon administrators, when not carnally, at least intellectually and spiritually. Few of their ideas were without precedent in the Spanish Enlightenment. They were exponents of what Jean Sarrailh has termed a "culture utilitaire et culture dirigée." They wanted to implant practicality, in part as a means of preserving social order. Spanish Bourbon administrators and New Granadan elites alike believed that maintaining social order required more than moralistic preaching. The masses would live virtuously only if their energies were engaged by productive activity; this meant that the state and the elite must channel them into profitable employment through technical training.[8]

Like the Spanish Bourbons the early republican elite sought to direct the upper classes as well as the poor toward technology and economic enterprise. Just as Gaspar Melchor de Jovellanos denounced the idleness and vacuity of the Spanish aristocracy and called for their redirection from sterile "literary careers" toward scientific and technical ones, so nineteenth-century Colombians like Lino de Pombo, Pedro Alcántara Herrán, and Mariano Ospina Rodríguez harped on the same theme. In late eighteenth-century Spain and nineteenth-century Colombia the enlightened elite attempted to introduce a new technical orientation in the upper class by importing foreign science instructors and by sending well-born youth abroad to scientific centers. In both cases the elite's stated interest was more in the practical, the technical, and the productive, than in the theoretical, the scientific, and the intellectual. Although they were not averse to nurturing creative scientists, their first concern was to create a corps of technicians and entrepreneurs who could help them catch up economically with the more advanced countries of the Western world. They recognized, however, that technical and economic advances require more than simply absorbing a received technology. It was necessary to inculcate a scientific approach to knowledge, emphasizing the development of reason rather than the memorization of authoritative truths. There was a limit, of course, to their enthusiasm for scientific rationalism. Both the Spanish lights of the eighteenth century and the New Granadan conservatives vigorously rejected the atheistic-materialistic aspects of the Western Enlightenment. As traditional, yet modernizing, elites, they wished to appropriate only those new ideas that were necessary for the economic advancement of their countries.

While the New Granadan neo-Bourbons shared many attitudes of the Spanish Bourbons, they also diverged from them in some respects. William J. Callahan has argued that eighteenth-century Spanish writers promoted practical occupations for the nobility without abandoning the traditional condemnation of profit pinching and the ideal of public service as a justification for class privilege. The Spanish Bourbons simply redefined public service to include large-scale commerce and the arts.[9] There was something of this in New Granada's neo-Bourbons. Certainly in their rhetoric public service was an obligation inherent in upper-class status, large-scale merchants were viewed as workers of the public weal, and the appeal to patriotism figured heavily in all their preachments for an upper-class turn to the practical. On the other hand, the New Granadan upper class was only the palest shadow of the Spanish nobility; and from the very start of the republican era they had begun to fall under British bourgeois influences. As Jaime Jaramillo Uribe has pointed out, one of the central themes of Colombia's nineteenth century was the struggle of upper-class conservatives as well as liberals to make their society over in the image of the "Anglo-Saxon bourgeoisie."[10] Consequently, the New Granadan neo-Bourbons were not markedly hostile to the idea of profit. While they condemned usury in public rhetoric, they did not shy away from money lending or speculative profits. In general their argument for economic enterprise took the form of a decorous compromise between the aristocratic ideal of public service and the capitalistic goal of private profit. The usual formula was that upper-class youths should turn to practical occupations so as to serve their country, their families, and themselves.

New Granadan republican leaders, unlike their Spanish predecessors, did not at first take any special measures to build the prestige of economic, as opposed to political, occupations. For much of the first half of the nineteenth century, New Granada's neo-Bourbons either exhorted other members of the upper class to take new paths or they attempted to coerce them. Until at least 1847 they made no effort to endow technical skills or business enterprise with formal marks of prestige. Perhaps they did not realize how much their society continued to operate within a system of honor; more probably, having English and North American bourgeois models in mind, they assumed that economic virtue would provide its own reward.

While the New Granadan elite undoubtedly was aware of the Spanish Enlightenment heritage so evident in their attitudes and actions, they rarely appealed to it except in its colonial New Granadan manifestations. Such men as Lino de Pombo may well have read Benito Gerónimo Feijóo, Pedro Rodríguez de Campomanes, and Gaspar Melchor de Jovellanos, but in their public pronouncements they made little or no reference to these Spanish sources. Undoubtedly it was more politic in the first decades after Independence to cite institutional or ideological models taken from France, Great Britain, or the United States. But it is also true that the New Granadan leaders, like the Spanish savants before them, viewed Spain as an economic failure. It was, therefore, understandable that in promoting ideas already familiar to the Spanish world they should emphasize the French, British, or North American origins of these ideas.

In accord with this foreign orientation, most of the Colombian elite traveled abroad as soon and as often as possible. Of eighteen political leaders notable for their support of scientific and technical education before 1860, fifteen lived or traveled in the United States, the West Indies, or in Europe; in twelve cases the travel occurred early enough in their lives to have influenced their efforts on behalf of technical education (see Appendix 1).

Their motives and interests in traveling abroad were mixed. Politics was usually the occasion for their travel—most went as voluntary or involuntary political exiles; some went as ambassadors; some went on pleasure trips with perhaps some commercial activity on the side to help pay for the trip. Only one of the eighteen, Joaquín Acosta, traveled abroad primarily to receive scientific education. Their letters from abroad reveal that, while they had some interest in science and technology, it was not usually at the center of their attention. The dominant subjects were Colombian or New Granadan politics, European or U.S. politics, and general European culture. In this third category, European scientists drew their attention less than legal-political or economic thinkers and probably no more than literary lions. The fact that the New Granadan leaders for the most part were not entirely equipped to deal with scientific ideas probably had something to do with this. There are some variations in the pattern—Joaquín Acosta seems to have consorted with scientists as much as with literati and politicians, and José Manuel Restrepo took a particular interest in North American factories. But on the whole their interest in science and technology tended to be as much touristic as purposeful. They were interested in science and technology as symbols of power, but, with such exceptions as Acosta and Lino de Pombo, they lacked an intrinsic involvement with science.[11]

On the other hand, superficial as their interest might be, they did not omit the pursuit of the practical. In most cases aesthetic and utilitarian values mingled. While they often put themselves to learn Italian for its beauty and its cultural associations, they more frequently tried to learn English for its usefulness. They delighted in knowing European nobility, but they took similar pleasure in meeting European scientists. They visited not only the Vatican and the British Parliament but also educational and correctional institutions, banks, and merchants' houses. In hostelries and at dinner parties they discussed the latest operas and contemporary European politics, but they also were interested in the technical marvels and economic achievements of the age. On their return they brought new patterns of consumption as well as new types of seed and breeding stock. Their aim was self-improvement—primarily as individuals but also implicitly as agents of a new nation. To some degree their experiences in Europe and the United States provided them with ideas and models for educational and technical innovations in New Granada. They were not merely passive recipients of these ideas; they actively sought them out.

The men who promoted technical education before the 1860s were predominantly on the conservative side in New Granada's political wars. Some liberal members of the political and educational elites supported scientific and technical instruction—most notably Gen. Francisco de Paula Santander, José Duque Gómez, Vicente Lombana, Lorenzo María Lleras, and Francisco J. Zaldúa. Others, like Gen. Tomás Cipriano de Mosquera and Manuel Ancízar, were associated with conservatism in the 1840s but evolved toward liberal connections during the period of liberal dominance after 1849. But most of those who actively promoted scientific and technical training before 1860 formed part of a political group that in the first half of the 1830s was known as the *moderados*, by the end of that decade as the *ministeriales*, and after 1849 as the Conservative party. Most of these leaders figured importantly in the moderate-conservative administrations of José Ignacio de Márquez (1837–1841), Gen. Pedro Alcántara Herrán (1841–1845), and Gen. Tomás Cipriano de Mosquera (1845–1849). Most of those who survived to see the years of liberal control after 1849 were in the opposition.

That political conservatives played a somewhat larger role than liberals in promoting education in the sciences before 1865 is partly attributable to their political dominance during many of these years, only partly to lack of interest among the liberals. The conservatives possessed the national executive from 1837 to 1849 and between 1857 and 1861 and enjoyed a bipartisan coalition government in 1855–1857. And in the administrations of the liberal Francisco de Paula Santander (1819–1827 and 1832–1837), which did try to implant scientific education, the key cabinet ministers happened to be men of decidedly conservative leanings: José Manuel Restrepo in the first case and Lino de Pombo in the second.

Although political circumstance had something to do with the relative importance of conservatives in the Colombian pursuit of technical training, there also was a philosophical consonance between political conservatism and technical education. Conservatives viewed education as an instrument for preserving the social order. They supported universal public primary education, at least verbally, on the ground that an educated citizenry was necessary to a moral social order. Technical education served moral order as well as economic growth. Training in the manual arts helped to instill the habit of labor. If an individual had acquired the habit of work and practical skills, then his economic productivity would increase. Lured by profit, he would be engaged by his work and thus become a moral, responsible, and orderly individual. Conversely, a member of the lower class who lacked training in a useful skill would be easily distracted into drunkenness and crime, while a member of the upper class could be drawn into disruptive political activities.

Liberals as a group were by no means hostile to technical education, but on the whole they did show less interest in it than did political conservatives. Liberals in general were more concerned with expanding conventional primary instruction in order to develop the educated citizenry needed to sustain a liberal republic. Liberals also tended to favor the extension of secondary schools into the provinces, thus providing avenues of mobility for new political elites. They came to resent scientific instruction when it was used by conservative regimes to constrict secondary and university instruction. Further, liberals, at least by mid-century, did not see the need for the kind of institutional discipline that technical education represented to conservatives. At least in rhetoric, liberals were willing to rely instead on the discipline of the market, with all of the upward (and, though it was mentioned less frequently, the downward) mobility that it implied. At certain times liberals devoted little attention to technical education because they were absorbed in the process of revolutionizing political, social, and economic institutions. This was particularly true when liberal forces swept the conservatives out in 1849–1853 and again in 1861–1863.

While purportedly revolutionizing Colombian society, the Radical liberals of the 1850s actually developed a new system of upper-class control, one that for a time did nothing more to encourage technical development than the system employed by the Conservatives. Until the early 1840s the elite in Bogotá, for the most part conservatives, pursued the goal of limited industrial development with the government providing support to manufacturing enterprise. But the elite of the 1850s, with the Liberals at their head, were convinced that New Granada was destined to specialize in export agriculture and that the protection of national manufacturers was misguided. Further, as dogmatic Manchesterian liberals, they objected to government involvement in any sort of economic enterprise. Under Liberal control in the 1850s all government-sponsored activities, including technical education and public works, declined. Further, the Liberal program weakened New Granada's artisans who would have to play a key role in technical development. Having allied themselves politically with Bogotá's artisans in 1848–1849, the Liberals once in power pursued a low tariff policy that tended to undermine the artisans. When the artisans in 1854 revolted against Liberal free trade policy, the Liberals joined the Conservatives to repress the rebels, sending them to die in the jungles of Panama. In subsequent decades Liberals viewed the artisans as a dangerous group to be kept in leading strings if possible and under constraint if not. Thus the Liberal establishment repressed the artisans politically, sapped them economically, and, for a time, gave little more than lip service to the goal of technical training.

After 1864, when they had consolidated their party's control and confronted the responsibility of national economic development, the Liberals began to relent in their dogmatic opposition to positive government. Technical schools and public works projects created in the last third of the century made possible the emergence of technical professions in Colombia. But while Colombia toward the end of the century developed an engineering elite, this elite tended to be more bureaucratic than entrepreneurial in behavior. Colombia remained, and remains, weak in middle- and lower-level technicians. The effort to inculcate practical orientations had been only partially successful.

Part One

Colombia:
Its Geography
and Society

Chapter 1   Opportunities and Incentives

To understand the problems involved in introducing technical orientations to New Granada, it is necessary to discuss some of the salient characteristics of the country and its society in the eighteenth and nineteenth centuries. The country's geographic structure, the economic and social patterns developed in the colonial period, and the many problems of the nineteenth century tended to limit economic opportunities, channel energies in unproductive directions, and frustrate efforts at national development.

Geographic Constraints

The two central facts about New Granada's geography are that it is tropical and mountainous. Lying entirely within the heart of the tropical zone, the country's lowlands were disease-ridden areas. At least until the twentieth century, the lowlands were avoided by most of the population, which resided in the healthier temperate highlands. The hot low country of the Magdalena valley and the Caribbean coast, which might have offered commercial possibilities in the form of plantation production for world trade, also presented the constant danger of illness and death from yellow fever, malaria, and dysentery. In the colonial period and throughout the nineteenth century the great bulk of New Granada's population lived in the cooler climate created by the three branches of the Andes that run in a northerly direction through the country from the Ecuadorean border. The densest population clusters were located in the cool eastern highlands, generally at altitudes of more than seven thousand feet, and in the relatively temperate climate of the mountains of Antioquia and the upper Cauca valley.

All these highland population centers were deep in the interior, connected to the outside world by the sand-clogged, rapids-bedeviled Magdalena River. While sweating travelers huddled miserably, at the mercy of the mosquitos, the poled boats that plied this tropical river made their slow progress more than six hundred miles to the headwater of navigation below

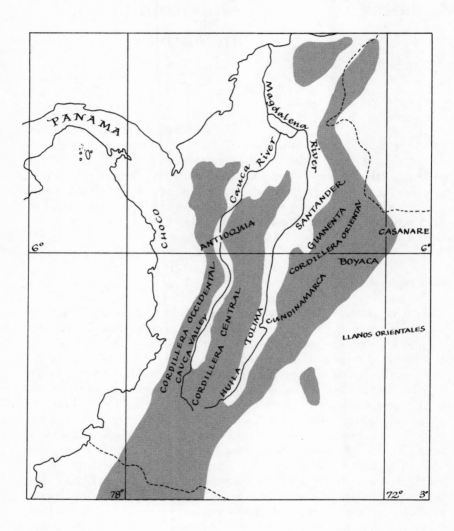

Map 1. Physical Map of Colombia

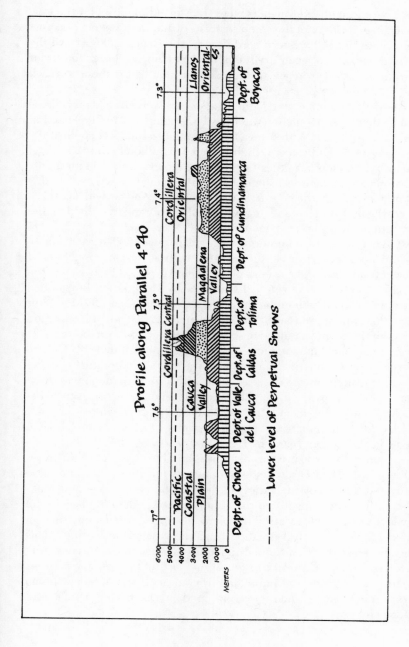

Map 2. Topographical Profile of Colombia (based on Banco de la República, *Atlas de economía colombiana*, cartograma 1)

Honda. There freight and travelers were transferred to mules for the long haul over several ridges of the steep eastern cordillera to Bogotá or across the even more difficult western cordillera to the Cauca valley. Until the middle of the nineteenth century it might take as long as three months for goods from the coast to reach the capital, six months for them to reach Popayán in the upper Cauca region.[1]

The country's mountainous geography also kept New Granadans isolated from each other. Her population was fairly large compared to those of other parts of Latin America. With somewhat more than a million people at the beginning of the republican era, slightly over 1.6 million in the 1830s, and more than 2.2 million at midcentury, New Granada ranked behind only Brazil among South American states.[2] Yet this population was widely dispersed and sparse for the country's vast area. The Andes, with its three major north-south chains and many difficult subbranches, divided the country into many separate economic pockets.

New Granada contained numerous very small towns (200 to 2,000 inhabitants), but no large urban center. Bogotá, with an urban population of about twenty thousand at the end of the colonial period, was by far the largest city; no other was even half that size. By 1870, when Bogotá had slightly more than forty thousand inhabitants, its only rival was Medellín, with less than thirty thousand. The dozen next largest towns, scattered widely about the country, ranged in size from seven to thirteen thousand.[3]

The combination of mountainous terrain and tropical climate obstructed commercial connections in a number of ways. As temperatures in the tropics vary not according to the season but with altitude, Colombia's three mountain ranges provide great differences in climate within short distances. Foods for a diversified diet can be grown within a closely circumscribed locality. The *sabanas* ("mountain plains") to the north of Bogotá produce wheat, potatoes, garden greens, flax, and wool; a few miles down the mountain maize, sugar cane, plantains, and bananas and other tropical and subtropical fruits grow; and some seventy miles away rice and cacao are cultivated. Struck by the variety of the Bogotá market, one mid-nineteenth-century visitor suggested that "there is not perhaps a place in the world which can provide for itself the elements necessary to enjoy such an absolute independence and isolation from the rest of the world."[4] This superficially ideal situation tended to stultify the economy, discouraging the development of a national market. Many parts of the country, neither having to reach outside the immediate region for basic foods nor being able to sell much outside the region, operated on a far-from-dynamic local subsistence basis.

As it was possible to get along using the products of the immediate area, there was not a strong imperative to improve roads. Furthermore, physical conditions in the tropical mountains made it difficult to do so. It is not merely that the terrain is abrupt. Equally important, most of the Colombian Andes have prolonged seasons of heavy, often torrential, rain. If road improvements on mountain slopes were not finished before the rain hit or if the roads were not adequately drained, as was often the case, they simply washed away, leaving treacherous sloughs. Until the last third of the nineteenth century not one of the roads over mountainsides was more than a mulepath. Travel over such routes was difficult in the dry periods and almost impossible in the rainy season. On one of the most-used roads in the country, from the Magdalena River to Bogotá, in many places mules sank to their girths in mud holes and in others they skittered over slippery clay slopes. The high risk to both cargo and animals made it almost prohibitively expensive to transport anything but high-value items. Very heavy or bulky objects could not be carried by mules at all and had to be shouldered by teams of *peones*, at even greater cost. There were, of course, a few level places in the country. But, possibly for lack of traffic, only one cart road was built before the 1860s. Transportation was also impeded by the general lack of bridges except in and around Bogotá. Until the 1880s almost all rivers had to be forded or ferried, or, in the case of deeply cut mountain gorges, travelers and freight were pulled across on rope traverses while horses, mules, and cattle swam.[5] Through most of the nineteenth century freight costs were generally above twenty-five cents per ton mile over level ground. Over mountain roads rates ranged from thirty to fifty cents per ton mile in the dry season and double those amounts after heavy rains.[6]

While high transportation costs and the vertical economy of the tropics tended to discourage interregional trade, in the colonial era there was some exchange of selected products. Because of the restrictiveness of the Spanish trade system and the expense of transportation up the Magdalena River by poled boat, costs of moving goods into the interior of the country were high enough to protect domestic producers and to provide some leeway for overland freight charges. In the eighteenth century Antioquia, a region specializing in gold mining, procured cattle, mules, and pigs from the Cauca valley and textiles from Pasto and the Socorro region. Socorro's cotton and canvas goods were sold as far away as Popayán. The woolens woven by more than fifty Indian communities around Tunja found widespread markets at least until the end of the eighteenth century. The mountain plains of the eastern region—from Bogotá to Tunja—grew wheat that was sold in the Socorro area, the upper Magdalena valley, and sometimes

Antioquia and the Caribbean coast. There was also some fairly long distance trade in cacao (from Cúcuta or Neiva to Bogotá; from Popayán to Antioquia).[7]

During the eighteenth century and, at a more rapid pace, in the first half of the nineteenth, this limited "national" market broke down under the pressure of foreign imports. After the British won the right to import African slaves and with them flour and cloth in 1713, the highlands in the interior effectively lost the coastal market for these products. Only with the aid of strong viceregal protection was flour from the interior sold from time to time in Cartagena. The disintegration of the New Granadan market was accelerated by the republic's increasingly liberal trade policies and the navigation of the Magdalena River by steamboats (sporadically between 1825 and 1847, continuously after that time). Both of these developments lowered the cost of bringing foreign goods to the interior, while producers in the highlands continued to depend upon expensive mule transportation. As it became no more costly to ship from Liverpool or New York to Honda (at the head of navigation of the Magdalena River) than from Bogotá, less than a hundred miles away, New Granadan products could not compete with foreign goods. British manufacturing and North American agriculture, both of which were becoming increasingly productive, took over the regional markets; the wheat growers and textile weavers in the mountains were forced back into production on a local subsistence basis.[8]

The retardation of two traditional economic sectors in the interior provinces tells something about the country's economic problems in general. One critical observer reported that at the end of the colonial period, when the domestic market was already contracting, many large landowners still used rude wooden plows because of the high cost of importing iron. While Bogotá had water-driven grain mills, flour was still prepared and packed ineffectively; domestic flour often arrived at the coast black and vermin-ridden after passing through the hot, humid Magdalena River valley. In textiles human power operated all looms (except for a brief experiment at the end of the 1830s) until the middle of the nineteenth century and hand looms remained the majority to the end of the century.[9] Efforts were made to improve the efficiency of both of these segments of the economy during the first half of the nineteenth century. In the 1830s the Colombian elite attempted to adapt foreign wheat seed to fight disease that had spread from the warmer mountain areas to the cool highland plains between 1800 and 1825, but *polvillo* was still taking its toll at midcentury. In the same period Bogotá imported some foreign plows, but the cost of bringing large objects up the Honda road impeded the introduction of more elaborate agricultural machinery even in the second half of the century.[10] Similarly, efforts to establish a water-powered cotton factory in the 1830s and a woolen mill in the 1850s were complicated by transportation costs. Being entirely dependent upon foreign technology, the entrepreneurs in each case faced the problem of hauling heavy machinery up from the Magdalena River. Then they found that, although they had set up more efficient weaving processes, they could not compete with the industrial countries either in access to raw materials or in transporting the finished product to the various corners of New Granada.[11]

While New Granada's geographic structure clearly limited its capacity to respond to the foreign challenge, its nineteenth-century failures can also be linked to the character of its society. While some agricultural experimentation did occur, large landowners in the highlands could not be said to have met the test aggressively. In textiles upper-class efforts failed in part because a supporting technical culture, a skilled and reliable workforce, and entrepreneurial persistence were lacking.[12] One must turn then to an examination of the country's social characteristics in order to understand the country's nineteenth-century economy.

Social and Economic Patterns

While New Granada's geographic structure constricted economic opportunities for all of its inhabitants, the character of class relationships and the control of important economic resources by a small upper class also limited incentives, for both the upper and the lower classes. Upper-class control, however, was not simply a matter of landownership. In some areas large holdings did not predominate. And, in any case, a property-owning class could not sustain itself without the aid of other instruments of power. Several forms of cultural control, varying in their relative importance over time, helped to support, first, the power of the Spanish population in general and, second, that of a small group within that population. Military and related means of cultural dominion exercised by the upper class gave way during the sixteenth and seventeenth centuries to subtler forms of control—religion, a monopoly of literacy and administrative functions, and a continuing cultural differentiation between dominant and subordinate.

For both economic and cultural reasons, there was some variation in class relations among the population centers of New Granada. Some places of importance early in the colonial period had relatively substantial Indian or Negro slave laboring populations that supported a small class of large

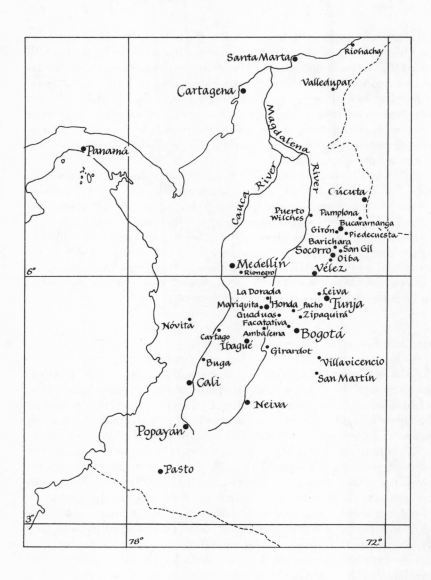

Map 3. Political Map of Colombia

landholders and mineowners and a civil and ecclesiastical administrative elite living in a few principal towns. Notable among such towns were Santa Fe de Bogotá and Tunja in the eastern highlands, Popayán in the upper Cauca valley, and Cartagena on the Caribbean coast—all founded in the 1530s. Because they were the homes of the administrative elite as well as of substantial property owners, these towns tended to accumulate pious endowments that served to found church-run secondary schools. In these well-established communities, class relationships were marked by a clear pattern of domination and obeisance. Some regions that were settled later, in the eighteenth or even the nineteenth century, tended to be less aristocratic in style. These newly developed areas did not have long traditions as important centers of civil or ecclesiastical administration. And some of them either were less dominated by large landholdings or offered other economic opportunities permitting some social mobility. Antioquia in the central cordillera and the Socorro region in the eastern zone are salient examples of less aristocratic societies.[13]

Bogotá and Tunja, located in the eastern highlands, became prominent early because this area contained the most numerous, sedentary, and docile Indian population. Spanish settlers tended to gravitate to the highlands and Indian labor. With them came ecclesiastics who served as auxiliaries of, and competitors with, the Spanish lay settlers in controlling the indigenous population. Aside from the indigenes, the only other important resource of the eastern cordillera was its series of fertile, flat highland basins. During the colonial era Spanish settlers seized control of much of the flatland in the mountain valleys, using much of it for raising cattle. The indigenous peasants retained many community holdings but increasingly were reduced to the cultivation of hillside *minifundia*, though in the region around Tunja they also raised sheep and wove woolens on home looms. During the eighteenth century the peasant communities became substantially less "Indian." Spanish and mestizo penetration, economic and sexual, was turning many of them into largely mestizo communities by the latter half of the eighteenth century.[14]

At the beginning of the republican era, wages in this region were among the lowest in the country—about ten centavos per day for agricultural labor.[15] Upper-class economic domination was carried a step farther when in the 1830s the republican government began to break up the remaining Indian community lands, which were gradually sold to large landowners. The cattle of the estate owners replaced the crops of the peasants and food prices rose, while the limited demand for peasant labor kept wages down. As their situation steadily worsened, the peasants, while necessarily hard working, tended to be depressed, fatalistic, withdrawn. In the nineteenth and even in the twentieth century, peasants continued to acknowledge their considerable social distance from the upper class by using such forms as *"mi amo"* or *"el señor."*

In the Cauca region, dominated by Popayán, but with lesser centers at Cali and Buga, the geographic circumstances differed, but upper-class domination was at least as pronounced. Here an Indian population, operating under the forced labor *repartimiento* system until the latter part of the eighteenth century, remained significant in the highland regions immediately around Popayán and along the borders of the valley elsewhere. But in the sugar-producing valley and, particularly, in the Popayán patricians' gold mines in the Chocó, an African slave labor force was important in the colonial era. The republican government gradually abolished slavery between 1821 and 1850, but, as the upper class continued to monopolize the better land, there was no important change in class relationships. The dominant white population, living in seigneurial ease, showed little inclination to economic activity; and the poor black workers, like their Indianoid counterparts in the eastern highlands, lacked opportunities and incentives.

The port of Cartagena was a kind of Caribbean counterpart of Popayán. As Cartagena in the colonial period had held a monopoly over all legal maritime trade, it had been the point of entry for African slaves, and a slave-supported aristocracy was deeply rooted there. Because of its commercial and strategic importance in the Spanish trade system, Cartagena was also a significant military and administrative center. As in the case of Bogotá and Popayán, its many conventual establishments symbolized its centrality in the colonial era. Between 1820 and 1850, however, Cartagena fell into decline as its canal communications with the Magdalena River deteriorated. The rival port of Santa Marta captured the bulk of the import trade. Like Popayán, Cartagena continued to be important politically but lacked a substantial economic base.

In the areas that had developed more recently and were administratively less important, an aristocratic style was less apparent and upper-class domination less complete. In the abruptly broken terrain of the Socorro region the Indian population during the eighteenth century was overwhelmed demographically by Spanish and mestizo colonists who starting from the town of Vélez, moved northward, establishing by cellular division a series of small communities. The tiny pockets of arable land in this rugged area supported a society of spirited smallholders and weavers.[16] Though there was an identifiable town elite in this Guanentá region by the time of Independence, the area would not support much in the way of upper-class pretensions.

Located in the western part of the country, Antioquia had become significant as a mining region during the sixteenth century, but none of its cities was an important administrative center. The governor in Popayán ruled the area in civil matters until the last third of the sixteenth century, and long after that time its ecclesiastical governance was divided among the bishops of Popayán, Cartagena, and Bogotá. Medellín, the city that emerged as the focal point of Antioquia, was not founded until 1675, and much of the area was settled by colonization in the eighteenth and nineteenth centuries. Large landowners dominated some parts of Antioquia, but not the region as a whole. The region's gold-mining economy created occasional opportunities for rapid enrichment and social mobility, in trade perhaps more than in gold mining itself. Medellín developed essentially as a commercial center catering to the mines. In Antioquia, as in the Socorro region, the population tended to be more engaged and aggressive economically and to value work highly.[17]

Several indicators depict the extent to which regional differences in social structure as well as in general economic possibilities produced varying degrees of incentive in the lower classes. A community's success in establishing primary education depended not only on raising money for schools and teachers but also on having a populace that could perceive some reason for attending school. As one might expect, the areas with the haughtiest aristocracies and the most stagnant economies did rather poorly in developing primary education, while more egalitarian, later-developing regions did better. Antioquia was consistently in the vanguard of primary education throughout the nineteenth century. The city and province of Santa Marta were also among the educational leaders, while their unsuccessful competitor, the down-at-heels aristocrat Cartagena, ranked consistently in the rear. The patricians of Popayán had more students than most in the early days of the republic, but by midcentury Popayán's enrollments had fallen in relation to those of other provinces. Conversely, the poorly endowed but relatively egalitarian Santander (Socorro) region lagged early in the republican era, but before the last quarter of the century it was among the leaders. Directly to the south, very few of the depressed Indianoid peasant population between Tunja and Bogotá attended school. The situation improved somewhat around Bogotá in the 1870s when the capital initiated a vigorous drive to promote education.[18] That popular interest in education was an important factor in school at-

TABLE 1. *Primary Education: Statistical Comparison by Region*[a]

	1835 Public	Primary Students as Percentage of Population			Teachers per 1,000 Population, 1870
		1847 Public & Private	1873–1874 Public	1873–1874 Public & Private	
Antioquia	1.79	2.16	3.71	5.41	0.7
Bogotá (Cundinamarca)	1.01	1.54	3.41	4.58	1.1
Cartagena (Bolívar)	1.00	1.98	1.84	3.04	0.3
Popayán (Cauca)	2.56	1.90	1.88	2.28	0.6
Santa Marta (Magdalena)	2.66	4.03	2.71	3.48	0.3
Socorro (Santander)	1.01	0.91	2.13	3.13	0.3
Tunja (Boyacá)	0.87	0.94	1.69	1.95	0.3
National	1.19	1.53	2.16	3.10	0.6

Source: Calculated from figures in Memoria de lo Interior y Relaciones Exteriores, 1836; *Anuario estadístico de Colombia, 1875*, pp. 78–79; Jorge Rodríguez, "Sinopsis estadística de Antioquia," in Antioquia, Dirección de Estadística Departamental, *Boletín de Estadística Departamental*, July 20, 1920, p. 6.

[a]Educational statistics, like all others for nineteenth-century New Granada, are not very trustworthy. The above figures should be taken as merely suggestive.

tendance in Antioquia, Santa Marta, and the Socorro region seems confirmed by the fact that in the 1870s their enrollment rates ran ahead of their supplies of teachers. The Bogotá, Popayán, and Cartagena regions, on the other hand, tended to be relatively well provided with teachers in relation to the numbers of the students (see Table 1).

Constricted regional economic possibilities may have played as great a role as class structure in dampening lower-class aspirations. During the nineteenth century almost the entire eastern cordillera stagnated economically. Such stagnation is reflected in the numbers of servants and vagrants in the area. The latifundiary regions of Boyacá contained high proportions of servants and vagrants, but so did neighboring Socorro, where land was not so much badly distributed as too scarce. The Cauca valley and other notably aristocratic areas in other parts of the country, on the other hand, had fewer servants and many fewer vagrants.[19]

A few colonial administrators and an occasional member of the creole elite were aware that the unequal distribution of land was restraining the country's development. Pedro Fermín de Vargas, a creole lawyer-administrator, noted in the 1790s that the unequal division of the land left some people with much more land than they could cultivate, while the poverty of the many held back population growth. Archbishop-Viceroy Antonio Caballero y Góngora, in 1789, ascribed the vagrancy of his era to the "too great accumulation of lands" in the hands of a few, and the proprietors' "tyranny" that caused the landless peasant population to become uprooted. Another viceroy, Pedro Mendinueta, described another leg of the same elephant in 1803. While denying that landholdings were too concentrated, Mendinueta admitted that rural wages were too low to provide any incentive to workers.[20] For the most part, however, in the colonial period and in the nineteenth century, the New Granadan elite did not recognize or preferred to ignore the negative effects of *latifundia*. Upper-class leaders in the middle of the nineteenth century said they wished to increase the purchasing power of peasants, but they could not bring themselves to admit that inequalities in the distribution of land were a primary factor depressing consumer power.[21] Similarly, they wanted the peasants to attend primary school and to adopt better agricultural techniques. But they generally failed to notice, or at least to acknowledge, that the land system had something to do with the peasants' lack of interest in education and their failure to embrace the latest agricultural innovations.[22]

Nor did the elite perceive a connection between the latifundiary system and undesirable attitudes in the upper class. The New Granadan elite did believe, however, that certain values in their society needed reforming.

Newspapers in the first half of the nineteenth century occasionally carried fulminations against gambling and the value of saving was conjured in frequent incantations.[23] As the century wore on and New Granadans stumbled from one economic failure to another, the elite became acutely aware that they and their kind lacked perseverance. The degree of this awareness can be measured by their pronounced tendency in the middle of the century to idolize Englishmen and North Americans for their possession of this virtue. One can also infer from the many obituaries praising the *laboriosidad* of the deceased that hard work was a value the literate elite wished were more in evidence. And, as the rest of this study emphasizes, the elite were generally concerned with orienting the upper class more toward practicality and even with helping its members overcome their mandarin distaste for manual labor.

While the values of the New Granadan upper class tended to be anti-economic and unmodern in many respects, this point should be qualified. In the late colonial period, there was substantial evidence of the ascriptive orientation that characterized most of Spanish America. In the latter half of the eighteenth century, even in the relatively egalitarian Socorro region, members of the local upper class felt it necessary to establish the "purity of their blood" with documentary evidence from Spain.[24] After the achievement of Independence, however, this convention was abandoned in all formal respects with remarkable rapidity. Under the republic, designations of caste were no longer applied to infants at the time of registry, and entry into the university did not require "purity of blood." Once *pureza de sangre* ceased to have a legally defined importance, it lost much of its social power.

Although lineage continued to carry some weight, individuals could now win entry into the upper class solely through achievement. Achievement, of course, can be defined and measured in many ways. Some men sought distinction in literary creation and proved incredibly prolific in that pursuit. Many more turned to political careers. Some conservatives and many liberals of modest origins were awarded the highest professional distinctions. One of the principal attractions of politics probably lay in the fact that it offered the possibility of relatively rapid upward mobility, in contrast to economic enterprise, in which opportunities were constricted by the high cost of loaned money in the nineteenth century.

Nonetheless, money was the most widely accepted coin of social prestige, and many men, therefore, turned to those economic activities that were most likely to yield a profit. In the nineteenth century this was most likely to mean commerce. The Colombian upper class, having a strong pecuniary propensity, was far from scorning commerce or those who took it up. In the last decades before Independence the brothers Gutiérrez Moreno, sons of distinguished landed and legal-bureaucratic families in Santa Fe de Bogotá, took considerable risks importing contraband. Francisco José de Caldas, a member of Popayán's upper class, at the same time forsook a professorship in law to take up the wandering life of a retail merchant.[25] In the republican era it was standard for a large landowner or important public figure to spend much of his time behind a store counter. In the early 1830s a French diplomat was astonished to discover Vicente Borrero, a great landowner in the Cauca valley and a leading jurist and politician, in his shop in Bogotá, "selling cloth, measuring it himself with the yardstick in his hand," the day after resigning as secretary of foreign relations.[26]

Commerce provided a good avenue for upward mobility, mainly because it was possible for a shrewd man to make rapid profits. Artisans were much less likely to advance into the upper class, perhaps not so much because of prejudices against manual work as because artisans tended not to make enough money to qualify. Some foreign artisans, whether as foreigners or as possessors of scarce skills, were able to rise quickly to the upper sector of the society.[27] The contrast between opportunities for most artisans and those for merchants is illustrated by the case of the progenitors of a twentieth-century president, Alfonso López—his grandfather, an artisan, obtained much notoriety but little status as a leader in the artisans' rebellion of 1854; the artisan's son, however, was taken in as a clerk by an upper-class merchant family, and they extended him credit for commerical ventures that took him to the pinnacle of Colombian society.[28]

Though the upper class was highly acquisitive, most of its members in the first half of the nineteenth century were not very rich by the standards of European or North American bourgeoisie. Little is known as yet about the incomes of individuals in commerce or agriculture, and almost nothing about the artisan class. But government salary scales suggest that upper-class incomes seldom exceeded three thousand pesos a year and that they generally were no higher than one thousand pesos. These figures, of course, do not take into account possible incomes that government officers may have received from estates or rents. Bogotá's middle group of clerks, teachers, and lower-level army officers earned between three hundred and eight hundred pesos, while the urban lower class earned two hundred pesos or less. The servants' pay of forty-eight to seventy-two pesos is, as one might expect, in line with the daily wage earned by rural workers (see Table 2).

TABLE 2. *Representative Government Salaries, 1836–1839*

Political	Judicial	Military	Other
President $12,000			
Secretaries of state (4) $3,200			
Councillors of state (7) $2,000	Supreme Court justices (4) $2,400	Generals, when in service (3) $2,400	Treasurer of the tithe, Archbishopric of Bogotá $1,200
Provincial governors (20) top $3,200 low $1,500 mean $2,000			
Chief comptroller $2,000	Regional appellate court judges top $2,300 low $1,800	Colonels (14) $1,728	
Director of the mint $1,800		Lt. cols. $1,248	
Director general, tobacco monopoly $1,600			
Administrator of the mails $1,500			Treasurer of the tithe, Bishopric of Santa Marta $600
Oficial mayor, govt. depts. $1,400			
Jefes políticos cantons		Sgt. majs. $1,008	

Position	Salary	Position	Salary
Chiefs of section, govt. depts.	top $1,200 / low $400		
Chiefs of section, govt. depts.	$800	Captains	$708
Provincial adms. of the mail	top $900 / low $150		
Secretary, Supreme Court	$800		
Archivists, govt. depts.	$600	Surgeons	$600
Clerks	top $600 / low $400		
Secretary, *dirección general de instrucción pública*	$500	First lts.	$528
		Schoolmaster Bogotá	$400
National librarian	$500		
Second and third officers govt. depts.	top $700 / low $400	Ensigns	$420
		Prof. military school	$400
		Chairs in *colegios* & universities	top $400 / low $179
Clerks	top $360 / usual $300		
Doormen (guards)	top $200 / low $100	Doormen — top $200 / low $80; Arsenal guard $192	Boat on Magdalena River:
		Sgts. (1) $192	*Patrón* $120
		Sgts. (2) $168	Oarsman $96
		Cpls. (1) $144	
		Cpls. (2) $132	
Servants	$72	Servants $48; Soldiers $108	

Source: Budget for 1836–1837, Law of June 6, 1836, *CN*, VI, 174–193; Law of June 8, 1836, *CN*, VI, 207–208; Budget for 1837–1838, Law of May 30, 1837, *CN*, VI, 345–379; Budget for 1838–1839, Law of May 30, 1838, *CN*, VIII, 97–155.

Scattered evidence suggests that incomes in the private sector were not often superior to those of the higher-level government employees. Between 1820 and 1850 no more than a half-dozen landowners and merchants in Bogotá could claim a mobilizable capital of a hundred thousand pesos. Such men were viewed with awe as *capitalistas*. In 1842 a distinctly aristocratic family in Bogotá was elated when one of its daughters married a man with a capital of fifty thousand pesos.[29] In the same era property valued at ten thousand pesos was a good upper-class dowry. One may surmise that even rather well fixed *bogotanos*, whether landowners with a hundred thousand pesos worth of land or merchants with half that much in more liquid capital, did not have a net income of more than five thousand pesos per year.[30] Many members of the upper class may well have lived on a thousand pesos per annum.[31] To European visitors the New Granadan upper class was a sorry lot indeed, hardly up to the level of European tradesmen.

Because of its relatively low income levels and its colonial isolation from the Atlantic world, the upper class's consumption standards were not very high at the beginning of the republican era. Foreigners who visited Bogotá in the 1820s and 1830s were struck by the low standard of living of the capital's upper crust. Bogotá's best houses were carpeted with rush mats, furnished with rude leather and wood chairs, and in general lacked the European amenities. The dress of the upper class was far from elegant, and its diet differed only slightly from that of the poor.[32] One highly reliable observer concluded in 1837 that "the middling and better classes cannot be called even ordinary good livers. The few respectable foreigners here, and about three or four Bogotanos, are the only individuals who come within my ideas of comfort within the whole place."[33]

This situation changed, of course, during the nineteenth century. As New Granada's foreign trade increased after 1845, so did the incomes of its shrewder merchant-capitalists—though many who were included in the aristocracy continued to lag far behind. At the same time consumption standards changed dramatically, particularly in Bogotá and the other substantial towns. As New Granadans traveled to New York, London, Paris, and Rome—generally mixing business with pleasure—they became immersed in the latest modes, whether intellectual, sartorial, or bibular. By the middle of the century upper-class credentials were beginning to include having a Paris tailor; imported carpets, mirrors, and other furniture were gracing Bogotá parlors; and staggering *peones* were hefting pianos up the boggy trail from Honda to the capital.[34] These developments greatly increased the social distance between the upper class and the lower. And they created standards of consumption more difficult to attain for those at the margins of the upper class who sought to emulate and enter it.

The Politicization of the Upper Class

During the colonial era the creole upper class predominantly engaged in agriculture, commerce, and, in the western provinces, in gold mining as well. But while land, mines, and commerce constituted the economic base of the upper class, the royal administrative structure, socially as well as politically, formed its apex. During much of the colonial period, administrative posts were so dominated by Spaniards that few members of the creole landowning class could hope to penetrate this structure. Some creoles entered the lower ranks of the priesthood, but civil administration tended to be monopolized by the Spanish. In the eighteenth century, however, more bureaucratic opportunities began to open up for creoles, and the local upper class took an increasingly pronounced interest in legal careers.

The key to bureaucratic careers was education. Through most of the colonial period, almost no effort was made to develop systematic primary education. Nevertheless, primary instruction, usually provided by parish priests, was available to the upper class in most localities. Before the expulsion of the Society of Jesus in 1767, Jesuit-run *colegios* ("secondary schools") existed in various provincial towns. But there was a tendency for students to gravitate to Bogotá and Popayán, where substantial pious endowments and a concentration of educated ecclesiastics and administrators provided a financial and cultural base for higher education. After the expulsion of the Jesuits the cultural monopoly of Bogotá and Popayán was even more secure. Upper-class youths in the Cauca valley and Antioquia often went for their secondary work to Popayán and then to take university degrees in law or theology in Bogotá. Students from the eastern cordillera, of course, and also some from Antioquia, took all their work in Bogotá. Many of them then went on to ecclesiastical or, in fewer cases, civil bureaucratic careers.

The achievement of Independence opened up a wealth of new opportunities in politics and government. It was not merely that the Spaniards at the top of the system had been displaced. In order to function, the republic required a much larger educated elite. With a Council of State, cabinet posts and staff appointments in administrative departments, an elaborate judicial system, diplomatic posts, provincial governorships, a bicameral national congress, and provincial legislatures, the number of political positions available multiplied manyfold. Such numerous political opportunities, rather than quieting creole ambitions, only fed them. No matter how many posts were created, there never were enough to go around. *Empleomanía*, along with ideological factors, encouraged violent struggle for possession of the state, which created still other new possibilities for political enterprise in the military.

What did these political opportunities mean to the men who pursued them? For some among the political elite who did not possess significant properties, government salaries were worth seeking on economic grounds alone (see Table 1.2). For large landowners, however, these salaries, while substantial enough at the higher levels, were merely supplementary and primarily of symbolic importance. Indeed, for most politicians, whether rich or not, public office probably had a primarily honorific significance.

Even though renown was important to these men, it is nevertheless possible to ask whether those who sought political office might not have been drawn, under certain circumstances, to the alternative of economic enterprise. At some point even men who are oriented toward dramatic vanity-satisfaction may find economic activity psychically rewarding. In most parts of New Granda, however, attractive economic opportunities were not very evident, even for the upper class. The Cauca valley, isolated by two ranges of the Andes, could not export effectively to world markets or to the population centers in the eastern part of the country. Finding few opportunities in agriculture or commerce, the Cauca's upper class tended to look to politics to satisfy ambitions. Throughout the period from 1830 to 1880 the Cauca proved the republic's most fertile seedbed of rebellion. Had opportunities in business or local development been available such notable political entrepreneurs as Gen. José María Obando and Gen. Tomás Cipriano de Mosquera might have devoted less of their energies to political warfare. The contrasting case of Antioquia seems to support this possibility. Antioquia's gold mining offered that province, alone among Colombia's regions, effective economic opportunities. Significantly, while the *antioqueños* proved very aggressive in economic enterprise, they were relatively uninterested in civil war.

Unfortunately, Antioquia was very much the exception. In every region of the country there were practical men among the upper class, men who shunned politics, indeed cursed it as the bane of commerce. But in most regions they were overwhelmed by the political torments. Only in Antioquia were they strong enough to make their voices prevail much of the time. Almost everywhere else a significant proportion of the upper class, frustrated in their economic ventures, embraced political enterprise. And the pursuit of politics, with its sequels of civil war, insecure property, disrupted markets, flight of capital, high interest rates, and generally weak economic institutions, further constricted economic opportunities. Thus, until the twentieth century political careers remained a compelling option for ambitious young men.

Nineteenth-Century Economic Stagnation

For the creole upper class Independence in 1821 seemed to bode the fulfillment of a promise barely perceived in the last decades of the colonial era. Now the native upper class was undisputed master of church and state; now it could carry on trade with the British completely untrammeled. The British capital market for its part reacted bullishly. Both Britons and New Granadans assumed that the removal of incompetent Spanish rule and an influx of skilled British merchants and workmen would bring a new prosperity to the country. In this belief, British investors acquired Colombian bonds with a face value of 6.7 million pounds sterling by the end of 1825; a British mining company began making major investments to resuscitate abandoned silver mines in New Granada; and the first wave of British merchants and craftsmen established themselves in the country.[35]

The promise, however, remained unfulfilled for the New Granadans as well as the British. The British mining company, despite its heavy investments, was unable to turn a profit in the Santa Ana mines for decades. Nor was the speculative optimism of the British bondholders repaid. The republic of Colombia foundered from the first. The heavily discounted loans it had contracted to carry the Wars of Independence to conclusion could not be repaid or even serviced. During the years of political crisis when Gran Colombia dissolved (1826–1830), no payments were made on the debt. By the end of the 1830s, when the national debt was divided among the constituent parts of Gran Colombia (New Granada, Ecuador, and Venezuela), the share that fell to New Granada amounted to more than 52 million pesos; of this more than 32 million represented foreign debts contracted in London. At the 6 percent interest rate that most of these obligations were supposed to earn, annual interest payments on the foreign debt alone would have amounted to three-quarters of New Granada's total national revenues. Although all the Latin American countries became encumbered with debts in this period, New Granada's burden was the heaviest in the area. As of 1841, in per capita terms the debt was twice that of

Chile and three times those of Mexico and Brazil; in relation to the countries' foreign trade and fiscal resources, the disparity was even greater. Again and again in the nineteenth century, New Granada renegotiated its debt only to fail in its payments. A relatively satisfactory and enduring settlement was not achieved until the twentieth century.[36] In the interim British capital was not much interested in New Granada, and the new republic could not obtain loans for national development projects on reasonable terms.

New Granada was no more successful in attracting foreign skills. Elaborate efforts were made to attract skilled workmen and agriculturalists, as well as men of capital, from Europe. From the beginning of the 1820s Colombia offered easy naturalization, ample grants of more-or-less free land, and at least temporary exemptions from taxation and military service. But after the first flush of interest displayed by British merchants and craftsmen in the optimistic 1820s, immigrants from the advanced countries came in the merest dribbles. As of 1844 Bogotá province could boast no more than 275 Europeans and North Americans, about 0.1 percent of its total population. By 1851 Europeans and North Americans accounted for less than 0.05 percent of the province of Bogotá, and in the country as a whole, excluding Panama, there were less than 450 Europeans and North Americans, about 0.02 percent of the population.[37]

New Granada's failure to attract immigrants can be explained partly in cultural terms. European and, particularly, North American Protestants were disturbed by the fanatical Roman Catholicism of the populace. Others were discouraged by the country's economic limitations. Its market could not support manufacturing, as some foreign entrepreneurs discovered. And for the semiskilled immigrant, the country's low wages could not have been appealing. Finally, for all classes of immigrants, New Granada's unstable politics promised economic disruption, if not insecurity of property.[38] It should be noted, however, that there were opportunities for skilled craftsmen; those few who came found their skills so much appreciated that some of them, like the blacksmith Samuel Sayer, soon vaulted into the ranks of the upper class. A few others were able to establish substantial agricultural enterprises. Most of the several hundred foreigners in New Granada, however, were merchants and artisans catering to the developing taste of the upper class.

Thrown back on their own resources in the 1830s, New Granada's leaders attempted to start various manufacturing enterprises, protecting them with tariffs and giving them special marketing privileges. But the native labor force was unskilled and not entirely reliable. And even those few skilled foreigners who arrived sometimes proved unruly employees. In addition, the high cost of capital in New Granada and the country's non-existent transportation system made the idea of competing with the industrial powers a fantasy.

In the 1840s the New Granadan elite became convinced that—given the country's terrain, its unskilled, illiterate labor force, and its meager capital resources—its future lay entirely in tropical agriculture. Not all regions of the country were able to share equally in this enterprise, however. The upper Magdalena valley and the Caribbean coast were well situated for exporting tobacco, cotton, indigo, and other tropical products. But because of transportation costs, the eastern highlands and the Cauca valley were barred from competing effectively in European markets and tended to stagnate during most of the period before 1870. In addition, the areas that could export tropical products were afflicted with considerable economic instability as markets for first one crop and then another would appear and disappear with startling rapidity. Steady economic growth in the middle of the nineteenth century was largely limited to Antioquia. The improved mining techniques introduced after 1825 enabled this province to produce enough gold to dominate the nation's exports through the first half of the century; and between 1850 and 1880 Antioquia's gold remained consistently one of Colombia's three largest exchange earners as well as the most dependable one. Antioquia, therefore, was something of an exception to the general stasis.[39]

Although foreigners who visited New Granada in the nineteenth century were uniformly impressed by its backwardness and poverty, the country's economic stagnation cannot be described accurately in quantitative terms. Economic statistics, when collected at all, were incomplete and unreliable, a situation that is in itself indicative of retardation. In the 1820s a French traveler guessed the value of cereals, fruits, and vegetables produced to be about three pesos per capita (probably an underestimation). Cattle production represented at least an equal value, and agricultural goods and minerals produced for export amounted roughly to another two pesos per capita. Even adding a small amount of artisan manufacturing, the New Granadan product was not very significant.[40]

Colombia was a notably weak exporter before 1870. Even among Latin American countries she generally ranked no higher than seventh, though she possessed the third-largest population in the area. In the 1830s and 1840s exports per capita approximated 1.50 to 2.50 pesos. Between 1850 and 1870 exports expanded somewhat, reaching a value between 3 and 4 pesos per capita. Nevertheless, even in this period of growth, Colombia compared most unfavorably with such countries as Argentina, Chile, and Peru, all of which had exports per capita more than three times as high.[41]

This weakness in foreign trade meant that Colombia lacked capital, both private and public. Private capital was drained off in exchange payments for imported goods, which generally exceeded exports. The generally low level of foreign trade played a part in holding down government revenues, which increasingly depended upon customs duties. Attempts to supplement the customs with direct taxes in the 1820s and again in the 1850s failed as citizens refused to make property declarations. The partial decentralization of national revenues in 1850 further undermined the financial position of the national government. Not until the 1870s did national revenues reach five million pesos, and combined national-state income more than seven million pesos. National revenues per capita amounted to less than 1.50 pesos before 1850 and only about 2.50 pesos in the 1870s.[42]

New Granada's fiscal and credit problems were greatly aggravated by the political wars that characterized its nineteenth-century history. Major civil conflicts occurred in 1831, 1839–1842, 1851, 1854, 1859–1862, 1876, 1885, and 1899–1903. In addition, between 1864 and 1880 there were many localized upheavals. Provincial rebellion and the constant threat of rebellion kept military expenditures high. This was particularly true in the period from 1832 to 1845, when the military absorbed about half of the national budget. After 1845 the army's share in the national budget declined to about one-quarter. By the end of the 1850s it was down to less than 12 percent in peaceful years.[43] But, though the military's proportion of the budget declined on the whole, in times of crisis army expenditures necessarily rose sharply. At the same time, as economic paralysis and rebel seizures decreased available revenue, the state became less able to support the army. Civil war therefore meant that New Granada had to suspend interest payments on the national debt and at the same time borrow heavily. And this happened at a time when native capital was fleeing and in scarce supply and when the government's own credit was particularly shaky because of political and fiscal uncertainties. In the years between 1830 and 1855, therefore, the government was forced to take domestic wartime loans at usurious rates, often as high as 24 percent per annum. Thus, even after a war crisis had passed, New Granada found its revenues eaten away by wartime debts.

The dilapidation of government finances, the failure to generate capital through taxes, the flight of private capital, and the general insecurity meant that almost no major step toward economic development could be undertaken successfully. It was next to impossible to obtain foreign loans to build roads and railroads or to found a national bank. The combination of insecurity, financial weakness, and lagging foreign trade also delayed the successful establishment of commercial banks until the 1870s. Lack of a banking system in turn hampered the mobilization of private capital and constricted investments. Before 1870 interest rates for men of credit were generally 12 to 18 percent per annum, and for small-fry they were often more than twice as high.[44] Hence, most farmers, large or small, could not afford to make expensive technical improvements unless there was some assurance that investment would bring immediate and spectacular profit. As long as both overland transportation and credit remained expensive, private entrepreneurs lacked incentive for improving production methods.

New Granada's political instability during the nineteenth century not only brought physical destruction and economic insecurity but also fostered abrupt changes of policy. Throughout the nineteenth century the country was afflicted with a fatal inconstancy. Along with the country's frequent alterations of name, constitution, and administrative organization, there were constant policy changes in such critical fields as education and transportation. Whether it was road building or steamboating, one administration's contract was often the next one's cancellation.

Particularly when it came to building roads and railroads, the government found it hard to develop priorities and even harder to adhere to them. Rough terrain, financial difficulties, and a dispersed population, which attracted only sparse freight along mountain trails, all deterred the improvement of communications. But flabby government policies also played a role. With the partial exception of the 1840s, road construction was left largely to provincial and local governments and to the initiative of private enterprise until the last three decades of the nineteenth century. As each province had only minuscule resources at its disposal, no large project that might make a significant breakthrough could be mounted. At best the localities were able to maintain their mulepaths against the annual assaults of torrential rain.

In the first Mosquera administration (1845–1849) national road-building funds were reserved for projects considered important by the central government. But this attempt at a vigorous program of transportation development was soon abandoned, as the López administration in 1850 returned both the revenues and the responsibilities for road construction to the provinces. Not until after 1864 did the central government again attempt to move toward a national policy for the development of transportation.

In part because of the physical, financial, and political factors that inhibited road building and other areas of development, the demand for technicians in New Granada was rather limited. Until at least 1841 no communications project was large enough to support the service of an engineer. The factories created in Bogotá in the 1830s did depend on the services of foreign technicians. But these enterprises for the most part did not last long enough to encourage the training of Colombian mechanical experts. Only in the field of mining was there a clear requirement for small numbers of trained engineers.

As a result, the history of technical education in Colombia contrasts markedly with that in the United States. In the United States a vigorously growing economy created a strong demand for engineers for the construction of canals between 1785 and 1840 and for the building of railroads after 1830. In North America engineering and other technical education developed in response to a clearly established need.[45] In New Granada, on the other hand, the elite attempted to establish technical education in advance of a clear economic demand. They hoped that the nurture of a new, more technically competent, and more technically oriented generation might in itself be an important factor in furthering development.

Part Two   Moral and Industrial Education

Chapter 2   Learning to Work

LABOR economists who have studied the manpower resource problems of less-developed countries have concluded that the worst scarcity is that of skilled workers and middle-level technicians.[1] Members of the Colombian elite in the early republican period were well aware of the need to instill more skills in the lower and middle sectors of the society. They also were strongly concerned to "moralize" the population, an aim that included inculcating the discipline of labor in the upper classes as well as the lower. Through primary and basic industrial education they hoped to attain two closely related ends—social order and economic progress. This chapter is concerned primarily with the forms of industrial education that were attempted in various sectors of the society during the first half century of the republican era. But, as conventional primary instruction was fundamental to the same cause, it also will be treated briefly.

Primary Education

Primary instruction is, if not indispensable, still an extremely useful first step in effective industrial education. The Colombian elite recognized its importance to economic growth, but the strength of their desire to implant it is questionable. It is often alleged that the Latin American upper classes have neglected primary education, concentrating instead upon institutions of higher education that serve only the elite. In Colombia this tendency has been identified particularly with the political conservatives.[2]

Some evidence supports this allegation regarding early republican New Granada, though some of the data is susceptible to other interpretation. In legislating on education in the 1820s Colombia's leaders created a centralized system incorporating all levels of instruction. But secondary education was much more centrally controlled and received much more elite attention—measured in the number and length of laws, executive decrees, and administrative communications—than did primary instruction. Reliance in primary education upon local leadership, which was scarce, ill educated, and often not highly motivated, may have amounted to neglect. It may indicate the elite's greater concern with secondary schools, which trained the sons of the upper class and provided them with some of their ideological furnishing, than with public primary schools, whose pupils had little to do with the potential exercise of power. Similarly, there was a notable disparity between expenditures for secondary education, some of which came from the national government, and those for public primary education, which were generated locally and by the provincial governments (see Table 3). On the other hand, some of these differences in the treatment of primary and secondary education may have been inherent in their character and not the result of deliberate policy. Because of the large number of the primary schools, they necessarily were more dependent upon local leadership and were less susceptible to central government support and direction. And in any system the higher levels of instruction are more expensive to maintain.

While most members of the upper classes may have cared more about the education of their sons in secondary schools than they did about the sons of the masses in public primary ones, they showed a strong interest in primary education, particularly in the first two decades after independence was definitely established. The liberal Gen. Francisco de Paula Santander provided substantial symbolic leadership in this cause during his administrations of 1819–1827 and 1832–1837. During these years the cause also interested a number of prominent members of the political elite.[3]

In general the elite saw public primary instruction as an instrument for the inculcation of religion, morality, and social order; for propagating knowledge of and allegiance to republican government; and for fostering economic development. But the emphases on these various elements shifted from time to time. For example, Colombia's first general education laws, issued by the Congress of Cúcuta on August 6, 1821, emphasized religion, morality, and politics: public primary schools were necessary for Colombians to learn the "sacred obligations imposed upon them by religion and Christian morality, . . . [and] the rights and duties of man in social life." And secondary schools were justified as well on the ground that "public education is the fundamental basis of representative government."[4] By 1826, however, Colombia's legislators apparently were somewhat less concerned about religion, morality, and the salvation of the republic and more interested in promoting economic development. The general education law of March 18, 1826, provided two reasons for supporting public instruction. First, "the country in which instruction is most widespread, and the education of the numerous class destined to cultivate

TABLE 3. *Educational Investment, 1847*[a]

	Number of Institutions	Number of Faculty	Number of Students	Faculty/ Student Ratio	Expenditure per Student (in pesos)
Universities	3	24	747	14	96.60
Seminaries	5	18	571	32	52.49
Colegios provinciales (public)	11	47	861	18	61.78
Private primary schools	659	659[?]	7611	11[?]	n.a.
Public primary schools	474	474[?]	21517	45[?]	2.79

Source: Calculated from figures in Felipe Pérez, *Geografía general de los Estados Unidos de Colombia*, pp. 278–281.

[a]The purpose of this table is to suggest relative investments of money and personnel among the various types of institutions. The figures are approximate at best. The numbers given (number of institutions, number of faculty, number of students) do not represent totals. More than 70 percent of the students listed as attending the universities were studying at the secondary level. Seminaries and *colegios provinciales*, for which revenues but not students were listed, were excluded from the calculations. Both private and public primary schools are here assumed to have had one master each. The funds listed for the public primary schools were also spent for other purposes.

the arts, agriculture, and commerce most generalized, is that in which industry most flourishes, at the same time that general enlightenment in the sciences and useful arts is a perennial . . . and inexhaustible fount of wealth and power for the nation that cultivates them." Second, education would foster "public morality and . . . useful knowledge, which make the people prosperous."[5]

The early enthusiasm of Colombian legislators for primary education is indicated by the high goals they established in this area. The Congress of Cúcuta in 1821 decreed the establishment of a public school for boys in every town of one hundred or more families. In 1826 the Congress decreed that every parish in the country, no matter what its size, was to have a primary school.[6] The legislators also attempted to establish attractive salaries for schoolmasters. "If funds permitted," they were to be not less than three hundred pesos per annum (the level of most secondary instructors), ranging upward to six hundred pesos or more for those teaching more than a hundred students. The legislators also provided for pensions at full salary for those who taught for twenty years.[7] These provisions doubtless remained a dead letter, but they provide some evidence of intent.

Colombian leaders of the 1820s confronted the problem of having to expand primary instruction from a very small base. As public instruction was negligible in extent and of recent arrival at the end of the colonial period, the number of citizens equipped to teach school was very small. And those individuals sufficiently educated to teach were largely absorbed in the complicated business of republican government or in commercial enterprises. The Santander government attempted to finesse this problem by adopting the Lancasterian mutual-instruction method, in which student teaching was supposed to help compensate for the lack of sufficient adult instructors. To introduce the method the Colombian government in the 1820s imported Joseph Lancaster himself (who worked briefly in Caracas) as well as two other foreign practitioners of the system.[8] During the 1820s and 1830s the mutual-instruction system was viewed as the key to rapid educational expansion. As of 1827, 10.7 percent of all primary schools and 18 percent of the students were under the Lancaster system; by 1835, 18.8 percent of the schools and 34.5 percent of the students were under it. Using the Lancasterian method and conventional instruction, the government made substantial progress in extending primary education in the years up to 1837. Starting from the insignificant base of the colonial period, primary enrollments by 1837 had managed to reach more than 25,000, roughly 1.46 percent of the national population and 8.7 percent of the school-age population.[9]

The extent of elite concern about primary education in the 1820s and the 1830s is further demonstrated by the variety of their efforts to implant it. In addition to attempting to create primary schools for children in every parish, the earliest general laws on education called for schoolteachers to hold Sunday classes for adults and youths who could not attend weekday school sessions because they were working. The same laws also provided for instruction in basic literacy for soldiers in the army, with military schoolteachers to be given the rank and salary of first sergeants.[10] During the 1830s one leading military officer, the liberal Gen. José Hilario López, took a notable interest in primary schooling for soldiers, and basic instruction spread from his units to others.[11] In cases other than this one, however, it seems that most efforts at adult education did not get far beyond the pious words employed to proclaim them.

The same can be said for the works of the various philanthropic societies established by leading upper-class figures to promote and encourage primary instruction in Bogotá, Popayán, and elsewhere.[12] The societies to promote primary education, particularly in vogue during the second Santander administration (1832–1837), generally adopted as their principal function the raising of money for texts and school materials. Of the various sorts of philanthropic societies organized in the early republican period, those for primary instruction were the most numerous and seemingly also the most effective and long-lived (some lasted several years). Their success was only relative, however. It appears that the participants entered into them partly out of a sense of social obligation, partly for honorific reasons. They were more or less an early nineteenth century equivalent of the Junior League and must have had no better results.[13]

After 1837, when Santander left the presidency, the wave of interest in primary instruction subsided. In contrast with the dynamic expansion of primary instruction in the 1820s and 1830s, little progress was made in the 1840s and 1850s. Under the protoconservative administrations of José Ignacio de Márquez, Pedro Alcántara Herrán, and Tomás Cipriano de Mosquera (1837–1849), school enrollments remained at about the 1837 level while the population grew by about 25 percent (see Table 4). Substantial progress in primary education did not resume until the administration of the Radical Liberals in the period from 1864 to 1880, when enrollment levels reached nearly 3 percent of the total population and 18 percent of the school-age population by the middle of the 1870s.[14]

These statistics seem to confirm the dictum that conservatives were less interested than liberals in primary education. Looked at more closely, however, the situation is less simple. Many of the protoconservatives who

TABLE 4. *Total Enrollment in Public and Private Primary Schools, Selected Years, 1834–1852*[a]

Year	Enrollment	Comments
1834	20,931	All 22 provinces (where data for 1834 missing, secretary of interior filled in data for previous year)
1838	27,108	20 of 22 provinces reporting; lacking Panamá and Veraguas
1844	26,528	20 provinces reporting
1846	23,926	21 provinces reporting; lacking Mariquita province
1848	24,418	19 provinces reporting; lacking Barbacoas, Casanare, and Veraguas provinces; cantons of Honda and Castrolarma
1850	19,627	Statistically useless; does not include Bogotá, Cartagena, Casanare, Mariquita, Ocaña, Panamá, Túquerres, Valledupar, and Veraguas provinces
1852	21,997	Statistically useless; does not include Antioquia, Bogotá, Buenaventura, Casanare, Zipaquirá, Chiriquí, Mompós, Panamá, Sabanilla, Valledupar, and Veraguas provinces

Sources: Memorias de lo Interior y Relaciones Exteriores, 1839, Cuadro 9; 1845, Cuadro 21; Memorias de Gobierno, 1847, Cuadro 8; 1849, Cuadro 9; 1851, Cuadro 8; 1853, Cuadro 5.

[a]Enrollments are as of August 31 in each year.

governed between 1837 and 1849 were among the most prominent promoters of primary education during the Santander periods. And the long period of relative stasis after 1837 also included some years of apparently slow growth under Liberal auspices (1849–1854).[15] Finally, the most notable advances in primary education occurred in the conservative-dominated province of Antioquia.

To understand the decline of primary education between 1837 and 1864, therefore, one must look beyond political labels or attitudes toward education to more fundamental problems in the polity and the economy. The period between 1837 and 1864 was one of extreme political instability, including two major nationwide civil wars (1839–1842, 1859–1863) and two less damaging ones (1851 and 1854). There were also years of peaceful administrative disorganization as the country went through an almost continuous process of political reconstitution, most notably an evolution from a centralist to an extreme federalist system between 1850 and 1863. Much of the period, particularly between 1837 and 1845, was one of pronounced economic stagnation everywhere except in the province of Antioquia. Political warfare, administrative reorganization, and economic stagnation limited revenue collections at the national and local levels.

The problem went beyond having the will or the wherewithal to provide primary education. There was also the problem of getting the populace to accept it, in particular of motivating peasant families to send their sons to school. Peasants in mid-nineteenth-century Colombia manifested the conservative tendencies of small subsistence farmers in many cultures. A stagnant agricultural economy and a highly stratified, urban-dominated society discouraged peasants from investing time in education. Education represented not merely the loss of a son's laboring time but also the risk of losing his labor permanently. Nor could one expect a return in the form of new income-earning capacity, for a half-educated son, while perhaps ruined for farm work, would remain unintegrated in the dominant urban society. Given the hierarchical structure of Colombian society, it was impossible for the mass of the population to conceive of primary education as a means of preparation for social advancement. Primary instruction therefore seemed to many country folk an irrelevant, if not dangerous, system constructed by urban elites and, no matter what their intentions, oriented toward urban needs and social forms.[16]

In the twentieth century social revolution has enabled some governments in the emerging nations to break through peasant conservatism and to mobilize the people toward education. In nineteenth-century Colombia, of course, the political elite never contemplated such an approach—not only because it was against the interest of upper-class leaders but also because none of the European or Anglo-American models that they followed suggested such a course. Under the liberal Anglo-American model, pecuniary interest was presumed to be a sufficient stimulus. But in Colombia's static economy and highly stratified society, that pecuniary interest was not clearly discernible for the mass of the people.

Industrial Education for the Masses

The problem of motivation was also evident in the field of industrial education. The New Granadan elite, particularly between 1832 and 1849, through a variety of mechanisms attempted to encourage the development of an orderly, moral, industrious, and industrially skilled population. Most of their efforts focused on the unskilled, unemployed, and vagrant among the lower classes, though some also aimed at potentially feckless sons of the upper class. In most cases the elite based its argument for the work ethic upon the assumption of pecuniary reward. Once an individual learned orderly habits, the discipline of labor, and a skill, these virtues would earn him increased profits which would bind him more tightly to an orderly, workerly mode of living. But in the Colombian context the pecuniary advantages of industrial training were not evident, and the elite turned to other means of motivation—sometimes a rather unenticing carrot of honorific incentives, sometimes an equally ineffective stick of coercion.

Among the instruments chosen for uplifting the lower classes were a workhouse in Bogotá; the forced apprenticeship of vagrant or homeless youths; the instruction of peasants through newspapers read to them by parish priests; "philanthropic societies," which attempted to propagate moral maxims and, in some cases, the practical arts; and industrial expositions. Some of these experiments had Spanish Bourbon antecedents, but these were rarely recognized. For political reasons, French, British, or North American models of the same institutions were proclaimed instead. The origin of the model was, in fact, unimportant, as the aims and the spirit of the institutions were rather similar throughout the Western world. The New Granadan elite, like their counterparts in Europe and North America, hoped to use industrial training both to foster economic growth and to shore up the existing social order.

Industrial training based upon coercion and honorifics was most characteristic of the period between 1832 and 1849. And it is particularly identifiable with the men who were politically dominant in that period, men who for the most part became known as conservatives. Most members of the political elite who emerged as Liberals in 1849 were not much involved in the neo-Bourbon crusades and in general devoted little attention to technical training for manual workers. Instead, liberals, particularly as they began to come into political prominence in the 1840s, stressed basic literacy and political education. This difference in emphasis can be explained in at least two ways. On the one hand, in the years before 1845, when the *moderados* (later Conservatives) were clearly in the saddle, the hope that New Granada might develop as a manufacturing country was still alive. It was possible therefore to think that industrial training would prove at once economically useful (in terms of productivity) and socially useful (in terms of moral order). By the middle of the 1840s, when the

Liberal party was emerging as an effective force, it had become clear that New Granada could not compete with Great Britain and the other more advanced nations in manufacturing; this country would have to specialize in tropical agriculture, importing its manufactured goods. Consequently, the promotion of industrial education did not seem appropriate given the developing pattern of the economy. Nor did industrial training make as much sense politically to liberals as it did to conservatives. While the conservatives sought to keep order through industrial discipline, the liberals were trying to break through to power, using urban workers as political allies. Thus, they tended to stress not technical training but political mobilization through the inculcation of liberal political and economic doctrines.

The Casa de Refugio

The first of the neo-Bourbon institutions, the Casa de Refugio, was actually established, in its republican incarnation, by the chief liberal figure of the 1820s and 1830s, Gen. Francisco de Paula Santander. But it was not a typical liberal effort. With a few exceptions liberals were not conspicuous supporters of the Casa de Refugio. Rather, its principal sponsors through the 1830s and 1840s were such men as Ignacio Gutiérrez Vergara, Rufino Cuervo, and José Ignacio de Paris—neo-Bourbon *moderados*, later to be known as Conservatives.

The Casa de Refugio, or *hospicio* ("workhouse") as it was also known, originated during the Bourbon reform era of the colonial period. Throughout the second half of the eighteenth century, modernist intellectuals and administrators in Spain expressed alarm at the backwardness of the Spanish economy and the prevalence of vagrancy, idleness, and mendicity; they looked to technical training, often compulsory, as the cure for social disorder and economic weakness. Between 1776 and 1790 newly created upper-class economic societies in at least seven Spanish cities attempted to maintain instructional workhouses, spinning schools for girls, and schools of agriculture, industrial arts, or design for boys.[17]

The Spanish Enlightenment's assault upon idleness was echoed by colonial administrators in New Granada. During the last four decades of the eighteenth century, the viceroys of New Granada, like their counterparts in Spain, expressed concern about the many vagrants wandering in the wilderness, the beggars in the city streets, and a general shiftlessness of the laboring population. To handle those vagrants who straggled into Santa Fe de Bogotá, the viceregal governments of Pedro Messía de la Zerda (1761–1773) and Manuel de Guirior (1773–1776) devoted some of the property that belonged to the Jesuits before their expulsion to the creation of two sexually segregated workhouses, with a foundling home attached to the women's section. Succeeding viceroys worked to build up the endowments of these institutions by soliciting charitable donations from the wealthier residents of Santa Fe de Bogotá. By the beginning of the nineteenth century and the last decade of the colonial period, the Bogotá *hospicio* was maintaining some 260 individuals, including foundlings.[18]

The viceroys appear to have viewed the *hospicio* primarily as a way of clearing the streets of the idle and mendicant. The occupants of the institution engaged in some industrial activity, principally the spinning and weaving of cotton and wool. But the viceroys considered these labors a means of helping to sustain the poorhouse and paid little attention to its training function. In the early 1790s, however, one of Bogotá's first newspapers, the *Papel Periódico* (1791–1795), sponsored by Viceroy José de Ezpeleta, articulated the dream of the local *hospicio* as an industrial school. The newspaper admitted that Santa Fe's poorhouse would not soon measure up to European models, primarily because it was more difficult to sell *hospicio* products in the stagnant New Granadan market. Nevertheless, the *Papel Periódico* voiced the hope that the local poorhouse "someday would . . . [become a] general office of the Arts, and that . . . the *Hospicio de pobres* would be converted into a famous Seminar of industry, education, and Virtue." But until the end of the colonial period, the primary purpose of the *hospicio* remained simply to get the beggars out of sight. Craft training for youths, while recognized as one of the institution's several goals, held no especially high priority.[19]

The Bogotá *hospicio* collapsed in the turmoil of the Independence period. In 1833, however, Pres. Francisco de Paula Santander sought to reestablish it, but on a new basis, with a much clearer focus on the training of youths in industrial arts. Although there existed a colonial model for an instructional workhouse, the inspiration for Santander's new model, by his own account, came from abroad, principally from the United States, where he had spent some time in 1832. In 1824 and 1826 New York City and Philadelphia had set up the first publicly supported schools specializing in juvenile reform, and Santander during his short stay in the United States had managed to visit both of them.[20] In these "houses of refuge" inmates received primary instruction for four hours a day and spent the rest of the time in industrial work. Santander recorded very favorable impressions of both establishments. Both were teaching the elements of citizenship—reading, writing, morality, and the Constitution—as well as various crafts.[21]

The institution created in Bogotá at President Santander's request was quite similar in form and spirit to those he had seen in New York and Philadelphia. Like them, it was to be supported by the provincial (rather than the national) government and supervised by a public commission. Like the American houses of refuge, it was based on two assumptions: first, that a child could be nurtured either into criminality or into social responsibility and, second, that social responsibility could be sustained in adulthood only if the individual found a stake in society through some economically rewarding activity. Society therefore had an interest in the moral education and productive training of neglected children. Like its American counterparts, the House of Refuge represented an attempt to endow a semipenal institution with constructive educational and corrective functions that emphasize the instruction of youths in basic literacy as well as artisan skills.[22]

Santander emphasized that the institution should not be merely an almshouse. Its purpose was not simply to rid the citizenry of the nuisance of *pordioseros* in the street but, more important, to make useful citizens of youthful vagrants before they became totally corrupted:

> It is not the principal interest of a society to gather up the poor and the feeble, so that, instead of wandering through the most public streets displaying their misery and misfortunes, and disgusting the citizens with their daily demands, they are collected in a place where they at least do away with their idleness. . . . the principal and most important [object] is to attack the evil at its origin, to collect the youth of both sexes in a house of correction or instruction, where learning the principles of religion, some useful trade, and good morality, they may leave prepared to live with profit to themselves and to the state.[23]

In accord with Santander's emphasis on the instructional function of the workhouse, the decree creating it expressed the hope that the institution would prepare the younger inmates to become apprentices to artisans or "some respectable person."[24]

From 1833 through the end of the 1850s, the provincial administrators charged with supervising the Casa de Refugio continued to stress its function as an educational institution for youth, with particular emphasis on learning the habit of work and a useful trade. These administrators were unable to concentrate on this function, however, because Bogotá had no other effective institution for handling its various public charges. *Bogotanos* continued to view the Casa de Refugio as a convenient dumping-place for social nuisances. In the 1830s some members of the upper class refused to pay the sums they had pledged to the Casa because large numbers of older vagrants and *pordioseros* were still on the streets. The administrators of the institution were under constant pressure to sacrifice the training of youth in order to perform this police function.[25] Consequently the Casa de Refugio became burdened with more functions than its scarce re- sources could support, including the care of foundlings, the aged, and all other unemployables. A decade after its founding, these latter activities were absorbing almost the entire budget, leaving the education of youths in the discard.

In its early years in the 1830s, the institution functioned more or less according to Santander's plan. In January, 1835, when it began operations, the 19 vagrant boys who had been rounded up were being given primary instruction, and most of the 90-odd adult inmates were occupied in clean- ing, spinning, and weaving wool and cotton. By 1839 the Casa was main- taining 39 boys, 22 of whom were studying in the school run by the chap- lain of the institution, while the rest preferred to work in the tailor, shoemaking, and carpentry shops along with the 23 adult males. In 1842 a Bogotá philanthropist donated two spinning machines to the workhouse and offered the services of two Italian workmen as instructors. Neverthe- less, during the 1840s practical instruction collapsed completely. When the value of its manufactures fell below the cost of production, the Casa's directors decided to suspend all the work in the shops.[26]

The Casa's instructional efforts were undermined in part by the prodi- gious growth in the number of foundlings for which it had to care. In the late colonial period, when Bogotá had a population of about 20,000, the *hospicio* had cared for only 35 to 50 foundlings—less than 20 percent of its total number of charges. In 1835, when the population of the capital had risen closer to 40,000, the Casa de Refugio still maintained less than 50 foundlings, representing only 26 percent of its 190 charges. After that, however, the number of infants rose steeply, and their care became the institution's greatest concern during the 1840s and 1850s[27] (see Table 5).

Patrocinio Cuellar, the governor of Bogotá province in 1851 and 1853, summed up the situation in this period. In 1851, having received a total of 254 foundlings, the Casa "only [had] fulfilled its purpose as a house of maternity." Most of the institution's income was employed in paying foster mothers and in feeding some 60 or 70 persons "who, because of their age and misery, could not even beg for bread." The aged were not fit for any kind of work, and those school-age children in the institution were too few in number to justify the hiring of craftsmen to teach them. Consequently,

TABLE 5. *Foundlings in the Casa de Refugio at Date of Annual Report*

Years	Number of Foundlings	Total Charges	Foundlings as % of Total
Ca. 1788	47	269	17
1796–1800 (av.)	37	258	14
1835	50	190	26
1836	70	190	37
1839	82	204	40
1848	109	170	64
1849	116	167	69
1850	150	219	68
1851	179	251	71
1852	149	230	65
1853	141	212	67

neither a training program nor any kind of economic activity was being carried on in the workhouse.[28]

After the artisans' revolution of 1854, a number of efforts were made to revive craft instruction and manufacture in Bogotá's Casa de Refugio. At the urging of José Manuel Restrepo, a factory-school for the manufacture of straw hats was established in the Casa in 1855. The factory lasted no more than a year, however, because the institution failed to attract the external apprentices that it was hoped would sustain the operation. This occurred because "to the class of the people from which apprentices might come, the idea of their children going to the workhouse [was] repugnant," even though it was only for instruction.[29]

In 1856 the provincial government of Bogotá attempted to make a contract with the textile firm of Sánchez, Ponce y Compañía that would have turned the Casa into a factory under their management. But the Sánchez, Ponce arrangement fell through because the provincial legislature imposed terms the entrepreneurs considered too restrictive. A cigar factory finally was established in the Casa and maintained for several years. The cigar factory, however, was primarily a device for employing the older women in the Casa. According to its administrators, the aim of instructing youth in craft techniques and the habits of work was not satisfactorily fulfilled, primarily because the Casa did not have sufficient resources to take on a substantial number of abandoned youths.[30]

It is unlikely, however, that the Casa de Refugio ever could have fulfilled the broader technical-training function that Santander and others envisioned for it. Because it grouped together vagrants of all ages, the old and unredeemable tended to confirm the corruption of the young.[31] And, as it was created for the correction of vagrants, its training services could not be extended to other elements in the lower class who shunned identification as vagrants or with an institution thought of as having a penal character. In part because of this identification as well as because of scarce resources, the Casa de Refugio was never transformed from a mere poorhouse into a school for the industrial arts.

Forced Apprenticeship

Contemporaneous with the Casa de Refugio and similar in intent was a scheme for forced apprenticeship (*concertaje*) of youths between the ages of seven and eighteen. According to a typical *proyecto* for forced apprenticeship, such devices were necessitated by the "inconstancy and lack of foresight which are characteristic of early years and cause youths frequently to abandon the haciendas, houses or workshops in which they could acquire knowledge and skill in some useful art or work, and laborious habits for the rest of their lives." Society needed to assure itself of the perseverance of youth in occupations profitable "for themselves, for their families and for the community in general."[32]

Even more clearly than in the case of the Casa de Refugio the advocacy of forced apprenticeship in the 1830s was connected with the contemporary efforts to establish manufacturing in Bogotá. Among the most vigorous proponents of forced apprenticeship were the empresarios and investors in the capital's recently established factories. These small factories—including a textile mill, a paper mill, and a porcelain manufactory—were attempted by leading members of the upper class in many cases for philanthropic reasons as well as to make a profit. In 1839, twenty-two of these upper-class entrepreneurs signed a petition in support of stronger forced apprenticeship laws. The petition admitted frankly their interest in the cheap labor that forced apprenticeship would make available, but it also emphasized the program's educational and philanthropic purposes, aiming as it did at the technical and moral education of the country's youth. Forced apprenticeship had a double importance, "because the good morality and the good government and the order of the population are highly interested in it, as well as the advance of the arts and the gradual progress of industry."[33]

Several laws providing for the the forced apprenticeship of vagrant youths were enacted, the principal one being that of April 6, 1836. This law defined as vagrant not only prostitutes and the unemployed, but also those who were only partially employed and those who, even though they may have had money on which to live, were habitually in the company of vagrants, criminals, gamblers, and prostitutes. It also included minors (*hijos de familia*) who scandalized society "by their bad customs and little respect for their parents, without showing any application to the career chosen for them." In addition, the law considered vagrant those students who refused to obey their teachers, failed to fulfill their "scholastic obligations," and were delivered over to idleness. These various classes of vagrants, "according to their various aptitudes," were to be condemned to the army or to forced public labor (adult males). They could be required to form new colonies (all adults) or to serve forced apprenticeships with private entrepreneurs or public establishments for two to six years (youths).[34]

The forced-apprenticeship law of 1836 proved ineffective. Most of the people condemned for vagrancy were too recalcitrant to provide usable labor, and private entrepreneurs refused to take them on. For this reason it was increasingly emphasized that only youths, who had not yet been entirely corrupted, should be destined to apprenticeship. Despite various efforts to make the vagrancy laws more effective, it appears that they did not yield the expected fruits.[35]

Voluntarist Efforts

Along with the coercive mechanisms of the Casa de Refugio and forced apprenticeship, upper-class Colombians also attempted to create some positive stimuli to the habit of work and useful employment. During the 1830s and 1840s various efforts were made to disseminate useful knowledge among the lower classes. One of these involved the publication of a newspaper focusing on agricultural questions, which was to be read by parish priests to their peasant congregations. This project—rather sensible given the role of the clergy as an elite, practically *the* educated elite, among the peasantry—also had Spanish Bourbon precedents. From the 1770s onward Enlightenment intellectuals had attempted to encourage Spanish priests to provide economic leadership at the parish level. The ultimate expression of this idea in the Bourbon Enlightenment era was the publication in Spain between 1797 and 1808 of a weekly newspaper, the *Semanario de Agricultura y Artes Dirigido a los Párrocos*. At the end of the colonial period New Granada had something vaguely like this. The *Semanario del Nuevo Reino de Granada*, published by Francisco José de Caldas, while not specifically directed toward parish priests, did serve as an organ for the diffusion of useful knowledge among at least a few of the more enlightened provincial clergy.[36]

In the early 1830s the idea of an agricultural journal aimed at rural priests and their parishioners was revived in New Granada. The newspaper's founder, Rufino Cuervo, then governor of the province of Bogotá, was a typical neo-Bourbon. Educated in the law, he spent much of his life as a public official and as a private citizen promoting public education and various works of public welfare. Like most neo-Bourbons he was also a strong supporter of New Granadan manufacturing, as well as of agricultural improvement. The provincial newspaper that he sponsored as governor, *El Cultivador Cundinamarqués*, discussed agricultural problems and techniques and also contained lessons in *urbanidad* and moral homilies. Cuervo's intention, perhaps imperfectly carried out, was that the journal would be distributed or read to members of rural communities by the parish priests, *alcaldes*, and other local officials.[37]

Some parish priests, even without the stimulus of the short-lived *Cultivador Cundinamarqués*, worked to diffuse new agricultural and manufacturing techniques among the peasant population. In the late colonial and early republican periods, Fr. Eloy Valenzuela of Bucaramanga promoted the use of improved varieties of pasturage and sugar cane. A contemporary curate in Antioquia introduced cane cultivation to the environs of Marinilla. From 1834 through the 1850s Fr. Francisco Romero required his parishioners to plant coffee as an act of penance and thus helped to found an export industry in his part of northern Santander. Though most priests naturally promoted agricultural improvement, some also encouraged various types of home manufacturing. A Father Posada in Marinilla brought new looms to Antioquia in an effort to improve cottage weaving. An Ecuadorean friar taught bookbinding in Bogotá in the 1830s and early 1840s. And in Santander the straw hat industry that flourished in the 1850s and 1860s is said to have been started by a priest. During the 1820s Fr. Felipe Salgar of Girón employed a Pasto hatter to train his female parishioners in the art in order to provide them with an economic alternative to prostitution.[38]

Philanthropic societies similar to those promoting private education undertook the diffusion of useful knowledge, though not very successfully. These societies were of various sorts, almost all based upon French, British, or Spanish Bourbon models. One type was the National Academy established by the national government as an official body to promote morality as well as the arts and sciences. The first of these, created in 1826 by the Santander regime, collapsed during the political crises of the late 1820s. It was revived very briefly with Santander's return to power in 1832. The idea of a national academy was resurrected by the Mosquera administration with the creation of the Instituto Caldas, which endured from 1848 to 1850. The members of these short-lived academies, generally selected by government ministers, tended to be those upper-class individuals most known for an interest in science, technology, or education and included a goodly sprinkling of political and religious leaders chosen because of their leadership roles.[39] With the possible exception of the Instituto Caldas the accomplishments of these official academies are not perceptible.

Other philanthropic societies were locally created groups, generally formed with the encouragement of the provincial governor, but not considered official government bodies. These societies, in design and membership, were less clearly oriented toward the natural sciences and their applications than the national academies, though some of them showed some interest in artisan education. The Temperance Society, promoted during a two-month period in 1835 by the brothers Joaquín and Tomás Cipriano de Mosquera, simply sought to propagate morality in the most direct and obvious ways.[40] Of those societies directed toward the education of artisans, it is not clear how many were concerned with technical, as distinguished from literary, skills. Two that apparently attempted industrial training in the 1830s were the Sociedad Patriótica de Amigos del Pais of Cartagena, founded in the fall of 1831, and a similar society in Panamá, active from 1834 to 1835. The Cartagena society, after a refounding in 1835, attempted to publish a monthly to "disseminate useful knowledge," significantly entitled *La Abeja de Cartagena* [*The Bee of Cartagena*].[41]

These local bodies, particularly those concerned with morals and industrial education, were characteristically promoted and dominated by conservative patricians like the Mosqueras of Popayán and the Gutiérrezes of Bogotá. With the exception of a few men like Lorenzo María Lleras, liberals tended to be skeptical of these bodies, even though they were drawn into them because of their political position. Such liberal notables as Francisco de Paula Santander and Vicente Lombana, both associated with the "national academy" of 1832, tended to take some of these societies rather lightly, considering them excessively pompous and not very effective.[42] Most of the societies were, in fact, short-lived—usually enduring only as long as the principal promoter remained in office (as president or governor) or in town. The other members apparently tended to lose interest once a society had been organized, its officers elected, its statutes written, and its committees named.

Interest in philanthropic societies appears to have been greatest during the 1830s. The efforts of this decade were soon interrupted by the civil war of 1839–1842. But the war also stimulated renewed attempts to "moralize" the masses. Some upper-class conservatives, viewing the war as new evidence that traditional social constraints were loosening, turned increased attention to the promotion of the industrial arts as an instrument of social discipline. The postwar association of public morality with the industrial arts had its earliest manifestation in Bogotá with the celebration in the fall of 1841 of a "civic festival" to commemorate the conservative victory over the liberal forces that had threatened the capital the year before. Ignacio Gutiérrez Vergara, an influential *ministerial*-conservative, suggested an industrial fair as the most appropriate way to celebrate the triumph of the forces of order.

The son of one of the most prestigious families in colonial Santa Fe de Bogotá, Gutiérrez was descended from the lawyer-bureaucrats, *hacendados*, and large merchants who composed the colonial elite. His greatgrandfather, Francisco Antonio Moreno y Escandón, as a colonial official had played a leading role in the founding of Bogotá's first workhouse as well as in efforts at university reform. Gutiérrez Vergara's grandfather was one of the largest landowners in the Bogotá region, and his father had been both a colonial officeholder and one of the aristocratic leaders of the early independence era. Ignacio Gutiérrez, himself, after securing the standard law degree, began his career in Bogotá in the 1830s as a government administrator. One of his early appointments was as the first director of the Casa de Refugio of 1833, a post that some in Bogotá thought belonged to him by inheritance.[43]

The idea of establishing an industrial fair was in keeping with Gutiérrez's role in the Casa de Refugio. The scheme apparently was prompted, however, by a foreign model. The French Directory, under what Gutiérrez viewed as somewhat similar circumstances of revolutionary disorder, had established industrial fairs, which he believed had helped to promote both public morality and industrial development in France. He hoped that similar fairs in New Granada might bring about the "destruction of turmoil and political revolutions."[44] To promote the industrial fairs and the social goals they embodied, Gutiérrez and two other conservative politicians, José Eusebio Caro and José María Galavis, published pamphlets exhorting the lower classes to strive for the intertwined virtues of industrial competence and domestic and public morality.[45] In the industrial fairs held in Bogotá during the 1840s, prizes were awarded not only for achievements in the arts and crafts but also for demonstrations of exemplary moral behavior.

Individuals were invited to appear before the fair judges to proclaim virtuous deeds previously unknown to the public. Students, public employees, soldiers, domestic servants, and others were urged to present certificates of good behavior from their teachers and masters. Gaming was forbidden during the fair, and those who denounced gamblers before public authorities were to be rewarded with prizes.[46]

Bogotá's industrial fairs, contrary to the hopes of the elite in the capital, were not widely emulated. They survived, though with declining public interest, through the 1840s, and they were held occasionally in the 1850s. The effects of the fairs were limited at best. There is no evidence that public morals were dramatically improved. And certainly none of the mechanical contrivances and other works of human art that were exhibited ever merited attention outside of Bogotá. Nevertheless, the fairs represent another example of conservative interest in promoting the industrial arts.

In the early years of relative glory of the industrial fair, its founders attempted to pursue the goal of social order through economic progress by creating another society, the Sociedad Filantrópica, established in the fall of 1842. Its members, chosen in part by the provincial governor, were among the capital's leading conservative politicians, ecclesiastics, and merchant-capitalists.[47] The society does not appear to have been a very practical body. Members viewed its functions as largely hortatory, its principal concern being to publish pamphlets and periodicals dedicated to the propagation of morality. Even this function was not very actively pursued.

Nevertheless, the establishment of the Bogotá society apparently stimulated the creation of many provincial societies, some of which did work effectively. These varied somewhat in character. In Antioquia they tended to promote primary education.[48] On the Caribbean littoral, on the other hand, they were markedly oriented toward material progress. The Sociedad de Fomento Industrial of Cartagena, established in 1844 by the provincial governor, Pastor Ospina, had commissions devoted to the encouragement of the arts and manufactures, as well as of mining, agriculture, and domestic economy.[49] The philanthropic society of Panama, founded in 1843 by its *antioqueño* governor, Col. Anselmo Pineda, similarly concentrated on the promotion of artisan industries. Sunday schools were established for workers. Schools for instruction in shoemaking were created in two Panamanian towns, and in three communities instruction was offered in the weaving of palm-leaf hats. For the latter purpose Pineda brought instructors from the hat-weaving regions of the upper Magdalena valley. Pineda's promotion of hat weaving proved particularly fruitful; according to Panamanian sources, these schools were the origin of hats that from the middle of the nineteenth century onward were sold in the United States.[50]

A third wave of interest in philanthropic societies was fostered by Manuel Ancízar during the Mosquera administration (1845–1849). Ancízar was born on a hacienda near Bogotá and as a child was taken to Cuba by his father, a Basque merchant who had compromised himself by serving as a corregidor during the Spanish reconquest of 1816–1819. After a legal education in Havana, Ancízar moved to the United States and ultimately to Caracas. In 1846 through the influence of a leading New Granadan neo-Bourbon, Lino de Pombo, Ancízar was brought into the Mosquera government in New Granada; by 1847 he was serving in the cabinet as interim secretary of foreign affairs and internal improvements.[51] In this post and later as editor of a semiofficial newspaper, Ancízar undertook a variety of projects for the diffusion of useful knowledge, among them the printing of scientific and technical articles, the hiring of foreign science professors, the resurrection of the Bogotá observatory, and the execution of the republic's first systematic geographical survey (Comisión Corográfica).

One of Ancízar's efforts on behalf of technical training for the masses was the Instituto Caldas, established by a Mosquera decree at Ancízar's request in December, 1847. Ancízar, like Santander in 1833, pointed to a U.S. model for his institute, an artisans' school in New York.[52] Nevertheless, the Instituto Caldas, like the earlier philanthropic societies of the 1830s and 1840s, was clearly in the Spanish Bourbon tradition. The decree establishing the institute stated that its purpose was the "development of intelligence, the conservation of morality, and the perfection of industry among the Granadan masses [*el pueblo granadino*]." And its principal objects in the field of morality were to "restrain . . . the laboring classes [*morigerar a fondo el pueblo jornalero*], eradicating vices [and] crimes," and the "social improvement of the Republic, founded on family morality and punishment of the delinquent." The first of the ways these aims would be achieved was through the promotion of apprenticeships in the arts and crafts.[53]

Despite its similarities to the earlier Bourbon and neo-Bourbon societies, the Instituto Caldas also bore some of the distinctive marks of the Mosquera administration. It was less pious and moralistic in spirit and more clearly focused on material progress: its membership included two foreign technicians and only one clergyman. In addition, it was organized with a certain specialization of function. Members were divded into sections according to their expertise. Men who had taught in *colegios* or were interested in industrial education composed the education section. The section on benefaction appropriately included the archbishop of Bogotá and the city's most notable lay philanthropist. Manuel Ancízar, joined by a Scottish "architect" and a local construction entrepreneur, comprised a section on material improvements. The section on roads, immigration, and statistics included a French engineer, Antoine Poncet, who was serving as a director of roads for the government, along with three politicians who had experience in the Ministry of Finance.[54]

As in the case of the Sociedad Filantrópica, some of the provincial branches, with their more obscure memberships, accomplished more than did the central body in the capital. In the Santander region, for example, schools for instruction in the weaving of hats were established in Pamplona, Oiba, and other places. In the early 1850s Barichara, a town of four thousand inhabitants, was maintaining eight shops in which a hundred young women were given free training in the weaving of palm-leaf hats.[55] The Santander hat-weaving schools helped to introduce a new industry that in the 1850s began to take the place of the region's declining cottage weaving of cottons and canvas. As in the somewhat earlier case of Panamá, the new hat-weaving industry soon provided an important export item for the Santander region. Aside from the limited achievements of the Santander area, there is no indication that the Instituto Caldas was more successful than its predecessors. In most places the institute died in 1849, with the administration that had founded it.

Despite repeated beginnings, the New Granadan elite between 1833 and 1849 achieved only limited and scattered success in introducing new techniques to manual workers. This failure may be ascribed in part to certain fundamental and intractable socioeconomic problems and in part to the weaknesses of aristocratic leadership. In any society like that of New Granada—marked by a great distance between a small dominant class and a poor and ignorant peasantry—the implantation of innovations would have been difficult. The ignorance of the peasantry and other manual workers made them suspicious of change, and their poverty limited their willingness to take risks. Further, a long history of often arbitrary domination by the creole upper class had created a deeply rooted (though partially concealed) lower-class distrust of anything emanating from the aristocracy. No matter what tack the innovating elite took, they were unlikely to encounter an enthusiastic response.[56] That the neo-Bourbons so often couched their proposals in patronizing terms—"the moral correction of the poor"—undoubtedly did not help to allay lower-class mistrust.

There is also reason to question the depth of elite commitment to the technical instruction of the lower classes. In the case of the philanthropic societies, as in that of their predecessors, the Spanish economic societies, many members of the upper class appear to have joined as much for honorific reasons as out of concern for the cause at hand.[57] Even the dozen or so individuals who cared deeply about artisan education tended to operate on a somewhat lofty level. They contributed a good deal of pious exhortation. But upper-class leaders remained largely uninvolved in the process of technical instruction, except as financial administrators. Only one case has emerged in which an adult member of the upper class set an example by taking practical instruction in the manual arts. Serving as patrons, not participants, the upper-class leaders did nothing to modify the negative class associations connected with manual trades, and they probably reinforced the notion that this program was an upper-class imposition.

While a blatant paternalism was congenial to the upper class, the tendency to reform-by-imposition can also be viewed as a reflection of the country's unprepossessing economic situation. Because the small, poor, isolated local markets offered little economic incentive, there was little choice but to try imposition as an instrument of progress. That the gestures at imposition were so feeble is itself an indication that the economy offered few opportunities, even to the upper class.

On a few occasions when the neo-Bourbons tried innovations with economic possibilities they were somewhat successful, despite their aristocratic style. Beginning in the middle of the 1840s they established savings banks in Cartagena, Bogotá, Medellín, and various smaller places. These savings banks were explicitly advertised as instruments of the upper class for the moral and economic correction of the lower. With the cream of the upper class serving as volunteer administrators, the savings banks did attract numbers of lower-class depositors. At least in the larger cities they flourished for nearly two decades, an astonishing longevity for any institution in mid-nineteenth-century New Granada.

The relative success of the savings banks cannot be ascribed to greater commitment on the part of the elite. In the savings banks most of the upper-class participants played much the same role as they did in the philanthropic societies. They were symbols of respectability. By the same token their motives for taking part might often have had as much to do with the satisfaction of vanity (in being chosen one of the dozen or so most respected individuals in the city) as did membership in other types of philanthropic association.

It seems rather that there was a clear economic need for the savings banks. When they were established, there was no alternative savings institution, nor was there any significant secular institution providing credit. This function had been exercised by church organizations in the past. But with the seizure of some church properties during and after the Independence period, church economic power deteriorated. To a great extent borrowers were at the mercy of individual moneylenders who were charging interest at such high levels (often 2 or 3 percent per month) that borrowing became a sure road to disaster. Thus, the utility of a savings bank was evident to many.

In the case of technical instruction, however, the advantages were not always clear. Frequently upper-class leaders conceived of such instruction as training in the use of textile machinery. Yet in the 1830s and 1840s, it was becoming increasingly obvious that cottage weavers as well as upper-class entrepreneurs in the textile industry, under pressure from British and French imports, were facing a dead end. It is notable that where a substantial economic benefit could be realized from learning a craft, training programs were quite successful. The schools for the manufacture of palm-leaf hats that were established in Panamá and Santander in the 1840s had no difficulty attracting apprentices as there were considerable markets for these hats in the United States, Cuba, and Brazil. The peasant population of Santander, while sometimes leery of primary schools, responded favorably to training in domestic manufactures that promised an immediate pay-off.[58]

The importance of an evident and effective economic interest is further suggested by the success of an artisans' school in Caracas. By the early 1850s more than five hundred students—carpenters, stone masons, blacksmiths, tinkers—were studying not only reading and writing, but also mathematics and applied science in the evenings and on Sundays. Possibly the Venezuelan founder of this institution provided more compelling leadership than his New Granadan counterparts. But it is also true that the economy of Caracas in the middle of the nineteenth century was much more dynamic than that of any city in New Granada. Located close to the coast, Caracas could export coffee and sugar profitably, and its plantations had developed on a grand scale. In this part of Venezuela, plantations were using sugar-refining and coffee-curing machinery of a size and complication virtually unknown in Colombia until the last quarter of the century.[59] Caracas's growing agricultural economy therefore provided a basis for the development of a vigorous industrial artisan class.

In isolated, economically stagnant Bogotá the agricultural economy had hardly reached the iron age. Many implements—including plows and machinery for sugar mills—were still wooden and of the rudest construction. As there was little demand for the services of industrial mechanics, the artisan class was limited largely to the production of luxury consumer goods. And Bogotá's consumer-goods craftsmen (cobblers, tailors, furniture and cabinetmakers, etc.) faced the depressing prospect of increasing importations of fine ready-made clothes and fixtures from England and France. The drastic lowering of the tariff on finished goods in 1847 simply served to make these artisans aware that the future held little for them. The economic climate in Bogotá was not propitious to the development of the vigorous, confident artisan class needed to sustain a successful program of worker education. Certainly the artisans of Bogotá were sufficiently numerous to support an artisans' school. In 1847 the Bogotá artisans' society had three hundred members and by the end of 1849 the society claimed fifteen hundred (probably including some university students and other upper-class affiliates).[60] But among the artisans of Bogotá the atmosphere was one of desperation and crisis rather than one of sanguine confidence in future prosperity rewarding present effort.

Artisan Organization and Education after 1849

Artisan organization and education after 1849 was oriented much less toward technical improvement than toward political action. The principal organ of artisan education after 1849 was the Sociedad de Artesanos (later Sociedad Democrática). This was formed by the artisans of Bogotá in 1847 (and subsequently in many other communities) in opposition to the lowering of the tariff in that year. In 1848 the society began a self-administered educational program that included instruction in reading, writing, and math, but that placed increasing emphasis on political discussion. In 1849, the artisans of Bogotá formed a political alliance with the upper-class Liberal party. At that time young Liberal university students and university graduates offered lectures to the artisans. These lectures, however, were distinctly nontechnical, consisting primarily of Liberal economic dogma and political indoctrination (some of which was not well received by the ardently protectionist artisans).[61] Ultimately, political agitation among the artisans led to the artisans' revolution-military coup of 1854 and to partisan political ferment from the 1860s through the 1880s. Thus, the conservative ideal of technical proficiency and subordination gave way to politicization and political turbulence.

After 1849 upper-class attempts to promote the material and moral progress of the poor through the typical neo-Bourbon institutions fell into relative disfavor. The Liberals who controlled the government from 1849 to 1854 consciously rejected Bourbon models. Under their rule such Bourbon instruments as government coercion of vagrants and philanthropic societies were abandoned. In 1851 Liberals moved to eliminate the vagrancy laws of the 1830s and 1840s. And in 1853 the Liberal-dominated Senate ignored a request by the citizens of Cartagena for permission to create a house of refuge.[62]

Like the Conservatives, the Liberals sought labor discipline and wanted to inculcate values supportive of economic productivity. But they favored an entirely different strategy for the pursuit of these goals. First, the Liberals, unlike the Conservatives, did not believe that orderliness and laboriousness could be imposed. Rather, these virtuous habits must develop as a response to perceived economic opportunities. Thus, in the bill repealing vagrancy laws, the Liberals proclaimed that "vagrancy is not subject to the action of laws or the persecution of the magistrates and authorities of the Republic." The government could prevent it only by "protecting industry, opening new sources of wealth, and stimulating work and instruction."[63] While the Conservatives tended to believe that people were shiftless because of the disintegration of traditional social values, the Liberals believed that idleness was primarily a reflection of economic stagnation. Industrial morality and labor discipline would come not through official or semiofficial coercion but through opportunities generated by the free operation of the economic marketplace. If all institutional constraints on free enterprise were eliminated, new and more productive activities would spring up, and these would provide higher wages (incentives) to the worker. Second, though this was less frequently mentioned, in a free market situation workers would either become productive or be driven under. Liberals considered the traditional coercive institutions, such as antivagrancy laws and poorhouses, to be based on erroneous economic conceptions. Furthermore, as a general principle Liberals of the 1850s were suspicious of government leadership in any field on the ground that it interfered with the operation of the free market and usually favored vested interests.

While Liberals of the early 1850s were leery of active government leadership and guidance, they did accept the idea of action by private associations. Their conceptions of useful types of private association differed, however, from those of the Conservatives. From a Liberal point of view the neo-Bourbon philanthropic societies were too *overtly* paternalistic. The

word *overtly* is emphasized because the Liberals clearly wished to manipulate the artisans and other working-class elements as much as did the Conservatives. But, under the influence of democratic romanticism in general
and the Revolution of 1848 in particular, they adopted an egalitarian style,
attempting to guide the workers in the guise of revolutionary comrades
rather than as traditional upper-class *patrones*.

Although Liberals wished to control and manipulate the workers, it was
toward different ends than those of the Conservatives. The Conservatives
sought to inculcate technical education for the double purpose of achieving industrial development and social order. The Liberals of the 1850s,
however, were not interested in industrial development. Believing that
New Granada's proper and necessary role was to specialize in the export of
raw materials, they considered the Conservatives' efforts to develop industry futile and therefore pernicious. And, as for the Conservatives' idea
of the social order, the Liberals, as a politically emergent group, were more
interested in using disruptive tactics to secure power (in the early 1850s)
than they were concerned about the danger of social disintegration. Also,
during this early period they viewed social disruption as necessary to the
process of destroying the many remaining features of the colonial system.
The Liberals, therefore, did not sustain Conservative efforts in technical
education.

Philanthropic societies also fell into discard during the period of Liberal
strength (1849–1870) because the Liberal political program was so highly
distracting at best and disruptive at worst that it tended to divert Liberals
and Conservatives alike from the enterprise of education or, in fact, from
any sustained community social or economic activity. During the early
1850s the Liberals were preoccupied with the expulsion of the Jesuits and
a frontal attack on the remains of the colonial fiscal system. The Conservatives, for their part, were occupied in defending church interests and the
fiscal system; and, especially after the abortive Conservative rebellion of
1851, a number of Conservative leaders who had supported philanthropic
societies went into exile. Subsequently, New Granada was disrupted by
the military-artisan revolution of 1854 and by the Mosquera-led Liberal
revolution of 1859–1863. In part because of the chronic disorder of this
period, serious efforts on behalf of the industrial arts could not be resumed
until the end of the 1860s. Concerted efforts to train workers were not resumed until the early 1870s, when the various states of Colombia established schools of arts and crafts. By this time not only was there relative
public order but also Conservatives and Liberals could now agree on the
necessity of governmental leadership in this field.

Teaching the Upper Sectors to Work

The neo-Bourbons of the 1830s and 1840s were anxious to "moralize" not merely the lower class but also the sons of the upper class. A number of New Granadan conservatives wanted their children, as well as those of the plebeians, to become more responsible, more practical, more technically skilled, more positive toward manual work, and generally more oriented toward economic productivity.

In the Sisyphean labor of reforming upper-class values, the political elite of the 1830s and 1840s used many of the instruments that were applied to the lower classes. The industrial expositions and the work of the philanthropic societies, for example, were aimed at encouraging youths in the upper class as well as in the lower to study the mechanical arts. Some upper-class adults who would not think of engaging in manual labor did not hesitate to place their sons in artisans' shops as a moral corrective.

In 1843, when Col. Anselmo Pineda, as provincial governor, organized several philanthropic societies in the city of Panamá, one of his concerns was to encourage among the upper classes a higher valuation of, as well as greater skills in, the manual arts. One of Pineda's collaborators, Mariano Arosemena, a member of a leading Panamanian family, happily reported to Pres. Pedro Alcántara Herrán that they had succeeded in inspiring "appreciation of the [mechanical] arts in the class of the society most notable for its education and fortune." Considering the examples of Colonel Pineda's nephew, who had entered a tailor shop, and two military officers who were receiving practical instruction in a carpentry shop, he concluded that "cultivated youths [*juventud de finos modales*]" were beginning to go to the "workshops . . . to learn the craft of their inclination." The establishment of a straw hat factory in Panamá, Arosemena hoped, would help to "generalize the learning of all kinds of profitable industry among those who judged themselves degraded by the use of their hands in the mechanical arts."[64]

Arosemena's account seems a trace optimistic. It tells more, undoubtedly, about the hopes of conservative political leaders than about the attitudes of the youths. The great class divisions between a small, relatively leisure endowed upper class and an exploitable, cheap labor force provided strong and enduring support in most of New Granada for the belief that manual labor was demeaning. For the most part upper-class youths stoutly resisted all efforts by their parents to overcome their children's deeply ingrained horror of physical labor. At the beginning of the century, when Joaquín Acosta was a youth, his very aristocratic mother (the widow of a *corregidor* and a great landowner herself) attempted to lessen his hauteur by sending him on errands that would oblige him to carry home heavy objects. Young Acosta, who later was to become known in New Granada as an ardent practitioner of academic science, invariably evaded this requirement. Each time he paid a *peón* to carry his burden to the house for him; then, so as not to provoke his mother's wrath, he would walk through the door carrying the burden himself.[65]

In spite of the efforts of leaders of Acosta's generation to modify this upper-class attitude toward physical labor, the youth of each successive era remained constant in their resistance. At the end of the 1840s, after more than two decades of neo-Bourbon propaganda on the virtues of laboriousness and practicality, the class connotations of physical labor remained much the same as in the colonial period. This is suggested by the fate of the "architectural" school that the Mosquera administration attempted to establish in Bogotá as part of the national university. In August of 1846, Thomas Reed, a Scot of Danish citizenship, was contracted to construct the new national capitol building on the Plaza Bolívar. Taking advantage of Reed's presence in Bogotá, Manuel Ancízar induced him to instruct New Granadan youths in "theoretical and practical architecture." Accordingly in November of 1847, a chair in architecture was established for Reed in the central university in Bogotá. The Mosquera government asked each provincial governor to contract two youths who would be sent to the capital to study with Reed for a period of four years.[66]

The architectural school failed to achieve much, in part because its founders did not have a well-defined conception of its purpose or of the social groups that were to participate in it. It was not entirely clear whether the school was expected to train men of lower-class origins destined to work with their hands or upper-class professionals. Most aspects of the program suggested the former. Government circulars specifically solicited artisans' sons;[67] the students were contracted as apprentices;[68] and the government's stated aim was to produce trained masons. In other ways, however, the program seemed to involve elements of upper-class status. Entrants were supposed to have completed secondary school and to have received the bachelor's degree in philosophy, qualifications that tended to restrict participation to individuals of relatively high social status and perhaps even higher social aspirations.[69] In addition, the national government provided insufficient funds for transportation from the provinces to Bogotá, thus making it unlikely that very poor provincials would attend.[70] This combination of criteria and conditions made it probable that the school would attract students neither embedded in the working class nor firmly established in the upper class, the uncertainty of whose social position might make them particularly sensitive to questions of status.[71]

The consequences were predictable. As Reed sadly reported to the government, the boys had assumed that the course would be limited to academic instruction in design and had not imagined that it would involve manual labor in construction trades. When they were asked to perform physical labor, they became insolent to the master building foreman, who resigned rather than suffer their arrogance. For their part, the students were justifiably disappointed that their "instruction" was limited to a few branches of masonry, work on the capitol not being sufficiently advanced for them to work on other aspects of construction. Reed concluded that of the fifty-odd youths who had studied with him in 1848–1849, only six would ever be of use to the country in the construction of buildings.[72]

Not long after Reed's discouraging report the new López government abolished the school. The students were not doing well, and in any case the Liberal administration rejected the manual-labor approach to industrial education. Victoriano de Diego Paredes, the government minister who liquidated the school, pointed out that the students lacked the preparation needed to "receive theoretical instruction in the art" and that the "practical notions" they were acquiring were not worth any expense from the national treasury, as they consisted of "the rude work of a common laborer."[73]

Despite such meager results, members of the Colombian elite persisted in attempting to make their sons less mandarin and more practical through manual labor. Some of these efforts were absolutely heroic. One *bogotano* of a notable and well-connected family, confronted with an incorrigibly indolent and irresponsible son, took him out of secondary school and placed him in a carpenter's shop "with the . . . hope that hard work . . . of a mechanical character . . . would make him change his course." Unfortunately, a series of such experiments did no good. The first craftsman he tried, a German, was too impatient with the boy, who for his part had "no inclination to work." New Granadan artisans' shops were not satisfactory either, partly because (in the view of this upper-class conservative) of the increasing "demoralization and corruption" of the native artisans; "familiarity . . . with this kind of people could complete his perdition." Finally, in desperation, the *bogotano* decided to send his son to work in a shop or factory in the United States, where, isolated from his family and thrown upon his own resources, he might learn that he "must work to live" and might acquire the "habit and love of work, thus becoming a substantial man, useful to his family, to society, and to himself."[74]

Such attempts to use craft training to discipline sons of the upper class were doomed to failure. By the time they were tried many upper-class youths had already been spoiled by the obsequious servants and doting females in their households and had learned to emulate the elegant style of their aristocratic fathers. Given their fathers' behavior, outward assertions of the value of labor could not have been very convincing. Further, no matter what model the father provided, the aristocratic milieu in which these youths lived provided little support for these remedial disciplinary efforts.

While New Granada's political Liberals were also concerned with instilling economic values, they did not favor such Draconian devices as the artisans' shop. In part this was because some Liberals did not have to compensate so much for the home environment. The recent experiences of many Liberal families, impoverished by political adversity or for other reasons, made it easier for them to transmit economic discipline to their sons. Some of the more notable Liberals of the 1850–1880 period had had to work as youths (generally as clerks or merchants) to help support their families.[75]

Many Liberals felt, nonetheless, that it was necessary formally to inculcate the work ethic in upper-class youth. But in saying so they employed symbols different from those of the neo-Bourbons and used them in a different way. The Liberals of the 1850s, having discarded the neo-Bourbon objective of industrialization in favor of single-minded concentration on export agriculture, saw the plantation and the merchant's warehouse, rather than the shop and factory, as appropriate work places. And rather than emphasizing the subordination of youths to authority (the shop foreman), the Liberals were committed to furthering the ideal of the free individual subject only to the discipline of the marketplace.

Men of such liberal persuasions had to confront a dilemma, however. What if building the economy entailed taking risks for which profitable return was far from certain—which was generally the case in New Granada? Could one depend on the enticement of the market in a country where the failure of enterprises was much more conspicuous than their success? Liberal writers clearly doubted that they could rely so heavily on the profit motive, for they often supplemented it with inspirational exhortations.

Inspirational pieces lauding the economic virtues—hard work, enterprise, persistence (but not discipline in the Conservative sense)—are sprinkled through the leading Liberal newspapers of the years between 1850 and 1875. The inspirational approach is epitomized in *Los trabaja-dores de tierra caliente*, a retrospective work written toward the end of the century by a typical Liberal of the 1850s, Medardo Rivas. Rivas's book is a paean to the dozens of upper-class Colombians of all ages (most of them Rivas's Liberal friends) who in the years after 1850 left the comforts of Bogotá to descend into the torments of the upper Magdalena valley hot country to carve new tobacco, indigo, and cotton plantations out of the wilderness. Rivas fulsomely and repeatedly praises each of these *"trabaja-dores"* (of which he was one) for their willingness to take on hard, uncomfortable work and physical and cultural deprivation and to risk financial disaster, tropical disease, and death—all of this self-sacrifice in the cause of national economic development.[76]

No doubt Rivas's account—like other, shorter ones of the same sort—exaggerates the economic virtues of the upper-class *trabajadores* in the *tierra caliente*. Rivas often gives the impression that his heroes were out, machete and ax in hand, personally laying waste the forests, whereas in most cases they probably supervised gangs of *peones* who did the work for them. But the fact that Rivas chose to portray his plantation entrepreneurs in this way is significant. Fictional as his picture may have been, he was trying to instill the work ethic in the coming generations by dramatizing many men of an earlier period as tropical Stakhanovites.

Few of the nineteenth-century elite's efforts to instill a work ethic and practical skills in upper- and lower-class youths were successful. Whether the instrument was coercive training or pious exhortation, the effect appears generally to have been negligible. The elite could not prevail against the values inherent in the structure of the society, particularly as they fundamentally believed in the continuance of that structure and many of its values.

Part Three   Academic
Science for the
Upper Class:
Bourbons and
Neo-Bourbons

THE Colombian political elite's efforts in craft training represent only one aspect of their interest in technical education. On another level they sought to increase secondary and university instruction in science and applied science for upper-sector students. The elite's motives for promoting academic science paralleled those behind their interest in manual training. By providing upper-class youths with technical education the elite hoped to make them more practical and productive. As in the case of craft training, they saw academic science as an instrument for securing social order.

Imbuing the upper class with technical orientations required attacking several interdependent parts of the project simultaneously. It was necessary to introduce science into the curriculum, which in turn required a scientific elite to staff educational institutions. The effectiveness of the new science courses, moreover, depended on the development of widespread interest in science and technology. Upper-class interest could be sustained only if the new scientific knowledge was of demonstrable economic and social utility for individual careers.

The initial impetus for introducing scientific and technical orientations came from abroad. Spanish Bourbon administrators encouraged scientific and technical instruction while European scientists, coming to investigate the natural phenomena of the country, aroused an interest in science among a few of the native born. By the last two decades of the colonial period a handful of creoles, with royal encouragement, were actively engaged in scientific research—particularly in gathering data about their environment—and in the diffusion of modern scientific knowledge in their society.

The trauma and triumph of Independence, however, aborted the development of a native scientific and technical elite. In the nineteenth century, scientific activity received formal approval but had no real institutional support. Political instability robbed the republic of the resources needed to support research or significant scientific instruction. Few individuals could pursue scientific careers, and they lacked the reinforcement of a community of peers. Until the latter half of the nineteenth century, science in New Granada was in no way self-sustaining. The country continued to be no more than a consumer of foreign scientific ideas. And it depended upon periodic injections of foreign instructors to maintain some elements of modern science in the university curriculum. Similarly, foreigners supplied most of the technical expertise employed in the economy. In these respects New Granadan science and technology remained entirely colonial.[1]

Success in inculcating an interest in science and technology depended fundamentally on the structure of opportunities in the society. For several reasons, other than lack of institutional support, science was not attractive. The erection of a republican government created new career possibilities for the educated elite; of those few who developed an interest in science, most were drawn into political and administrative careers. Moreover, the country's economy was not sufficiently advanced or vigorous to provide the sustained demand for technical skills that would make engineering or other science-based careers imaginable. Thus, while most members of the upper class could see in the abstract the usefulness of science to their society, it was difficult for them to envision how any individual might effectively apply it in a career.

Chapter 3

The Enlightenment in New Granada

THE work of education in colonial New Granada, as in Spain, was at all levels predominantly the work of the clergy. Until at least 1789 the religious orders and secular priests provided almost all primary instruction. As of the middle of the eighteenth century the Jesuits ran the majority of *colegios menores* ("secondary schools"); the Society of Jesus administered ten of the fourteen preparatory schools believed to have existed at this time. The expulsion of the Jesuits in 1767 collapsed secondary instruction in most of the provincial towns that had possessed it, though to some degree Franciscans, Dominicans, and secular clergy moved into the vacuum. While some of the more substantial towns, such as Popayán, were able to offer preparatory work with some consistency, students seeking university degrees had to travel to Santa Fe de Bogotá. There they worked either at the Jesuits' Colegio Real Mayor y Seminario de San Bartolomé or at the Colegio Mayor de Nuestra Señora del Rosario, which was under the patronage of the viceroy but, having been founded by a Dominican, was formally committed to the propagation of Thomist doctrines. Both of these institutions offered preparatory work in Latin and philosophy, as well as university studies in theology and law; el Rosario on occasion provided courses on medicine. One anomaly persisted from the Hapsburg era. El Rosario and San Bartolomé, which gave all the public university instruction, could not grant professional degrees. This privilege was reserved for the Dominicans' Universidad de Santo Tomás, which gave no public classes and was little more than a degree-granting mechanism.[1]

The clerical cast of the *colegios* necessarily shaped their curricula. Preprofessional studies consisted of four years of Latin, followed by three of philosophy—a year of logic, a second of metaphysics, and a third of physics, all taught in the scholastic mode.[2] Few students took the physics course. The *colegios*, including San Bartolomé and el Rosario, began the philosophy cycle every three years, and there was a tendency to exempt students from the third-year physics course if their careers were being excessively delayed by the slow triennial revolution of the cycle. As Francisco Antonio Moreno y Escandón commented in his reform plan of 1774, "it appears that the examination of nature has been forgotten on purpose." As science was limited to the concepts of the ancients, based on a priori reasoning and encased in rigid formulations, it did not provoke the interest of students. In addition, the existing system of social rewards provided no stimulus for such an interest. "A taste for modern philosophy," Moreno noted, "has not reached the palates of youth, and it even appears to them a vain fantasy and useless vanity, opposed to the authority of their ancestors."[3]

Stimulus for changing this sytem, like the educational system itself, came from Spain. Spanish interest in the promotion of useful knowledge became notable in the middle of the eighteenth century when the writings of Fray Benito Gerónimo Feijóo received royal approval. Denouncing the dominion of Aristotelian scholasticism in Spanish higher learning, Feijóo called for the introduction of Newtonian scientific ideas and, just as important, of the experimental approach to knowledge that underlay Europe's recent scientific discoveries. By the middle of the eighteenth century Feijóo's views began to have considerable currency, and the promotion of science and "useful knowledge" became a primary concern of some royal administrators. In the 1750s and 1760s the Spanish Crown created a botanical garden and natural history museum, erected several observatories, and encouraged public lectures on contemporary science. Before 1767, however, the clerically controlled institutions of higher learning in the Spanish world remained relatively unaffected by the new scientific knowledge. The expulsion of the Jesuits in that year served as a catalyst for efforts at a general reform of higher education. At the time of the expulsion Charles III ordered royal officials throughout the empire to use the Jesuit properties to create new educational and other institutions under civil control. When the royal governor of Seville, Pablo Antonio Olavide, took over the Jesuits' establishments in that city, he elaborated a new plan of education that called for a secular university with a curriculum strongly emphasizing natural science and mathematics. Inspired by Olavide's example, the Council of Castile in 1770 ordered all Spanish universities to draw up new curricula including chairs in mathematics and experimental physics.[4]

In Spain, the paired reforms of bringing the universities under royal control and introducing modern science had the support of some of the secular clergy and of some regulars also, most notably Franciscans and Augustinians. But the Bourbon program was vigorously opposed by the Dominicans, the official defenders of Thomism, and to a lesser degree by some other religiou̇s. Reform of the curriculum, both in Spain and America, was stymied to a considerable extent by Dominican opposition and (in descending order of importance) by the financial weakness of the universities, the lack of faculty trained in modern science, and a lack of adequate texts.[5]

Nevertheless, throughout the Spanish world two important changes did occur. Although the overall curriculum was not dramatically reformed and scholasticism remained firmly entrenched to the end of the colonial period, elements of the new science crept into the three-year philosophy courses taught at the preparatory or *colegio* level. Second, outside the cloistral walls, some of the civilian elite developed an interest in science that led them to acquire knowledge substantially in advance of that propagated in the universities. In Spanish America royal scientific expeditions sent out in the 1770s and thereafter, at a cost of more than half a million pesos, played an important role in stimulating creole curiosity.

"Useful Knowledge" versus "the Schools"

During the 1760s New Granada began to feel the first effective impulses emanating from the Spanish Enlightenment. The first agent of the Enlightenment to exert notable and enduring influence, José Celestino Mutis, arrived in Santa Fe de Bogotá in 1761 to serve as personal physician to Viceroy Pedro Messía de la Zerda. After studying medicine in Seville, Mutis between 1757 and 1760 had steeped himself in botany at the new botanical garden in Madrid. Although he was selected by the Spanish Crown as a young talent to be sent to the major scientific centers of Europe for further study, Mutis decided instead to go to New Granada in the hope of making known to the world the as-yet-unstudied wonders of its natural history. Soon after his arrival in New Granada he began to send plant specimens to Carolus Linnaeus. But, as Mutis proved unable to secure royal patronage for a major botanical study during the 1760s, much of his attention was drawn to other subjects.[6]

Between 1762 and 1766 he taught mathematics and astronomy in the Colegio del Rosario, asserting views strongly reminiscent of those of Feijóo. Mutis condemned Spain's backwardness in matters scientific and held as his first principle the abandonment of the suppositions and systems of the Peripatetics. Apparently the Dominicans in Bogotá considered Mutis a dangerous challenge to their authority. Taking exception to the public exposition of the Copernican system by Mutis's students, the Dominican order in 1774 announced a public disputation in which the Copernican doctrines were to be attacked as contrary to sacred writings and the prohibitions of the Inquisition. Incensed, Mutis complained to Viceroy Manuel de Guirior, and the Dominicans in turn denounced Mutis before the Inquisition.[7]

The dispute over Copernicus served to intensify a conflict over the control of higher education that had begun in New Granada, as in Spain, with the expulsion of the Jesuits in 1767. Royal instructions to convert the Jesuits' many enterprises to secular uses had been committed to the hands of an ambitious young *criollo* administrator, Francisco Antonio Moreno y Escandón. Born in Mariquita and educated in the law by the Jesuits at San Bartolomé, Moreno had recently returned from a successful venture to Madrid to advance his career with an appointment to the office of protector of the Indians. In the spirit of the royal instructions, in 1768 he proposed using some of the Jesuits' properties to create a centralized public university under viceregal control like those in Mexico and Lima. One of the principal aims of this measure was to tighten the standards for degrees in jurisprudence so as to cut down the "excess of lawyers" in New Granada. Moreno's project immediately drew the fire of the Dominicans, who jealously guarded their degree-granting privilege. By 1774 the objections raised by the Dominicans and other religious orders, along with a shortage of funds, had stalled Moreno's reform project. The conflict between Mutis and the Dominicans, however, brought the question of educational reform sharply into focus. Provoked by the retrograde friars, Viceroy Manuel de Guirior supported a new Moreno plan calling not only for a secularized university but also for a greatly increased emphasis on science and scientific approaches to learning.[8]

Moreno proposed a greatly strengthened emphasis on natural science in the introductory philosophy course. By combining the revenues of San Bartolomé and the Colegio del Rosario, the new public university could provide instruction in all segments of the philosophy sequence every year. All three years, including mathematics (through trigonometry) in the first year and physics in the second year, were required without exception for students going on to higher degrees.

Moreno, echoing Feijóo, considered the Peripatetic curriculum useless, in part because of its irrelevance to the economy but more because of its mind-crippling effects. The religious orders, in constant competition with each other, devoted themselves to inculcating their particular dogmas. The "spirit of faction" that pervaded the orders encouraged doctrinaire disputes, in which intellectuals were preoccupied not with discovering the truth, but with "sustaining their caprice against reason." The religious orders were not merely filling the heads of students with useless and antiquated doctrines; the scholastic method was destroying the students' capacity to think. The study of physics would give students a "solid knowledge of nature, supported by observation and experience," free their minds from "superstitition and credulity," and make their reasoning more exact. Like other Bourbon administrators, Moreno of course saw economic utility in the study of science. He particularly recommended geography, natural history, meteorology, agriculture, and mineralogy to students for the priesthood; as curates they would be in a unique position to offer economic leadership in rural areas.[9]

Viceroy Guirior immediately put the plan into effect on a provisional basis with Moreno in charge as the royal director of studies. The new plan survived for only six years, however. Crown officials objected to the projected university's dependence upon public revenues. At the same time the religious orders, with the Dominicans at their head, rallied to defend their vested interests. The Colegio del Rosario and the Dominicans in the Universidad de Santo Tomás were probably most concerned with preserving the autonomy of their institutions. But while the defense of corporate privilege was a central issue, there were also objections to the Copernican cosmology and the new scientific curriculum. The two issues were actually entwined, for the introduction of higher mathematics and a new cosmology implied a partial displacement of all university graduates who were trained in the old schools and were unequipped to handle the new sciences. Some alumni of San Bartolomé protested the diminished role of logic and metaphysics and the banishment of the scholastic method. Moreno's excessive emphasis on mathematics, they claimed, was leaving students in fearful ignorance. "Parents lament the perdition of their sons, and this realm fears the total extermination of letters . . ."[10]

By October, 1779, the ecclesiastical reaction had succeeded in scuttling the Moreno plan. The Spanish Crown, unwilling to provide funds for a new public university, had referred the Moreno plan to a junta in Santa Fe de Bogotá for reconsideration. The junta, which included representatives of the various institutions of higher learning in Bogotá, as well as Moreno and other civil officials, moved quickly from a discussion of funds to a debate over the intrinsic merits of the Moreno plan. The junta concluded by ordering philosophy to be "explained and taught in the scholastic manner as before," using the text of Fray Antonio Goudin, a seventeenth-century Dominican to whose trustworthy Thomism the Dominicans clung throughout the Spanish world. The new program returned the study of natural philosophy to the third year so that students might pass on to the study of law or theology after the second year "without the necessity of burdening themselves with the study of physics." Meanwhile, Mutis having gone to supervise mining operations near Ibagué in 1777, the chair in mathematics remained unfilled.[11]

Despite these defeats, later viceroys continued to promote the idea of a public university with more science in the curriculum. The Archbishop-Viceroy, Antonio Caballero y Góngora (1782–1788), reinstituted the mathematics chair in 1786 and in the following year resurrected the idea of a public university completely under viceregal control. Like Moreno's, the Archbishop-Viceroy's new plan came to naught. But it is of interest for its strong assertion of the need for "useful knowledge." The object of the plan, Caballero y Góngora explained, was "to substitute the useful exact sciences for the merely speculative ones, in which so unfortunately time has been wasted until now; because a realm full of the most precious products to utilize, of forests to clear, of roads to open, of swamps and mines to drain, of waters to control, of metals to purify, certainly more needs subjects who know how to comprehend and observe nature and to operate the calculus, the compass, and the ruler, than those who understand and discuss the nature of reason, the prime matter and the substantial form."[12] His plan called for industrial arts training for the sons of artisans and peasants and the study of medicine, mineralogy, agriculture, and industry in the universities. Caballero y Góngora provided for four university chairs in mathematics and science (natural philosophy or physics, mathematics, botany, and chemistry) and required that their holders give particular attention to the industrial application of these sciences.[13]

Another theme that runs through the Caballero y Góngora plan is the idea that to teach effectively the professor must excite the students' curiosity and hold their attention. To increase the effectiveness of teaching he urged the abandonment of Latin as the language used in the classroom in favor of Spanish except in ecclesiastical studies. And he assumed that the university would have such teaching aids as a botanical garden, a natural history museum, a chemistry laboratory, and instruments for experimental physics and applied mathematics.

The viceregal curriculum reforms were frustrated for the most part during the colonial era. But critics continued to snipe at the scholastic system, often with the apparent approval of the viceroys. Bogotá's first substantial newspaper, the *Papel Periódico* (1791–1797), edited by a protégé of Viceroy José de Ezpeleta, attacked the "gibberish" and "puerile subtleties" of "*ergotismo.*" It called for a new scientific education calculated to produce not "ridiculous pedants," but useful citizens capable of applying themselves to mining, agriculture, commerce, and the crafts. In the same vein it urged the substitution of Spanish for Latin in the classroom.[14]

Although the educational system remained much the same in form, natural science was infiltrating *filosofía* courses in the 1780s and 1790s. Change was facilitated by the fact that the *filosofía* courses often, if not generally, were taught by young men who were still finishing their professional degrees in law or theology or had just finished them and were awaiting higher appointments. These young men were more likely to be responsive to the new science than were older men operating according to a long-established routine. It is possible to construct a kind of intellectual genealogy showing how Mutis's influence spread from one student generation to the next. Thus, Mutis taught Felipe Vergara y Caycedo in the 1760s and Eloy Valenzuela in the 1770s; both of these men transmitted their knowledge in mathematics or *filosofía* courses in el Rosario.[15]

In the latter half of the 1770s, José Félix Restrepo, a young *antioqueño* studying law at San Bartolomé, became a devotee of modern philosophy. Between 1778 and 1781 he taught a scientifically oriented philosophy at his alma mater and then carried it to the Colegio-Seminario of Popayán. With the strong support of the rector of the *colegio*, a secular priest who was interested in medicine and botany, Restrepo taught a "useful physics" in the 1780s and in later years.[16] At least ten of his students developed a continuing interest in science. The most notable of these was Francisco José de Caldas, an impressively active and inventive geographer, meteorologist, astronomer, and botanist. Another, Francisco Antonio Zea, ultimately became director of the Botanical Garden at Madrid; and a third, José María Cabal, later studied chemistry in Paris. The others were no more than amateurs of botany or meteorology.

The interest displayed by these few men should not be taken to mean that "modern philosophy" had carried the day in Popayán. Traditionalists continued to compete for the philosophy chair and occasionally won it. In 1791 Restrepo felt compelled to refute the opinion, "still too rooted in many superficial minds," that mathematics and modern physics were in conflict with religion. Natural philosophy, as the "study . . . of the works of God, far from being contrary to religion [is] useful, favorable, and necessary to it." As late as 1801 the modernists were making elaborate efforts to defend themselves against charges of encyclopedic impiety for teaching physics with the texts of Jean-Antoine Nollet and Peter van Musschenbroek. The new science also remained under attack on religious grounds in the viceregal capital. In 1796 a *filosofía* professor at el Rosario who had taught Copernican doctrines was forced to resign his chair. And in 1801 Mutis still found it necessary to defend these teachings against clerical objections.[17]

Useful Knowledge Takes Root

Long before the proponents of modern science overcame the defenses of academic scholasticism, there was outside the cloistral walls an increasing interest in applying science to the economy. One of the first manifestations of this interest was in mining, gold being New Granada's principal export. During the 1770s and 1780s the Spanish government and private citizens made several efforts to import the most sophisticated European mining expertise. José Celestino Mutis was active in this field, as in others. Having failed in a mining venture in Pamplona in the 1760s, Mutis and one of his partners sent a young New Granadan, Clemente Ruíz, to Sweden to study mining and metallurgy at their expense. On his return in 1777 after four years of study, Ruíz joined Mutis in a new mining enterprise near Ibagué.

Soon afterward Spanish administrators began to make efforts to promote technical improvements in mining. Early in the 1780s Minister of the Indies José de Gálvez sent a number of mining experts from the leading European centers to Spanish America. Gálvez designated Juan José D'Elhuyar —a Basque mineralogist who had trained for eight years in Paris, Freiberg, and Uppsala—to serve as director of mines in New Granada. D'Elhuyar arrived in 1784, accompanied by three Spanish assistants, one of whom had also been trained in Paris. Their principal mission was to implant improved refining processes in New Granada. In 1788 Spanish authorities reinforced these mining engineers with eight skilled Saxon mineworkers, whose Protestant faith was overlooked in the interest of greater mining production, but whose lack of formal education D'Elhuyar found more difficult to tolerate. The D'Elhuyar mission and its Saxon adjunct bore little fruit. Most of their attention was devoted to the silver mines of Mariquita, which after consuming heavy investments produced very little silver. Nor did the mission leave a lasting legacy of improved technology. Since D'Elhuyar spent most of his time in isolated Mariquita, he contributed little or nothing to the training of a colonial technical elite. (One of the Saxon miners, Jacob Wiesner, did survive into the republican period, discovering and beginning the development of the iron mines of Pacho.) Another effort at mining improvement seems to have yielded more significant and enduring changes. A French mining engineer, Louis Laneret, who served as director of mines in Antioquia after 1784, introduced new ore mills that later came into general use. In this case, however, the technical and capital requirements for success were much less challenging, and the resource base much more propitious.[18]

Along with mining experts the Spanish Crown also sent a series of military-civil engineers in the 1780s and 1790s. In the Bogotá region Col. Domingo de Esquiaqui and Carlos Francisco Cabrera drew up plans of the city and built churches, bridges, roads, and fortifications. And in Cartagena other engineers worked on improving the port's fortifications. There is no indication, however, that the Spanish engineers of this period had any influence on creole upper-class youth.[19]

The botanical work begun at about the same time as the efforts to improve the technology of mining ultimately aroused more curiosity among the intellectual elite. Although Mutis's first petitions of the 1760s for royal support of a natural history survey were ignored, he continued to pursue his interest in botany as best he could. In particular he was concerned with discovering plants of commercial value, such as cinchona and various spices. Mutis's botanical pursuits became particularly significant in the 1780s when he finally found an effective patron in Archbishop Antonio Caballero y Góngora. In 1782 Mutis was sweltering in the heat of the mines of Ibagué when Caballero y Góngora made an episcopal visitation there. Besides celebrating a Mass together, the two apparently chatted about botany and mining. Caballero y Góngora immediately created a royal natural history survey with Mutis as its director. The following year, in 1783, Charles III confirmed Caballero y Góngora's dispositions and provided Mutis with substantial financial support. Called the Botanical Expedition, the survey actually involved much more than the name implies—its mission included astronomical and meteorological observations as well as geographical research and the elaboration of a map of New Granada. In addition, it came to be charged with supervising the collection and export of cinchona bark and cinnamon as well as the planting of indigo and nutmeg.[20]

The Botanical Expedition deeply affected a small portion of the New Granadan elite. Under Mutis's direction about a dozen creole investigators and a larger number of illustrators fanned out across the viceroyalty between 1782 and 1810, examining its fauna and flora as well as other aspects of the environment. Others not officially connected with the expedition were stimulated by it. The New Granadan *botánicos* manifested a wide-ranging curiosity, encompassing everything from orchids to snakes. But their attention focused primarily on the discovery and development of plants of possible economic value, such as the cinchona tree, "Bogotá tea," cochineal, and improved varieties of pasturage and sugar cane. Along with an interest in practical botany, the handful of creoles surrounding Mutis displayed considerable zeal in the fields of meteorology, astronomy, and economic geography. Ultimately, creoles who were much influenced by the Botanical Expedition wrote New Granada's first substantial treatises exploring the country's economic possibilities and defending its economic interests.[21]

The pursuit of science in colonial New Granada reached a climax in the first decade of the nineteenth century. The arrival of Alexander von Humboldt and Aimé de Bonpland in 1801 provided a new stimulus to Mutis and his *criollo* disciples. In the same year the son of a large estate owner, Jorge Tadeo Lozano, who had studied chemistry while waiting at court in Madrid, undertook a series of enterprises that helped to draw the vice-royalty's scientific community together. While teaching mathematics at el Rosario, he published a journal, *El Correo Curioso, Erudito, Económico y Mercantil*, which stimulated the exchange of ideas between the *aficionados* of Popayán and those in Bogotá. Mutis and Lozano also promoted the abortive Sociedad Patriótica del Nuevo Reino de Granada. In 1802 and 1803 Mutis constructed an astronomical observatory in the garden of the Botanical Expedition in Bogotá. There he and his associates gave lessons not only in astronomy and botany but also in other branches of science. In these years a school of "physicomathematical sciences" was functioning in Bogotá, with instruction provided by Bernardo Anillo, an engineer and mathematician sent from Spain as the vice-royalty's director of public works.[22]

The most notable of the upper-class creole scientists who appeared at this time was Francisco José de Caldas of Popayán, who, despite the fact that he worked for a long time in virtually total isolation, managed to make some truly original contributions. After studying *filosofía* with José Félix Restrepo at Popayán's seminary, Caldas took the standard law degree at the Colegio del Rosario. Caldas, however, was not interested in the law and soon began to carry on independent investigations in the environs of Popayán and Quito—measuring altitudes by a method of his own invention, studying the cinchona tree and other useful plants, and making astronomical and geodesical observations with instruments that he constructed unaided to carry out his solitary studies. When Caldas arrived in Bogotá in 1805, Mutis turned the newly constructed observatory over to him. After Mutis's death in 1808 Caldas became the professor of mathematics at the Colegio del Rosario. Meanwhile he continued to write on a wide variety of topics—from the influence of climate on human development to the culture of cochineal in New Granada. And from 1808 to 1810 he published the *Semanario del Nuevo Reino de Granada*, a journal dedicated to science and the promotion of material progress.[23]

The *Semanario* is of particular interest as a measure of the diffusion of scientific interest at the end of the colonial period. The picture that emerges from its pages is of a small group of enthusiasts amid a largely indifferent upper class. In a brief survey of the educational scene in Bogotá, José María Salazar admitted that some advances had been made in the teaching of "useful things" but lamented the lack of instruction in chemistry and mineralogy, of instruments for teaching physics and the mechanical arts, and of many important books. Not only had institutional development been inadequate, but intellectual attitudes also had failed to change sufficiently. Certain professors of *filosofía* had dedicated themselves to orienting students toward science. But this was not enough. It was "necessary that this become the dominant taste," so that ideas would be "fixed for the future." As yet too much time was still being lost in useless metaphysical disputes, and "philosophical authority" retained its ascendency over "reason and experience."[24]

The mixed picture described in Salazar's article is confirmed by the history of the journal as a whole. The *Semanario* contained meteorological observations, economic and population statistics, discussions of cures for diseases, geographical sketches emphasizing economic problems and possibilities, articles on useful plants that might profitably be introduced and cultivated, and other suggestions for improving productivity. These contributions were submitted by about two dozen creoles. More than a third of these were resident in Bogotá, but contributions also came from at least nine other communities, including Cartagena, four towns in the northern provinces of Pamplona and el Socorro, and three in the Cauca region. This indicates a certain spreading of the interest in science and its economic applications. The surviving subscription lists of the *Semanario* show 108 subscribers in thirty-two communities located in each of the major regions of New Granada.[25]

One may suppose that few of these subscribers paid more than passing attention to science. In Popayán in 1801 Alexander von Humboldt noted "an intellectual effervescence which was not known in 1760, a desire to own books and know the names of celebrated men, a conversation which dwells on objects more interesting than birth or quality." On the other hand, while science had become something of an upper-class vogue, the scientific knowledge of the university educated did not match their pretensions or go beyond the superficiality of the dilettante. With the notable exception of Caldas, few demonstrated a deep scientific curiosity. Humboldt attributed the lack of scientific vigor to the aristocratic tenor of the society, more marked in Popayán than anywhere else—"What can be expected of youths surrounded and served by slaves . . . who flee work, who count always on tomorrow, and who are terrified by the slightest discomfort . . .?" Such youths would be "incapable of the sacrifices required by science and society."[26]

Humboldt was probably right in pointing to a connection between aristocracy and dilettantism. But the extension of science was also inhibited by other difficulties, most notably the lack of a clear economic function for the scientifically trained. José Antonio de Plaza noted that at the time of Humboldt's visit, when the scientific movement was at its height, the mathematics classes at el Rosario were "almost deserted," among other reasons because "youths did not find in these studies a secure means of undertaking a lucrative career."[27]

An End to Small Beginnings

The Independence era completely disrupted and ultimately destroyed the small New Granadan scientific elite. With the removal of the strong supporting hand of Spanish royal authority, the frustrations and failures of the nineteenth century began. Caldas was able to continue publishing memoirs and, in 1811, to offer some scientific instruction. But for the most part the energies of the creole elite, including its handful of scientists and more numerous scientific amateurs, were absorbed in the problematic task of founding and defending a republic. The political disruption and civil war that characterized New Granada after its independence was secured really began in the period from 1810 to 1815. Centralists in Bogotá and federalists there and in other parts of the republic struggled, first peacefully in 1811 and then violently from 1812 to 1813. These disputes were no sooner papered over than the creoles found themselves fully engaged by royalist forces to the north in Venezuela and to the south in Ecuador. In these years the zoologist Jorge Tadeo Lozano was at the center of the governmental whirl—as president of the constitutional convention, as president of the state of Cundinamarca in 1811, and, after his resignation, as a participant in various political intrigues and negotiations. José Félix Restrepo and other scientific amateurs played leading roles in the governance of Antioquia. At least four creoles with scientific interests were occupied by the military struggle. Caldas served as a military engineer for the federalist faction from 1812 to 1813; then, a political refugee, he worked for the government of Antioquia from 1813 to 1815. In Antioquia he applied his talents to a variety of projects—the establishment of an academy of military engineers; the manufacture of powder, cannons, and rifles; and the creation of a mint. He was not able to return to his scientific work in Bogotá until the end of 1815, at which point the Spanish Pacification cut short his life and works, as well as those of others of the creole scientific elite.[28]

The thoroughness with which the Spanish generals extirpated the creole scientific elite is astonishing. Aside from those who were priests or too socially obscure to trouble with, few escaped. Lozano, Caldas, and practically everyone else whose name had appeared in the *Semanario* went down before the firing squads in 1816. Among them was José María Cabal, who, after having been sent to prison in Spain among a group of supposed conspirators in 1795, had studied chemistry in Paris between 1802 and 1809. Cabal's later service as the leading general in the campaigns against royal forces in the South logically placed him on the execution list. But his death, like those of Caldas and Lozano, certainly contributed to New Granada's scientific impoverishment in the first decades of the republican era. Men executed at this time included at least four lawyers who had contributed geographical sketches, meteorological observations, and various disquisitions to the *Semanario*. The firing squads also cut down Miguel Pombo, who had served in the smallpox vaccination campaign from 1801 to 1805, and Crisanto Valenzuela and Custodio Garcia Rovira, both of whom are thought to have taught the new philosophy in Bogotá before 1810.[29]

Only a handful of those who engaged in scientific research and teaching before 1810 survived into the republican era. And, living more or less in isolation, their scientific activity was not particularly significant. Fr. Eloy Valenzuela labored quietly as a parish priest in Bucaramanga promoting local material development until he was murdered in 1833. Benedicto Domínguez, a student of Bernardo Anillo as well as of Caldas, carried on the astronomical observations he had begun before Independence, serving in the 1820s and 1830s as director of the Bogotá observatory. He also attempted, with little success, to establish a paper factory between 1834 and 1840. About the only other individual whose late colonial scientific efforts were carried on for some time into the republican era was Francisco J. Matís, one of the illustrators for the Botanical Expedition, who taught and wrote articles on botany from time to time in the 1830s and 1840s and had some impact on at least a few young New Granadans.[30]

Some other creole savants who escaped execution were diverted into political leadership and permanently lost to science. Francisco Antonio Zea, at one time director of the Botanical Gardens of Madrid (1805–1808), became vice-president of Colombia and later the new republic's emissary in Europe, where he died in 1822. Sinforoso Mutis, who had briefly carried on his uncle's botanical work after 1808, was entirely involved in politics from 1810 until his death in 1822. José Félix Restrepo, who had taught natural philosophy to Caldas and Zea, divided his time between instruction and the Supreme Court from 1823 through 1825. But, heavily occupied with his judicial duties and then with service in the Congress, he stopped teaching after 1825, though the lectures he gave from 1823 to 1825 were published as a text that was used for some years thereafter.[31]

Throughout the first three decades of the republican era New Granada could claim very few scientists or scientific amateurs, fewer than at the end of the colonial period. This abrupt decline was attributable in part to Gen. Pablo Morillo's terrible swift sword. At least equally important was the tendency of republican politics to absorb the attention of a high proportion of the educated elite. Not only were the savants from the colonial era drawn into politics, but also most of the university-educated youths of subsequent generations eagerly embraced the opportunities in law and politics that were offered by republican government.

Chapter 4   The Neo-Bourbons, 1821–1845

TWO strains competed for dominance in New Granadan attitudes and policies toward higher education during the first half century of the republican era. On the one hand, the social tendencies as well as the political needs of the new republic suggested the need for a more open and extended university system than had existed in the colonial era. New Granada had to raise up a new political elite to replace the expelled Spanish administrators as well as the creole ones who had died during the Independence era and to fill the multiplicity of posts created by the republican system. From a social point of view, the republic offered new, previously undreamed of, opportunities for those with the requisite educational preparation. Thus, there were strong pressures, especially from the provinces, to make higher education more readily available. Interest in legal education was particularly strong, because traditionally and functionally the law was the path to public office.[1] Furthermore, as the republic eliminated some formal social distinctions observed in the colonial era, the doctorate became more important as a sign of upper-class status.

At the same time there was a contrary tendency to impose centralist restrictions on professional education. This restrictive tendency was motivated in part by a desire for quality control. But another element was the neo-Bourbon conviction that large segments of upper-class youth must be channeled away from the traditional literary professions and into more practical or technical careers. The neo-Bourbons hoped that, by discouraging the younger generations from entering legal-bureaucratic careers, they might raise up a new, complementary, scientific-technical elite, which, rather than engaging in disturbing political adventures, would stay in traces and build the strong economy needed to support the state. The Bogotá administrators therefore pursued a policy of restricting legal, medical, and ecclesiastical education to three university centers, while encouraging the implantation of scientific and technical education in the provinces.

With the changed political context, the neo-Bourbons who promoted scientific education from the 1820s through the 1840s faced somewhat different obstacles than their Bourbon administrator predecessors. During the Independence era the religious orders were greatly weakened and no longer raised any effective opposition either to civil control of higher education or to curriculum reform.[2] In the early republican period the major problems rather were, first, to reconstitute the scientific elite recently extinguished by the Spanish Pacifiers and, second, in the face of the political opportunities of the period, to motivate students to take up scientific and technical careers.

Despite the honorable precedent established by Mutis and his companions, both of these endeavors failed. The initiatives undertaken by the royal government could not be carried on by the new republic. The New Granadan leaders who had had some acquaintance with the Botanical Expedition tended to assume at first that the republican government could support science as handsomely as the Bourbons. But the republic was too weak politically and fiscally to provide either the financial support or the continuity of policy needed for building a scientific establishment. The New Granadan elite thus indulged in a phenomenon frequently observed in Latin America in the republican era—*proyectismo*, the tendency to dream up elaborate programs completely out of proportion to the resources available to support them.

The problem of motivating youth to study science was closely related to that of weak institutional support. As the republican government could not provide for secure, well-remunerated careers in science, the field could hardly be very attractive. It was even less so when the alternative was a career in law and politics.

The tendency for talented members of the elite to be engaged by the work of government is manifest in the lives of the very men most concerned with promoting science and technology. Each of the secretaries of the interior who served for substantial periods in the years between 1821 and 1845 had an active interest in science and its teaching but found himself drawn into the vortex of politics. José Manuel Restrepo of Medellín, after obtaining the standard law degree in Bogotá at the beginning of the nineteenth century, became one of the satellites of the Botanical Expedition. Informally he studied surveying, astronomy, meteorology, and botany with Caldas and Mutis, and in 1807 he published a geographical study of Antioquia in Caldas's *Semanario*. During the Spanish Pacification of 1816–1819, he made political exile the occasion for a visit to the United States to study manufacturing techniques. After Independence, Restrepo continued his active interest in the mechanical arts and manufacturing. But his energies were largely absorbed in politics and public administration; he devoted much of his free time to another type of nation building, the creation of national pride through the writing of patriotic history. Similarly, Lino de Pombo, who was inspired by Caldas, and Mariano Ospina Rodríguez, who was deeply affected by José Félix Restrepo, dedicated much of their effort to teaching and to the promotion of useful knowledge. Yet the one found himself constantly called to high public office, and the other, absorbed in the political passions of the period, spent much of his active life as a party leader.[3] If men closely linked to the late colonial Enlightenment were distracted from the pursuit of scientific knowledge, how much more likely were youths of later generations to choose law and politics as their careers?

Scientific Instruction, 1822–1839

To replace the savants lost in the Independence era, Colombian leaders early turned to the idea of importing European scientists. In 1821, when Colombian independence was still quite tenuous, Francisco Antonio Zea, the former director of Madrid's botanical garden and now Colombia's representative in Europe, contracted a Mexican engineer, José María Lanz, to make a map of the new republic.[4] The following year Zea, aided by his connections with Humboldt, Georges Cuvier, and others in Paris's scientific community, gathered a group of five scientists and technicians who were to establish a mining school and a museum of natural history in Colombia. The head of this expedition, Mariano Rivero, a young but notable Peruvian metallurgist and mining engineer, agreed (for a salary equal that of the vice-president of the republic) to take charge of bringing a science library and laboratory equipment to Bogotá and, once there, to establish a natural history museum and a national school of mines and to serve as national director of mines. Jean-Baptiste Boussingault, then recently graduated from the school of mines of Saint-Etienne, took a four-year contract to teach mineralogy or chemistry in the school of mines and to serve as a research mineralogist and mining engineer. A French physician, François Desiré Roulin, agreed to spend six years teaching physiology and comparative anatomy in the museum of natural history. In addition, two technicians skilled in handling zoological specimens were hired to work in the museum.[5]

Stimulated by Zea's success, the Colombian Congress outdid itself. In its decree of July 28, 1823, approving Zea's contracts and creating the proposed mining school and natural history museum, it authorized courses in practically every branch of science conceivable at that time. The museum was to offer studies in mineralogy and geology, general and applied chemistry, botany, mathematics, physics, astronomy, agriculture, zoology, comparative anatomy, entomology, conchology, and drawing. At the same time the mining school would provide instruction in mathematics and its applications to machines, physics, mineralogy, and geology, the exploitation of mines, analytical chemistry and metallurgy, descriptive geometry, and drawing. Bogotá's science instruction was to approximate, insofar as possible, that in France.

These plans must not be taken too literally. The congressional authorization, a typical expression of the high aspirations and optimism of a new nation, must be viewed as a declaration of good intentions. As usually occurred in such cases, the Congress left it to the executive branch to cut the plan down to the scale that fiscal circumstances might permit.[6]

Even in its modified form, however, the plan was not executed. In the turmoil of the 1820s Colombia could not adequately use, let alone retain, the services of the foreign scientists. Partly because the necessary laboratory equipment was late in arriving from Europe, the French scientists did very little teaching, spending most of their time on scientific excursions to various remote corners of the republic. Some of their research was clearly geared to practical applications, particularly Boussingault's work inspecting mines, assaying metals, and conducting geological surveys in Antioquia, the Chocó, and Mariquita. Boussingault is also credited with introducing a new amalgamation process that increased the productivity of Antioquia's gold mines.[7]

Two of the degree-holding scientists left the republic soon after their contracted terms had expired. Rivero, who was required to stay only one year, departed in 1825 to return to his family in Peru, where Simón Bolívar appointed him director general of mines and public instruction. Roulin went back to France in 1828, the moment his time was up. Boussingault lingered a while, evading Bolívar's proposal to make him head of a planned military-polytechnical school by leaving Bogotá on a scientific excursion. Contemptuous of Colombia's society, yet fascinated by its natural wonders, he remained in the northern Andes until the middle of 1832, occupied primarily with scientific expeditions.[8] The biological technicians, Jacques Bourdon and Justine-Marie Goudot, stayed on in New Granada, the latter working as a druggist in Bogotá; but their lives are wrapped in obscurity.[9]

It is difficult to conceive how Colombia could have sustained a scientific establishment in this period. The financial drain of the War of Independence, political disorder, and fiscal weakness made it difficult for the Colombian government to meet even its most basic obligations. Colombian government employees were taking sharp salary cuts, and in these circumstances the government's liberality with foreigners was bound to be strictly limited. Roulin at least appears to have been bitterly disappointed by nonpayment of or discounts on his salary, which left him hanging on the edges of respectability. Neither his efforts at offering medical services nor his portrait painting sufficed to sustain his family in its accustomed manner; ultimately he walked the streets of Bogotá in a coat his wife made from old curtains with a floral design.[10]

Probably at least as important as financial considerations was the fact that Bogotá could offer neither the laboratory facilities available in Europe nor the stimulus of a scientific community. For the European scientists, Colombia had only one attraction. It represented to the botanist, zoologist, or mineralogist a new field for observing unusual phenomena and collecting rare specimens. Boussingault, by his own account, was primarily attracted by the opportunity to see active volcanos.[11] Once the phenomena were observed and the specimens collected, however, the European scientists naturally looked to the scientific communities that they had left and that provided their professional frames of reference. Boussingault and Roulin had never looked upon their venture to the New World as more than an extended field trip.

From a New Granadan perspective the scientific expedition was not strikingly productive.[12] Only Boussingault made a substantial contribution, and this was not to the creation of a technical elite but to the development of improved mining techniques. As so often is the case today, the expedition contributed more to the careers of the foreign experts than to the development of the client country, in this case by providing the foreign visitors with the raw material for numerous scientific memoirs.[13] The French scientists did leave behind a well-organized and well-stocked natural history museum. But as New Granada passed through its time of troubles it was not maintained, and many of the specimens were lost.[14]

After the scientists of the 1822 expedition departed, nothing of any consequence occurred on the scientific scene until the middle of the 1840s. Or perhaps more appropriately a "scientific scene" could not be said to exist until the middle of the 1840s. The few Colombian enthusiasts who remained after the slaughter of 1816 were pathetically isolated. Between 1830 and 1845 only about a half-dozen Colombians in Bogotá were engaged in the study of science. The principal practitioners in this era were Benedicto Domínguez in astronomy; Francisco Javier Matís, Pbro. Dr. Juan María Céspedes, Dr. Manuel María Quijano, and Dr. Francisco Bayón, in botany; and Col. Joaquín Acosta, who had some knowledge of several fields. Acosta, the son of a *corregidor* and large landowner, had the advantage of immersion in the scientific world of Paris. But the educational opportunities for most of these men were rather limited.

Matís was not a broadly educated man. He had come to the study of botany by serving as an illustrator for Mutis, who ultimately taught him the Linnaean system of classification. But, without the stimulus of the intellectuals of the Botanical Expedition, Matís did not keep up with newer developments in the field. He did transmit a good deal of botanical lore to a few younger New Granadans. But, as he lacked a university degree and the polish and presence that went with it, he was incapable of providing the kind of leadership required to bring about the revival of a scientific community like the one that revolved around Mutis.[15]

Contemporaries had a much higher regard for the priest, Dr. Juan María Céspedes, who in the 1830s was the principal professor of botany in the university, even during the prolonged periods when he was absent from Bogotá, tending his parish in Charalá. The case of Céspedes (1776–1848) is illustrative of the overwhelming isolation in which the few New Granadan practitioners of science worked. As a priest in the Cauca valley, he was infected by the scientific enthusiasm of the last decade of the colonial period. He became interested in botany after reading a copy of Linnaeus that he found in a *posada*. Unable to make contact with the savants of the Botanical Expedition, he pursued his studies alone until he came to know Matís at the beginning of the 1820s. At this point he began working with the scientific expedition of 1822, teaching in the natural history museum and joining Rivero, Boussingault, and Matís in an exploration of the San Agustín region. Céspedes is said to have been much more aware of current European developments in botany than Matís. In 1842 he recommended that students learn a modification of the Linnaean system of classification and the then generally accepted approach of Antoine Laurent de Jussieu. Nevertheless, Céspedes also suffered quite obviously from the isolation of Bogotá.[16]

As the number of scientific amateurs was limited, so necessarily was the amount of scientific instruction available. In Bogotá in the early 1830s the only science courses beyond basic natural philosophy were the botany classes of Céspedes, or in his absence Matís, and the lectures on chemistry and experimental physics given by Joaquín Acosta from 1833 to 1836. Recently returned from study in Paris, Acosta apparently stirred at least momentary interest, for it is alleged that his classes were attended at first by more than sixty persons, including a number of professors from the traditional faculties. Two years later Acosta still had enough students for ten of them to make a public presentation. Acosta also taught or offered to teach mineralogy in the Colegio del Rosario in 1837. At the same time el Rosario's vice-rector, Juan Nepomuceno Núñez Conto, introduced "an elementary course on agriculture" into the third year of philosophy. Some of these plans remained on paper, however, for Acosta was often called away from Bogotá on government service. Beginning in 1837, Benito Osorio, a professor of physiology, taught chemistry in Acosta's absence. Not long afterward, Bogotá's Colegio de San Bartolomé and its ancient competitor, el Rosario, sporadically offered some chemistry and botany. None of the chemistry courses appears to have offered much in the way of laboratory demonstration. Outside the capital, science offerings were even more limited. The university at Cartagena awarded degrees in medicine but had no classes in botany, chemistry, mineralogy, or any of the other "new" technical subjects. The university in Popayán also presented nothing on these subjects, although Lino de Pombo and, after 1832, José Rafael Irurita, his student and successor, offered mathematics instruction at relatively high levels. Pombo made some effort to teach engineering applications of mathematics.[17]

Bogotá generally had a good deal more to offer than the two other national universities, and all three universities as well as the private *colegios* in Bogotá tended to be well in advance of most of the provincial *colegios*. The latter in their "philosophy" courses of the 1830s rarely offered more than basic mathematics and some rudimentary physical theory. The quality of *colegio* instruction, of course, varied a great deal. At Vélez, Cerbeleón Pinzón tried to include zoology, botany, and mineralogy in the second year of natural philosophy, and the *colegio* in Panamá offered chemical principles in the third year. In Medellín, Mariano Ospina taught a staggeringly elaborate physics course, which included a surprisingly sophisticated treatment of electricity and a strong emphasis on the use of instruments and other practical applications. The *colegio* in Tunja emphasized experimental demonstrations as well as the practice of surveying. A number of smaller places provided a rather limited diet of physical theory but made sure not to omit surveying. At the lower end of the scale were such *colegios* as those in Santa Marta and Pasto, which taught nothing about electricity and magnetism or even, in some cases, light and sound. At the end of the 1830s the experimental physics of Nollet was still used in poorer provinces.[18]

The effectiveness of these natural philosophy courses was limited in many places not only by the scarcity of adequate or modern texts but also by the kinds of instructors available. The philosophy classes were often taught by men who must have considered this function marginal to their careers. In the more important educational centers the philosophy instructors, as in the colonial period, frequently either were law or theology students who were finishing their professional degrees or were professors of law or medicine or theology who taught natural philosophy on the side. In the latter category was Dr. José Dionisio Araujo of the university at Cartagena, who in one year taught four courses in medicine and two in natural philosophy. In the provincial *colegios* the philosophy instructors were less likely to have other academic occupations. As these instructors often donated their time, the local rectors were in no position to require a high standard of teaching.[19]

Perhaps the greatest difficulty with the philosophy courses lay in the fact that the natural science portions were irrelevant to the pursuit of any career in New Granada. The literary parts were clearly related to the law, and arithmetic was obviously necessary. But it was not clear that algebra and the higher branches of mathematics or the principles of physics or other sciences were of any professional utility. As a result many students endured these courses much as many American students labor under current college science requirements.

One place in which technical knowledge seemed relevant was Antioquia, where gold mining was experiencing foreign-induced technical change and growth. In 1833 some of the provincial political leaders began to work toward establishing courses in chemistry and mineralogy in the provincial *colegio* in Medellín. While the idea originated among the political elite in Medellín, it had rather broad support throughout the province. When public funds laboriously scraped up from a variety of sources proved inadequate, some 225 citizens in twenty-one communities pledged contributions to support a chair in chemistry.[20]

For the brief period from 1838 to 1840, Medellín enjoyed the services of an Italian chemistry professor, Luciano Brugnelly. This project proved very expensive, however. Before Brugnelly had passed a year in Medellín the total expenditures on the chemistry chair had mounted to more than five thousand pesos: about two-fifths of this was the Italian's salary from time of contract; the rest was the cost of buying books and laboratory equipment and transporting them into Antioquia's mountainous interior. Two years of sustaining the chemistry chair completely drained the province's resources for the support of secondary education. The experiment collapsed along with the *colegio* under the impact of the civil war from 1839 to 1842. Brugnelly, for his part, was undoubtedly relieved to be released from the rude environment of Medellín. Aside from having been beaten publicly by one of his students, he had found it a boring place and pined for Paris or even the relative civility of Bogotá.[21]

Antioquia had better incentives and greater resources than most provinces for taking on the importation of a foreign science professor. But its experience illustrates some of the difficulties of such projects. There was the problem of financing, which was sometimes complicated by the necessity of obtaining authorization from administrators or the Congress in Bogotá for special fiscal expedients. Then in most cases the costs turned out to be even greater than anticipated. Until the 1870s it was necessary to pay the foreigners two or three times the salary deemed appropriate for a native professional teaching philosophy and letters, jurisprudence, or medicine.[22] Higher still was the cost of chemicals and laboratory equipment. Virtually none of these were produced in the country. They were purchased in Paris and then transported by poled boat up the Magdalena River and by mule or *peón* over the mountains, at great risk to the glassware. And then the whole project was likely to be curtailed by political disruption, during which the foreign scientist, his contract up, would quickly make his escape. Finally, such experiments produced few dedicated Colombian scientists to carry on after the foreigners left—in the Medellín case two youths later served as chemistry professors.

Moreover, the intended beneficiaries of the foreigners' scientific knowledge often were not interested. While some upper-class adults felt strongly that the younger generations ought to be practically educated, the youths themselves were not persuaded. Only eleven students enrolled in Medellín's chemistry course in 1839, in contrast with thirty in jurisprudence and nineteen in theology. At the end of the year only three students remained in chemistry, and only one made a public presentation of his accomplishments, the others having been absent from class too often to claim any knowledge of the subject. In Bogotá in the same period upper-class youths were displaying the same lack of interest in practical fields: courses in accounting and commercial math offered by the central university had to be suspended because fewer than ten students attended.[23]

The Neo-Bourbon Campaign for the Practical

The years from 1826 through 1845 were marked by a concerted effort on the part of the Bogotá authorities to channel students away from the study of law and other traditional careers and into scientific studies that would profit their local economies. This campaign by the political and educational elites met steady, and sometimes heated, resistance. In the resulting conflict, many Colombian youths and some adults publicly questioned the value of scientific education.

After the effective defeat of the Spanish forces but before central administrative mechanisms were firmly established in Bogotá, the Congress of Cúcuta set forth a national education policy that aimed at extending higher education but was not particularly oriented toward science. The law of August 6, 1821, declared that every province was to have a *colegio* regulated by the national government but supported if possible by local revenues, primarily the income from properties confiscated from local convents. The provincial *colegios* were expected to provide the standard introductory courses of the colonial period (Spanish, Latin, natural and moral philosophy, elementary mathematics). The law said nothing more about the natural sciences. There was, nevertheless, one important innovation. Whereas university studies had been limited to Bogotá in the colonial period, the law of 1821, obeying the imperatives of the republican system, permitted any *colegio* to give courses leading to degrees in law.[24]

As secretary of the interior (1821–1830) and thus the first man charged with the national administration of education, José Manuel Restrepo pressed for a more scientific and practical orientation. Encouraged by the arrival of Rivero and the other foreign scientists, Restrepo in 1824 called for a "revolution" in Colombian *colegios* and universities "as complete as that which we have made in the political organization of the republic." He emphasized the need to teach mathematics, physics, and chemistry (along with religion and morality) instead of the "so many useless things" then being taught in Colombian secondary schools. Restrepo advocated the establishment of "Central Schools of Agriculture and the Arts" (probably based on French models) in the three major cities of Gran Colombia (Caracas, Bogotá, and Quito), with the expectation that these would serve as seed schools for the areas surrounding them.[25] Even before these hopes were avowed, the Congress provided for chairs in mineralogy in the newly authorized *colegios* of Medellín, Cali, and Ibagué.[26] These paper programs for scientific instruction reached their apotheosis with the Plan of 1826, which called for each of the three universities (in Bogotá, Caracas, and Quito) to maintain an astronomical observatory, a natural history museum and botanical garden, physics instruments, and a chemical laboratory and to provide instruction across the gamut of contemporary science.

The 1826 plan also reversed the liberal policy toward professional studies adopted in 1821 and returned to something like the colonial system of centralized control of education. The legislators prescribed the establishment of an educational pyramid that was, in conception at least, highly symmetrical. Communities were to have instructional institutions scaled according to their political category (and thus, presumably, their size and resources). The idea was to have a clear division of function between the most important political and cultural centers, which were to provide elaborate university programs for the formation of professional elites, and the provincial towns, which were to dedicate themselves exclusively to providing the basic education required for loyal and productive private citizens. In the humblest communities (*parroquias*) primary schools would give instruction in reading, writing, grammar, simple arithmetic, religion and morality, and the "political constitutional catechism." At the next step up, cantonal administrative centers were to have *casas de educación* with more ample programs emphasizing the natural sciences most useful to the local economies, such as geometry for the mechanical arts and "practical agriculture." In the largest city of each of the country's departments the university was to provide an extremely elaborate preparatory program. Instruction in the natural sciences was to include mathematics, physics, the three branches of natural history, chemistry, and experimental physics. Completion of these courses, as well as the literary ones in French, English, Latin, and Greek, was a prerequisite for undertaking professional studies in law, theology, or medicine. The provincial *casas de educación* or *colegios* might also give these preparatory courses. But unlike those given in the universities, such provincial courses would not automatically lead to entrance into professional studies, for graduates of the provincial schools were required to undergo a rigorous examination of their qualifications in the university towns to gain admission to the university. Professional studies of law, theology, and medicine, according to the 1826 plan, were limited strictly to the universities in Bogotá, Caracas, and Quito. (After the breakup of Colombia in 1830 the three-university system remained, with Cartagena and Popayán joining Bogotá in the triad.) To maintain educational standards at all levels, and most particularly in the *colegios* and universities, the legislators created a national Dirección General de Instrucción Pública, a committee of three serving under the Ministry of the Interior. This strictly regulated hierarchical system was the ideal pursued by Colombian government authorities and educational administrators throughout the period from 1826 to the latter part of the 1840s.[27]

The provinces, however, successfully challenged the attempt to confine professional education to the universities. In November, 1827, Simón Bolívar granted the right to teach jurisprudence to the provincial *colegio* in

TABLE 6. *Chairs Authorized or Reauthorized by Congress,*
September, 1832–September, 1838

Grammar	10
Languages	8
"Philosophy"	16
Chemistry	2
Jurisprudence	21
Medicine	13
Theology	6
Total	76

Source: *CN*, V–VIII; see also note 31.

Medellín.[28] And in March of 1832 the right to give courses in the *facul-tades mayores* was conceded to all the provincial *colegios*.[29] Finally, the law of May 30, 1835, provided explicitly that these courses could be credited toward university degrees. The result was a proliferation of provincial chairs in the traditional professions, with very little increase in advanced science offerings.[30]

Between September, 1832, and September, 1839, Congress authorized, or in a few cases reauthorized, some seventy-six chairs in twenty-one *colegios* (see Table 6). A fifth of these were in "philosophy" (including natural philosophy) and an equal number in grammar and languages. These professorships in introductory subjects were in accord with the intentions of the 1826 plan. But more than half were chairs in provincial *colegios* for professional courses, the bulk of these being in law. Only three institutions, in Medellín, Cali, and Cartagena, asked for chairs in chemistry;[31] and these came to naught because the necessary funds were committed to traditional fields.

Many of these chairs were authorized for short terms of one or two years; others never were filled. These statistics, therefore, are not a measure of what actually was created and persisted, but of the directions in which the provinces and their legislators were trying to move. If one looks at the instruction actually offered, the same pattern emerges. As of August 31, 1837, there were forty-four chairs in law, thirteen in medicine, and fifteen in theology. Only three chairs existed in advanced science—two in chemistry and one in botany.[32] At the end of the 1830s, therefore, scientific instruction for the most part was limited to those rudimentary principles expounded in the introductory three-year *filosofía* courses.

The expansion of professional studies in the provinces and the lack of corresponding growth of the sciences alarmed neo-Bourbon leaders in Bogotá. During the latter part of the 1830s and in the 1840s, a number of politicians and some newspaper writers railed at New Granadan students and their parents for their lack of interest in technical or practical education. Two of the individuals who expressed most concern were Lino de Pombo, who served as secretary of the interior for almost five years (1833–1838), and Mariano Ospina Rodríguez, who in the same post dominated the Herrán administration (1841–1845).

Pombo was the scion of one of New Granada's most distinguished families. At the end of the colonial period members of the family held positions of wealth and prestige in all three of the major centers of Popayán, Cartagena, and Bogotá.[33] Several Pombos had played active roles in the scientific activities of the era. Lino de Pombo's uncle, José Ignacio, founded and led the merchants' Consulado of Cartagena and vigorously promoted export agriculture and commerce, transportation development, scientific instruction, and material improvements in general. José Ignacio figured among the patrons of Mutis and Caldas.[34] Lino de Pombo had been closely associated with Caldas. As a youth he hung about the Bogotá observatory, which was then under Caldas's care, and at the dawn of the Independence era he had studied mathematics and military engineering with the creole savant in the Colegio del Rosario.[35]

Lino de Pombo's university education, like that of his contemporaries, was interrupted by the struggle for Independence; nevertheless, with the aid of family connections, he managed to feed his scientific interests during and following the worst of the fighting. Captured by the Spanish while he was serving as a military engineer, Pombo was sent to prison in Spain. His mother's family, well placed in the Spanish aristocracy, secured his freedom, enabling him to continue his study of mathematics at the University of Alcalá de Henares.[36]

In 1829 he established himself in Popayán, where as professor of mathematics in the university (1829–1833), he denounced the colonial curriculum; extolled the examples of Mutis, Caldas, and their companions; and urged his contemporaries to continue their efforts as a means of achieving economic development.[37] Pombo, himself, did what he could for scientific education and material progress. From 1833 until 1858 he was heavily occupied in high political or administrative office, in special diplomatic missions, and in editing two of the principal legal compilations of this period.[38] In addition to his many public duties, Pombo served as a professor of mathematics and published two mathematics texts.[39] In the realm of economic development Pombo made contributions both as an officeholder and as a private citizen. As secretary of finance for four months in 1846, he was so rambunctiously reformist as to stir considerable opposition among his fellow conservatives in Congress, who considered him utopian. As a private citizen he founded, and between 1845 and 1859 usually directed, the Bogotá savings bank; in newspaper articles he promoted the establishment of a national bank and a mortgage bank.[40]

Pombo first articulated the principal elements of the neo-Bourbon academic reform in a series of articles written in 1832 while he was teaching mathematics in the Universidad del Cauca. Writing at the beginning of the period during which professional studies were spreading through the provincial *colegios*, Pombo issued a sharp warning against this process. Pombo argued for higher standards in general. In the philosophy course mathematics ought to be prescribed during all three years, rather than only one, taking up fully half of the course, with additional instruction being given in experimental physics and architecture. The law course should also be more thorough. Pombo urged that it be extended from five to eight years, so that a law degree would truly be significant. In addition to a general tightening of standards, Pombo also called for a shift in priorities, with more emphasis on useful knowledge, less on legal studies. The nation did not need so many isolated jurisprudence courses in the provincial *colegios*. These provincial courses could not provide a high standard of instruction. And they robbed educational institutions of the funds needed for studies of "a general utility," such subjects as modern languages, history, geography, mathematics, and natural philosophy, which taught youths to think clearly. Pombo argued for the restriction of legal studies to the three national universities and the promotion in other places of the study of useful knowledge. He pointed to the United States as a country that stressed the study of these "classical" subjects in preference to jurisprudence. Finally, he called for the creation of a higher technical institute, modeled on the French Ecole polytechnique.[41]

Immediately after publishing these opinions, Pombo had what would seem to have been an excellent opportunity to apply them, for in 1833 he was named secretary of the interior and foreign relations. He was thwarted, however, by the law of May 30, 1835, which not only permitted provincial *colegios* to give accredited courses for professional degrees but also allowed students to speed up their careers by taking several required courses at once. Under Pombo's administration the proliferation of law chairs in the provinces and of superficially educated lawyers continued unimpeded.

In 1836 Pombo again issued a strong public denunciation of the prevailing tendencies in New Granadan education. New Granada suffered from an excessive number of lawyers and physicians, a reflection, he noted, of traditional and still-prevailing social values. Few citizens believed that their children would be "men of reputation and of merit" if they did not obtain the *doctorado* in medicine, law, or theology. All other studies were looked upon with a "painful indifference." Again Pombo called for the restriction of professional studies to the three universities, with the provincial *colegios* giving preferential attention to subjects of useful application. Pombo acknowledged that the dominant opinion of the day would oppose any effort to restrict studies in the traditional careers. But, he asserted with aristocratic aplomb, "these opinions are not the best ones," nor were they in the true interests of the public or of the individuals who held them.[42]

Pombo was by no means alone in holding these views. They were substantially shared by what might be called New Granada's educational establishment. After his service as secretary of the interior in the 1820s, José Manuel Restrepo worked with Pombo as director general of public instruction throughout the 1830s; in this post he consistently used his influence to press for as taut standards in the provinces as the law permitted. Toward the end of the 1830s the Pombo-Restrepo attitude spread more broadly among the tight little group of men who alternated in the principal posts of educational administration. In varying degrees it was held by almost all who served as secretary of the interior and as director general of public instruction in these years. The rectors of the central university, the Bogotá *colegios*, and the universities of Cartagena and Popayán generally formed part of this neo-Bourbon establishment. All agreed on the need for central standards; and many wanted to use them to cut down on the number of law graduates, to require more science courses, and to introduce modes of instruction based on scientific reasoning rather than rote learning.[43]

Toward the end of the 1830s a developing consensus for a major academic overhauling found expression in various ways. In 1839, Gen. Pedro Alcántara Herrán, Pombo's successor as secretary of the interior, raised the fear that the provincial *colegios*, by creating chairs in professional fields, were overextending themselves. Herrán therefore advised the provinces to restrict themselves to giving courses only in practical subjects of use in their respective regions. Perhaps responding to Herrán's suggestion, the provincial legislature of Antioquia in 1839 voted to abandon the study of law in Medellín, substituting work in civil engineering. Finally, in 1840 the university establishment conducted a searching self-examination, as a result of which Pombo's principles were generally affirmed.[44]

The consensus was well expressed in an April, 1840, report of José Duque Gómez, rector of the central university. Duque Gómez, a professor of law, complained that the 1835 law had extended the teaching of jurisprudence courses too broadly throughout the provinces and had made law degrees too easy to obtain. As a result the country was afflicted with a surfeit of lawyers and physicians, while it lacked practical men who could grow crops, exploit mines, or build bridges scientifically. Duque Gómez and other educational administrators objected to this state of affairs for two contradictory reasons. The proliferation of law and medical degrees meant that young men were being drawn out of productive pursuits at a time when the country was foundering economically. The growing horde of underemployed lawyers would contribute nothing to economic growth and perhaps a great deal to political instability. On the other hand, having posited the need to steer youths away from the traditional professions, at the same time the Bogotá educators worried that the excessive numbers of poorly trained lawyers would diminish the prestige of the degree. However paradoxical this position, they agreed on the need to restrict study for the three traditional careers to the national universities in Bogotá, Cartagena, and Popayán and to make these studies more rigorous everywhere. Duque Gómez and some others strongly urged that more attention be given to natural science and its applications. But the natural sciences were not the primary preoccupation of all the neo-Bourbons. Some gave this cause no more than lip service, their principal interest being in tightening up studies in law and medicine.[45]

Bogotá was thus well prepared for sweeping academic reform when Mariano Ospina Rodríguez entered the cabinet of the Herrán administration in 1841. A relatively insignificant figure up to that time, Ospina as secretary of the interior became the foremost spokesman of neo-Bourbonism. While he was not the originator of its doctrines, he quickly became the focus of opposition to neo-Bourbon educational policies because of the forceful, dogmatic, and indeed utopian way in which he applied them.

Ospina's background was less patrician than Pombo's. His father was a middling landowner in the district of Guasca (about 30 miles northeast of Bogotá).[46] Ospina came from the provincial landed element of the upper class, which at the end of the colonial period and in the republic tended to look to the legal profession as a vehicle for attaining power, mobility, and status confirmation. Indeed, after preliminary instruction in Guasca and Bogotá, he studied jurisprudence at San Bartolomé. Although he never actually practiced law, he formed part of the alleged surplus of lawyers that Pombo and he later so resoundingly denounced.

Ospina's interest in science, by his own account, was stimulated by José Félix Restrepo, in whose last course in *filosofía* Ospina was enrolled between 1823 and 1825. After taking the socially required law degree, he followed Restrepo into teaching, taking a job in a private *colegio* in Bogotá. At about this time Ospina apparently learned of and hoped to duplicate Philipp Emanuel von Fellenberg's manual labor and agricultural school in Switzerland. He planned to earn enough money to go to Europe, where he would study French, English, and German ("the foreign languages most adequate for the propagation of the applied sciences"), as well as mathematics, physics, chemistry, geology, "and particularly the parts of these [which were] applicable to agriculture, mining, and industry in general." He also intended to study, among other subjects, hygiene, the rules of public administration, and the "economic construction of buildings, bridges, and roads." Living frugally, he would travel by foot through Switzerland, Holland, and other countries known for their agricultural progress and political enlightenment. There he would learn in detail how to administer a model farm and would acquire "practical notions of the city and rural life of laborious, economic, and honorable peoples."

Ospina hoped to establish in a rural area near Bogotá a "scientific and industrial" *colegio* that would feature hard work, severe discipline, rural simplicity in living styles, and practicality. On the ancient premise of a "sound mind in a sound body," students were to employ their time alternately in academic study and in farmwork, swimming, gymnastics, hiking, and other physical activities. All students were to work on the school farm and in the school shops, not only to support the school, but more importantly to gain practical experience in useful activities. Among the instructors would be experienced artisans, who would teach the various mechanical arts. The academic curriculum would give preference to the modern languages; only especially good students would be taught some Latin. The course would also feature "principles of municipal and administrative organization" and judicial and parliamentary procedures. Ospina's aim was to "educate men of energetic and resolved will, sound, robust, austere, moral, laborious, patient, . . . apt for organizing and running a colegio, for setting up an hacienda, for exercising with expertness and honor any governmental function or administering a commercial house or an industrial, agricultural, or mining company; men in the true sense of the word, able to gain their living honorably for having acquired habits of laboriousness, temperance, honor and exactitude."[47]

This plan was aborted in a manner characteristic of nineteenth-century Colombia. Ospina, the exponent of discipline, patience, and civic virtue, became involved in the assassination attempt against Simón Bolívar in September, 1828. He had to flee to Antioquia and, lacking money, was forced to abandon his trip to Europe. Nevertheless in Antioquia he took up the work of practical education. As secretary to the governor (1833) and later as rector of the provincial *colegio* in Medellín he was one of those most responsible for carrying forward the project of importing a chemistry professor.[48]

Ospina's ideas and activities in the 1820s and 1830s indicate that he already conceived of technical education as an important instrument for economic development and general social improvement. After 1839, however, he began to see it as a political device as well. He, like many others of his generation, was horrified by the War of the Supremos of 1839–1842. Ospina interpreted the outbreak of this war as a sign of galloping moral decay in Granadan society. Ospina saw the handful of students and young lawyers who joined the rebel forces as evidence that a surplus of underemployed professionals was one cause of New Granada's persistent political disorders. In his 1842 report to Congress he quoted an unnamed "illustrious Granadan" to the effect that there existed hundreds of graduates in medicine and jurisprudence, "discontented with themselves and with the society that does not provide them with work and easy means of subsisting." These unemployed professionals were likely "to afflict their families, torment themselves, and disturb the country."[49] An article in a Bogotá newspaper put the argument even more explicitly. From the surplus of professionals issued "the desire for novelties, to find by means of political disturbances the posts that others occupy." The excessive number of lawyers was also the reason "that everyone is preoccupied with politics, with new systems, new constitutions, while no one directs his attention to agriculture, to mining, to any kind of industry."[50] This theme, repeated endlessly by Ospina and other leading *ministeriales*, became a dogma that lesser politicians felt compelled to adopt at least outwardly until the latter years of the 1840s.

The *ministeriales* of the 1836–1845 period thus pursued several distinct, but in their minds linked, goals—the inculcation of science and scientific reasoning, quality control for higher degrees, and, through a reduced number of lawyers, political order. In advocating their aims the neo-Bourbons displayed a certain ambivalence toward both science and the traditional professions. Despite their praise of the utility of the sciences, their own words failed to conceal an implicit acceptance of the "superiority" of the traditional professions and of literary and political careers. In urging that secondary education be clearly separated from "superior" education, Pombo explained that in this way "the generality of citizens" might acquire notions of geography, history, the living languages, and the natural sciences, but only "a part of them might continue with profit the careers of the forum, the church, and medicine, cultivate literature in its different branches, and give flight to lively genius with the study of the good models and of the great masters, for the good and lustre of their country."[51] When higher education was described in such compellingly elitist terms, how could any provincial youth of good family fail to want to come to Bogotá to take part in these Athenian doings? To stick to practical secondary training was necessary and good for the provinces but apparently a lower order of activity. Advocating the mission of practicality in such terms could hardly excite much enthusiasm for it.

Beginning in the war year of 1840, the neo-Bourbons moved by stages to give the Pombo doctrine institutional form. At first the Bogotá authorities tried suasion. The Congress of 1840 conceded the right of the provincial legislatures to determine the courses their *colegios* would offer. But it again suggested a functional division between the three university centers (Bogotá, Cartagena, Popayán), which were to give preference to professional studies, and the provincial *colegios*, which were to devote their attention primarily to modern languages, geography, history, and to those branches of the natural sciences that could be usefully applied in their regions. The national congress attempted to encourage the provincial legislatures to fulfill Neo-Bourbon goals by giving them a general authorization to spend their funds to import foreign science professors and laboratory equipment.[52]

The Herrán administration, with Mariano Ospina as its secretary of the interior (1841–1845) adopted a more coercive approach. The national authorities countered the provinces' substantial financial autonomy by aggressively using the central government's control over the granting of degrees. A law of May, 1841, suggested somewhat tentatively and ambiguously that the provincial *colegios'* courses in law and medicine might not be credited toward university degrees if the schools did not attend first to the "preferred subjects," that is, literature, natural philosophy, and locally applicable natural sciences.[53] This policy was more clearly and strongly set forth in Ospina's comprehensive educational plan of 1842, which erected a Procrustean bed for the provincial *colegios*. In the name of standards, Ospina declared it impossible for a *colegio* to give accredited courses in any of the traditional professions unless it could sustain a faculty of ten (four in literature and philosophy, three in natural sciences, and three in any traditional university field the *colegio* chose to offer).[54]

The faculty stipulated by Ospina's program challenged the financial resources of its three universities, and it clearly was an impossibility for almost all the *colegios*. The greatest stumbling block was the prescribed science faculty, as science teachers were both expensive and unavailable. While lawyers and physicians were willing to teach cheaply (200 to 400 pesos) or even on a volunteer basis, Ospina's own experience in Antioquia had shown that hiring a single foreign professor with apparatus might cost 5,000 pesos within the space of two years. This was more than the total annual revenues of most provincial *colegios*. At this time only the provincial school in Tunja had revenues and expenditures of more than 10,000 pesos per year. Only two other schools, those in Panamá and Cali, could claim revenues of more than 5,000 pesos, and they could not depend upon even that much. Their actual, collected incomes were often considerably less. Eleven other provincial *colegios* for males had paper resources of less than 5,000 pesos and actual collections of less than 3,000. Seven of them, in a relatively prosperous year, were not able to collect even 2,000 pesos per year, and four were below the level of 1,200 pesos.[55]

The same story is told by the provincial *colegios'* expenditures on salaries. In 1846–1847 Tunja spent 4,500, Cali 3,500, and Panamá 2,400. The other eleven provincial *colegios* had salary disbursements of 1,500 or less, and three spent only a little more than 500 pesos.[56] The funds of the eleven poorest institutions might support from one to three New Granadan instructors of grammar or law. But they would not suffice to employ one foreign chemistry professor.

As the *colegios* could not afford to provide accredited courses, the new plan meant that provincial students would have to take all their professional courses in Bogotá, Popayán, or Cartagena, at great and perhaps prohibitive cost to their parents. In addition to financial problems, the program involved other new burdens for students. Ospina's plan of 1842 included an elaborate introductory program, seemingly modeled on the French *lycée* system. The new literature and philosophy program greatly increased the number of subjects required of students. The exhaustive list of twenty-seven subjects included not merely French, English, and natural philosophy, but also a smattering of chemistry, mineralogy, geology, topography, and drawing. Ospina tried to force all students to take all these courses irrespective of their relevance to the students' intended careers. The new seven-year curriculum was to be enforced by a general examination for the degree of *bachiller* in literature and philosophy, which was now a prerequisite for entry into professional studies. In addition, students could get credit for courses given in provincial or private *colegios* only by taking a long series of examinations on each of them in a university town.[57]

There were also many incidental complications. The courses had to be taken in a certain prescribed order. As Ospina's plan changed the sequence of the courses, many students had to repeat courses that they had already completed. And then it appeared they would have to delay their graduation until they had completed other newly required courses not offered when they began their studies.[58]

Ospina's program so thwarted the ambitions of parents and youths and created so many headaches for provincial administrators that it stirred widespread resistance. Most provinces made no move to increase their introductory offerings or to establish higher schools of science. Ospina at first attributed this, with some reason, to the fiscal difficulties of the provinces, which had been greatly augmented by the civil war of 1839–1842. Because of these problems, he commented dryly in 1843, it was "not yet time" to attribute lack of provincial action to "negligence or incapacity."[59]

A few provinces tried to respond positively to the Ospina program. In 1843 the relatively well endowed Colegio de Santa Librada in Cali sent to France for two science professors. The provincial *colegio* of Medellín, which lacked the funds required for such an effort, tried another expedient. After the expensive experiment with Luciano Brugnelly at the end of the 1830s, the former governor, Juan de Dios Aranzazu still hoped for a technically oriented *colegio* in the province. But, convinced that Antioquia could not afford any more French professors, he suggested that Medellín's provincial *colegio* be turned over to the Jesuits, who "as men who don't earn salaries [and] live on little," might provide cut-rate instruction in modern languages and the sciences. The governor tried this recourse, but it did not work out.[60]

Mariano Ospina, a noted proponent of the Society of Jesus as an instrument of social order, was soon forced to recognize that the Jesuits were not apt for teaching the sciences or other subjects of utility in the modern world. While serving as governor of Antioquia in 1845, Ospina reported sadly that the Jesuits were unwilling to take over the provincial *colegio* in Medellín, in his opinion because they felt unable to cope with the curriculum that Ospina had created. "The old fathers," he commented, "do not know anything more than their Latin and their Spanish theology, and perhaps Greek and metaphysics, things of little profit to us." Knowing only these subjects, "they find the teaching of modern languages, mathematics, physics, chemistry, etc. distasteful."[61] Rather than taking over the public *colegio*, the Jesuits created a private *colegio* in Medellín, the curriculum of which was notably lacking in science.[62] Meanwhile the province's public *colegio* was unable to fulfill Ospina's requirements, and Ospina, like other provincial authorities, was forced to ask Bogotá for a special dispensation so that Antioquia's sixty students might gain entry into the university.[63]

While Medellín and Cali made honest efforts to comply with the Ospina program, most provinces balked. Ospina concluded that his countrymen simply were uninterested in science instruction and incorrigibly addicted to professional degrees. Provincial resistance had shown "sufficiently that public opinion in favor of the teaching of sciences of industrial application" still had less force in New Granada "than the preoccupation that favors the multiplication of physicians, lawyers, and ecclesiastics."[64]

That this judgment had some merit is suggested by the behavior of leaders in the province of Tunja, whose richly endowed *colegio* was probably the only one in the country that could come close to sustaining the Ospina program. The authorities in Tunja, while establishing three chairs in jurisprudence, asked to be exempted from supporting a school of natural sciences and even from offering the English, French, chemistry, mineralogy, and geology required in the introductory curriculum. The governor of Tunja predictably argued that no one in the province could teach chemistry and the other new science courses in the preparatory program. And, even though the *colegio* had surplus funds, he rejected the idea of importing foreign science teachers. He ridiculed the curriculum of the higher school of natural sciences, which he suggested could not be taught in the capital itself. "Besides this, I do not believe that in the state in which our society finds itself, the knowledge of differential and integral calculus, applications of algebra or geometry . . . and other subjects of this school would be very useful." These subjects, he asserted, were for schools in developed societies, not for those in a poor one that had not yet broadly extended primary education. Yet he wanted a full-fledged school of law in Tunja.[65]

A continuing orientation toward the traditional professions was clearly an important factor in the failure of the neo-Bourbon efforts. But the Tunja governor's comments indicate the difficulty in disentangling lack of interest in or hostility to science from resentment at the neo-Bourbons' heavy-handed approach in implanting it. Mariano Ospina was not simply introducing new science courses; he was also using them, rather obviously and successfully, as a means of professional birth control.[66] Students, their parents, and the provincial authorities who represented their interests were perfectly aware of this. Their attitude toward science instruction was not improved by their realization that inability to obtain science professors was the principal barrier to the accreditation of their *colegios*. As the mandatory study of chemistry and mineralogy blocked the fulfillment of the aspirations of a whole generation of students, it is not surprising that the waves of public opinion dashed furiously against these subjects.

A manifesto penned by some Cali students in May, 1845, suggests that they objected to the increased burdens of the Ospina program as a whole and to natural science simply as the most evident obstruction to their careers. The new curriculum required learning a "multitude . . . of useless and unnecessary subjects." And, even if these subjects were useful, their implantation would be impracticable because of the impossibility of finding or supporting all the professors needed to teach them. The program discouraged students with the "immensity of years the courses must last" and the "multiplicity and extraordinary severity of the examinations." Thus it had dealt a "mortal blow" to public education and left large numbers of youths unoccupied, "all with the not very important aim of diminishing the numbers of physicians and lawyers." The students heaped scorn on Ospina for so heavily emphasizing the mechanical arts, which they contended New Granada was too backward to be able to utilize. They questioned whether Ospina himself really believed that his program could be implanted in a "poor country, lacking . . . professors, elementary books, . . . and scientific establishments with the necessary instruments and machinery, even supposing a surplus of patience in its youth." The students concluded that Ospina's main purpose was simply to impress people in foreign countries with a false picture of New Granada's progress.[67]

There is reason to question, as the students did, the appropriateness of Ospina's program. In his plans was a good deal of keeping up with the Joneses. He was attempting to introduce the latest modes in instruction, ones already practiced in Europe and being implanted in the United States, but without the necessary underpinnings. In the United States at this time liberal arts colleges were going through much the same process as Ospina was prescribing for New Granada. Increasing specialization in science was leading to a proliferation of courses. In most American colleges, as in Ospina's plan of 1842, the tendency was not to drop older courses to make room for new ones but rather to cram the new ones into the older curriculum. Along with this curriculum dilation came significant increases in the science faculty at leading North American institutions— typically from one professor of mathematics and science early in the 1820s to three or four by the end of the 1840s. At the same time the American colleges were making substantial investments in the scientific equipment needed to teach experimentally.[68]

In a variety of ways the United States' dynamic and relatively advanced economy of the first half of the nineteenth century provided a supportive environment for increased scientific activity. One detail is suggestive: by the 1840s the United States' glassmakers were able to produce skillfully and cheaply almost all the laboratory glassware that New Granada had to import at great expense.[69] In the United States many transportation projects and growing industrial centers had a stimulating effect on both educational institutions and their graduates. One thinks of the impact of the Erie Canal and manufacturing in Troy on the Rensselaer School and Union College, of the vital role of the Philadelphia–Delaware–New Jersey industrial community in the development of technical research and technical professions, of the interconnections between the industries of the Connecticut Valley and the emergence of the Yale Scientific School, and of Massachusetts textiles and Harvard's Lawrence School.[70] Obviously all this was missing in New Granada. Ospina, however, unwilling to bow to the economic realities, attempted to turn the country around by the negligible force of his decrees.

The expansion of the science curriculum in the United States is believed to have been aided by the competitive character of the North American college system, each college seeking to match the offerings of its rivals in order to attract students.[71] It might be assumed that a laissez faire approach could have produced the results the neo-Bourbons sought through centralist control. But the North American model does not apply very well to New Granada, even by inversion. Although regional isolation tended to cut down competition among New Granadan secondary institutions, some did exist, particularly between the various provincial *colegios* and the nearest of the three universities. But the generally accepted coin of competition was the chair in law or medicine, not the natural sciences.

Ultimately, students were not much interested in science, because in the context of their society it did not seem very practical. For economic as well as institutional reasons, there was no place for scientific professionals. In his decree of 1842 Ospina had attempted to give science more status within the university system by creating a *facultad mayor* in the natural sciences to accompany the three traditional ones. All degrees available in the traditional fields, including the treasured *doctorado*, were also to be offered in the natural sciences.[72]

In creating doctoral degrees in science, Ospina tried to deal with the problem of prestige. But he left unsolved the problem of careers. Though the concept of an engineering profession was not unknown in New Granada, Ospina seemingly did not conceive of this possibility. If the putative graduates in the natural sciences did not apply their talents to private economic enterprise, they were expected to become science teachers.[73] Given the low salaries in the *colegios* and the lack of any other clear prospect for scientific specialists, few young men were likely to start down the path to such a profession. One young New Granadan science instructor, who was entirely sympathetic to Ospina's aims, made this point to Ospina rather explicitly in 1844: "[In] the present state of the country, and in that which we might anticipate in our patriotic dreams, [the physical and mathematical] sciences will not become a profession whose labors will be rewarded by society, not even with honor and esteem, less still financially, and . . . without these stimuli, the spirit of progress will be extinguished here and the faculty of physical and mathematical sciences will remain established only on paper."[74]

Chapter 5

The Decline of
Neo-Bourbonism

THE administration of Gen. Tomás
Cipriano de Mosquera (1845–1849) shared many goals with its predecessor, but it differed somewhat in style. While the Herrán government, dominated by Mariano Ospina, depended almost entirely on coercive decrees, the Mosquera administration displayed more positive leadership. The contrast in the spirit of the two administrations is partly a reflection of the differing circumstances under which they governed. Herrán and Ospina came to head the government in the middle of a civil war, and their efforts were devoted substantially to restoring order. Mosquera's administration began with domestic peace relatively secure and ended with a small commercial boom in tobacco exporting underway. But if General Mosquera governed in an era of greater confidence, this was partly his own doing. Ospina, a man of modest means and rather Puritanical attitudes, emphasized discipline and constraints, while Mosquera believed that the way to achieve something was to support it handsomely with government appropriations. Through his commitment to innovation and his willingness to use government largess, Mosquera, the glory-seeking second son of an aristocratic Popayán family, helped to stimulate a general spirit of change, an interest in progress and profit, and a general optimism in the upper class as a whole.

In his four-year term the national government became, for nineteenth-century New Granada, a remarkably dynamic force. The Mosquera administration established a new, more vigorous road-building policy and provided subsidies that permitted the definitive establishment of steam navigation on the Magdalena River. It tried to reform the currency, weights and measures, and government accounting methods. It turned the government tobacco monopoly over to the country's largest merchant-capitalists so that they might develop its export potential.

The Mosquera government approached the development of academic science with much the same zest. It established a military school oriented toward civil engineering (see chapter 7), gave increased financial support to the Bogotá observatory and the national museum, and recruited foreign professors, some of whom were employed in a new Institute of Natural, Physical, and Mathematical Sciences in the capital.

But, while the Mosquera administration relaxed some of the devices by which Ospina tried to coerce students into the study of science, his government retained many others. The spirit of change that Mosquera promoted, widespread resentment of continued academic controls, and the fiscal crisis that resulted from Mosquera's extravagance ultimately combined to undermine the neo-Bourbons' edifice of centrally directed academic science. During the last years of the Mosquera administration and the Liberal government of Gen. José Hilario López (1849–1853) Liberals and Conservatives joined in dismantling the neo-Bourbon system. From the middle of the 1850s to the middle of the 1860s the national government gave virtually no support, financial or moral, to the mission of science.

Academic Science in the First Mosquera Administration

From its inception the Mosquera administration began to contract science instructors from Europe and neighboring South American countries. Through the agency of Manuel Ancízar and Lino de Pombo, the government secured the services of a Neapolitan chemistry professor, Giuseppe Eboli, who came from Caracas to the university in Popayán, where he began teaching in September, 1846. Ignacio Gomila, a Jesuit brought by General Mosquera on his return from a diplomatic mission in Chile and Peru (1842–1844), became a professor of physics in Bogotá. Others were obtained from Paris, the usual source of foreign science professors. To staff the Institute of Natural Sciences created in 1847, the government contracted Aimé Bergeron, a mathematician, and Bernard Lewy, a Dane with a Paris degree, who was to teach chemistry and serve as director of the institute. In addition, Eugene Rampon, a French physician, taught pathology in the university during the Mosquera period. At the same time the administration contracted two European engineers, Antoine Poncet and Stanislas Zawadsky, and an architect-builder, Thomas Reed, to supervise construction projects. All of these men added to the locally available store of technical information.[1]

While the national government was procuring foreign science instructors for the national universities, at least one province was taking similar steps for its *colegio*. In October, 1843, the assembly of Buenaventura province, in compliance with the aims of the Ospina plan of 1842, authorized the hiring of two European professors of science for the Colegio de Santa Librada in Cali. In 1846 Manuel María Mosquera, New Granada's envoy in Paris, finally contracted two French science instructors for periods of five years. François Chassard was to teach mathematics and its industrial applications, in effect, the fundamentals of mechanical and civil engineering. Edmond Charles agreed to teach the physical and natural sciences "in all their branches." Their contracts heavily emphasized their obligation to provide laboratory experiments and practical instruction in the applications of science.[2]

The efforts to import scientific knowledge during the Mosquera administration involved considerable expenditures. All the specially contracted Europeans enjoyed salaries of at least 1,000 pesos per annum, plus travel expenses. Col. Agustín Codazzi, a Piedmontese military engineer who came from Venezuela at the end of the Mosquera period, was paid the extraordinary annual salary of 8,500 pesos for his work on the republic's first geographical survey. In addition to paying substantial salaries the government purchased scientific equipment and texts worth 8,000 to 9,000 pesos along with works in history, geography, and law worth another 4,000 pesos. The Cali *colegio* also invested its own funds on a smaller scale in laboratory equipment, mineral samples, and texts. The scientific equipment obtained at this time would have to last for a long time; no significant investments of this kind were made again until the last quarter of the century.[3]

The visits of the science professors were complicated by conflicts that illuminate some of the problems typically encountered in the use of foreign instructors in the traditional Latin American university. In Popayán Giuseppe Eboli entered an environment in which the members of a distinctly aristocratic upper class were accustomed to being treated with solicitude by their instructors in the local universities. While Eboli was well received by many of his students, he soon fell afoul of the Urrutia family, long prominent among the priests, lawyers, and humanist educators in Popayán.[4] When Francisco Urrutia failed to complete the three years of chemistry newly required as a prerequisite for the law degree, he and his friends decided to rid themselves of Eboli; if there were no chemistry professor, the requirement could not be enforced. The Urrutias mobilized their forces, sending petitions and printed manifestos against Eboli to the capital.[5] Though the university rector, his faculty, and some twenty students defended him, the Italian chemist soon found it convenient to leave Popayán for another job in Peru.[6]

A more general problem with the foreigners' science courses was that of finances. In addition to the high salaries normally demanded by European science instructors, the universities faced the high costs of maintaining and operating chemistry laboratories, costs that Colombian university rectors and European science professors viewed from quite different perspectives. The foreigners came to New Granada with European conceptions of standards of operation, which the New Granadan universities were hard put to afford. In some cases the foreign experts were unable or unwilling to recognize the strict financial limits within which these institutions had to operate. For their part university administrators were cost conscious, particularly as the extravagances of the Mosquera administration began to result in cutbacks in funds in 1848 and 1849. With the national government constricting rather than expanding its contributions to the universities, the extraordinary cost of the chemistry courses was very difficult to absorb in the budget. Furthermore, the rectors and the members of the academic councils that advised them were for the most part lawyers. They were accustomed to operating in a system in which they and other lawyers taught for minimal compensation, if not entirely without charge. The lawyer-rectors therefore found it hard to accept both the high pay of the science professors and their incomprehensibly high laboratory costs. As one rector pointed out, either the science professor's salary or the laboratory expenses alone would serve to support three professors of other subjects.[7]

The problem of adjusting European standards of operation to New Granadan limitations was further complicated by the arrogance of at least one foreign expert, Bernard Lewy, the chemistry professor and director of the new science institute in Bogotá. Manuel María Mosquera, the president's brother serving as ambassador in France, had been so eager to contract Lewy's services that he had conceded everything he demanded. Lewy came to New Granada with an unusually high salary, even for foreigners (1,400 pesos per annum as against the standard 1,000) and with a carte blanche for the purchase of books and instruments and for laboratory expenses. Conscious that he had conceded Lewy a great deal without binding him to very much, Mosquera suggested hopefully that "the moderation and mildness" of Lewy's character would permit the government to take full advantage of his services.[8]

This proved to be a rather considerable misjudgment. In Paris, Lewy insisted on purchasing expensive instruments already available in Bogotá on the chance that those in New Granada might be broken. On his arrival in the New Granadan capital Lewy demanded further large-scale expenditures not only for the repair and maintenance of the laboratory but also for the decoration and furnishing of the residence the government provided him. When the rector of the university began to object to some of Lewy's expenditures, the Dane made them without the required authorization. Lewy refused to take part in academic councils as his duties as director of the institute required. He began his course months late, taught it infrequently, and spent enormous amounts on fuel. The rector refused him funds for laboratory expenses, whereupon the chemist declined to teach at all.[9] When the faculty governing board rebuked Lewy for his offenses, he threatened to resign and took his case directly to President Mosquera. President Mosquera, like his brother before him, attempted to conciliate the chemist. Later the vice-president of the republic and the French chargé tried to mediate between Lewy and the university authorities. But the battle went on.[10]

Lewy never did much teaching, and that which he did was ineffective. Arrogant in all respects, he taught his classes very casually, reading from notes in badly pronounced Spanish. In his laboratory demonstrations, which were limited to a brief period after the lecture, he did not deign to make clear what principles were being dramatized. After the first two months of the course attendance dropped from thirty-seven to less than half that number. Finally, in 1850, after two years of tribulation, the government suspended his contract. Incredibly, after this prolonged and scandalous drama, a private *colegio* organized by leading Bogotá Conservatives planned to employ Lewy upon his release by the government.[11] To obtain the precious light of science, a portion of the Bogotá elite was apparently willing to absorb any amount of punishment from this difficult foreigner.

Lewy undoubtedly presented a challenge to the tolerance of all who had to deal with him. But the various ways New Granadan leaders responded to him suggest a divergence in value orientations among the national elite. President Mosquera, a well-traveled man who fancied himself something of a scientist, considered this spiny foreign expert so important that he was willing to go to some lengths to appease him. The university rector, José Ignacio de Márquez, saw events differently; his rectoral ego was at stake. But his actions toward Lewy also bespeak his more limited commitment to the mission of science. Born on a hacienda in the highlands of the eastern cordillera, Márquez seems to have rarely strayed far from Bogotá; unlike many leading politicians of the day, he had not traveled abroad. And as a man who had achieved his reputation as a jurist-politician, he epitomized the previously existing sense of order and professional standing in the university and in the broader society. To such a man it was a good idea to improve the country by importing foreign scientists but not at too great a cost, either in money or in dignity.[12]

Lewy's case is of interest as an extreme example of the hazards of employing European scientists. But, while in certain respects he characterized the worst aspects of the foreign expert, his actions do not speak for all the instructors who came to New Granada during the Mosquera administration. Most of the foreigners labored, at substantial salaries it is true, but with patience, dedication, and some success. Giuseppe Eboli instructed without laboratory equipment during most of his time in Popayán (1846–1850). But he was able to train several young *payaneses* who taught chemistry and other aspects of the natural sciences in the local university after his departure. François Chassard, facing similar difficulties in Cali, had to teach French to maintain his equipment.[13] But at least two of his students became leading engineers in the Cauca valley.[14] Aimé Bergeron served well as a mathematics professor in Bogotá until the end of 1853, even though his salary was in arrears during the last third of his six-year stay.[15]

Despite all their rhetorical and regulatory efforts, the neo-Bourbons were only slightly successful in developing science education along the lines conceived by Ospina. A few gains were made in the direction indicated by the academic reforms of the early 1840s. Higher mathematics, physics, and elements of chemistry and mineralogy were now being taught in Cali, first by the two French professors and then by their students. Chemistry classes were established in Popayán, with Eboli's students able to carry on after his departure. In Bogotá, Lewy's egregious behavior impeded the development of instruction in chemistry, but its future growth was nonetheless fed by the acquisition of new equipment. Finally, at least for a brief time, higher mathematics was taught in Panamá by a Colombian educated in Europe. But this was the sum of the innovations of the 1840s. In the fragmentary educational statistics of the 1840s, various provinces—Medellín, Vélez, Socorro, Buga, Cartago—are occasionally listed as giving courses in "physical and mathematical sciences." But it is doubtful that these amounted to anything more than the algebra, geometry, and principles of physics already given in most *colegios* in the 1830s.[16] With the exception of the Cali case, the gains made can be attributed more to the financial support and enthusiasm of the Mosquera administration than to the administrative prescriptions of Ospina's period in power.

In addition to the fact that the new courses were few in number, their significance was reduced by the fact that in many cases they bore no relationship to later careers. The chemistry courses were of interest to medical students. Otherwise the new courses were merely irrelevant preliminaries to study for the traditional professions, which remained the primary goals. The neo-Bourbons succeeded in temporarily obstructing the path to the liberal professions, but not in diverting upper-class youths into new channels[17] (see Table 7).

The effort to redirect the country's youth ultimately contributed to something like a revolution against neo-Bourbon rule. As more and more youths found themselves frustrated by elaborate and constantly changing requirements, pressures steadily built up against the system. The neo-Bourbon administrators in the Mosquera government gradually retreated from the extreme positions staked out by Ospina. But they fought rearguard actions, which only served to increase the antagonism of students, parents, and many provincial officials.

In September, 1845, the curriculum in literature and philosophy was again reformed, generally in the direction of fewer requirements. The length of the program was cut from seven to six years. The courses that caused the most grief—chemistry, mineralogy, and geology—were dropped temporarily, on the ground that no *colegio* had the necessary instructors. (The chemistry requirement was reinstituted in 1846 when the foreign science professors began to appear.)[18] The 1845 decree eliminated the written general examinations introduced by Ospina, and it permitted provincial *colegios* to give courses in law, medicine, and theology without the full complement of professors in these subjects.[19] On the other hand, the 1845 curriculum introduced new courses and altered the order in which existing ones were to be given. It meant more changes and more uncertainty for the students and kept alive resentment of centralist bureaucratic meddling.[20] As Ezequiel Rojas, a law professor and a leader of the liberal opposition, suggested, the Bogotá administrators would be well advised to practice a greater "economy of innovations."[21]

The extent to which the neo-Bourbons in Bogotá antagonized provincial elites is suggested by the case of the Colegio de Santa Librada in Cali. Having hired two European scientists, local leaders assumed they were fulfilling the intent of the neo-Bourbon program, even though they could not measure up to every one of its provisions. Nevertheless, the authorities in Bogotá kept them waiting for accreditation for three years. Then, finally, in August, 1846, Mosquera's secretary of government, Alejandro Osorio, ordered the *colegio* to drop its chairs in theology and to replace them with more courses in the natural sciences, including a chair in mineralogy.[22]

This order and similar ones following it infuriated the citizenry of Cali, and local leaders began to turn against the neo-Bourbon system. Their communications with the Bogotá authorities reveal an increasing rejection

TABLE 7. *Enrollments in Public Institutions of Secondary and Higher Education, by Field*[a]

Year	Secondary[b]			Natural Sciences[b]	Law	Traditional Professions[c]		
	Literature	Philosophy	Total			Medicine	Theology	Total
1835	813	756	1,569	39	385	138	65	588
1838	1,036	965	2,001	79	581	306	112	999
1842	643	531	1,174	104	254	159	139	552
1844	n.a.	n.a.	1,336	69	112	71	56	239
1845	n.a.	n.a.	1,095	9	148	82	38	268
1847	n.a.	n.a.	512	71	114	49	44	207
1850	n.a.	n.a.	1,072	253	190	52	156	398
1851[d]	n.a.	n.a.	323	245	576	87	n.a.	663

Source: Memorias de lo Interior y Relaciones Exteriores, 1836, Cuadro 3; 1839, Cuadro 10; 1843, Cuadro 16; 1845, Cuadro 24; and Memorias de Gobierno, 1846, Cuadro 1; 1848, Cuadro 4; 1851, Cuadros 9, 10, 11; 1852, Cuadro 14.

[a]These statistics are evidently incomplete in all cases, probably somewhat deficient in all, but they are the most complete data available.

[b]For the years 1835–1842 the natural sciences group is composed of students enrolled in chemistry, botany, nautical, or military mathematics courses. After 1842 the figures are for "physical and mathematical sciences," a category by the end of the 1840s applied to many classes formerly in "philosophy" (e.g. algebra). The growth in the natural science category is therefore much less significant than the figures would suggest.

[c]The figures indicate a general constriction of secondary education during the neo-Bourbon campaign (1838–1847), with the most severe contraction in professional studies. The large number of law students in 1851 represents a response to the freedom of instruction laws of 1848 and 1850.

[d]*Colegios nacionales* only.

of the authority of the central government to control provincial education and a distinct cooling in their attitudes toward the science program. Once rather sympathetic to neo-Bourbon aims, the province's leaders were beginning to take the students' position that Bogotá's expectations were exaggerated. In his assertions that the two French professors would offer sufficient work in science, the rector in Cali began to refer to them, with more than a trace of irony, as *"los sabios del viejo mundo"* (the sages of the Old World). He suggested, as the students had nearly two years before, that it was "delirium" to think that a young and poor republic could sustain a science program like those of older, more developed nations. He ridiculed the incredibly numerous course requirements in *literatura y filosofía*, arguing that it would be many years before New Granada would have "so many enlightened men" to staff the courses as stipulated in the central plan. And he pointed out that the excessive requirements merely had the effect of depressing and alienating upper-class youth.[23]

The Collapse of the Neo-Bourbon Program

In their pursuit of increased central control over education, higher standards, and an increased scientific content, the neo-Bourbons overreached themselves. During the latter part of the 1840s there developed a general revulsion against central controls, which led to the disintegration of the science program they sustained. In 1847 and 1848 the growing antagonism toward administrative restrictions and superfluous requirements began to find political expression. Dislike of the centralist system undoubtedly was most strongly felt in the provinces, where fiscal poverty made it impossible to obtain accreditation. Only two provincial *colegios*—in Cali and Tunja— came close to meeting Ospina's standards, and they were in continuous dispute with the Bogotá administrators over whether they might teach law or theology.[24] Neo-Bourbon policies were also resented in Bogotá and the other university towns where students had become befouled in changing degree requirements.[25] Many families in the capital and in the provinces viewed the neo-Bourbon system as simply a mechanism for preventing poor youths from obtaining a professional education. Even those who shared the neo-Bourbons' goals and could meet their standards objected to the excessive governmental meddling. Lorenzo María Lleras, master of Bogotá's most respected private *colegio*, became increasingly irritated at the changing rules for accreditation and at the government's insistence on dictating every detail of the curriculum. In these years Lleras, an influential politician as well as educator, began to push hard for more freedom from government regulation.[26] Finally, there was a reaction among congressmen against the arbitrary use of authority by administrators.[27]

Liberal politicians provided the most vigorous and most united opposition to the Ospina system. Most accounts of midcentury politics emphasize differences between liberals and conservatives over such questions as the church and economic organization, but it seems likely that educational issues also played an important role in shaping attitudes and ideologies in both parties. Upper-class political leaders, after all, were as likely to feel the effects of government policy in education as in any other social institution. There is a direct relationship between the social location of many conservatives and liberals, their attitudes on education, and their general ideologies. The conservatives' political strength was concentrated in the three university towns of Bogotá, Cartagena, and Popayán; for them a centralized system with the universities lording it over the provincial *colegios* seemed sensible. The system represented social discipline and the defense of standards. Many liberals, on the other hand, came from provinces that had been relatively poor or unimportant in the colonial period; lacking substantial conventual establishments, they were not endowed with the incomes needed to support elaborate secondary education. Such liberal provinces as Casanare, Socorro, Neiva, Mariquita, and Santa Marta were among the least likely to obtain accreditation under the centralized system. For men from these places the neo-Bourbon emphasis on standards meant the denial of opportunity; experience with Ospina's system suggested the necessity of breaking down all centralized controls and asserting the freedom of the provinces and private entrepreneurs to provide such education as they would and could. There was thus considerable harmony between liberal views on economic, fiscal, and political matters and their attitudes on education. They sought to open up increased social opportunities through provincial autonomy, laissez faire in all aspects of economic and social policy, abolition of the most obvious forms of privilege, and a rhetorical egalitarianism.

Liberals viewed the neo-Bourbon centralist policies as a general system for the suppression of political liberalism as well as for the denial of individual opportunity, for Ospina, along with his prescriptions for science instruction, forbade the use of texts by Jeremy Bentham and other liberal favorites in the curriculum. Ospina also introduced an intensified academic and social discipline in the university. Liberal youths, who had to learn European liberal theory on the sly, resented the repressive atmosphere that characterized the university at the height of neo-Bourbonism. In addition, Ospina's introduction of the Jesuits as agents of political conservatism, the single most inflammatory issue of the period, was associated in liberal minds with the neo-Bourbon educational system, as Ospina and some of his political friends had promoted the use of the Jesuits in secondary instruction. Some of the more radical politicians of the 1850s later contended that their extreme liberalism occurred partly in reaction to Ospina's restrictive system.[28]

Liberals also objected to the attention that conservatives lavished on higher education. High standards in secondary and university education meant a concentration of expenditures at this level. An elaborate state-supported system of higher education represented a form of special privilege for the upper classes. A truly democratic policy would focus on primary education, leaving the upper classes to take care of themselves.[29] Midcentury liberals tended to believe strongly that the universities needed to be cut down and placed more on a par with the provincial *colegios*.

A welling tide of liberalism in the latter part of the 1840s had much to do with the destruction of the neo-Bourbon system. But the liberals could not dismantle the system without some conservative support, for in 1848 the conservatives held not only the executive branch, but also an unquestionable majority in the Senate. The conservatives, however, fell into increasing disarray during the Mosquera period. Some younger conservatives on some issues were militantly liberal. Julio Arboleda, for example, supported both the expulsion of the Jesuits and the end of central government control over education. Some other conservatives, becoming convinced of the impossibility of maintaining the centralist policy, supported its abolition, allegedly hoping the Jesuits would dominate an uncontrolled system. Ospina and some less notable conservatives fought rearguard actions in Congress. But ultimately they had to accept a compromise between absolute central control and the absolute abandonment of control.[30]

The law of May 8, 1848, undermined the centralist system by making it unnecessary for *colegios* to meet Bogotá-prescribed standards on faculty and curriculum. The concept of such standards, the *régimen universitario*, still existed. But the law provided ample means of giving degrees in the provinces or in private institutions without meeting all the university requirements. In effect, the law replaced a government-backed university monopoly with a more freely competitive system.[31]

After the Liberals came to power in 1849 this "freedom of instruction" was carried to an extreme in the law of May 15, 1850, which made it unnecessary even to obtain an academic degree to practice law or medicine.

To complete the annihilation of the Ospina system and all its symbols, the law of 1850 "abolished" the three national universities, renaming them *colegios nacionales*.[32] Thus, the Liberals sought to reduce further the psychological distance between the three established cultural centers and the *colegios* in the poorer provinces.

Liberals also attacked the financial bases of the three universities. In so doing they found themselves playing a role comparable to that of the religious orders during the late colonial period. In 1842 Mariano Ospina had attained one of the objectives that had escaped the Bourbon reformers. To increase the resources and expand the programs of the universities, he had incorporated in them various formerly autonomous institutions. The central university in Bogotá was greatly augmented through the total assimilation of the Colegio del Rosario and its revenues. As in the late colonial period, el Rosario's alumni reacted against this measure. In the law of 1850 the Liberals removed el Rosario once again from the university's embrace. At one stroke the university lost more than a third of its income as well as free access to its chemistry laboratory, which the authorities had shortsightedly located in the Rosario building.[33] Throughout the period from 1850 to 1868 the former university of Bogotá was an educational nullity.

Academic Science during the Liberal Revolution

In the latter part of the 1840s, General Mosquera and his administration devoted considerable attention to refurbishing Mutis's astronomical observatory. Mosquera bought new instruments and encouraged the use of the observatory for both teaching and research. In the middle of the 1850s, however, the observatory was taken over by an enterprising woman who used it to prepare and sell ices. Somewhat later it became a daguerreotype studio.[34]

The fate of the observatory symbolizes the state of science under the Liberal governments of the 1850s. It was not that the Liberals felt an animus toward science. The López administration carried forward a large-scale geographic survey under the charge of Col. Agustín Codazzi. And in educational policy the Liberals followed the neo-Bourbon example of giving the first priority to science. Under the López administration, the Congress ordered that the nation's three universities (*colegios nacionales*) create schools of arts and crafts to function alongside the science faculties ordered established in the 1840s. The Liberals further declared that, if financial stringencies required any course to be omitted from the *colegios nacionales*, those dealing with the traditional professions rather than the science classes would be the first to go.[35]

But if Liberals manifested positive attitudes toward science and technology, they gave these pursuits very little institutional support. While they conceded science a high priority within secondary instruction, neither science nor higher education in general stood very high among Liberal concerns in the 1850s. Their most urgent causes were to satisfy their supporters and to keep themselves in power by attacking the complex of institutions and power relationships inherited from the colonial period. Creating a Liberal New Granada meant abolishing slavery. It meant cutting down church power and privileges. It meant restructuring the political system along the lines of the North American model and economic policies according to liberal economic dogmas. The López administration introduced reforms of such a far-reaching nature that the Liberals were heavily occupied in carrying them out, the Conservatives in fighting them. The Liberal revolution of the 1850s thus necessarily pushed the mission of science to the margins of public concern.

The content of Liberal policies as well as the distraction of the Liberal revolution adversely affected scientific institutions. Liberals wanted to break with the colonial tradition of centralist government, cutting back the power of the national government and granting more freedom to the provinces and to individual citizens. The freedom of instruction law of 1850 was only one expression of this commitment. In economic policy it was represented in the fiscal decentralization of 1850. When the Liberals came to power in 1849, they inherited a financial crisis. The Mosquera administration had spent extravagantly and then had abandoned the central government's second largest source of tax revenue, planting a time bomb for the succeeding administration. In 1848, during Mosquera's tenure, the Congress had declared that in 1850 the official tobacco monopoly, which provided roughly a quarter of the central government's income, would be abolished. Confronting the ensuing financial crisis, the Liberals, from principle as much as from expediency, carried fiscal disintegration one step farther. They considered a number of traditional taxes—among them the *aguardiente* ("cane liquor") monopoly, the tithe, the king's fifth on precious metals—restrictive of individual enterprise and therefore harmful to the economy. In 1850 the Liberals ceded these taxes to the provinces, hoping that many of them would be abolished. Those taxes that the provinces retained would help the regional governments provide the few services that Liberals were willing to admit were the responsibility of government. Liberal policies, calling for weakening the central administration and its financial base, necessarily impaired the functioning of scientific institutions supported by the national government.

The three *colegios nacionales* quickly felt the effects of fiscal collapse and Liberal attitudes as the national government suspended the subsidies due them. By October, 1852, the national treasury allegedly owed the *colegio nacional* in Bogotá nearly fifty thousand pesos. Forced to operate entirely on their local incomes, the former universities in Bogotá, Popayán, and Cartagena reduced their programs drastically. The *colegio nacional* in Bogotá managed to save its course in chemistry, but to do so it had to sacrifice its seven chairs in jurisprudence, its four in medicine, and its three in arts and crafts, as well as posts in anatomy and cosmography. By 1853 the former central university was no more than a preparatory school, offering five courses in modern languages, geography, and chemistry, but no mathematics.[36] The *colegio nacional* in Cartagena was better endowed with local funds than those in Bogotá or Popayán and so was able to sustain a more elaborate program.[37] But even there the rector wanted to abandon four higher mathematics courses as well as cosmography, astronomy, physics, chemistry, and arts and crafts.[38]

Liberals clearly hoped that the decentralization of revenues and its educational analogue, freedom of instruction, would help provincial *colegios* become more competitive with the three *colegios nacionales*. This occurred to a degree, but only because the established institutions declined, not because those in the provinces improved very much. There is no clear indication that any public *colegio* in the provinces offered calculus during the 1850s. Trigonometry appears in only about half the course lists and surveying in about a third of them. Chemistry was rarely taught outside Bogotá or Popayán.[39] In Medellín's provincial *colegio* a Spanish chemistry professor served a three-year contract (1856–1859) with the acrimony and fragmentary results that so frequently attended the use of specially contracted foreign instructors.[40]

The weakness of the public institutions at the center and in the provinces placed private ones in a relatively favorable position, strengthening an ominous tendency to rely on private schools for most secondary instruction, a tendency still quite noticeable in Colombia. The private *colegios* generally offered a more ample curriculum than the public ones in the provinces, but they usually did not reach much higher levels in the sciences. Trigonometry and surveying were commonly the limit in mathematics and engineering sciences. Two private *colegios* offered calculus, and another may have included it under higher mathematics. Between

1853 and 1868 four private institutions had chemistry courses, and two of these also gave work in mineralogy, geology, or agronomy. All these classes were taught by Colombians with some claim to proficiency. The courses could not have lasted long, however, as most of the private schools, like many other institutions in this era, were rather short-lived.[41]

Just as the Liberals' fiscal decentralization brought a shift in the educational balance between the university centers and provincial and private institutions, their demolition of the academic degree structure had some significant effects. There was one positive result. The end of government controls over the granting of degrees turned the field of education into an absolutely free market. All institutions, public and private, had to compete for customers. Responding to the demands of the consumers, *colegios* began to experiment with variations in the curriculum. Some schools created special curricula for each profession, requiring students to take only those courses that were strictly necessary for the profession. Others simply permitted the students more-or-less complete freedom to determine their curriculum.[42]

The Liberal free market may have encouraged experimentation, but it also had some negative effects. With degrees no longer required to exercise the professions, young men were under less pressure to enter and stay in secondary schools. Almost immediately after the 1850 law, enrollments in both public and private institutions began to decline drastically. The public *colegio* in Medellín, which had attracted as many as a hundred students in the years between 1837 and 1845, by January, 1853, had only seven resident students, and a campaign to recruit more proved fruitless. The following year Medellín's *colegio* was forced to suppress all its professorships, leaving instruction entirely in the hands of the rector and vice-rector.[43] The enrollment of Lorenzo María Lleras's Colegio del Espiritu Santo, the best-equipped and most-patronized private *colegio* in Bogotá, dropped from 150 students in 1850 to 72 in 1851. Having invested 65,000 pesos in a new building and equipment for teaching physics, chemistry, and mineralogy and having set up an elaborate program including civil engineering, he was forced to close the school for lack of customers in 1852. For the same reason other public and private *colegios* remained in a tenuous situation throughout the 1850s.[44]

The removal of the pressure to acquire degrees also made it difficult to discipline those students who did enroll. The rectors of the *colegios nacionales* complained that students came to class only when they felt like it, disrupted those they attended, and often refused to take examinations. According to a foreign observer the public *colegios* in Bogotá and Cartagena practically disintegrated; in the capital, classes were sometimes suspended for months.[45]

By 1853 educational administrators, Liberal and Conservative, had concluded that the relaxation of curricular and other disciplines had particularly impeded the study of science. Because the law no longer required mathematics or science as a prerequisite for professional degrees, students tended to pass these courses by. This complaint, voiced by the Conservative rectors in Bogotá and Popayán, was echoed by the Liberal Patrocinio Cuellar, the secretary of government at the end of the López administration. Cuellar commented sadly that the knowledge of mathematics and natural sciences remaining in New Granada was attributable to the fact that "before 1850 they [students] were required to obtain the degree of doctor."[46]

The educational administrators may have been exaggerating somewhat. Enrollment statistics point in both directions. In Cartagena the law courses often drew twice as many students as those in the natural sciences, and sometimes the science courses had to be closed for lack of students. In Popayán enrollments were quite low in all subjects, but science enrollments were proportional to those in other fields.[47] Actually, it might have been viewed as hopeful that anyone took the science courses at all, considering that most of them had absolutely no professional payoff. That some educators were chagrined at low science enrollments is a measure of their own frustrated aspirations for the development of the country.

The many changes introduced by the Liberals struck so deeply at established institutions and so disturbed class relationships that they provoked violent conflict that disrupted scientific education along with every other public enterprise. To win and keep power and to effect their reforms, the Liberals introduced a new political style, emphasizing the mobilization and manipulation of the masses. They encouraged turbulence among certain elements in the lower classes, most notably the artisans of Bogotá and the rural workers of the Cauca valley. At the same time Liberal measures so deeply affected the Conservatives that they attempted armed rebellion in 1851. Later Liberal efforts to cut the army down to size provoked a military coup that led to another full-scale civil war in 1854. The conflicts between Conservatives and Liberals over power and principles brought devastating civil war between 1859 and 1863.

It was standard practice in time of war to use *colegio* buildings for barracks, with predictable damage to furnishings and educational materials. This happened to the public *colegio* in Medellín in 1851, 1860, and 1867, and war caused the school to close during three other school years before

1886. In the civil war from 1859 to 1863 the public *colegio* in Popayán suffered first from the loss of its subsidies from the national government and then from the seizure of its income-earning real estate by the Liberal forces under General Mosquera. Finally in 1861 the school building was turned into a barracks, and the occupants destroyed everything they encountered, including the laboratory equipment and the library, many of the volumes of which were sold as wastepaper. In the Cauca region the Liberals were the destroying force; in Santander it was the Conservatives. There the bishop incited local fanatics to destroy the laboratory, botanical garden, and all else in the widely respected private *colegio* of the Liberal Victoriano de Diego Paredes in Piedecuesta.[48]

With the drastic institutional changes and civil conflicts of the 1850s and 1860s, government leaders lacked either the composure or the financial resources needed seriously to promote technical development. Even the period after 1863, which saw some beginnings in this direction, was marked by tension between General Mosquera and his former allies, the Radical Liberals. Only after the Radicals eliminated Mosquera from the scene through a coup in May, 1867, were effective steps taken to reconstruct a national university system with a significant scientific and technical program.

Part Four

The Origins
of a Colombian
Engineering
Profession

WITH the failure of the academic science program of the 1840s, the Bogotá elite took up other instruments for turning upper-class youths toward the technical and practical. When New Granada's system of higher education deteriorated under the impact of the liberal revolution, Conservative leaders and some others began sending their sons to Europe and the United States for training in commercial methods or engineering. Simultaneous with the outward flow of upper-class youths, another, more fruitful, experiment was made with the creation of a Bogotá military school (1848–1854), which was strongly oriented toward civil engineering. Both of these efforts were hampered by the continuance of some of the obstacles of the 1840s—political disruption, fiscal and financial weakness, the dominance of politics and political careers in upper-class culture, and, most important, the lack of professional or business opportunities for those who did acquire technical training.

Before the middle of the 1840s, neither modern civil engineering nor an economic base for such a profession existed in New Granada. At the beginning of the republican era the country had, for example, almost no trained surveyors. And, as landowners were accustomed to using natural landmarks to demarcate their properties, there was little effective demand for surveyors. In the 1830s government attempts to distribute Indian community lands allegedly were delayed by the lack of surveyors; ultimately much of the job was done by Venezuelans, who stayed in the country only long enough to take advantage of this opportunity. While the distribution of Indian lands stimulated some momentary interest in surveying, it alone could not provide sufficient employment upon which to base a native engineering profession.[1]

Similarly, until at least the 1840s road building offered no place for an engineering profession. The country clearly needed better roads. The mule paths that carried the country's commerce traversed their routes inefficiently and, being poorly drained, often were washed out. Until well past the middle of the century, the country was virtually without bridges. But, no matter how evident the need for improvement, road building was not organized so as to employ trained engineers. Many of the country's mule paths were cut by private concessionaires, who supervised their own projects, being unwilling or, in most cases, unable to afford to employ professionals.[2] The road works that the government financed were insignificant. The tax assigned for road construction produced no more than thirty thousand pesos per year in the 1830s, and this money was distributed among many small projects in every corner of the country. These public works using corvée labor amounted to little more than repair and maintenance of existing routes. They were supervised by local officials, who were at best commonsense practitioners, and were generally badly done and rarely finished.[3]

In the middle decades of the century this situation began to change. Toward the end of the 1830s such notable neo-Bourbons as Lino de Pombo, José Ignacio de Márquez, and General Herrán argued strenuously in favor of a concentration of national public works resources so that the government might undertake one significant improvement using trained engineers and bring it successfully to a conclusion.[4] In 1842 the Herrán administration began to move in this direction, appropriating one-third of the national road tax and mobilizing the nation's convict labor to cut a single road through the central cordillera.[5] With General Mosquera's accession to the presidency in 1845, public works schemes ballooned. Bogotá's elite conceived of a system of national roads to which the road tax would now be entirely devoted. To promote the development of this national system, the administration was authorized to contract the services of three foreign civil engineers and a hundred skilled foreign workmen. Army sapper battalions were organized for use in road construction. Mosquera's plans for public works were so expansive, however, as to explode the concept of priorities; el Gran General, as well as the legislators of the era, found it hard to deny that any road was of national importance. Between 1845 and 1849 Mosquera undertook road construction on such a scale that, with the aid of some other less useful expenses, he drove the national government into a fiscal crisis. The response of the Liberal governments after 1849 was to decentralize both revenues and road-building responsibilities.[6] As a result few large road-building projects were undertaken before the end of the 1860s. Thus, the middle decades of the century represented both a beginning and a time of frustration for professional engineering.

During the 1850s the idea of engineering as a profession began to spread among the upper class. There began to exist, at least as a mental construct, an acceptable professional channel for a technically trained aristocracy.

The foreign studies of Colombian youths contributed something to the development of such a conception and to the membership of the engineering corps that embodied it. But the Colegio Militar of 1848–1854 played a much more important role in providing students with a clear sense of identity as engineers, particularly by offering them some hope of government employment in the new profession. The expectations raised by the military school were not realized at first. Although engineering existed as a concept, the economy was still too weak to support it as a real profession before 1870.

During the 1870s and 1880s, however, the economy began to move, if somewhat jerkily. The beginning of railroad construction provided Colombia's new engineers with a larger field for professional endeavor. It provided jobs and technical challenges that encouraged the development of a small, but at least partly self-sustaining, community of scientific and technical professionals.

Until the 1880s Colombia stood in an unequivocally colonial relationship to Western scientific centers. All of its scientific and technical ideas originated abroad, and many of its science instructors and engineers were either foreigners or trained in Europe or the United States. There existed almost nothing in the way of institutional support for indigenous scientific or technical activity. After 1880 Colombia's technical dependency remained quite evident, but technically trained Colombians were beginning to move toward at least a marginal autonomy. During the 1880s Colombian science teachers and engineers began to create the scientific institutions needed to sustain a Colombian technical community. By the 1880s a number of upper-class Colombians were well abreast of Western engineering, and a few were capable even of minor innovations in mathematics and engineering.

Chapter 6   Study Abroad

DURING the first three decades after New Granada secured her independence, her political leaders attempted to introduce new technical knowledge to the country by importing foreign scientists and technicians to teach in the *colegios* and universities, build roads, navigate steamboats, and establish factories. They also paid some attention to an alternative mode of acquiring modern technologies—sending young New Granadans abroad to observe and learn the techniques at the places of origin, the United States and Europe.

A few gestures had been made toward study abroad before the 1840s. In 1825 the Santander administration granted the request of Joaquín Acosta, an artillery captain, to receive his military pay while studying technical subjects in France. Acosta's personal initiative became public policy when the 1826 educational code provided for government subsidies for Colombian youths who wished to study useful subjects in foreign lands. Applications were occasionally made for advanced medical studies in Europe during the 1830s, though it is probable that they were denied for financial reasons. In 1832 a semiofficial newspaper in Popayán proposed the establishment of provincial agricultural societies, one of whose functions would be to send youths to study agriculture in Holland, Switzerland, Saxony, England, and other countries known for scientific agriculture, as well as in plantations in the European tropical possessions. This plan, never carried into effect, called for three years of subsidized study on the farms of advanced European cultivators, with the youths possibly serving as "paid farm workers." On their return to New Granada, the beneficiaries would be required to present reports and give instruction on animal breeding and other aspects of scientific agriculture.

In 1835 Domingo Acosta suggested that President Santander send five youths with appropriate secondary training to Paris to study mathematics and mechanics so that each would develop expertise in some useful branch of the arts and applied sciences, such as manufacturing and agricultural

Note: An earlier version of this chapter appeared in *Hispanic American Historical Review* 52, no. 2 (May 1972), Copyright 1972 by the Duke University Press. I am grateful for permission to use this material.

machinery, civil and hydraulic engineering, and civil architecture. The following year President Santander put forward the same proposal and in 1837 Lino de Pombo, as secretary of the interior, repeated it in the name of Santander and his successor as president, José Ignacio de Márquez. In the same period the governor of Antioquia, considering the many obstacles to obtaining a foreign professor of chemistry, urged the provincial government to send one or two youths to study the subject in France or Germany.[1]

Although no action was taken on any of these proposals for government-sponsored foreign study, a few young Granadans studied at their parents' expense in England and France before 1845.[2] These, however, appear to have represented no more than scattered individual cases. Before 1845 study abroad could not be said to have come into vogue.

But at the end of the 1840s, and increasingly during the 1850s, Colombians turned to the idea of sending their sons abroad for technical training. In doing so, they conformed to a general Latin American pattern. A growing Latin interest in technical study in foreign lands is reflected in the records of the Rensselaer Polytechnic Institute, which attracted extraordinary numbers of Latin Americans, presumably because it was one of of the first American civilian institutions to establish a degree program in civil engineering (1835) and to advertise itself as a polytechnic institute (1837).[3] Before 1847, during Rensselaer's first quarter-century of existence, not one Latin American attended the institution. But in the twenty-five years between 1850 and 1875 some ninety youths from the Hispanic world studied there, accounting for more than 10 percent of the graduates. In the next decade (1875–1885) another sixty Latins attended Rensselaer, making up slightly more than 9 percent of the student body.[4]

Latin American attendance at Rensselaer and other technical schools in the United States is particularly striking when compared with the record of other less-developed areas of the world. The Latins were not only the most numerous foreign group at Rensselaer, but also the first on the scene. The first trickle of Japanese students did not arrive at Rensselaer until the middle of the 1870s, by which time ten political entities in the Latin world boasted Rensselaer alumni and seven Latin countries could claim graduates.[5]

After 1850 young Latin Americans were carried abroad by the swelling current of foreign trade that both increased contact with foreign lands and gave the upper class the cash needed to support overseas education. The Rensselaer figures show (not surprisingly) that those countries with the most intensive trade relations with the United States (Brazil, Cuba, Puerto Rico, Mexico) sent youths there earliest and in the greatest numbers. An interest in engineering education developed rather later in Peru as that country was lured into railroad construction by the income from the guano trade and the attraction of its rich mineral deposits in the Andes (see Table 8).

In these developments New Granada was among the laggards. Because its foreign trade was relatively insignificant and its mountainous interior offered no spectacular resources requiring special transportation development, New Granada entered the railroad era very late. Nevertheless, the country was affected by the quickening pulse of international commerce. Between the beginning of the 1840s and the latter half of the 1850s, the average annual value of exports from New Granada tripled.[6] New Granadan newspapers in the latter half of the 1840s began to run regular price quotations on commodities in domestic trade, and in the second half of the 1850s reports on foreign markets became common. During these years articles on economic topics tended at least partially to displace political commentaries.[7] Increasing numbers of the upper class traveled to Manchester and New York on business as well as to Paris and Rome for their edification. Curiosity about new techniques in mining and agriculture stirred, and interest in learning English and English commercial practices became quite marked. After 1850 Colombian youths began to flow in greater numbers to the United States, England, France, and Germany to take up practical studies.

Although foreign trade was undoubtedly the most important stimulus, politics also played a role in some Colombians' decisions to send their sons abroad. With the decline of the university system at the end of the 1840s, many Conservative families had placed their trust in Jesuit schooling. But the Liberals' expulsion of the Jesuits in May, 1850, cut off this alternative. Rather than consign their children to *colegios* dominated by the Liberal ideologies current in the period, a number of Conservatives educated them at home. If they could afford it, Conservative parents sent youths abroad, thus removing them entirely from the evil influence of Liberal doctrine as well as from the dangers and distractions of partisan conflict.[8]

A few Conservative fathers explicitly stated their fear that in New Granadan *colegios* their sons would be corrupted by Liberal doctrines and would probably be infected with the national political fever. Mariano Ospina, at the end of 1850, urged a friend to send his son to a Jesuit school in Jamaica or to one in the United States, so that he would be well trained to become an "industrialist." If the child stayed in New Granada, he would surely enter politics, which would "become worse and worse in this country . . . Our *colegios*, all of them, have the very grave defect of inoculating youths with political spirit, and as politics is the devourer [*polilla*] of wealth, it could be said that a youth who can count on some capital to

TABLE 8. *Students from the Hispanic World Who Attended Rensselaer Polytechnic Institute, 1850–1884.*

(Numbers to the left in each column represent total attending; numbers in parentheses represent graduates.)

	1850–1854	1855–1859	1860–1864	1865–1869	1870–1874	1875–1879	1880–1884	Total
Brazilians	2 (1)	2 (1)	1 (1)	5 (3)	3 (1)	5 (2)	7 (3)	25 (12)
Cubans	1 (0)	8 (3)	10 (3)	30 (6)	5 (4)	7 (2)	5 (4)	66 (22)
Spaniards?			1 (1)				1 (1)	2 (2)
Puerto Ricans		1 (1)	1 (1)	4 (0)		2 (2)	2 (0)	10 (4)
Mexicans				4 (0)		3 (0)	3 (0)	10 (0)
Costa Ricans					1 (0)		1 (1)	2 (1)
New Granadans				1 (1)	1 (1)	1 (0)	2 (1)	5 (3)
Venezuelans			2 (2)			1 (0)		3 (2)
Ecuadorians					1 (0)		1 (0)	2 (0)
Peruvians					5 (2)	2 (1)		7 (3)
Chileans			1 (1)			1 (0)		2 (1)
Origin unknown						4 (0)	2 (0)	6 (0)
Total[a]	3 (1)	11 (5)	16 (9)	44 (10)	16 (8)	26 (7)	24 (10)	140 (50)

Source: Data assembled from *Semi-Centennial Catalogue—Officers and Students of the Rensselaer Polytechnic Institute*, bound with *Proceedings of the Semi-Centennial Celebration of the Rensselaer Polytechnic Institute. . . 1824–1874*, pp. 14–66; Henry B. Nason, ed., *Biographical Record of the Officers and Graduates of the Rensselaer Polytechnic Institute, 1824–1886*, pp. 448–458, 574–582.

[a] Graduates as well as nongraduates are included in the total attendance figures. Graduates are placed in the five-year period of their graduating class even though their actual attendance may have occurred primarily in the preceding five-year period. The figures for 1880 to 1884 exclude eight men who attended in 1884 but graduated in 1885.

begin to work . . . is incapacitated . . . by the studies of our *colegios.*" Ospina went on to suggest that, in a school in England or Germany, a youth would acquire habits and ideas of order, economy, and work. He would not entrust his son to the politicized schools of Bogotá. "It seems to me that a youth leaves none of our *colegios* with a desire to work," he concluded, "but rather all want to . . . become poets, public writers, representatives and presidents, all occupations of little profit."[9]

The pattern of Conservative flight from the contrarieties of Liberal politics to technical activity in foreign havens was repeated at the end of the decade. Mariano Ospina, as president, reestablished the Jesuits and their *colegio* in 1858, only to have his work brought to the ground by the Mosquera-Liberal revolution in 1861 when the Jesuits again were ejected. After Mariano Ospina and his brother Pastor escaped from prison into exile, they busied themselves with planting coffee and operating a "Scientific and Industrial College" in Guatemala. One of their sons studied mathematics and natural sciences at Georgetown.[10]

Until 1880 Colombian efforts to assimilate technology through foreign study were entirely private in character. It was a matter of the upper class attempting to educate its sons in ways that might be profitable to their families. Nevertheless, many of the parents who sent their sons to study abroad also thought of their efforts, at least secondarily, as directed toward national development. What was good for the family was bound to be good for the country.

Some insight into Colombians' study abroad can be gained from the papers of Gen. Pedro Alcántara Herrán, who served as guardian for some four dozen young Colombians who studied in the United States, principally in New York state and Connecticut, between 1848 and 1863. Comparison of the names in Herrán's records with those in the records of leading American institutions suggests that as many as sixty New Granadan youths studied in the United States during this period. Information on students in western European countries is much less ample, so that it is difficult even to hazard a guess at their numbers. Scattered evidence makes it clear, however, that some Colombians studied in England, France, Spain, and Germany, and perhaps a few in Belgium.

A word should be said about the man who offered the extraordinary service of standing *in loco parentis* to so many youths. Pedro Alcántara Herrán was of less notably upper-class origins than many other *ministeriales*. His father was of the lowest stratum of the upper class and might properly be considered middle class. He held the rank of captain of infantry and served in the rather lowly post of *guarda-almacén* in Bogotá. Toward the end of the colonial era, Herrán's father engaged in medium-scale commerce, buying imported goods in Cartagena and bringing them to Bogotá to sell.[11] Pedro Alcántara Herrán studied law at San Bartolomé for one semester but dropped his studies in 1814 to join the patriot armies, and it was as a military man that he rose to prominence in the 1820s. Between 1830 and 1834, Herrán traveled in Europe, first as a political exile, then as a diplomat. While there he applied himself to learning English and French, as well as the military arts. His interests, however, ranged far beyond military affairs. Toward the end of the 1830s he was an active participant in an attempt to establish a cotton mill in Bogotá. As secretary of the interior and foreign relations from 1838 to 1839, he followed the example of Lino de Pombo in attempting to orient Colombian students more toward scientific and technical education. And as president of the republic between 1841 and 1845, he was ultimately responsible for the university reforms elaborated by his secretary of the interior, Mariano Ospina. Herrán's services as a guardian of Colombian students began with, and more or less as an adjunct of, his appointment as Colombian ambassador to the United States, a post that he filled during the Mosquera administration between 1847 and 1849 and again from 1855 to 1862.[12]

The youths Herrán supervised cannot be taken as a representative sample of Colombians studying abroad. As he was a Conservative general and a politician from Bogotá, most of the boys were the sons of Conservative politicians, military men, or *bogotanos*. His services, first extended to political friends at their request, became more-or-less public in character after November, 1851, when he put out a circular advertising his availability as an educational agent in the United States. But of course Conservatives were most likely to turn to him—the November, 1851, circular was issued not long after the suppression of a Conservative rebellion.

Of the Herrán clients who can be identified, twelve were lawyers and politicians, and eleven were merchant-capitalists. Five were landowners or landowner-politicians, and three were military men or military-politicians.[13] In accord with this pattern, the youths came mainly from places involved in foreign trade or otherwise affected by foreign influences. Of forty-three youths whose origins can be identified, twenty were from Bogotá, ten from the Caribbean coast (including Panamá), and nine from the *antioqueño* commercial centers of Medellín and Antioquia. Only three of the fathers lived in the interior in towns that could not be classified as commercial centers.[14]

The principal concern of the fathers who sent sons abroad was that their studies be practical, in particular that they be of utility in their homeland.

The first man to use Herrán's services, a large landowner in Valledupar, asked that his ward be taught surveying.[15] Most of the rest of Herrán's clients hoped that their sons would become chemical, mining, or civil engineers, or that they might learn the ropes of international commerce. A few wayward youths were sent without any more specific aim than the hope that they would learn some self-discipline.

The emphasis upon practicality was such that some parents cautioned their sons against the temptation of studying the pure sciences. They were instructed to concentrate on that which was immediately and obviously applicable. Mariano Ospina, writing instructions to his sons Tulio and Pedro Nel in the 1870s, stated this view quite strongly. Ospina said that in two or three years of "serious and continuous study" they could make themselves civil or mining engineers. But he expressly instructed his sons not to take up "the most overrefined" aspects of analytical mechanics or higher mathematics. They should devote themselves preferentially "to that which is applicable in practice and attempt to acquire the knowledge of those who are called mechanical engineers." Ospina went on to warn specifically against the study of those sciences that were intellectually "very attractive, but not very profitable," like botany, zoology, and astronomy, "which ought to be left to the rich."[16]

Mariano Ospina also warned his sons to stay away from novels and verse. If they were to advance in the applied sciences, it would be necessary to renounce fine literature, "which takes up time and tires the mind without profit."[17] Ospina went so far as to enjoin his son Pedro Nel not to write poetry or even to write elegantly, but rather to prefer a "noble simplicity of expression, which produces thought with clarity and precision."[18] In this pronounced concern for practicality and self-discipline in economic action and personal style, there is more than a hint of the attitudes commonly associated with the Protestant bourgeoisie.

The fathers' desire for practical training often went beyond the idea of learning technical subjects in the classroom. Many particularly wished their sons to obtain practical experience in merchants' houses, shops, and factories in the United States. This concern was well expressed in a letter written by Pastor Ospina regarding the education of his son Sebastián:

> My object in sending him to that country is that he learn some branches [of knowledge] which may be useful in this one. But most especially I desire that he learn mechanics and machinery, not so much theoretically as practically and in the part of most immediate application to our necessities; like the use of pulleys, capstans, [illeg-

ible] to move great weights, the construction of water wheels, the arrangement and management of saws, mills, sugar mills and other machines used in agriculture, the construction of wooden bridges, etc. Of course these branches [of knowledge] in particular can not be learned in a secondary school and much less practically.

Pastor Ospina's intention was not for his son to obtain a degree as a mechanical engineer, but rather to achieve a practical capacity in the field. He suggested that his son study mathematics, mechanics, and hydraulics for a few months. In this time he would learn enough of the theory of these subjects so that he might "dedicate himself exclusively to practice." Ospina's particular concern was that Herrán place his son as an apprentice in a shop where machines were made or used, in a mill, sawmill, or some other mechanical establishment. And if this were impossible, he should be placed in some commercial house to learn bookkeeping and commercial operations.[19] Pastor Ospina saw no point in sending a son abroad simply to go to a secondary school for formal general education; this could be obtained in Colombia. Only practical apprenticeship in industry would justify study in the United States. Although they did not articulate it in precisely these words, a number of upper-class Colombians viewed study abroad, particularly in the United States or England, not simply as a formal educational process but more as a means of immersing their children in a technical culture so evidently lacking in Colombia.

Many upper-class fathers, in fact, dispensed entirely with formal schooling in their projects for education abroad. Often youths would be sent to New York, or more commonly to England (where it was easier to get a position), to obtain clerking jobs in which they might gain valuable commercial experience.[20] The Colombian fathers did not expect these clerking jobs to pay salaries; the value lay in the mercantile education. Business experience in the Western world's leading emporia was considered of such importance that even a political leader like José Eusebio Caro, in the ripeness of his thirties, was delighted to become an unpaid clerk in a New York house.[21]

Some of the boys sent for commercial training were, of course, the sons of merchants. But it is striking how many lawyer-politicians (presumably men in the traditional mold) put their boys to practical studies of commerce. Rufino Cuervo—landowner and lawyer; at various times rector of the National University, Supreme Court justice, and vice-president of the republic; and one of Bogotá's leading literati—sent his eldest son to England to learn his commercial ropes. Manuel María Mallarino, a lawyer-politician and landowner from the Cauca valley, attempted to put his sons into a merchant's house in New York between 1855 and 1857, the very years when he served as New Granada's vice-president. Many other lawyers and landowners, less famous but nevertheless respected members of the aristocracy, did the same.[22] These lawyer-politicians, without explicitly denigrating their own careers, nevertheless were urging their sons down a path they themselves had not taken. José Manuel Restrepo, who served as a government administrator and ate at the public trough continuously from 1821 to 1860, sent his son Manuel to England to "complete his practical mercantile education" with the comment that he "never [had] thought that his children should live off public offices that only produce a scarce subsistence and salaries that always are expended in their totality."[23]

Although their first interest was in practicality, some Colombian parents were also concerned that their sons not lose their Roman Catholic faith during their sojourn in the land of the Anglo-Saxons. Some specified that the youths be enrolled in Roman Catholic institutions.[24] Accordingly, Herrán at first placed most of his charges in the grammar school of St. John's (Fordham), a Jesuit school. But some of his wards considered the Jesuit discipline too severe; and others were distracted from their studies by the diversions offered by New York City. As a result, Herrán constantly experimented with new institutions. By 1851, he was sending many of his wards to Protestant or secular institutions, and he came to prefer Protestant schools in small towns in New York state and Connecticut to Catholic ones in New York City. Although Herrán placed students in eighteen different private schools, most of them not Catholic, in only one case did religious belief or practice become a problem.[25]

In the first years of Herrán's guardianship, Granadan parents had almost no knowledge of American educational institutions. Consequently, they left the choice of schools and colleges, and in some cases even of their sons' courses of study, to his judgment. Herrán's procedure was to place the youths in a private school, particularly to learn English, but also to study French, mathematics, physics, and bookkeeping. If students presented disciplinary problems, Herrán attempted to send them back to their parents. Those youths who were merely dull or whose parents specifically had ordained a commercial career were directed to train for commerce. The good students were encouraged to go on to American universities to study chemistry, mineralogy, agriculture, and civil and mechanical engineering.

While Herrán seemingly found no preparatory school entirely satisfactory, he discovered quickly where to place the good students for university studies in science. In 1850 and 1851 Brown University, under the leadership of Francis Wayland, instituted a new program emphasizing applied science. One of Herrán's charges was among the first to seize upon this opportunity; he enrolled at Brown in March, 1852, to study engineering with William A. Norton. During the summer of 1852 the Brown program began to crumble as Norton and John A. Porter, his colleague in applied chemistry, left for Yale. Herrán's protégé, like many of the other science students in Providence, immediately followed them to New Haven.[26] After 1852, Yale's scientific school was the institution General Herrán favored most, sending four of his wards there before 1859. Yale was undeniably a good choice in these years.[27]

During the 1850s, a few Colombian parents began to acquire some information about American institutions and thus to express more precise desires about the placement of their sons. A merchant in the Magdalena river port of Honda in 1856 asked that this two sons be sent to Yale, one to study "mineralogical chemistry," the other engineering, under Benjamin Silliman, "the celebrated professor of natural sciences and mathematics." Although the Honda merchant was misinformed as to what Silliman taught, bits of information were evidently seeping into the Colombian interior.[28] In a similar case two important New Granadan politicians sought unsuccessfully in 1855 and 1856 to place their sons in the United States Military Academy, a school that was well known for its excellence in engineering but that had not accepted a foreign student for more than three decades.[29]

By the end of the 1860s Colombians were beginning to show considerable sophistication in their choices of institutions. In 1869 the first Colombian graduated from Rensselaer; between 1877 and 1886 five others studied there. José María Villa, from the small town of Sopetrán, Antioquia, graduated from the Stevens Institute in 1878, only eight years after it was founded as the United States' first institution specializing in mechanical engineering. At about the same time two sons of Mariano Ospina Rodríguez took their degrees in mining engineering and metallurgy from the University of California at Berkeley, a school that was also less than a decade old. They were followed by various *antioqueños* interested in mining. Similarly, Colombians in the 1870s and 1880s were studying mining engineering at Columbia, the first American institution to develop this specialty.[30]

By the 1880s Latin Americans studying technical subjects in the United States had become so common that agencies specializing in the preparation, care, and placement of foreign students had emerged in North America. In 1882 a Springfield, Massachusetts, agency offered such services to Colombians who wished their sons to study commerce, agriculture, or other practical fields. Foreign study was further facilitated in 1887 with the founding of the Sociedad Colombiana de Ingenieros, whose journal provided a steady flow of information on North American technical schools. The journal's editors kept their readers up to date on ideas about technical education under discussion in the United States. The journal made frequent mention of the established American schools, such as West Point, Rensselaer, and Stevens, and carried descriptions of other institutions, such as Purdue, as they began to become significant. Any substantial change in the curriculum or facilities of a leading institute like Stevens or the founding of a new engineering school, such as the "Polytechnic School of Terre Haute, Indiana," was duly noted in the pages of the *Anales*. In its obituaries and other articles the journal also showed some awareness of the careers of American, as well as European, scientists.[31]

Ironically, at about the time American institutions were beginning to develop real strength in technical fields and were becoming known in New Granada, as well as the rest of Latin America, General Herrán became convinced that they were inferior to European ones. Despite the recent development of "special schools" of engineering at Harvard and Yale, he believed instruction in engineering was better in France. His growing objections to American colleges, however, were based at least as much on moral grounds as on technical ones. By 1855 he had concluded that the "control and discipline of the European colleges is preferable to that observed in this country," where students of engineering in the "principal colleges" lived off campus, without institutional supervision. Possibly for this reason, possibly on educational grounds, by 1856 Herrán was declaring flatly that he was "every day more disgusted with the secondary and primary schools of the United States: all are 'humbug.'" Accordingly he began to advise parents to send their sons to Europe for technical training.[32]

Although some of Herrán's friends followed his advice, Colombians by no means gave up on the United States. They continued to be fascinated by its industrial plant and to believe they could learn something from it.[33] And Colombian youths, including Herrán's own sons, continued to attend American institutions in ever greater numbers.[34] But, while many upperclass Colombians sent their sons to the United States because they identified it with industrial practicality and business sense, others turned to Europe because of its established scientific superiority.

From the beginning of the republican era Granadans, along with the rest of the Western world, had looked to the Continent in general and to Paris in particular as the mecca of the natural sciences. One of New Granada's first students abroad, Joaquín Acosta, studied in Paris between 1827 and 1830 and returned there to continue his work between 1845 and 1849.[35] Colombia's scientific eminences of succeeding generations—for example, the botanist José G. Triana—also gravitated to the Continent and particularly to Paris. Another Colombian who devoted much of his life to practical education, Eustacio Santamaría, studied chemistry for four years (early 1850s) in France and Germany. In addition it was not uncommon during the period from 1840 to 1880 for Colombians to go to France for advanced medical studies, particularly clinical work, after they had received their medical degrees in Bogotá.[36]

After 1850 Colombians began to look to Paris not only for scientific enlightenment but also for technical instruction. A number of men who had done some work in engineering, either in the United States or in Colombia, attended one or another of the special schools of engineering in France. Juan Nepomuceno González Vásquez of Zipaquirá, one of the better students in Bogotá's military school (1848–1854), took further work at the Ecole centrale des arts et manufactures from 1857 to 1860, and a second *zipaquireño* studied there in 1864. Still another notable Zipaquirá alumnus of the military school, Manuel H. Peña, attended the Ecole des ponts et chaussées from 1873 to 1874, after he was already established as one of Colombia's most notable engineers.[37]

While the preeminence of France in academic science and civil engineering was generally recognized, it was not necessarily the best place for on-the-job studies of industrial technique. Some young Colombians, therefore, were sent to Germany and Belgium to gain practical knowledge of mining and manufacture. In the middle of the 1850s Tyrell Moore, a British mining engineer long resident in Antioquia, began to urge rich *antioqueños* to send their sons not to Bogotá or to Paris, where they were unlikely to receive a practical education, but rather to Saxony or Hungary, where they could learn mining and metallurgy, skills that were obviously of fundamental importance to Antioquia.[38] Toward the end of the 1850s Moore took several young *antioqueños*, including Santiago Ospina Barrientos (son of Mariano Ospina Rodríguez), with him to Germany. There they studied metallurgy and mining technology at the mining academy of Freiberg.[39]

The strength of Germany and Belgium in mining and industrial technology and that of France in mathematics, civil engineering, chemistry, and some other branches of science offered a convenient complementarity. Some Colombians took advantage of this by studying pure sciences in Paris and industrial applications in Germany and Belgium. In the mid-1850s

Vicente Restrepo of Medellín followed work in chemistry in Paris with the study of metallurgy in Germany. A quarter-century later the pattern could still be observed, as Pedro Nel Ospina, having graduated as a mining engineer from the University of California in 1879, spent two years studying mining techniques in Freiberg and analytic chemistry in Paris.[40]

After 1880 Colombian students in Europe, like those in the United States, began to test alternatives to the standard institutions of midcentury. Just as students in North America began to move west from the eastern seaboard, so their contemporaries in Europe began to look beyond France for academic instruction in engineering. At least one studied engineering in Turin in the 1880s, and several graduated from the University of Lausanne in the 1890s.[41]

A few Colombians studied medicine, mathematics, and engineering in Great Britain during the nineteenth century.[42] But British instruction in these subjects was considered inferior to that in the best Continental institutions; most Colombian students, therefore, gravitated to the Continent. On the other hand, England—as Colombia's primary trade partner and the world's leading commercial nation—was the preferred place for practical education in commerce.

The Fruits of Foreign Study

The results of the nineteenth-century experiments in foreign education were at best mixed. Particularly between 1850 and 1870, many of the Colombians who came to the United States carried on only preparatory studies. None of the twenty-two Granadan youths who studied at St. John's (Fordham) went beyond its "grammar" (preparatory) school, although some of them apparently did more advanced studies elsewhere. Four of the Herrán group and five other Granadans attended Yale, all of them studying in scientific fields. Only six of the nine students at Yale graduated, five in engineering and one in medicine. Three more under Herrán's care attended Georgetown; of these only one graduated.[43] At least six of the Herrán contingent, and undoubtedly some others, went on to Europe to finish their studies. Most, however, did not finish or did not go beyond secondary school; a few of these were placed in merchants' houses as apprentice clerks before being sent back to New Granada.

Failure to enter or to finish college should not necessarily be read as a sign of academic inadequacy. Like Pastor Ospina, a number of upper-class fathers never intended that their sons take degrees. For their purposes it was enough that the boys learn something practical—some English, some math, some bookkeeping, perhaps some technical trade. Frequently, because of the high cost of maintaining a son abroad, fathers planned only a year's dip in the pragmatic North American environment. Others with grander plans soon found they could not afford more than a year.

Many of the parents sending their boys to the United States did not fully appreciate the costs involved. While education in a private *colegio* in New Granada cost from 150 to 250 pesos per year, expenses in the United States tended to be about three times as great.[44] In most cases, the boys' fathers had budgeted far less than the actual cost, and, notable as they might be in Bogotá, Herrán often had difficulty in collecting money he had advanced for their sons. The father (a middle-rank military officer) of one of the best students in the whole group, a *bogotano* who ultimately graduated as an engineer from Yale, withdrew his financial support, and this student was apparently kept afloat only through Herrán's good offices.[45]

For the handful of Herrán's charges who attended American colleges, the rate of completion (58 percent) was actually rather high. During a considerable part of the nineteenth century most technical fields did not reach a stage of professional development in which degrees were required. Thus, many American youths either enrolled as special students with no intention of taking a degree or simply did not bother to finish the four-year course. Fragmentary evidence suggests that the rate of graduation among Latin American students in general was at least as high if not higher than that of their North American peers. At Rensselaer Polytechnic only 35 percent of all students in the first fifty years (1824–1874) were graduated. Of some eighty-seven students from the Hispanic world who attended Rensselaer in this period, slightly more than 36 percent finished. But if Cubans and Puerto Ricans (who seem to have constituted a special case) are not included, the Latin rate of finishing at Rensselaer was, as in the case of Herrán's protégés, above 50 percent.[46]

The long-term fruits of the Herrán experiment fell far short of spectacular. Only a few students of the Herrán group attained any eminence, and none of these ever became quite as important as his father. In evaluating the performance of the group as a whole, however, it should be remembered that, while some youths were sent to study in the United States because they seemed particularly apt, others were upper-class youths whose parents or guardians hoped might be reformed by foreign study. The most extreme case of this sort was that of Jesús Malo Blanco. When his perversities were not corrected after two years with the Jesuits in Bogotá, his desperate father sent him to New York. In the United States, the appropriately named Malo was expelled from four different schools in the space of a year, at which time Herrán shipped him back to New Granada. Malo capped his career in 1859 by murdering his older brother, a highly respected lawyer and politician and at the time governor of the state of Cundinamarca.[47] No other academic performance or later career was as spectacularly bad as that of Malo. But while many of those who studied in the United States were the cream of Granadan youth, in a number of cases the cream had soured before it was shipped abroad.

In general Colombian investments in foreign study produced their best return in the areas of commerce and medicine. A number of the young men who studied commercial practices in England or the United States later became important business leaders. Some were founders of banks and other new financial institutions, and others fostered the building of railroads or introduced new techniques of advertising.[48] Often, however, it is difficult to attribute business leadership directly to the influence of foreign experience. The role of these individuals may be attributable to the same family wealth that permitted foreign study in the first place.

In medicine a high return was likely because most of the youths who studied abroad did so on their own initiative, usually after they had already manifested a strong professional commitment. Most held a Colombian university degree and also had some experience practicing medicine in their native land.[49]

Colombian social traditions and the state of the Colombian economy, however, also had a good deal to do with the relative success of commercial and medical studies. Both were well-established and respected professions and offered substantial financial returns as well as high status. This was much less true of the newer profession of engineering, which offered some social respect but for some time not very clear financial and career perspectives.

A few of the Colombians who studied engineering abroad in the 1850s had technically productive careers. The studies of Manuel H. Peña and Juan N. González Vásquez at Bogotá's military school (1848–1854) and in Paris were followed by many years of service in railroad construction. More generally, however, foreign-trained engineers of the midcentury generations were diverted from the practice of engineering to theoretical, literary, or academic pursuits. An intermediate case is that of Vicente Restrepo. After five years of study in Europe, Restrepo for seventeen years operated a laboratory for metallurgical analysis in the service of Antioquia's gold-mining economy before moving to Bogotá, where he turned to more literary scientific activities and a career in politics. In some cases the tendency toward the literary and theoretical represented a purely personal propensity. Rafael Nieto Paris, educated at Boston University at the end of the 1850s, seems to have been propelled by his own genius into mathematical theory and the invention of scientific devices.[50] In many cases, however, Colombians turned from the practical to the literary or academic because a restricted economy combined with political upheaval to limit their field of action.

Of eighteen in the Herrán group whose later careers are known, only four became practicing engineers, and these were not full-time practitioners. One worked on road construction during the 1850s. Two others, Rafael Arboleda Mosquera and Eugenio J. Gómez, participated in the building of Colombian railroads. And several of these engineers had equally or more active careers in literature, politics, or education.[51]

A number who studied for engineering or other practical careers were drawn some distance from their intended paths. The traditional fields of literature and education attracted some. Of the Herrán group, three became known as literati, six as educators. The adoption of these careers represents a thwarting of their fathers' intentions—to keep their sons away from politics and literature and to suppress the traditional inclination toward genteel abstraction in favor of mundane affairs. Nevertheless, the students who took up careers in education may be considered to have paid off as investments in social overhead capital. As active participants in the efforts to build the national university and the school system as a whole in the period after 1868, they made some contribution to the future development of the country.[52]

Some of the more able Colombians educated abroad in scientific studies remained in Bogotá for only a few years and then returned to the research facilities and the scientific community that Europe offered. Ezequiel Uricoechea, who graduated from Yale in medicine in 1852 and then went on to study in Europe, returned to Colombia in 1857 for about ten years. In that period he served for a time as professor of chemistry and mineralogy in the Colegio del Rosario, founded a Sociedad de Naturalistas Neo-Granadinos and in 1867 briefly filled the post of director of public instruction. In 1868, however, he returned to Europe, where in 1878 he became a professor of Arabic at the University of Brussels. In 1880 he died in Beirut while on a research expedition. This was an extreme case of nineteenth-century brain drain, but it was not a completely isolated one. José G. Triana, New Granada's most dedicated botanist of the second half of the nineteenth century, was trained in Bogotá but spent more than two-thirds of his productive years in Europe (1857–1889). Admittedly, Triana devoted much of his thirty-two–year stay on the Continent to the study of New Granadan plants. But the return to his country might have been greater if he had conducted some of this work in Bogotá. Triana, like other Colombians of the era, undoubtedly was captivated by Europe's cultural possibilities, including association with renowned scientists and membership in European scientific societies.[53]

In contrast with some of the Colombians who turned to academic science, those who took up the practice of engineering showed surprisingly little tendency to be drawn into foreign careers. Young Colombians who had studied engineering in the United States or Europe often stayed abroad for a year, either to get valuable experience on public works in the advanced countries or, as was often the case, because civil war and economic paralysis had eliminated any immediate possibility of exercising their profession in their native land. But the Colombian engineers, unlike many of their Cuban counterparts, eventually came home.[54]

When they returned, however, the young South American engineers found few opportunities to use their training because of the economic stagnation that prevailed in many parts of their homelands. The case of the few youths from northern Brazil who graduated from Rensselaer during the 1850s is suggestive. They came home to take up such duties as principal of a girls' school and agent for a steamship line. Not until the 1860s did the Brazilian graduates of Rensselaer begin to find railroad construction jobs waiting for them. Cuba, whose rapidly expanding sugar economy was becoming closely integrated into the great North American market, was one of the few places where Latin American engineers were fairly sure to find jobs in the 1850s.[55]

Like northern Brazil (though for different reasons), New Granada suffered economic stasis and constricted opportunities; her economy was among the more retarded in Latin America at least until the end of the 1860s. Her first foreign-trained engineers, finding it difficult to exercise their professions, diverted their energies into other channels. José María Mosquera, who studied engineering in England in the 1840s, found on his return to Popayán that he could find employment only in architecture, "the only specialty which at that time offered a field for work in this environment." His only notable works, as a result, were churches.[56]

Along with Colombia's economic stagnation, the country's agitated political atmosphere hampered the pursuit of careers in engineering, in at least three ways. The unconstant policies of the two parties undermined large-scale projects that might have employed engineers. Engineers of both political tendencies found themselves drawn into the violent conflicts of the era. And partisan politics sometimes caused certain engineers, particularly those of Conservative affiliation, to be denied government jobs.

The damaging effects of Colombia's mercurial policies are reflected in the career of Rafael Espinosa Escallón. Perhaps the best of the Herrán group at Yale, Espinosa, after graduating as an engineer in 1853, had to struggle to find work in New Granada. With Herrán's support he obtained a job clearing the Canal del Dique connecting Cartagena and the Magdalena River from 1855 to 1856. The project, however, proved beyond the resources of the Compañia del Canal de Cartagena, and Espinosa ended up jobless and unpaid for his labors. In 1857 he worked on the road running from Socorro province to the Magdalena and then moved on to the Carare road, connecting Vélez with the river. Colombia's political vagaries helped to undermine this last project. When the states of Santander and Boyacá were created and the former province of Vélez was divided between them, Espinosa believed that the Carare road project would lose the support of any effective political organism. Convinced that interest in the road would collapse, Espinosa quit in discouragement. After this series of disappointments, Espinosa gave up the practice of engineering, taking refuge in university teaching.[57]

Some young engineers could not resist the siren song of the violent politics of the era. Isidoro Plata, a young Liberal with a B.S. from the Yale Scientific School (1856), spent the early 1860s in General Mosquera's military campaign against the Conservatives.[58] Five, and possibly six, of those eighteen Herrán protégés about whose careers something is known, were active in politics.[59] Two of the country's brightest hopes—Uladislao Vásquez and Sebastián Ospina—died fighting for the Conservative cause in the civil war of 1876–1879.[60]

Foreign-trained Conservatives found it particularly difficult to obtain government appointments during the period of Liberal hegemony from 1861 to 1880. José Cornelio Borda, of a notable Conservative family, studied engineering in Paris and is supposed to have been asked to serve as chief of engineers of a railway in France. When the Conservatives held the government in Bogotá (1857–1861), he returned to New Granada and was made director of the national observatory. But then came the Liberal revolution of 1859–1863, during which he tenaciously served the Conservative cause as an artillery instructor and staff officer. After the war, when the Liberals reestablished their hegemony, Borda found it necessary to move to the Conservative stronghold in Antioquia, where he obtained employment as a professor of physics in the state's *colegio*. Perhaps finding his field of action too confined in Medellín, Borda soon traveled to Lima, where, in the defense of the port of Callao against the Spanish fleet, he was killed by an exploding artillery shell.[61]

A similar case is that of Rafael Arboleda Mosquera, who studied under Herrán's tutelage at St. John's (Fordham) from 1853 to 1854. After finishing his studies, Arboleda spent the 1860s practicing engineering in Spain and Portugal, "for lack of a theater for it in Colombia." In all probability political considerations prevented his obtaining government employment in New Granada. As the son of an important, and notoriously partisan and bloodthirsty, Conservative leader, he could expect few favors from a recently triumphant Liberal government. On his return to Colombia at the end of the 1860s, the younger Arboleda became active in Conservative politics. It was only in the early 1880s that he secured an important engineering appointment to construct the Girardot railroad, and then his employer was not the government but a Cuban entrepreneur, Francisco Javier Cisneros. Arboleda died of yellow fever in Girardot in 1882, not long after beginning work on the railroad.[62]

While the careers of Conservative youths who studied abroad in the 1850s were constrained by Liberal domination during the years before 1880, later generations of Conservatives educated in the United States or Europe seem not to have been so adversely affected. Alejandro Manrique C. received training similar to that of José Cornelio Borda and Rafael Arboleda, but twenty-five years later. Educated as a civil engineer in Spain in the early 1880s, he worked there for seven years on railroads, roads, and bridges before coming back to Bogotá. In contrast with the Conservatives who returned in the 1860s, however, Manrique was embraced by the engineering fraternity in Colombia.[63] His warm reception may have reflected the fact that conservatives now controlled the government. It seems more likely, however, that he was well received precisely because Colombian engineers by the end of the 1880s had finally formed a fraternity. During the 1870s and 1880s sporadic public works activities were creating a small place for native engineers. As opportunities developed, those with technical training tended to turn away from party struggles and to focus more on engineering careers. The definitive founding of the Sociedad Colombiana de Ingenieros in 1887 marked and furthered the growth of the collective consciousness of the country's engineers. They increasingly abandoned partisan politics for a new politics of professional promotion.

Chapter 7   The Colegio Militar

NEW GRANADA's transitory military schools contributed at least as much as foreign studies to the creation of a science faculty in Colombia's universities and, more importantly, to the development of a source of practicing civil engineers. Bogotá's Colegio Militar joined military instruction and civil engineering and, in fact, emphasized the latter. In its first incarnations it survived for only a few years at a time. Nevertheless, during its brief periods of existence (1848–1854, 1866–1867, 1883–1885) the military college trained a large proportion of the engineers who worked on road and railroad construction and who taught mathematics and engineering during the second half of the nineteenth century.[1]

The combination of military instruction with civil engineering was rather generalized in the Western world. In Continental Europe civil engineering had developed as an offshoot of military engineering. Though separate schools for various branches of engineering—civil, military, mining, and others—were created in France during the eighteenth century, military and civil engineering remained closely related. At the Ecole polytechnique, established during the French Revolution, students in all fields of engineering shared the preparatory course.[2] New Granadan leaders, like others in Western countries, were undoubtedly impressed by the elaborate French system. But, lacking the financial or cultural resources required to create the specialized institutions found in France, the Colombians left civil engineering and military training joined in a single school much like the U.S. Military Academy at West Point.

The Colombian military school of the nineteenth century followed and embroidered on the North American pattern in having the more-or-less explicit function of training engineers for the civilian economy. The U.S. Military Academy evolved toward an emphasis on instruction in civil engineering as the years of peace after the War of 1812 tended to blight military careers while compelling opportunities held out by the dynamic American economy tended to lure officers from the service. Almost a quarter of West Point's alumni of the years 1802 to 1850 worked at some time or another on purely civilian projects.[3] The Colombian military school of 1848–1854 differed from the U.S. academy in that the function of training civilian engineers was adopted from the outset. And the alumni of the Colombian school pursued civilian careers in engineering in even greater proportions than those of the U.S. Military Academy.

As in France and the United States, engineering instruction in Colombia was affected by considerable stress between its civil and military functions. In France the character of the technical schools varied with each change in political dominion—becoming civilian under liberal or republican regimes and military under imperial or reactionary ones. Similarly, in the United States the Military Academy was criticized alternately for being either too civilian or too military in orientation. Between 1816 and 1830 the curriculum increasingly emphasized civil engineering and its graduates in considerable numbers served the civilian economy. Some members of the military establishment protested that this trend represented a perversion of the military functions of the academy. On the other hand, during the Jacksonian period several state legislatures, various members of Congress, and state militia leaders called for the abolition of the academy at West Point on the grounds that it was inconsistent with republican institutions and that it used public funds for the benefit of the rich and privileged and to create a "military aristocracy." Such attacks were ultimately silenced by the sudden need for trained officers during the Mexican War.[4] In Colombia, however, similar antagonism between civilian politicians and professional military led to the collapse of the country's first effective military academy (1848–1854) and continued to affect later efforts at engineering instruction.

Early Efforts at Polytechnical Training

Though a technically oriented military school was not established in New Granada in any substantial form until 1847–1848, the idea of an engineering school and a corps of engineers with combined civil and military functions was expounded in Bogotá at the end of the colonial period. Not long before the collapse of the Spanish monarchy in 1808, Francisco José de Caldas proposed the creation of a "military corps of mineralogical engineers" in the viceroyalty of New Granada. While its members were to be available for service during military emergencies, their primary purposes would be to increase mining production, carry on geographical surveys, make topographical and geological maps, and plan roads. Several members would be sent to Europe to study mining techniques. Caldas's plan of studies was correspondingly oriented toward civilian, rather than military, needs—the six-year course was to run the gamut from mathematics and experimental physics to botany, mineralogy, chemistry, and metallurgy and would pay scant attention to military training.[5]

The Independence era presented Caldas with the opportunity to establish a school and a corps of engineers, though not of the sort he had proposed. Responding to the exigencies of the moment, he and a few others with technical knowledge served as military engineers; and Caldas taught primarily military subjects in Bogotá (1811) and Medellín (1814–1815). At the end of 1815 he was called to Bogotá to establish a national military school. But the return of the Spanish Pacifiers in 1816 put an end to the republican government, its plan for a military school, and Caldas.[6]

During the first years after the expulsion of the Spanish from New Granada, creole leaders retained some interest in a military academy. In 1820 they attempted to start another one. This project was short-lived, undoubtedly overwhelmed by Colombia's many financial, administrative, and political problems of the early republican era. As the creoles' primary concern in these years was to consolidate independence by driving the Spanish from the rest of the American possessions, their projects for military schools in the 1820s heavily emphasized the purely military function of training army officers. A plan elaborated by Lino de Pombo at the request of the secretary of war in 1827 gave rather little attention to civil engineering. The scheme provided for instruction in the building of canals, roads, and bridges, but Pombo clearly presumed that all the graduates would enter military service.[7]

The years from 1827 through 1838 were marked by strong antagonism between civilians and the military, a conflict provoked at the outset by the Venezuelan military dictatorship of 1827 to 1831 and then sustained by continued disruptive activities on the part of some ambitious officers. The split between civilian and military leaders was reflected in their attitudes toward the idea of a military academy. Throughout the 1830s the secretaries of war urged the creation of a military school, conceiving of it as no more than an institute for officer training. During these years the civilian-dominated Congress just as consistently ignored these requests.[8] Not until 1836 did the Congress provide for the academic instruction of officers, and then this training was to take place in the civilian-controlled universities of Bogotá, Cartagena, and Popayán, rather than in a separate military academy. During these years one influential civilian, Lino de Pombo, advocated a technically oriented military school, "a minute imitation of the famous Ecole polytechnique of France." But Pombo's proposals stirred no response from other civilian leaders, even though his new plan gave much greater emphasis to the education of civil engineers than had his earlier formulation of 1827. By 1832 it was clear that Pombo was primarily interested in establishing an engineering school, to which military training would be no more than an addendum.[9]

The law of 1836 led to a small amount of military instruction. The nautical school in the university at Cartagena had difficulty obtaining professors, and the university in Popayán never obtained any military instructors. From 1837 through 1839 a Venezuelan, Blas Brusual, taught mathematics through trigonometry, as well as cosmography and topography, in the military class in Bogotá's university.[10] But this class had very few students. The 1836 law required all military students to provide bond to assure that they would give the six years' obligatory military service after graduation. Few youths whose families could afford the bond were willing to obligate themselves to six years' service. Consequently, the military class in Bogotá from 1837 to 1839 never had more than eight cadets. Even these few did not finish their studies. With the eruption of civil war from 1839 to 1842, they were sent off to the campaign, and their academic instruction ended.[11]

After the war, scientific officers' training existed only in the law; it was not even included in the national budget. The secretaries of war complained that the system of the law of 1836 was unworkable; with military training assigned to all three universities, resources were dispersed and nothing was accomplished. Generals José Hilario López, Tomás Cipriano de Mosquera and José Acevedo successively called for the centralizing of instruction in one military school to be established in the capital.[12]

At the same time a few civilians other than Lino de Pombo began to conceive of an institution that joined polytechnical and military training. In 1844 a young science instructor in Bogotá suggested that a military-polytechnical school offering the prospect of an army career would provide an "honorable stimulus" to the study of technical subjects.[13] The polytechnical-military idea did not fructify in Bogotá, however, until 1847, midway through the first presidency of General Mosquera.

Various factors worked in favor of the creation of a military-polytechnical school during the Mosquera administration. One was the strong-willed General Mosquera's commitment to the idea. More broadly, as president, General Mosquera provided dynamic leadership for the material development of the country, particularly in the area of road building. And, in so doing, Mosquera created visible opportunities for civil engineers. In November, 1845, the government offered to put up more than 300,000 pesos in cash and in convict and army labor and to take a loan of nearly 400,000 pesos more to encourage private companies to undertake four substantial road projects. The following year the government proposed to contract twenty-three different road jobs with an estimated cost of 1.2 million pesos. Along with its many schemes for road construction, the Mosquera administration undertook a variety of other public works, including the construction of a grandiose capitol building. Another major engineering effort was sponsored contemporaneously by the merchants of Cartagena—the clearing of the Canal del Dique, which linked that port with the Magdalena River.[14]

A few Colombians who had had technical training abroad were employed to direct some of these works. The largest projects and the best-paid appointments, however, went to foreign engineers especially imported for the occasion. While these foreign experts for the moment preempted the best positions, they also helped to stimulate among upper-class Colombian adults some interest in engineering as a possible career for their sons. New Granadan newspapers praised George M. Totten, the American directing the works on the Canal del Dique, as a titan of industry, holding him up as a model for the native upper class to follow. To a degree foreign engineers—like Antoine Poncet and the capitol architect, Thomas Reed, in Bogotá, Henry Tracy in the eastern region in general, and Stanislas Zawadsky in the Cauca valley—also helped to increase the supply of technical information.[15] Mosquera's public works activities in their several aspects and the creation of a polytechnical institute clearly complemented each other.

While the elaborate public works projects of the Mosquera administration created a favorable environment for polytechnic education, they could not be said to have determined the character of the military school that existed from 1847 to 1848. One individual, Lino de Pombo, played an extraordinary role in diverting the school from its military training function and turning it primarily into an institute for civil engineers. When Alejandro Osorio, Mosquera's secretary of government, proposed the creation of a military academy to the Congress of 1847, his project carried little suggestion of the polytechnical idea. As Osorio conceived it, the capital would have two separate schools, a military school and a civilian institute of natural, physical, and mathematical sciences.[16] After the idea had passed through the legislative process, in which Pombo took part as senator from Cartagena, the military academy was more clearly envisioned as an institute for civil engineers.

The 1847 law flatly provided for the training of civil engineers, who need not even pretend to enter the military. The law dropped the requirement of military service after graduation, and civil engineering students were not obliged to take courses on military subjects. The *colegio* as a whole was strongly oriented toward the technical. Entering students were expected to be soundly prepared in algebra and geometry and to be able to read French and English texts. The curriculum provided for three years of mathematics (through differential and integral calculus), cosmography, and principles of engineering. After the mathematics courses cadets took special instruction for particular careers as line officers in the artillery, as military engineers, or as civil engineers. For students choosing civil engineering, the fourth year was devoted to practical work in all the standard branches of that subject.[17]

The school's orientation toward civil engineering was by no means settled by the 1847 law. The academy's first year of operation (1848) was marked by a vigorous dispute among the faculty, essentially over whether military training or civil engineering would predominate. At the outset, most of the faculty viewed the school merely as a military academy. But Lino de Pombo, the professor of mathematics, strongly asserted his view that the institute's purpose was at least as much to train civilian engineers as military officers.[18]

Seemingly outnumbered by the military element, Pombo, through strength of personality and his prestige in Bogotá, proved able to give the school a technical orientation. In the fall of 1847 when the academy was being organized, Pombo requested a list of scientific books and instruments that the school's director, Gen. José María Ortega, considered "absolutely unnecessary." The secretary of war, however, overruled the director of the academy, giving Pombo most of what he wanted. A later shipment of books from Europe, probably ordered by Pombo, was composed primarily of French works on mathematics; thirty-seven of the titles were applicable to civil engineering and only twenty-four were on purely military topics.[19]

Throughout the school's first, formative year Pombo campaigned to ensure a pronounced orientation toward civil engineering. He vigorously protested the requirement instituted by President Mosquera that all students receive four years of instruction in military legislation and other forms of military training. The demands of these "essentially secondary" studies distracted students from the school's fundamental course in mathematics. When Pombo demanded the abolition of the chair in military legislation and a general reduction in military training, the other faculty members at first voted him down. Unlike Pombo, they considered the school a purely military establishment, the purpose of which was to train "scientific officers," with civil engineering its last concern. Denied by his peers, Pombo insisted that his views be communicated to the secretary of war. After nearly a year of hammering at his colleagues, he finally got his way. The mortified professor of military legislation resigned, and this course was relegated to a subordinate position. At the same time mathematics and its applications were further strengthened by the appointment, at Pombo's request, of a second mathematics professor, Aimé Bergeron, recently imported from France. The dominion of mathematics and engineering was extended at the end of the academy's second year when these courses were given an additional year in the curriculum.[20]

The records of the military academy make it clear that although Pombo was never the school's director, he was the soul of the enterprise. His leadership is everywhere apparent. Extremely meticulous in the instruction of his own classes, he set a high standard for his colleagues. And few faculty meetings passed without a strong statement from Pombo on the need to remedy some deficiency. Through the strength of his commitment Pombo turned the military school into the institution he had dreamed of for two decades.[21]

Pombo's dreams were fulfilled not merely in the curriculum but also in the career choices of the cadets. At the end of the second year, when the students chose the special courses that would prepare them for their particular careers, few of them opted for the military branches. Of the first group of students who confronted this choice, not one wanted to pursue a military career. The next year six decided for civil engineering; only four asked for any kind of military training.[22]

Probably some of these students were influenced in their choice of civil engineering by the passion for material progress that characterized the Mosquera years. The institute also operated in such a way as to select for civil engineers. While some parents at the outset looked upon civil engineering as the goal for their sons, more of them appear to have intended a career at arms.[23] The Colegio Militar functioned, however, in a way that tended to reverse this preference. Because of the heavily mathematical curriculum, many youths who hoped to pursue traditional military careers found the academy frustrating. Confronted with a rigorous scientific course, many of those who originally intended to become mere officers did not last through the first year. Either they were not sufficiently motivated, or not talented enough, or not well prepared. Many of these youths, becoming discouraged, asked to be released from the Colegio Militar and assigned as cadets in military units. As many of the students who were merely interested in a military career opted out of the school during their first year, there remained in the advanced classes a relatively select group who conformed rather well to Pombo's intentions.

Administration rhetoric as well as the curriculum tended to encourage this orientation toward civil engineering. After the school was founded, President Mosquera and his secretaries of state stressed its importance as a means of training road builders. During the succeeding administration of Gen. José Hilario López (1849–1853), this conception of the school took on more body, because of a continuing interest in material progress and for political reasons. The younger elements in the Liberal party (then called the Gólgotas, later the Radicals) were strongly antimilitary and were suspicious of the Colegio Militar as an instrument for the perpetuation of an officers' class. Before the Liberals had been in power a year, the director of the Colegio Militar, concerned about growing "prejudice" against the institution, began to emphasize strongly its civil benefits.[24] Following his lead, the secretary of war pointed out to the Congress that, although the school was no more than two years old, its utility was already being proven: two second-year students were teaching mathematics in Bogotá *colegios*. Subsequently, government spokesmen took care to note other civil contributions of the cadets, such as the mapping of Bogotá or work on the national geographic survey. Throughout the early 1850s the secretaries of war stressed that many cadets would become civil engineers.[25] In these years published invitations for applications to the academy made special notice of the fact that cadets were not expected to pursue a military career even though they were educated at government expense. The invitations now explicitly stated that the principal purpose of the institution was to spread mathematical knowledge so that the nation could be assured of engineers and trained craftsmen.[26]

To meet the objections of Liberal democratic ideologues, the war secretaries of the López administration repeatedly cited the example of West Point, a military school in the Liberals' model democracy. In 1853, when the *civilista* attack on the professional military became intense, Gen. Valerio F. Barriga pointed out that in time of peace many graduates of West Point had become civilian engineers rather than members of a permanent officers' class. He suggested that much the same thing was happening in New Granada, where, as of 1853, not one of the Colegio Militar's graduates had gone into the army; every one of them was practicing, or attempting to practice, as a civilian engineer. In any case, he argued, the way to avoid an officer caste was not to abolish the military school, but rather to make it possible for youths of all provinces and all classes to enter the school.[27]

The question of representativeness plagued the military school throughout its brief history. The academy was largely an upper-class institution primarily of benefit to the capital. This was not necessarily the intention either of the Congress or of the school's administrators. The legislators had sought to obtain geographical distribution by allotting one of thirty tuition-free places to each of the provinces. Not surprisingly, however, the Bogotá upper class dominated the school from the outset. In the academy's first four years, well over half the students were from Bogotá province. And the next largest groups came from the neighboring provinces of Tequendama, Zipaquirá, and Tundama or from such other eastern regions as Neiva or el Socorro. Relatively few students came from the western part of the country (Pasto, the Cauca valley, Antioquia) or from the Caribbean coast. In seven years the Chocó and Panamá did not send one. Even many of those who were listed as residents of the provinces had actually lived in Bogotá for some years before entering the Colegio Militar (see Table 9).

Bogotá's predominance to a considerable degree was simply a matter of physical accessibility. Residents of the capital were able to get in on the ground floor, mobilizing quickly to present the necessary documents for admission. The country being as far-flung and badly connected as it was, provincials often applied with too little and too late. In the first years they made up less than half of the application pool and of those who cleared the hurdles that led to the entrance examination.

Many *bogotanos* also were strategically located in social and political terms. Particularly during the Mosquera administration some special consideration was given to the descendents of men who had given notable service to the nation. Those who had played such roles were almost by definition upper class. In fact, notability may have been a more important criterion than patriotism, for while several of the first students were descended from *próceres* ("patriots") executed by the Spanish in 1816, one was the son of a leading royalist. What most of the first students had in common was undeniably upper class origins and some political or military connections. Three of the first nineteen were the sons of generals. Two of them were sons of Gen. Joaquín Barriga, then secretary of war. Four were nephews of Gen. José María Ortega, the head of the Colegio. Another was a son of Lino de Pombo.[28] Only one of the original cadets for whom data are available had clearly lower class origins.[29]

There were severe limits, however, to the application of ascriptive cri-

TABLE 9. *Provinces of Origin of Students Enrolled in the Colegio Militar*[a]

Date	Largest Group	Second Largest	Third Largest	Total
1848	Bogotá (12) (60%)	Tunja, Socorro, Antioquia (each 2)	Pamplona, Popayán (each 1)	20
1849	Bogotá (21) (66%)	Antioquia, Popayán, Neiva (each 2)	5 provinces (each 1)	32
1850	Bogotá (21) (58%)	Santander and Socorro (together 6)	Neiva (3)	36
1851	Bogotá (22) (59%)	Santander region— Santander, Pamplona, Socorro, Vélez (5)	Tundama, Neiva, Mariquita, Pasto (each 2)	37
1852	Bogotá (12) (41%)	Cundinamarca, Tequendama, Zipaquirá (together 5)	Tundama, Neiva (each 2)	29
1853	Bogotá (12) (41%)	Tequendama, Zipaquirá (together 4)	Tundama, Neiva (each 2)	29

Source: Calculated from figures in Gustavo Arboleda, *Historia contemporánea*, II, 338; Joaquín Barriga, *Memoria de Guerra, 1848*, Cuadro 2; ANCR, Guerra, tomo 768, fol. 460; V. S. Barriga, *Memoria de Guerra, 1851*, Cuadro 15; V. F. Barriga, *Memoria de Guerra, 1853*, Cuadro 13; V. F. Barriga, *Memoria de Guerra, 1854*, Cuadro 11.

[a]These figures represent students enrolled in the Colegio Militar proper; data on students in the *clase preparatoria* are not included.

teria, for intellectual competence was the first concern of Pombo and the other mathematics instructors who administered the entrance examinations. The concentration of upper-class *bogotanos* in the Colegio Militar was in part a result of the institution's high academic standards. To sustain an effective engineering program, Lino de Pombo insisted on the maintenance of high entrance and performance standards. Few artisans and not many provincials could obtain the preparation necessary to pass the entrance examinations and, once in the *colegio*, to stay abreast of the curriculum. From the outset the Mosquera administration sought to meet this problem by creating a preparatory class in which youths, many enrolled as recruits in the Bogotá garrison, could obtain remedial instruction in arithmetic and algebra. In its first year the preparatory class, along with a number of upper-class *bogotanos*, included several provincials and at least one youth from the artisan class. The faculty considered the preparatory class too much trouble, however. In Pombo's view it was another distraction from the main task of educating engineers; under his instigation the faculty convinced the Mosquera government to abolish the class at the end of its first year.[30]

A year later the faculty reversed itself and urged the reestablishment of the preparatory school. It did so partly on academic grounds—to make sure students would be sufficiently prepared to get through the first year. But there were also political reasons. The new López administration had its bases of power in two groups that were substantially excluded from the Colegio Militar—provincials from regions that were not well endowed educationally and artisans and others of the lower orders. The political imperatives of the López government were quickly felt by the military school. In November of 1849 the faculty recommended that preferential entry be given to artisans and others who "could not otherwise afford to provide their sons with an education." Miguel Bracho, the Venezuelan professor of drawing who proposed this measure, suggested that even artisans' sons who proved unfit for entry into the military school could use their preparatory instruction in later careers as craftsmen. The López government accordingly resurrected the preparatory class at the end of 1849.[31] The class was a modest success. For youths of any origin it was the surest way of obtaining entry to the Colegio Militar. With this mechanism Bogotá after 1850 lost some of its preponderance in the academy.

The Bogotá upper class predominated not merely in the number of students but also in successful performance. Students from the capital and from nearby provinces tended to be found in the upper half of each class, while provincials were more likely to be found near the bottom. Correspondingly, attrition, high for students of all kinds, was lower for upper-class *bogotanos* than for provincials.[32] In part this reflected a continuing effect of their superior preparation. A number of provincials also appear to have suffered from a certain disorientation in the capital. The Bogotá youths remained somewhat under the parental eye and therefore felt continuing pressure to meet their fathers' expectations. The provincials, suddenly released from family guidance, were only constrained by the more formal and less effective discipline of the institute. Academic mediocrity, adolescent fecklessness, and resentment of academy disciplinary measures worked together to alienate the students, many of whom dropped out after less than a year in the institution. To a degree these phenomena affected the Bogotá students, but a number of these were able to maintain a relatively steady course. As a result, though they were not necessarily the most talented students, *bogotanos* were more likely to finish the program. Almost all the students who graduated or even reached the fourth year of study were from Bogotá and its environs.[33]

The Colegio Militar was done in by several of the salient tendencies of the 1850s—fiscal disintegration, *civilista* hostility toward a professional military, and Liberal objections to the school's high standards and professionalism. The school somehow survived the radical reforms of the López administration (1849–1853), saved perhaps by the arguments that it contributed to economic development and to military responsibility. But as the central government's revenues dropped, so did the appropriations for the military school. By the fiscal year from 1851 to 1852 its budget was only 40 percent as high as the year from 1848 to 1849.[34] Fiscal difficulties certainly played a part in its ultimate demise during the civil war of 1854.

Liberal social and political ideologies, as well as Liberal fiscal decentralization, worked to undermine the military school. Liberal hostility toward the military, somewhat latent before 1853, in that year came strongly to the fore. One of its manifestations was an effort to demilitarize the military school by replacing it with "special schools for surveyors and civil and military engineers," by further reducing the military component of the curriculum, and by making military instruction entirely optional. The 1853 proposal put forward by two older Liberal leaders, Florentino González and José María Mantilla, also expressed another Liberal theme—federalism. It provided not merely for one centralized technical school but also for others to be located in the provinces.[35]

The González-Mantilla *proyecto* was approved by the Senate in 1853, but by 1854 it was considered insufficiently radical. By this time there was considerable support for a bill to abolish the Colegio Militar, leaving nothing in its place. Other leaders went further in the direction of the González-Mantilla plan, proposing a completely unrealizable scheme for a series of civilian scientific institutes located in six towns in every region of the country.[36]

By 1854 it had become clear that many Liberals objected to the Colegio Militar not simply because of its military affiliation but also because of its identification with conservatism and its elitism. Even though youths of Liberal families formed a high proportion of the student body in the 1850s, many Liberal politicians could not forget the institution's conservative origins. Liberals also disliked the Colegio Militar's academic elitism. Pombo had succeeded too well in establishing high educational standards. And, wherever high standards were proclaimed, Liberals saw the cause of aristocracy and charged to attack under the banner of democracy. Rito Antonio Martínez, from the poor and relatively egalitarian province of

Socorro, like many of the opponents of the institute, denounced the Colegio Militar as an extravagant expense for the benefit of a privileged few. Martínez said he would support such "generosity" on behalf of science if it were distributed with the greatest equality possible to establishments that were open to everyone, "whether poor or rich, of obscure family or distinguished, from the capital or from the provinces." Martínez urged the legislators to allow "nothing of obstacles, nothing of requirements which . . . permit injustice and . . . tend to promote favoritism." To Martínez it did not matter that the academy served to nurture "scientific men." This might be a good thing for "other countries and other governments," which, having the resources and "needing the support of privileged classes," had reason to encourage the development of professional careers. But, unlike these aristocratic states, the "Republic of New Granada has already said that it does not want decorations and titled professions: the republic . . . cannot have *specialties*."[37]

None of the Liberal proposals to abolish or create a substitute for the Colegio Militar ever became law. But in the intensified antimilitary atmosphere created by the coup d'état–artisans' revolution of April, 1854, the civilian politicians allowed the institution to die. Expelled from Bogotá by the local garrison and its plebeian allies, the politicians in their campaign capital in Ibagué simply voted a budget that made no reference to the Colegio Militar. When the upper-class Conservative and Liberal parties jointly retook power at the end of 1854, supporters of the military institute proved unable to revive the idea. Vice-Pres. José de Obaldía and his secretaries of government and war (Mariano Ospina and General Herrán) attempted to save the academy on the ground that it was the only means of educating engineers and surveyors in New Granada. Herrán argued that the institution should have a military character, not to give preference to military studies nor for the exclusive purpose of providing the army with trained officers, but simply because it would provide the discipline needed for profitable study. Nevertheless, he was willing to turn the *colegio* into a civilian institution in order to preserve a school that would enable New Granadan youth "to be useful to the country." In accord with this, Mariano Ospina submitted a plan for a civilian National Conservatory of the Sciences and Arts to replace the Colegio Militar should it be eliminated. The familiar appeal to utility was of no avail, however, amid the strong political emotions of the period. The Congress of 1855, as the administration had feared, permitted the Colegio Militar to die, and no civilian equivalent was created in its place.[38]

The Bogotá military school enjoyed several other brief lives. In 1866 and

1867 General Mosquera, in his last administration, resurrected the institution. In 1861, amid his revolution against the Conservative government, el Gran General had decreed the reestablishment of the military school. The institution he envisioned at this time remained on paper until he returned to office in 1866. The 1866–1867 "Colegio Militar y Escuela Politecnica" differed from its earlier incarnation in several important respects. It was at first placed under the direction of a civilian Liberal, Lorenzo María Lleras. Lleras's interests and expertise lay in the humanities, and he gave much more emphasis to these studies (particularly history and geography). Mathematics received less attention than Pombo had given it from 1848 to 1854. Furthermore, unlike the earlier academy, the 1866–1867 school had extremely lax academic standards. Whereas Pombo and his colleagues had admitted only those students who seemed prepared to take on higher mathematics, the new school accepted hordes of youths, many of them having little knowledge even of arithmetic or French and some of them scarcely able to read and write. By the end of 1866 the school had more than a hundred students, yet only twenty-two were found qualified to begin the first course in higher mathematics. The rest were taking essentially remedial or preparatory work.[39] No one could charge the new school with elitism.

Although the 1866–1867 institute conformed substantially to dominant Liberal tendencies, it also came to grief in the crosscurrents of Colombian politics. In May of 1867 General Mosquera was overthrown by his former allies, the Radicals. The military school, which was just moving beyond remedial education, collapsed almost immediately. Students of *mosquerista* families departed the school in protest against the coup. The Radicals for their part abruptly suspended the school on the ground of its excessive cost, later placing its technical courses in a School of Engineers in the newly created (or re-created) National University.[40]

The Radicals and their successors were not able to rest with this solution, however. During most of the rest of the nineteenth century, politicians continued to tinker with higher technical education and its relationship to military training. During the 1870s the Radicals moved step by step toward the resurrection of a technical military school independent of the national university. The outbreak of a Conservative rebellion in 1876 particularly contributed to this development. But an Escuela de Ingeniería Civil y Militar was no sooner created in 1879 than the regime of Rafael Núñez tried in 1880 to reincorporate military and polytechnical training in the university. In 1883 the government of José Eusebio Otálora re-created the Escuela de Ingeniería Civil y Militar with an elaborate seven-year program and more than two hundred students.[41] Soon afterward the second Núñez government again located engineering instruction in the national university, this time definitively.

Fruits of the Colegio Militar

Despite the brief periods during which they functioned, the Colegio Militar of 1848–1854 and its successor proved relatively fruitful, not in a quantitative but in a qualitative sense. It appears that in the period from 1848 to 1854 about a hundred youths attended the military school proper. Few of these finished, partly because of the severe attrition which occurred in the first year of study, but also because of the school's short life, which gave only the first three classes a chance to finish. At least six cadets graduated, and five others either completed or came close to completing their studies before the school collapsed.

Compared with neo-Bourbon efforts of the previous decade, the short-lived Colegio Militar was strikingly successful in attracting students. Most of them were on government tuition. Beyond this the Mosquera government's obvious commitment to the school undoubtedly made it appealing on both honorific and practical grounds. Although it was probably not a case of calculated manipulation, the Colegio Militar was established in a way that catered effectively to established status conceptions. Located in the capital and attended by the sons of many distinguished families, the military school enjoyed from the first a clearly elite designation. Further, the 1847 law promised military school alumni preference in government engineering and teaching appointments, thus speaking to their general desire for economic security as well as to the prestige elements in the phenomenon of *empleomanía*.

As a professional channel, the institution provided a convenient blend of the old and the new. It represented a complete break with the traditional university system. In Ospina's program, secondary students who were seeking law degrees had considered the science requirements simply an obstruction to their chosen careers. Entering the Colegio Militar, however, meant renouncing the traditional professions at the outset, and students in it were not burdened with obsessions about thwarted careers. Rather the military school raised the prospect of a career that was new to Colombia but of established honor in Continental Europe and the United States. It offered training for a profession bearing two kinds of prestige—

the traditional one of the military officer as well as the newer one of the scientist and technician. [42]

The elaborate public works plans conceived by the Mosquera administration undoubtedly made it appear that such a career would be possible and desirable. But by January, 1848, when the military school opened, the administration had already discovered that its grandiose programs could not be carried out. New Granadan capital had not come forward to take road contracts, nor was it possible to obtain a foreign loan. The government could hardly support its many schemes with its own revenues. The national budget at this time totaled no more than 3.2 million dollars; even devoting 277,000 dollars, or close to 9 percent of the budget, to communications improvements, the government had to cut back on most of its projects. By the beginning of 1848 it was providing funds for only three roads. Even these efforts, combined with extraordinary military expenditures, left the fisc exhausted by the end of Mosquera's term. [43]

The ensuing López administration (1849–1853), by decentralizing and effectively liquidating many sources of national revenue in 1850, cut the national budget almost in half. By 1851 work on the extravagant capitol building had stopped, not to begin again for years. The construction of twenty-five miles of macadam cart road and a few other lesser projects in the environs of Bogotá, all executed by untrained contractors, completely absorbed public works expenditures. During the life of the first Colegio Militar, no other significant road enterprises were in more than the dreaming stage. [44] Yet somehow the cadets looked forward to engineering careers. Apparently the Mosquera government, while unable to sustain its elaborate plans, had created an atmosphere of activity that encouraged a segment of the upper class to develop expectations of public employment as engineers.

In the decade from 1854 to 1863 civil disruption and fiscal weakness made it impossible for the national government to employ the military school alumni in the manner originally envisioned in the Mosquera administration. Most had to depend upon a private sector that was not yet particularly eager for their services. They tried surveying for landowners, teaching science and mathematics in *colegios*, and giving private lessons in surveying. Juan Nepomuceno González Vásquez, who later became one of the country's most notable road and railroad builders, spent most of these years in Europe seeking further education and employment. Nevertheless, the government, in every administration, gave preference to military school alumni in whatever appointments came up. Some of the better students seem to have been fully occupied by government jobs in the latter part of the 1850s. Between 1856 and 1859 Manuel Ponce de León did studies of roads in the Chocó, the upper Magdalena valley, and elsewhere and of the saltworks at Zipaquirá; between 1861 and 1866 he was in charge of publishing the maps worked up by Colonel Codazzi's geographic survey (Comisión Corográfica). Various others did road studies or worked for the Comisión Corográfica.[45] Whenever General Mosquera was in power, the military school alumni were particularly blessed, as he evidently took seriously the pledge made in his first administration. In each of his subsequent ventures in national administration he attempted to sustain the men of the Colegio Militar—validating their titles as engineers (1866), reestablishing the military school (in which they might teach), and installing them in a national corps of engineers (1866–1867). The other administrations of the era, controlled by the Radicals, seem to have felt less obliged to provide them with sinecures, but the Radicals did turn to them, more than to other Colombian engineers, with commissions for exploration and inspection.[46]

Aided by government appointments, they were able to give New Granada a good return on its investment. Of the handful of men who finished their course before 1854 or who came close, seven contributed substantially to road and railroad construction, and at least two more served in minor roles. Even when railroads were constructed by foreign engineers, the alumni of the military school played important parts exploring the routes or inspecting the finished works for the government. At least three former cadets helped to construct one or more long cart roads, and most of them at one time or another did some work on mule paths. They also put their hands to such various activities as surveying, making maps, assaying metals, observing astronomical and meteorological phenomena, building bridges, draining lakes, installing ironworks, constructing aqueducts, and managing enterprises from railroads to gasworks.[47]

Some of the same men provided the country with its first corps of native professors of science and engineering. In private *colegios* or the Colegio Militar in the 1850s, in the traditional institutions of San Bartolomé and el Rosario or the various schools of engineering of the last third of the century, the men of the Colegio Militar were likely to be the instructors in mathematics and physics. In the early 1870s, for example, four of six professors in the new National University's School of Engineering were products of the Colegio Militar.[48] As teachers of these subjects, they would work for less than a third of the salary generally required by their foreign counterparts.[49] Perhaps as important, they represented a pool of locally available expertise on which the government might readily draw on those occasions when it could sustain effective institutions of higher education.

In comparison with the contemporary experiments in study abroad, the Colegio Militar appears to have been more successful in attaining its object. The alumni of the military school were more likely to practice and teach engineering in Colombia. Among the successful students who went abroad, there was a greater propensity to move into academic science, rather than practical application, or into political or literary activity.

As students from the two groups had roughly the same social make-up—both being divided about equally between the Bogotá elite and upper-class provincials—it is tempting to believe that the two groups were affected by their differing educational experiences.[50] Those who went abroad had opportunities to learn about the latest scientific advances and to develop rather specialized and rarefied interests; thus they might have been expected to gravitate toward research and writing in pure science and to remain in the centers in Europe that were most notable for scientific investigation. The youths at the Colegio Militar, on the other hand, had a more limited, practically oriented education; thus they may have been less enticed by scholarly inquiry into abstract, exotic, or otherwise impractical subjects. It should be noted that some of the most actively practical of the Colegio Militar alumni spent a considerable amount of time studying in Europe; but their interests already had turned firmly toward the practical, for in France they chose engineering schools rather than the institutions noted for academic science.[51]

Ultimately, however, it seems that the military alumni may have pursued careers in practical engineering because they had the inside track to government engineering jobs. Those who studied abroad lacked the privileged standing granted in the law of 1847 and, in a number of cases, the Liberal party affiliations that were useful in the 1860s and 1870s.[52]

The services of the alumni of the first Colegio Militar were not spread evenly over all parts of the country. In accord with the centralizing tendencies that generally characterize Latin America, they did most of their teaching in Bogotá, and their engineering labors were most heavily concentrated within about a hundred kilometers of the capital. Even outside the Bogotá area, however, their operations were not equally distributed. They worked a great deal more in the eastern region than in the west or on the Caribbean coast. Cúcuta, about four hundred miles to the northeast of Bogotá, benefited much more from their energies than Antioquia, which was considerably closer. This pattern does not seem simply a reflection of the fact that most of the students came from the east, for the more active engineers were engaged far from their home areas.

Engineers based in Bogotá were not used in the west or on the coast partly because in these places foreign interests were dominant and foreign engineers commanded the available jobs. The eastern cordillera, being less attractive to foreign capital, fell to Bogotá's technicians by default.[53]

Political factors probably also had something to do with the greater use of these "official" or establishment engineers in the east. The Radical politicians who controlled the national government between 1864 and 1880 came overwhelmingly from the eastern cordillera region, particularly from Santander. They were naturally inclined to use the financial and technical resources of the national government more in their part of the country than in the Conservative bastion of Antioquia. Even after the Conservatives regained power in the 1880s, the division between Antioquia and the east continued for some time to be observable in the patterns of employment of Colombian engineers.

The Bogotá focus as well as the elitism of the Colegio Militar contributed to the political hostility that destroyed it as an institution. But the centralist concentration and elitism of the 1848–1854 academy may also have had certain advantages in promoting the development of a Colombian engineering profession. High standards of instruction permitted and encouraged several of its alumni to go on to advanced study in Europe and the United States, where they developed a high level of competence within the profession to which they were committed. In addition, the shared experience of intellectual and other disciplines in the military school, as well as the sense of being part of an elite engaged in something innovative, helped to produce a fraternal bond among the alumni. This shared experience and their geographical concentration around Bogotá ultimately facilitated the organization of an engineering society. The handful of engineers produced by the Colegio Militar and its successor institutions formed the core around which a self-conscious Colombian engineering profession came to adhere.

Chapter 8

Stumbling Progress, 1863–1903

COLOMBIAN attempts to promote technical education between 1821 and the middle of the 1860s were fitful and ineffective. The efforts of this period were negated to some degree by the drag of traditional social values. But even more substantial obstacles stood in the way. With little industrial activity or transportation development, few jobs existed for the technically trained. After 1863 this situation improved. Some of the factors that had retarded development—political disruption, weak fiscal resources, and a poor credit record—continued to operate, though in an attenuated form. Government policy, however, underwent a rather favorable change. Between 1850 and 1863 Colombian leaders focused single-mindedly on the export economy, which, they believed, had to be developed by private enterprise, with as little government involvement as possible. After 1863 the Colombian elite came to recognize that even an effective export economy required the development of overland transportation, which in that era was interpreted to mean railroads. Railroad construction in turn implied greater government intervention in the economy, the establishment of ironworks, and an increased demand for technicians. By the end of the century Colombian leaders had evolved toward the goal of a substantially industrialized economy supported by as much technical sophistication as they could muster.

In this era of initial industrialization, the weakness of the national government and political disruption remained serious problems. After the disastrous civil war from 1859–1862 the triumphant Radicals, ever fearful of their impetuous and uncongenial ally General Mosquera, reestablished constitutional government according to Liberal ideals. Their Constitution of Rionegro (1863) carried forward and consolidated the libertarian and federalist reform that Liberals had begun instituting in 1850. The Constitution prohibited the death penalty, decreed a ten-year maximum imprisonment, and explicitly sanctioned unrestricted commerce in arms. The writers of the constitution purposefully cut back national authority so as to approximate, even to surpass, American federalism. The state governments that had been created since 1855 now became sovereign states, possessing all powers not expressly delegated to the national government. The constitution greatly weakened the national president—his term was limited to two years, with no reelection, and his appointments were subject to Congressional approval for the first time. The Radicals restricted the powers of the national government to a minimum—the conduct of foreign relations, defense, and support of a national army, the collection of national revenues, and the management of public credit. The states now had independent military forces. And they bore primary responsibility for the development of education and communications within their boundaries, though the national government continued to carry a share of the burden in both areas.[1]

The liberal reforms of the 1850s, ratified in the Constitution of 1863, marked a radical break with the Spanish centralist tradition. To many Colombians then and since the Rionegro constitution represented the proclamation of a set of utopian ideals. The constitution, as the Liberal Miguel Samper commented four years afterward, "organizes anarchy."[2] Since that time Colombian Liberals and Conservatives have debated whether the system obtaining from 1863 to 1886 provided more organization or more anarchy. Liberals have contended that the new Radical order, by guaranteeing the autonomy of the states and by reducing the significance of the government in Bogotá, made the capital less of a prize for the warring political parties. Along with the powers of government, civil disruption was "decentralized." There were many small local struggles for control of the states. But between 1863 and the resumption of the centralist regime in 1886 only two national conflicts occurred, the Conservatives' rebellion of 1876–1877 and that of the Liberals in 1885. Conservatives, of course, turn these facts around, emphasizing that between 1864 and 1880, in addition to the major war of 1876–1877, there were more than a dozen local revolutions and almost continuous alarms and excursions verging on violent conflict.[3]

However one looks at it, political order clearly remained a major problem in Colombia, and not simply under the federal system. After the resurrection of centralism in the Constitution of 1886 the country continued to experience perfervid political agitation and two more national upheavals, the four-month rebellion of 1895 and the bloody War of the Thousand Days (1899–1903), which finally put the quietus on the violent politics of the nineteenth century. Nevertheless, amid the turmoil, there were moments of relative prosperity and progress, particularly between 1868 and 1875 and again between 1886 and 1895. The Radicals established a technically oriented National University in 1868, and in the early 1870s and between 1881 and 1895 Colombian and foreign engineers laid some railroad track.

An important change in the attitudes of the Radical leaders aided Colombia in its stumbling progress. During the 1850s some of the most influential Radicals had espoused a doctrinaire laissez faire position on communications development. Manuel Murillo Toro and his Radical associates in the state of Santander in the latter part of the 1850s had disavowed the responsibility of the state for road construction or even public education at any level. By 1864, however, Murillo as national president, under pressure from members of his own party, had forsaken the idea of leaving all to individual initiative as a policy practicable only in England or the United States. In countries in the Spanish tradition, he now believed, some government leadership was needed in the development of education and transportation.[4] Although the Constitution of 1863 limited the national government's purview to "interoceanic roads," Murillo interpreted this provision broadly. In 1864 his government adopted the first large-scale plan for national transportation development since the first Mosquera administration. It called, among other things, for cart roads connecting the country's various population centers with the Magdalena River and for the construction of a telegraph system. In the 1870s this proposal was followed by a series of even more elaborate ones, involving railroad construction.[5]

Expansion of the export economy between 1863 and 1875 encouraged interest in public works and other aspects of development. The export trade, which had begun to increase noticeably after 1845, continued its upward course after a period of crisis in 1858 and a very brief interruption in the war of 1859–1862. In the 1830s, according to admittedly deficient official figures, New Granada exported less than three million pesos per annum or about one and a half pesos per capita. By the middle of the 1850s, on the strength of growing exports of tobacco and cinchona bark and Antioquia's continuing contribution of gold, exports had reached levels of five to eight million pesos or between two and three pesos per capita. After 1863 exports jumped to a new level, averaging (with some violent fluctuations) perhaps nineteen million pesos between 1864 and 1885. Based on the 1870 population of three million inhabitants, this represented approximately six pesos per capita.[6]

The growth of Colombia's export economy was by no means continuous. The expansion of the period from 1850 to 1875 was followed by two serious setbacks in the 1870s and 1880s and a prolonged period of stasis in the last decade of the century. Even the period of growth before 1885 was marked by considerable instability in the marketing of individual commodities. Trade in Ambalema tobacco shot to the fore from 1845 to the middle of the 1860s and then rapidly declined. Cinchona bark became a major export item in the area south of Bogotá in the 1850s and then dropped to insignificance, only to reappear as a leading export commodity of the Santander region in the 1870s. Casting about for a profitable exchange earner, upper-class Colombians tried cotton in the middle of the 1860s and indigo at the end of the same decade, but they experienced only a few years of success. Coffee began to develop steadily as an export commodity only after 1870.

Because of its instability, Colombia's export economy first stimulated and then undid one development project after another. The emergence of the tobacco industry around Ambalema encouraged the conception of a cart road from that town to Bogotá at the end of the 1850s and the establishment in the capital of a British-owned commercial bank in 1864. But the downfall of Ambalema tobacco undermined the road scheme and played an important role in the collapse of the British bank in 1868. Similarly, Santander's cinchona boom at the end of the 1870s emboldened that state's leaders to found a bank and to start a railroad from the Magdalena River to the highland city of Bucaramanga; both projects were brought down by falling cinchona prices in London and subsequent civil war in 1885.

Particularly in the last two decades of the century, the instability of the export economy created an environment of frustration that fostered almost continuous political conflict. The rapid decline of the cinchona market in the first part of the 1880s is said to have stimulated Liberal rebellion in Santander, which in turn led to nationwide civil war in 1885.[7] The years 1883 through 1885 were also characterized by a rapid drop in the volume, though not in the price, of Colombian coffee exports. Between 1893 and 1902 the average price of Colombian coffee exported to the United States dropped steadily from eighteen cents per pound to five cents. These years were marked by another Liberal rebellion in 1895, followed by almost continuous political crisis, and capped by the disastrous War of the Thousand Days (1899–1903).

Because of the unreliable export economy and continuing political convulsion, Colombian development went forward fitfully. Nevertheless, the growth of the export economy did provide a base for a commercial banking system after 1870. And increased exports also supplied the freight required for building the country's first railroads. The first construction effort outside Panamá was a short line built in 1869–1871 from the river port of Barranquilla to the ocean port of Sabanilla (a part of present-day Barranquilla) to facilitate international trade. Most of the major works undertaken subsequently were spurred by the expectation that rapidly expanding coffee crops in Santander, Cundinamarca, and Antioquia would provide freight and in turn that the coffee trade would be benefited by greatly reduced transportation costs.[8]

A quickening of economic activity in the 1870s brought an increase in national and state revenues. Before 1860 the combined national and provincial revenues amounted to between three and four million pesos.[9] By the early 1870s, with increased income from customs duties and funds derived from the sale of church properties, national revenues alone amounted to about three and a half million pesos, and the states' incomes brought the total to between six and seven million. By 1880 national revenues, now without income from church property, had reached about ten million. In per capita terms this meant about a 50 percent increase in total revenues between 1850 and 1880, from about two pesos to three pesos per capita.[10]

Between 1868 and 1874, with increased exports, expanded revenues, and a national army scaled down to a thousand men, the central government was enjoying budget surpluses. In an atmosphere of optimism Colombian leaders elaborated plans for eight different railroads linking the interior with the outside world. Between 1874 and 1876 work on some of these lines actually began. The outbreak of the Conservative rebellion of 1876–1877 brought these efforts to a halt, however; railroad construction interrupted at this time in most cases was not resumed for five years. The national army swelled temporarily to perhaps twenty-five thousand men, and the ten million pesos spent on the war destroyed any hope of a balanced budget. After the war the Radicals, now feeling threatened by both the Conservatives and Rafael Núñez's Independents, continued to maintain a relatively large army.[11]

Deep in fiscal crisis in the latter part of the 1870s, Colombia's leaders responded by increasing budget deficits still further. In the face of mounting debts they refused to give up the dream of the railroads conceived in the more favorable years at the beginning of the decade. In 1881 work was resumed on four different lines and in the following year on four more. During these years the expenditures of the national government amounted to approximately three times its income. Public works outlays, most of them in subsidies to the projects of state governments, made up a large proportion of these inflated budgets. In 1879 and 1880 more than 41 percent of the national budget was devoted to material development, for the most part railroad construction. In subsequent years subsidies diminished somewhat, but much of the paper money generated by the new National Bank after 1881 went into loans for railroad projects.[12]

The extraordinary efforts of the first half of the 1880s once again were interrupted by civil war in 1885. Despite a great deal of elite preoccupation with the subject, only 206 kilometers of track had been laid between 1869 and 1885, and only two short lines had been completed. During the war military abuse and lack of maintenance damaged some of those stretches that were in service. And the country still faced two major bouts of political violence. During the War of the Thousand Days (1899–1903) almost all railroad work was suspended, and by its end the track and moving stock of three of the most important lines (Antioquia, Cauca, Girardot) had badly deteriorated.[13]

Civil war was only one of the many problems retarding railroad construction in Colombia. The country's geography presented great difficulties. Its steep mountains required many bridges and other elaborate works. And its rainy climate and vigorous vegetation turned any interruption of maintenance into a disaster. Colombia's hot, humid lowlands lacked a large local laboring population and threatened death to those who came from other places. Foreign technical assistance and even domestic labor, therefore, came at a relatively high cost.

Capital was also expensive because of the poor credit position of the Colombian government and Colombian businessmen, but perhaps even more because of the inherent risks of these enterprises. (Foreign companies had about as much trouble as the government in securing capital.) Some of Colombia's better informed leaders were aware from the start that the topography and the high cost of capital would make railroads twice as expensive in Colombia as they were in flatter, more developed parts of the world, and this indeed proved to be the case.[14]

Some thoughtful Colombians by 1880 questioned whether Colombia could support railroads. Its population of about three million in 1870 was widely dispersed. There was little commerce between the scattered population centers and not a great deal between them and the outside world. Very few places could produce enough freight to sustain a railroad.

The problem of population dispersion was reflected in and complicated by attempts to build many railroads at once rather than concentrating on one or two. This dissipation of resources was fostered between 1863 and 1886 by the federal system, under which both the central government and the several states could initiate public works projects. Funds were spread thinly over projects in all corners of the nation, and in the region of Bogotá national and state authorities were simultaneously building lines depending on substantially the same market. The centralist constitution of 1886 abruptly removed funds from the states' many enterprises, leaving them in temporary disarray. But centralization did not remedy the lack of rational planning in transportation development. In 1890 the national government within the space of fifty-five days made contracts for three different lines connecting Bogotá with the Magdalena River.[15]

Thus Colombia's nineteenth-century railroad building was notably unsuccessful. As of 1904 the country had only 645 kilometers of track in two widths. Effective expansion did occur during the political peace of the next decade when the amount of track doubled. But the Sabana de Bogotá was not connected by rail with the vital artery of the Magdalena until 1908, and the railroad linking Medellín with the river was not finished until a 3,700-meter tunnel was driven through the granite of the central cordillera in 1929.[16]

High transportation costs retarded the country's development by raising the expense of heavy machinery and, more important, by limiting the market. Nevertheless, Colombia experienced some movement toward technical improvement in the last third of the nineteenth century. At mid-century agriculture, even among large landowners, was still quite backward. Iron-shared plows were not unknown, but among the peasants rude wooden ones or hoes remained the most common cultivating devices. Even the large estates on the Sabana de Bogotá did not use threshing machines before 1855; the age-old hoof method was still in style. At the end of the 1850s and increasingly in the 1860s upper-class *bogotanos* began to import American plows, threshing machines, and other agricultural implements, as well as improved seed and breeding stock. In 1865 the *hacendados* of the Sabana marveled at a wheat-cutting machine that could do the work of two hundred *peones*. Deterred in part by the cost of bringing machinery up the mule road from Honda, large landowners in the highlands were cautious about such innovations.[17]

Manufacturing was hardly more advanced than agriculture. Since the 1830s an ironworks in the town of Pacho had produced cast and malleable iron; its capacity was modest (about 500 tons per year), but it met much of the demand of local blacksmiths and sugar mills. Other than the ironworks the Bogotá area had only light consumer manufacturing—a porcelain factory dating from the 1830s, a water-powered woolens mill set up in the 1850s, small manufactories of candles and soap operating in the 1860s. The steam engine was not put to industrial use around Bogotá until 1868, when a steam-powered flour mill was established. In Antioquia, the only place that could rival Bogotá, there was some technical activity, particularly in the mines run by Tyrell Moore and other foreign entrepreneurs. But Antioquia was far from an industrial state. It did not produce iron before 1865.[18]

After 1870 the Colombian elite for the first time since 1840 devoted serious attention to manufacturing and, in particular, to basic industries. In the last third of the century Bogotá in the eastern cordillera and Medellín in the west competed as industrial pioneers. Both attempted to develop substantial ironworks. In Antioquia after 1865 the Amagá ironworks and later other places produced simple iron parts for mining and agricultural equipment. After 1874 the national government in Bogotá encouraged the establishment of larger ironmills in the eastern cordillera. Such works were viewed as providing a general industrial foundation, but their primary mission was to support railroad construction through the production of rails. One of the mills, Samacá in Boyacá, failed by 1884. But La Pradera on the Sabana de Bogotá developed slowly, and by 1894 it was producing forty tons per day. Despite financial difficulties and war damage, its entrepreneurs constantly attempted to introduce more sophisticated techniques until the company's collapse in 1905. The 1870s and 1880s also were notable for efforts, both in Bogotá and Medellín, to establish chemical industries, particularly the manufacture of sulphuric acid, considered the key to many other enterprises.[19]

The period from 1864 to 1900 was one of fragmentary industrial development. In Bogotá and Medellín light consumer industries—beer, glass, soap, even some textiles—continued to unfold. Basic industries were established on a shaky footing, and railroad building suffered from the violent politics and fiscal weakness of the era. But the country was attempting new economic activities that required more sophisticated technical knowledge —including the installation of gasworks in the 1870s and electricity and telephones in the 1880s.[20] Although these ventures were by no means dynamic by North American standards, they did provide some support for equally spasmodic efforts in technical education.

Engineering Education, 1864–1900

By the last third of the century neo-Bourbonism no longer dominated the advocacy of technical education. After 1863 the neo-Bourbons were in exile, dead, or in their waning moments. As Liberals controlled the national government between 1863 and 1880, Liberals perforce figured importantly in the promotion of practical training. Men like Salvador Camacho Roldán, José María Samper, and Nicolás Pereira Gamba, once rebels against the system of Mariano Ospina Rodríguez, were now active proponents of scientific instruction. Their approach is distinguishable from that of the neo-Bourbons, however, because it was primarily economic in character with little of the paternalistic moralism of the first half of the century. This predominantly economic approach also characterized most of the efforts of Conservative leaders in Antioquia in the 1860s and 1870s as well as of the national administrations of Rafael Núñez in the 1880s. During conservative rule in the 1890s there was a resurgence of the old paternalistic style of manual training, but alongside it a more modern, secular spirit of technical professionalism continued to grow.

The 1870s were marked by a concern for educational growth in general, including the expansion of normal and primary school instruction. One part of this development was the creation of a vital national university with a strongly technical orientation. The reconstituted university had its genesis in a bill proposed in 1864 by José María Samper. Under the Samper plan all scientific studies were to be grouped together in one Instituto Nacional having three schools—civil and military engineering, natural sciences, and medicine and surgery. The Samper proposal was criticized for relegating the study of jurisprudence to an inferior station—one of his fellow Liberals detected in the proposal the shadow of Mariano Ospina, of the "Bolivarian and Bonapartist school, which is terrified at hearing the mere name of a *doctor* or an *ideologue.*" But the National University eventually created in 1867, while including a school of jurisprudence, retained Samper's emphasis on technical studies.[21]

The Congress encouraged technical education in the new university by requiring all government scholarship students to study in the schools of natural sciences, engineering, or arts and crafts (*artes y oficios*).[22] The policy favoring technical studies was at least temporarily successful. In the early 1870s more than half the students in the advanced faculties of the National University were studying in the schools of natural sciences or engineering. This figure is not an accurate indicator of the ultimate professional destiny of the students; in these years the faculty of natural sciences served to prepare students for the medical school, as well as, to a lesser degree, for engineering. Medicine, therefore, was by a considerable margin the preferred career choice of students at the National University in this era (see Table 10). Nevertheless, the predominance of engineering over jurisprudence at this time is noteworthy. While 22 to 35 percent of all advanced students were enrolled in engineering, less than a sixth were in law. This fact is particularly striking when one considers that in the United States during the same period, law remained the dominant profession of college graduates, making up about a quarter of the total until the 1880s; engineering was attracting less than 5 percent of the students at most American general universities.[23]

TABLE 10. *Students in the Escuelas Superiores of the National University, by Faculty*

	1870		1871		1874	
	Number/%		Number/%		Number/%	
Medicine	51	38	53	38	59	32
Natural sciences	44	33	40	29	30	16
Engineering	29	22	35	25	65	35
Jurisprudence	8	6	12	8	30	16
Total[a]	132		140		184	

Source: *Anales de la Universidad* 3, no. 13 (January 1870): 7, and 5, no. 25 (January–March 1871): 8; and *Anuario estadístico, 1875*, pp. 80–81. The figures for 1874 are averaged full-time equivalents in the various faculties, calculated from course enrollments.

[a]Percentages do not total 100 because of rounding off.

The relative strength of engineering in the early 1870s proved a temporary phenomenon. In 1874 the government eased the pressure on students to engage in technical studies by permitting scholarship students to enroll in any faculty.[24] Jurisprudence quickly recovered something of its former position, while medicine continued to be the most heavily enrolled faculty. By the early 1880s engineering lagged well behind both. In the early 1890s the Faculty of Mathematics and Engineering had enrollments fluctuating between 22 and 52, while the School of Natural Science and Medicine (now one unit) ranged from 144 to 197 students, and the law school rarely fell below 100.[25] These figures for the National University more or less reflect the relative strengths of the professions in the country as a whole. For, while additional instruction in civil engineering was given in the University of Antioquia (founded 1874), the Escuela de Minas in Medellín (1888–1894), and in the Universidad Republicana in Bogotá in the 1890s, the enrollments were overwhelmingly counterbalanced by the large numbers of students of law and medicine in the universities in Popayán, Medellín, and Cartagena.

Between 1876 and 1884 civil engineering in Bogotá was set back by a series of government decisions that brought the engineering school under military control once again. These changes seem to have been motivated by the Radicals' alarm at the Conservative challenge to their rule in the latter part of the 1870s. Suddenly seeing their control of the national government endangered, the Radicals in 1876 took a series of security measures, which included enlarging the army. The engineering school, which in 1870 had been entirely devoted to civilian purposes, was after 1876 required to provide full instruction for military careers. At the same time the government decided to sustain twenty-seven military students along with the seventy-two in civil engineering that it was already committed to support. [26]

In July of 1876 the threatened Conservative rebellion exploded. Although it was put down within nine months, the shaken Radicals were now acutely aware of the need for a loyal, professionally trained corps of officers. In 1877 the Congress called for the conversion of the engineering school to a military-dominated School of Civil and Military Engineering to be operated independently of the national university. In the reconstructed institution no more than half the curriculum had any bearing on civil engineering, and the title of civil engineer now meant simply that a student had taken those engineering courses that were required for any military officer. With the school now directed by military officers, students went into the field for tactical maneuvers rather than for practical work in engineering. Separated from the national university, the school had to provide its own preparatory courses, a function that absorbed much of the faculty's energy. [27] The decline of the institution as an engineering school is reflected in course enrollments. In 1880 with fifty-six members in the student body, courses on higher mathematics and engineering contained an average of only four students. [28] By 1883 Bogotá's small nucleus of scientists and engineers was vigorously protesting the collapse of the engineering school. Responding to their complaints, the government in 1884 again separated military and civil engineering, reincorporating the latter in the national university. [29]

Bogotá's instructors of science and technology, backed by the newly founded Sociedad Colombiana de Ingenieros (1887), complained that the frequent changes in the character of the engineering school severely disrupted technical education. Abelardo Ramos, an alumnus of the Colegio Militar of 1866–1867 and one of Colombia's engineers and science instructors, lamented the pernicious effect of Colombian politics on engineering instruction. Tied as it was to the "ephemeral existence of political sects that never had given the Nation peace nor credit," the teaching of engineering had failed to develop permanence or solidity. "Now, it is believed, correctly, that Engineering is the brain of Industry—synonymous with peace and well-being—and a School of Civil Engineering is founded; then, the thermometer of sectarian agitation rises, it is thought inconsiderately that Engineering was born to serve ballistics, fortification, strategy, and a Military School is founded." With such institutional vacillations, students could not be sure that they would be able to complete their course of study, nor, with curriculum and appointments so much affected by the shifting winds of politics, would men take up the teaching of technical subjects with any confidence of continuous employment.[30]

Throughout the rest of the nineteenth century the engineering school suffered from the institutional weakness that affected every area of Colombian life in the period. Its constant discontinuities were symbolized by almost yearly changes in its name.[31] More important, the faculty continued in flux. Of the seven professors teaching in 1888, only three remained in 1891, and none of these was handling the same courses. Nor did the school have a permanent location. At one moment (1887) it was lodged in the Instituto de Artesanos, then in the former convent of Santa Clara, then in a house in the barrio of Santa Bárbara, and not long afterward (1891) it was moved to the building of the School of Law.

As such a peripatetic existence would suggest, the engineering school had no adequate laboratories. At the end of the 1880s the school borrowed instruments from the defunct military school. But at the end of the century it still had no apparatus for teaching electricity. Rectors had had so little success in obtaining funds for equipment that they were reduced to making pathetically minimal requests.[32] They found it difficult to be demanding given the school's modest enrollments and the state of the national fisc, both of which were affected markedly by the political crises of the period. During the years of relative peace before 1895, enrollments in the Bogotá engineering school edged above fifty. Then, as a ten-year political torment ensued (1895–1904), the number of students dropped to thirty-five. Finally, during the War of the Thousand Days (1899–1903), the school of engineering was suspended completely; a small number of underemployed engineers took refuge in the Bogotá observatory, where the national astronomer, Julio Garavito, gave informal instruction and presided over most agreeable *tertulias*.[33]

While the years from 1877 to 1883 marked a low point in instruction in civil engineering in Bogotá, the same years were notable for a late-blooming interest in agronomy and veterinary medicine. Despite the preponderant role of agriculture in the Colombian economy, only at the end of the 1870s did the government begin to take systematic action to improve agriculture. Upper-class leaders in Bogotá were disturbed by the shaky position of their agricultural exports. First they were alarmed by the decline of tobacco and indigo produced in the Magdalena valley, and by the end of the 1870s they were threatened with the competition of cinchona produced on British plantations in Asia. In domestic agriculture highland farmers were worried by the spread of potato disease, and there was some belated agitation to improve wheat yields to defend local markets against American flour. Finally, some members of the elite felt a general concern to bring Colombia into line with the agricultural practices of the more advanced Western countries (breed improvement, crop rotation, use of fertilizer, and the latest agricultural machinery). Leaders of this movement were probably activated by the *idea* of Colombia's agricultural backwardness as much as by market pressures. Much of their attention was devoted to introducing new breeds of cattle, sheep, fine horses, and even dogs; in at least some of these cases there was no evident economic need for improvements in breed.

Leadership in agricultural improvement first came from the private sector. Salvador Camacho Roldán and Nicholás Pereira Gamba in the latter half of the 1860s began to import farm machinery, more from a sense of duty than because of prospects of commercial success. To promote its sale as well as the development of scientific agriculture in general, they began in 1868 to published *El Agricultor*, a weekly newspaper devoted to information and advice for farmers. Between 1870 and 1872 Salvador Camacho Roldán as national secretary of finance conceived and promoted Colombia's first agricultural expositions (1871 and 1872), which, according to contemporaries, played a critical part in the modest agricultural awakening of the subsequent decade. In 1872 and again in 1878 Camacho Roldán also led in founding the Sociedad de Agricultores Colombianos. As president of Bogotá's agricultural society, he was a chief organizer of follow-up expositions in 1880 and 1881.[34]

The first notable government initiatives for agricultural development occurred in the administration of Gen. Julian Trujillo (1878–1880) when Salvador Camacho Roldán served as secretary of the treasury. Beginning its labors just a month after the second founding of Bogotá's Sociedad de Agricultores Colombianos, the Trujillo administration's first message to the Congress pointed out the need for government leadership in this field. Granted an initial budget of thirty thousand pesos, the Trujillo administration embarked upon a broad program for agricultural research and development. Trujillo and Camacho Roldán hoped to establish stations to experiment in the cultivation of tobacco and cinchona. It was hoped that the work on cinchona could be directed by R. Clements Markham, already renowned for his work in creating cinchona plantations in India. Trujillo also created a National Department of Agriculture, under Camacho Roldán's treasury ministry, to oversee the experiment stations as well as to collect and publish data covering every conceivable aspect of Colombian agriculture, from commodity prices to land tenure patterns to modes of cultivation. The U.S. Department of Agriculture, whose functions were expanding rapidly at this time, was the model for the new Colombian agency.[35]

The Trujillo government also took an interest in agricultural education. From the beginning of the 1870s the National University had offered agriculture courses in its School of Natural Sciences; and in 1874 the state of Cundinamarca established Colombia's first agricultural school. The Trujillo administration attempted to expand these efforts by offering subsidies for agricultural instruction given in primary schools as well as in state or private secondary ones. This measure coincided with and stimulated the foundation of various state agricultural schools, most notably those in the eastern cordillera.[36]

Most of these early schools were heavily dependent upon foreign instructors. Cundinamarca relied on a German. Boyacá in 1878 attempted unsuccessfully to found an agricultural institute in the town of Leiva under a Spanish agronomist, José María Gutiérrez de Alba. The next year Boyacá established a similar school in the charge of two French professors. During these years the state of Santander also created an agricultural institute directed by Gutiérrez de Alba, with a staff including a Belgian agronomist and a French horticulturist, as well as various homegrown professors. As in earlier periods, dependence upon foreign instructors presented problems. While some labored at their tasks long, conscientiously, and effectively, others proved unable to adapt their work to the Colombian environment or for other reasons soon returned to Europe.[37]

Colombia's first national agricultural commissioner, Juan de Dios Carrasquilla, sought to increase the supply of instructors and scientific farmers by establishing a national institute of agriculture whose graduates would be obliged to teach in state and normal schools. He saw the establishment of a national institute as the foundation of a broad program, including agricultural training in primary schools and the establishment of agricultural colonies for homeless boys. In its final days the Trujillo administration created a National Institute of Agriculture and contracted Carrasquilla, a physician and *hacendado*, to serve as its director for a period of five years.[38]

The school endured for precisely this five-year period (1880–1885), serving a student body ranging in number from fifteen to thirty-seven. Despite aggressive leadership from Carrasquilla, the school suffered the early contretemps to be expected in any new venture. It was at first located on a country place that the part-time professors who came daily from Bogotá found difficult to reach, and the entire student body fell sick in its marshy atmosphere. The school lacked a chemistry laboratory and even agricultural implements. Its three Colombian professors were among the most able available—Francisco Montoya M. (physics and chemistry), Francisco

Bayón (botany and zoology), and Carrasquilla (agronomy and agricultural mechanics)—and apparently served well; but a specially contracted Belgian agronomist proved unable to adapt European techniques to tropical problems. The school was just becoming firmly established when the civil war of 1885 brought its deletion from the national budget. Surprisingly, professional instruction in agronomy was not attempted again for another twenty years and was not firmly established before 1916.[39]

Although the civil war of 1885 brought the collapse of the national agricultural institute, which was to be the keystone of a broadbased training system, some ancillary efforts continued. The late 1880s saw the emergence of instruction in veterinary medicine. Claude Vericel, a veterinarian contracted in France, taught, gave counsel, and carried on research continuously from 1885 through the end of the century. The government treated veterinary studies as a branch of the traditionally prestigious medical profession: the school was under the aegis of the national university's medical school. Nevertheless, interest in the career was limited. In the 1890s the veterinary students numbered from five to fifteen.[40]

During the fiscal emergencies of the 1880s the Colombian government proved unable to carry through on most of its projects for agricultural development. By 1880 the government, because of fiscal stringencies, had to suspend subsidies promised in 1878 to private *colegios* giving practical instruction in agriculture. For the same reason, it was unable to execute its plan to establish government-owned experimental cinchona plantations. In 1884 the government could not pay for chemistry equipment and agricultural tools ordered for the agricultural institute, had to abandon plans to send samples of Colombian plants to international expositions, and even had to withdraw its small subsidy to the weekly *El Agricultor*.[41] All this occurred even before the 1885 war, which brought the demise of the agricultural institute.

The Department of Agriculture managed to survive to the end of the nineteenth century under the direction of Carrasquilla's successor, Carlos Michelsen Uribe. But it never approximated the scale of operations envisioned by Carrasquilla and Michelsen, who held up the model of the United States' department, with its special sections on statistics, botany, chemistry, entomology, and meteorology. Colombia's fiscal stringencies could not permit so grand an establishment. The department's peak budget of 120,000 pesos in 1880 quickly dropped to less than 45,000 pesos in 1882, and even then it could not depend on its budgeted funds. Throughout the period the Department of Agriculture was a one-man affair. As the Congress withheld research funds, experiments and the supply of data depended entirely on scattered upper-class volunteers. By distributing free seed to a few dedicated *hacendados*, Michelsen was able to test various new fodders, acclimate Liberian coffee, and begin planting the eucalyptus trees now so notable in the Colombian highlands. Nevertheless, Michelsen was well aware that little progress could be made with voluntary research. Few Colombians were rich enough to sacrifice time and money in costly experiments. Nor were many moved by public spirit. In 1885 only eight individuals in the entire country were willing to keep meteorological records; the best were supplied by a Cúcuta priest who sent Michelsen copies of the reports he worked up for the U.S. Signal Corps. Agricultural censuses, depending heavily on the mailed responses of private citizens, were also incomplete and unreliable.[42]

The decline of agriculture's estate in the 1880s coincided with Colombia's first significant effort in mining engineering, the Escuela Nacional de Minas in Medellín. As with agriculture, instruction in mining engineering was surprisingly slow to develop, considering the importance of gold mining to the state of Antioquia and to the foreign exchange of the whole country. Possibly the small numbers of foreign technicians residing in Antioquia after 1820 satisfied the perceived demand. Early in the 1880s the national Congress authorized the creation of mining schools in Medellín, Rionegro, Popayán, and Ibagué, and there was some agitation for one in Bogotá. But all these projects were aborted by the civil war of 1885. After the war *antioqueño* politicians in Bogotá succeeded in getting the Medellín school into the national budget. Thus it emerged as a nationally sponsored institution but with some aid from the department of Antioquia.[43]

The Escuela de Minas suffered some of the same problems found in the early engineering schools in Bogotá. The first students were often inadequately prepared. Despite the availability of some foreign experts as well as a few *antioqueños* trained in the United States, it was sometimes difficult to staff the school. During the early 1890s the school possessed a French chemist, a Belgian metallurgist, and an *antioqueño* mining engineer trained at Columbia, but several of the faculty were local physicians. As in Bogotá, the directors of the Medellín school had to defend the curriculum's emphasis on higher mathematics: to parents in Antioquia as in Cundinamarca this sort of instruction seemed insufficiently "practical." The directors, all *antioqueños*, also complained of lack of local interest in the school.[44]

In retrospect, however, the *antioqueños* characteristically blamed many of their school's problems on Bogotá. Among its other unfortunate acts, the national government sent an engineering professor allegedly of such overwhelming incompetence as nearly to collapse the school. When the school was terminated on the occasion of the civil war of 1895, *antioqueño* leaders ascribed this setback to Antioquia's having fallen out of favor in Bogotá politics at the time. In fact, higher technical studies continued in Medellín at a newly created engineering school at the University of Antioquia.[45]

Medellín's Escuela Nacional de Minas, as its name implies, was conceived strictly as a mining institute. It was modeled on the School of Mines of the University of California, Berkeley, from which its first directors, Pedro Nel and Tulio Ospina, as well as several of its later moving spirits, were graduated. Despite a formal curriculum that emphasized mining, the school by the early 1890s in fact tended to give preference to civil engineering. Some local authorities thought this a mistake as the school's budget was too limited to sustain the expansion. But the curriculum continued to broaden under the pressure of local circumstances. Gold by 1890 was no longer the exclusive focus of Antioquia's economy. Railroad construction, stimulated in part by the new rapidly growing coffee industry, was the first priority. Medellín's development as a city and industrial center also began to pose problems in hydraulic, electrical, and mechanical engineering. There was therefore a much greater demand for the various skills of civil engineers than for those of mining experts. Regional interest, convenience, and *antioqueño* pride also argued for training all-purpose engineers at home rather than depending upon the increasingly resented Bogotá. When the school began its second life after 1904, it did not even pretend to an exclusive focus on mining; along with a mining degree, it offered a separate program in "civil" engineering, including industrial chemistry and electrical and mechanical engineering.[46]

The School of Mines therefore proved to be a seminary of technicians active in a wide variety of fields. Its alumni played important roles not merely in large mining enterprises like that of Zancudo and in the railways of western Colombia but also in the development of manufacturing in Medellín in the early years of the twentieth century. Of sixty-three alumni of the 1888–1894 period, sixteen worked in mining before 1912. But many more of the group had labored in other areas—thirty-one on roads and railroads, six in manufacturing, and ten in assorted other technical enterprises. A dozen had done significant work in both railroading and mining or in other combinations of quite distinct specialties.[47]

As the careers of the alumni of the School of Mines indicate, the Colombian market for technical services was not sufficiently developed to support the specialized training that the mining school was originally conceived to render. Both in Bogotá and in Medellín, engineers could not rely with any security upon steady employment in one specialty until well into the twentieth century. They needed to be prepared to handle any kind of job—to be *toderos* ("men capable of doing everything") as they put it. At the same time, as the state of the art developed in the Western world and as Colombian economic development created new demands, the number and complexity of the skills required constantly expanded. Between 1875 and 1900 a civil engineer might be called upon to build an iron bridge, install or administer an ironworks or other manufacturing plant, or to work in electrical or hydraulic engineering for developing municipal services.

This need for multiple skills presented a dilemma for engineering schools and their graduates. The schools lacked the resources to sustain many specialized programs, and given the engineering market it might not have been wise to do so. Bogotá's professors of science and engineering discussed the idea of offering various engineering degrees within a single institution. But they did not go far in the direction of specialization; instead new courses were simply crammed into one curriculum. Under the circumstances this was sensible. It meant that those graduates who were not able to latch onto an administrative post with a mine or railway might sustain themselves as all-purpose consultants. An engineering agency in Bogotá or Medellín at the end of the century typically found it necessary to offer its services in such various fields as civil and mining engineering, chemical analysis, and architecture and building construction.[48]

Industrial Training, 1867–1900

Along with the spasmodic development of university training of various sorts of engineers, Colombia after 1867 made efforts at scientific and technical education at lower levels. Undoubtedly the strongest theme in Colombian educational policy of the 1870s was the campaign for normal schools, which were established in every state. The primary concern in the normal school movement was the improvement of teaching methods—many foreign instructors, mostly Germans, were contracted to teach pedagogy—but the natural sciences also were well represented in the best normal schools. While the teacher training schools for girls and the branch schools for boys offered little natural science, the principal boys' normal schools in almost all states had physics, natural history, and mathematics through plane geometry; by 1875 two-thirds of these schools also provided chemistry courses. Two things are notable about this development. Virtually all of these science courses were taught by Colombians.

And for the first time such subjects as physics and chemistry were being taught to students who were not presumptive members of the local upper classes.[49] Thus, the 1870s marked an important step forward in the broader extension of scientific instruction.

Courses on the practical applications of science and in manual training were sometimes considered desirable for normal schools but were introduced only to a limited degree. In the 1880s some of the prescribed curricula for boys' normal schools included elaborate programs for agricultural science. But there is little evidence of such courses actually being given or of the establishment of school gardens in normal schools, though they often existed in private *colegios*. Only Bogotá's normal schools gave craft instruction (after 1880), and this was primarily in the decorative arts.[50]

While training in arts and crafts did not become an important part of normal schools, it did develop elsewhere. At the end of the 1860s some members of the upper class were seized by a fit of interest in artisan education. It was advanced in a different manner than it had been in the 1830s. Manual training for the most part now had less of a penal character. In some cases it was now linked to secondary institutions. In Bogotá the 1867 plan for the National University included a school of arts and crafts as one of the sections of the university for which government scholarships were reserved. Similarly, Medellín's school of arts and crafts was created in 1870 as part of the state *colegio*. This connection with higher education probably had the purpose of raising the level of instruction; but it may also have represented an attempt to give artisan training higher status by associating it more directly with the upper class.

Artisan training also now began to venture into instruction in high-level skills, particularly those necessary for basic industries. During the last two decades of the century such cities as Bogotá and Medellín stood on the threshold of their twentieth-century industrial careers. One indication of, as well as a positive factor in, this development was the emergence of training shops in the various branches of the metals trades. Another phenomenon of this protoindustrial period was the birth of interest in industrial management schools.

As the two largest cities, Bogotá and Medellín were the centers of much of the effort in artisan education. In this field as in others one detects a certain rivalry between the two, with Bogotá favored by the resources of the national government and Medellín backed by those of the politically subordinate but wealthy state of Antioquia. After the Radical-dominated national government prescribed a school of arts and crafts for the National

University in 1867, Pedro Justo Berrío, governor of Conservative-controlled Antioquia, in 1869 urged a similar institution for that state. In their early years, as at their creation, the two schools developed along parallel lines, with each taking cues from the other.

In both Bogotá and Medellín the artisans' schools began with rather elaborate programs of academic instruction and with aspirations for shop training that they were not immediately able to fulfill. With its superior cultural resources, Bogotá could provide its school extensive academic offerings; in 1872 sixteen of the country's most reputable men of science gave lectures on subjects ranging from grammar through industrial chemistry, industrial physics, applied mechanics, botany, geology, and mineralogy. These were probably public lectures rather than formally organized courses, as two years later the school had only five courses with numbered enrollments, all limited to basic education in literacy and arithmetic. The university appears not to have offered shop traning in the 1870s.[51]

The *antioqueño* school similarly relied at first more on courses in literary subjects than on shop instruction. This may have occurred in part because in the early 1870s it served as Medellín's substitute for an engineering school, the University of Antioquia not providing even an approximation of engineering education until 1874. The school probably did not offer all of its projected four-year program, which included mechanical drawing and mathematics, with an additional year of civil engineering for the most talented students. But its French-trained mathematics professor, Eugene Lutz, did provide instruction to a number of men, presumably members of Antioquia's upper rather than nether social sectors, who went on to become leading engineers and entrepreneurs.[52]

Workshop instruction in the Medellín school was initially confined to carpentry, cabinetwork, locksmithing—essentially the production of consumer goods. These activities did little for the basic development of the region; their principal effect was to arouse the hostility of already-established artisans producing consumer crafts.[53]

In 1874–1875 both the national and Antioquian governments decided to make more strenuous efforts at industrial training, sending to Europe for technicians who could establish "model shops." Bogotá sought a mechanical engineer and a master founder to direct shops specializing in carpentry (including wagonmaking), ironwork, and mechanics. Shop training was to be supplemented by instruction in mathematics, industrial mechanics, natural sciences, and accounting. The Bogotá plan, however, was aborted by the political crisis of 1876. Perhaps because of fears of artisan support for a Conservative rebellion, the Congress removed the artisans' school from the National University, an act that in effect terminated it. Artisan training sponsored by the national government was not revived until the beginning of the Núñez era in the 1880s.[54]

Antioquia's artisan school, on the other hand, survived the political crisis of 1876–1877 and under imposed Liberal rule (1877–1885) progressed quite notably. In 1876 the government of Antioquia contracted two Swedish ironmasters. Toward the end of the 1870s the school also began to benefit from the services of several *antioqueños* who had been trained abroad. (Among the latter was José María Villa, who after studying in the *colegio* in Medellín was sent on a state scholarship to study mechanical engineering at the Stevens Institute, where he graduated in 1878.) A period of significant mechanical development followed. By 1878–1879 the shops of the Medellín school, aided by steam power, manufactured lightning rods, sewing machines, and rifles and cartridges and repaired machinery used in mining and agricultural processing. From this time on the school's directors hoped to obtain furnaces and forges that would permit the founding of large pieces needed for the production of mining and sugar mills.[55] Evidently Antioquia's mining economy provided stimulus for this institution, which played a part in preparing Medellín for its emerging industrial leadership.

Medellín's school of mechanical arts was the most successful example of a more general movement for manual training. Lesser communities in the 1870s established *escuelas de artes y oficios* on scales appropriate to their resources. By 1870 Cúcuta's school taught experimental physics, while very small towns contented themselves with providing training in the manufacture of straw hats. Among the places that established shop training before the end of the 1870s were Pasto, el Socorro, and the state of Boyacá— all regions with long traditions of artisan manufacture. Mechanical training, as well as the development of heavy industry, was promoted with particular vigor at the end of the 1870s by José Eusebio Otálora as president of the state of Boyacá. During Otálora's regime industrial shops were established as annexes of schools in all of the principal districts of Boyacá. Otálora also attempted to convert the second-largest *colegio* in the state into a school of arts and crafts.[56]

During the 1880s the national government, under Rafael Núñez, began to make greater efforts in worker training. This movement was stimulated perhaps by Medellín's example and probably by Núñez's political relations with Bogotá's artisans as well as his interest in industrial development. Núñez's administrations (1880–1882, 1884–1886, 1887–1888) brought a variety of initiatives, including some craftwork in normal schools and worker training in building construction.[57] Among Núñez's initiatives in this area was his decision to send Colombian youths to the industrial centers of Europe to prepare themselves as masters of training schools in ironworking and mechanics. The single candidate who was found to be qualified, Juan N. Rodríguez, fulfilled his mission. In the 1890s he operated a government-supported model shop for metalwork (founding, boilerwork, lathework, gunsmithing, etc.). Between 1892 and 1897, 621 students were enrolled in Rodríguez's Escuela Nacional de Artes y Oficios.[58]

Meanwhile, a law of 1887 provided for the establishment of similar industrial training shops in up to three departments. By 1890 one was operating in Bucaramanga with seventy-two trainees engaged in ironwork, typography, and consumer crafts. By 1892 state-run schools of manual arts were also functioning in Tunja and Riohacha. And there were plans for others in Guamo (south of Girardot), Panamá, and Pasto.[59]

The several Núñez administrations were also responsible for Colombia's first efforts at training in business administration. At the beginning of the 1880s Núñez proposed to convert all *escuelas superiores* supported by national funds into industrial schools. The first of these converted schools, Barranquilla's School of Commerce, had a rather imaginative program, emphasizing experimental training in organization and management. Second-year students were to form commercial houses and actually to practice commerce; in the third year they were to liquidate these businesses, learning as they did the proper execution of suspensions of payment and bankruptcies, a useful skill in Colombia. The ten best students were to found, operate, and liquidate a bank. The 1884 plans for Bogotá's school of manual arts showed a similar interest in preparing students to cope with the realities of the marketplace. Under the 1884 plan good students were to receive salaries from the sales of school-made goods; sales also would provide all graduates with money for tools. Surprisingly, the 1884 plan emphasized that workers should be trained to organize cooperatives that could manage large industries "without need for capitalist control [*con prescindencia del patronazgo capitalista*]."[60]

Alongside these state-operated schools the conservative Holguín government (1888–1892) encouraged other institutions more in the neo-Bourbon mode—that is, "philanthropic" or church-run manual training operations. In the 1890s the Asylum of San José in Bogotá provided training in carpentry, leatherwork, and weaving to orphan boys, and a School of Domestic Service gave poor girls instruction appropriate to their station. In the capital and elsewhere the Sociedad de San Vicente de Paul also supplied limited craft training to poor children. The early 1890s also saw the implantation in Bogotá of shop schools run by the Salesian Order of Turin. Contracted by the Holguín government, the Salesians by 1891 had established eight shops in Bogotá, offering training in ironwork and mechanics as well as baking, printing, and bookbinding.[61] The Salesian brothers substantially fulfilled the neo-Bourbon ideal of fifty years before: operating within a context of religiously inspired social discipline, they were nonetheless technically capable. Through the twentieth century the Salesian schools have been favored repositories for wayward sons of the upper sectors.

The Foreign Study Mission, 1880–1883

The range of Colombian interest in technical development and the limitations on the country's capacity to develop are suggested by another phenomenon of the last quarter of the nineteenth century. In 1880 the Núñez government sent a few graduates of the National University to Europe and the United States to conduct technical studies on subjects of national interest. The government-sponsored study tour focused on new industrial processes that Colombia lacked almost entirely.

The four young Colombians whom the government contracted began with academic work in Paris and its environs. They studied chemistry, agriculture and agricultural chemistry, and meteorology as it applied to agriculture.[62] Then they moved into studies of industrial technology and the organization of labor. Much of this work was carried on in Belgium because of the concentration of mining, metallurgical, and other industrial activities around Liège.

The energy with which they pursued their investigations is suggested by their first reports in the fall of 1880. Rafael Espinosa Guzmán, during the space of one or at most two months, observed techniques of zinc metallurgy in five different plants in Belgium, mining operations in three coal mines, iron metallurgy in three places, machinery manufacture in another, iron lamination in two plants near Liège, and pipecasting at Dusseldorf. In the same period he also worked in a factory that produced chemical products in Liège, and, in the company of the manager of the chemicals factory and a professor of chemistry of the University of Liège, he visited industrial expositions in Brussels and Dusseldorf. Having reported in detail on many of these subjects, he was about to study the exploitation and refining of sulphur in Sicily. (The Sicilian sulphur deposits were the only ones in Europe similar to those at Gachalá in Cundinamarca, which the Colombians had been struggling to exploit since 1874.) He then proposed to learn about the manufacture of sulphuric acid, sulphate of soda, saltpetre, and nitric acid; the purification of fats; and the manufacture of candles, soap, hydrochloric acid, quinine sulphate, and other chemical products—all industries being considered or promoted at the time in Colombia. Later on he planned to examine iron pyrites in Luxembourg. Meanwhile, two of his colleagues were studying various other technical subjects, including Alexander Graham Bell's photophone and other aspects of electricity and its applications. For the next three years the group sent reports on a wide variety of topics—from artificial diamonds to potato disease to the exploitation of salt deposits in Michigan. But their primary focus remained on industrial chemicals and metallurgy.[63]

The Colombian government's attempt to assimilate the greater part of modern technology through four individuals typifies the aspirations of and the dilemmas faced by the country's elite. They were eager to absorb as many of the latest advances as possible. But with its limited economy, the country could not support elaborate development and the concomitant specialization. When institutions were created with more-or-less specialized purposes—like the school of civil engineering in the 1870s or the mining school in the 1890s—they inevitably were pressed to take on additional functions. With the country's meager resources thinly spread, each of Colombia's efforts to pursue the technical tended to be ineffectual and superficial. The Colombian economy permitted no alternative.

The major problems with Colombian technical development during this period lay, however, not in the institutions themselves but in the fundamental instability of the country's political life. Political ambitions led not merely to disruptive and budget-sapping wars but also to marked discontinuities in policy. Budgetary stringencies limited the possibilities and endangered the survival of all educational institutions. Moreover, the lives of a number of scientific and technical institutions were brief or agitated because they depended upon the sponsorship of one or a group of politicians. When the sponsors lost power, the institutions declined with them, while succeeding leaders devoted themselves to new ephemeral creations. With all its inconstancy, however, the Colombian elite was reaching toward technical sophistication.

Chapter 9   A Place for Engineers

WHILE Colombian leaders succeed-
ed in implementing some technical instruction in the last third of the nineteenth century, the country's growing number of native engineers still
faced the problem of finding professional employment in a politically disrupted, rather backward economy. It was necessary not merely to have a
political and economic climate that would permit the construction of public
works but also to ensure that political and business decisions would lead
to the use of Colombian engineers in the planning, construction, and maintenance of these works. Though by 1875 the country boasted about a hundred engineers, there was a continuing tendency to rely on foreign engineers rather than native ones in the supervision of major undertakings.[1]
Between 1864 and 1885 Colombian technicians gradually won a larger
place for themselves. Nevertheless, during the 1880s Colombian engineers in Bogotá became convinced that it would be necessary to form an
aggressive professional organization to promote their interests. The establishment of the Sociedad Colombiana de Ingenieros in 1887 marked the
emergence in the capital of a professional community imbued with a sense
of pride and determined to make its voice heard and its works respected
on the national scene. Colombia's engineers, however, did not form a
single fraternity. Rivalry between the eastern and western sectors of the
country and the differing experiences and functional roles of the two sections found expression in the development of separate professional communities with distinctive regional styles.

The Employment of Colombian Engineers, 1850–1900

The first Mosquera administration (1845–1849) brought the genesis of
Colombian engineering. The Colegio Militar provided a training mechanism; the large national projects envisioned by Mosquera created expectations of employment; and the foreign engineers contracted at this time
served as models and instructors through the 1850s. Because of the disintegration of the central government after 1850, however, most of the first

generation of Colombian engineers could find only marginal employment. Without official engineering posts, most had to depend upon teaching and odd jobs in surveying.

General Mosquera's revolution of 1859–1863 began a change in the fortunes of native engineers. Mosquera's provisional government and subsequent Radical administrations revived the idea of national government leadership in transportation improvement as well as in the establishment of a technically adequate university. These developments proved immediately advantageous to the alumni of the Colegio Militar, less so to engineers who had studied abroad. In 1863 military school alumni were being employed in surveys of possible railroad routes from the eastern cordillera to the Magdalena River. The disamortization and distribution of church lands in the 1860s also provided some graduates of the Colegio Militar with jobs as surveyors. In 1866 Mosquera formed a national corps of engineers, largely composed of military school alumni. Though the corps was abolished when Mosquera was turned out of office in 1867, many of its members found refuge on the faculty of the newly created national university.[2]

Though teaching positions helped to sustain some Colombian engineers, until at least the end of the century they complained of unemployment, or underemployment, in their profession. Their functions were limited by circumstances over which they had little control. Government policy in the 1860s was predicated on the assumption that road and railroad construction would be undertaken by private companies, albeit with government financial encouragement. The financial resources of the Colombian upper class, however, were extremely weak. Nor, when the Colombian government finally decided to play an entrepreneurial role in the early 1870s, was its capital position much better. Thus, railroad construction projects in the 1860s and 1870s were undertaken mostly by British or North American companies.

The foreign companies preferred to rely on their own nationals or other foreign engineers. On some occasions they did contract a few leading Colombian engineers to make preliminary surveys but only when their own men had not yet reached the scene. Most surveys and almost all construction projects of foreign companies were headed by imported experts, though some Colombians were employed in subordinate capacities.[3] The Cuban-American engineer-entrepreneur, Francisco J. Cisneros, who undertook the construction of five of the country's most important lines between 1874 and 1885, used more Colombians than most foreign contractors. But, with one exception, the most responsible technical positions in his enterprises were occupied by either Americans or fellow Cubans like the Rensselaer graduates Ernesto L. Luaces and Aniceto Menocal. While Cisneros used some nationals as assistant engineers, many of his Colombian employees were lawyers, journalists, and politicians whose influence he bought with jobs as administrators and agents.[4]

Even when Colombian entrepreneurs undertook railroad projects, they too at first imported foreign experts rather than trust the national product in railroad construction. When Nicolás Pereira Gamba initiated the construction of the Dorada railway along the banks of the Magdalena River in the early 1870s, his first step was to bring an engineer from England to mark out the route.[5]

The use of foreigners in technical positions may well have been dictated by more than prejudice. In some cases it probably responded to functional needs. It is significant that, while railroad companies would hire Colombian engineers to oversee some kinds of construction, they invariably used foreign craftsmen as chief mechanics and carpenters. Even the Cúcuta railway, which was owned, directed, and engineered by Colombians, employed a British mechanical engineer.[6] Whatever the capacities of Colombians as civil engineers, it appears that the society was producing very little in the way of skilled mechanics.

Thus, until about 1885, the principal roles of Colombians in railroad construction were to explore possible routes, to conduct feasibility studies (mostly of proposals made by foreign companies), and to inspect completed works for the government. Through the 1870s New Granadans were relegated for the most part to the opening of mule paths and cart roads and the construction of an occasional bridge for these roads. Although foreign experts had little to do with such secondary projects after 1870, even within this sphere Colombian engineers continued to suffer considerable competition. Local amateurs—merchants, landowners, military officers—continued to direct many of these smaller enterprises. As late as 1906 about half the men directing the construction of a major road from Bogotá into the department of Boyacá appear not to have had professional training as engineers.[7] The belief that one could get along well and cheaply by trusting to good sense and traditional routines pervaded many technical areas.[8]

Between 1863 and 1880 the Colombian engineers did find some employment surveying routes. The amount of surveying work available multiplied, probably more than was necessary, because Colombian leaders were unable or unwilling to decide which of many projects ought to be developed. In the eastern cordillera, the Cundinamarca and Santander regions jealously pressed their competing interests, each wishing to have priority in the development of improved communications with the Magdalena River. Within each of these two regions there was further division. In 1864 Bogotá politicians were debating the merits of six different routes between the capital and the Magdalena River; at the same time in Santander five different roads to the river were being promoted.[9] During the 1870s when railroads came to the center of Colombian interest, the elite in Bogotá remained at odds over which roads to build. At least four major railroad routes to the Magdalena valley (with several minor variants) were seriously considered.[10] Each of the routes had something to recommend it,[11] and each had influential supporters within the ruling Radical party.[12] The establishment of construction priorities was made no easier by some public-spirited capitalists in Bogotá who on occasion invested money in several competing roads at once.[13] With the continuing agitation in favor of the several options, the country's more favored engineers were kept relatively busy elaborating and evaluating the competing plans.

Between 1863 and 1874 foreign interests had built one short, predictably profitable line that connected the river port of Barranquilla with the ocean port of Sabanilla and thus greatly facilitated the export-import trade, but foreign entrepreneurs had made only feeble efforts when it came to projects in the mountainous interior. By 1874 no one had made an effective start on three major projects favored by the Colombian government—a railroad from the Pacific coast to the Cauca valley, one from Bogotá to the Magdalena, and a network connecting the entire eastern cordillera with the lower Magdalena valley. Another proposal—to connect coffee-growing Cúcuta with the Magdalena—had sparked no foreign interest whatever. The Colombian government therefore began to play a more aggressive role, encouraging the formation of Colombian companies when this was possible and undertaking construction under its own aegis when it was not. Between 1872 and 1900 Colombian engineers, usually headed by Colegio Militar alumni, constructed the railroad from Bogotá to Zipaquirá (1874–1876, 1884–1898), the line from Facatativá to Bogotá (1882–1885, 1886–1889), the extension of the Dorada railroad (1888–1890), various lines around Cúcuta (1872–1905), and parts of the Puerto Wilches railroad (1880–1885).[14]

At the same time Colombian engineers became involved in considerable construction of iron bridges and macadamized cart roads. And they were beginning to work on city water supplies, telephone service, electric lighting, and other aspects of municipal engineering.[15]

The Society of Engineers

Precisely at the point when Colombian engineers came to play an important part in substantial public works projects, they began to mobilize to demand an even greater role. Their increasing consciousness as a national, indeed to a degree a nationalist, professional entity was manifested in the organization of the Sociedad Colombiana de Ingenieros. The creation of this body had been attempted in the early 1870s but was aborted, according to one of its members, because of the "lethal . . . indifference" of Colombian engineers at that time to their interests as a professional group. The society's reorganization in May of 1887 was stimulated by the surge of public works activity which, except for the interruption of the civil war of 1885, dominated the 1880s. The Sociedad Colombiana de Ingenieros had the general purposes of promoting public works and technical education and of providing Colombian engineers with a more effective voice in guiding the nation's politicians in their decisions in these areas. More particularly, the founders of the society strongly asserted the claims of Colombian engineers to employment on public works in preference to foreigners and the many amateurs who continued to direct construction projects. For, while it was true that Colombian engineers were being used in greater numbers in the 1880s, many still remained without substantial employment as engineers. Linked to the aims of increasing the influence and employment possibilities of Colombian engineers was concern with strengthening their social prestige as a new profession. One of their first manifestos seized upon the figure of Francisco José de Caldas—upper-class *payanés* of the colonial era, Enlightenment savant, *prócer* of the Independence, and military engineer—as a kind of patron saint as well as model of the publicly engaged Colombian engineer.[16]

The Sociedad Colombiana de Ingenieros did not speak for all Colombian engineers by any means. It began with a nucleus of about fifty engineers and science professors in the capital, and, though individuals scattered across the republic joined before the end of its first year, it remained very much Bogotá centered. In 1898, of the full members (*socios de número*) subscribing to its journal, 73 percent lived in Cundinamarca. There were only six member-subscribers in the Cauca, four in Tolima, two each in Antioquia and Boyacá, and one on the Caribbean coast.[17]

Bogotá's dominant role in the society is hardly surprising. Most Colombian engineers lived in the capital. In the 1870s, excluding the 136 engineers in Panamá, most of whom were probably foreigners, 59 percent of the 139 engineers in the rest of the country resided in the state of Cundinamarca.[18] And, as the society was located in the capital, residents of Bogotá were naturally more actively involved in it than engineers in the provinces.

While one would expect the provinces to be underrepresented in the society, there are interesting variations in the degree of provincial participation. Discounting Panamá, Antioquia was second to Cundinamarca in the number of resident engineers in the 1870s with twenty-three, or nearly 17 percent of those counted; the Caribbean coast followed with thirteen, or nearly 10 percent. Yet these regions were less represented in the Bogotá society than such technically poor states as the Cauca and Tolima, in which, seemingly, a large proportion of the native engineers belonged to the society.

The aloofness of the engineers in Antioquia and on the coast to the Bogotá society probably reflected the well-known rivalry between *antioqueños* and *cundinamarqueses* and the less-celebrated antagonism of the *costeños* toward their unbending, slow-speaking governors in the distant interior.[19] Antioquia in particular during the latter half of the nineteenth century developed an intense rivalry with the capital, which formed part of a well-defined regional ideology. Antagonism toward the capital city, of course, was shared by other regions. But only Antioquia, with its gold mining and the concentration of mercantile capital in Medellín, was able to compete with Bogotá. In the last third of the century Medellín in fact, as well as in the minds of the *antioqueños*, stood as an economically based countercapital in the west. Conscious of their importance to the national economy, Antioquia's bourgeois leadership resented the powers, privileges, and preferences enjoyed by the parasitic, sybaritic, politicking *bogotanos*.

The *antioqueño-bogotano* rivalry was reflected in and augmented by the political divisions of the period. For most of the twenty-year (1861–1880) rule of the Radicals, who were predominantly from the eastern provinces, Antioquia in the west was the bulwark of Conservative opposition. Between 1864 and 1877 Antioquia was governed by Conservatives, remaining largely independent of rule from Bogotá. After a Conservative rebellion centering in Antioquia failed, the Radicals in 1877 seized control of the state government, but the Conservative majority in Antioquia continued defiantly dissident until they were able to reestablish their rule in 1885–1886.

While Antioquia's political isolation meant that the area was neglected when the national budget was drawn up, its economic strength (which may have been partly responsible for that isolation) enabled the state to forge ahead on its own. The mining economy induced some on-the-job technical learning as well as shop work and strengthened the School of Arts and Crafts founded in 1869; then Antioquia's first efforts at railroad construction after 1874 further stimulated an interest in industrial skills at the craft school; finally, all these activities provided a base for the successful School of Mines established in 1887. As a result of the region's economic strength and the technical development that it supported, Antioquia was able to stand independently of Bogotá—not only as a center of mercantile capital but also as a technical community. Thus it seems that *antioqueño* engineers took little interest in Bogotá's engineering society partly because they distrusted anything emanating from the capital and partly because by the end of the 1880s Medellín could sustain its own technical community. After 1888 this technical community cohered around the School of Mines; by 1915 it was large and sufficiently vigorous in its regionalism to found an independent Sociedad Antioqueña de Ingenieros.

Other provinces could not emulate Medellín's independence. In the Cauca valley, for example, the local upper class was as removed from Bogotá as the *antioqueños*. But, unlike the latter, technically trained men in the Cauca were too few to form a scientific community. Isolated in their verdant valley, they felt compelled to seek communication with the Bogotá society.[20]

While the *antioqueño* engineers were sufficiently numerous to maintain an independent scientific community, in other respects their career patterns and their attitudes were similar to those of technical men in the other western provinces. The professional tendencies of the westerners as a whole contrasted sharply with those of the engineers of the eastern belt, who dominated the Bogotá engineering society. In this regard as in many others the country divided along the north-south cleavage of the Andes' central cordillera.

The engineers in the east, focusing on Bogotá, were predominantly bureaucratic engineers. Generally they came from the capital or from the surrounding areas of Cundinamarca and Tolima. Some of them had been educated abroad, but most had been trained in Bogotá, either in the Colegio Militar during its several incarnations (1848–1854, 1866–1867, 1879–1885) or in the various schools of engineering of the National University after 1868. Through family and school associations, as well as by virtue of residence in the capital, they enjoyed political connections not available to engineers elsewhere. They therefore had the inside track for government technical jobs—teaching, surveying, constructing, or inspecting public works. The Bogotá engineers generally received appointments at the disposal of the national government, even when they involved work in the western part of the country.[21]

On the other hand, private enterprise in eastern Colombia offered the Bogotá engineers relatively few opportunities aside from occasional surveying and drainage work for local *hacendados*. Most foreign railroad enterprises in the region failed. Thus, not only were foreign engineers employed whenever possible for preliminary surveys, but also the railroads rarely reached a stage where local technicians might be employed as subordinate construction engineers. In the end much of the railroad construction in the eastern cordillera took place under government management. The Bogotá engineers, therefore, were confirmed in their tendency to look to the government for employment. And, among Colombian engineers, they most markedly resented the use of foreign experts.

Engineers in the western provinces had a quite different career experience. Lacking ready access to the technical schools in the capital, most attended provincial *colegios*. Then they either studied abroad or trained themselves, perhaps working their way up in the employ of a foreign mining company or railroad. Very few engineers from Antioquia or the Cauca studied in Bogotá's engineering schools.[22] Lacking connections in Bogotá, they could not obtain government appointments. If they could not establish a connection with a foreign enterprise, they not only had to train themselves but also had to assume the entrepreneurial function. The engineers in the western provinces, therefore, tended to be much less politicized and bureaucratic than the *bogotanos*. They relied more on private enterprise, in many cases their own.

This pattern applies above all, of course, to Antioquia. But it was also true of other regions, such as the Cauca valley. One salient figure in the Cauca, Zenón Caicedo (1827–1901), learned some mathematics at the Colegio de Santa Librada in Cali, taught himself bridge building and actively practiced this art on local projects for many years. In a later generation, Julián Uribe Uribe studied in the provincial *colegios* of Medellín and Buga and then worked his way up as a railroad employee (conductor, stationmaster, etc.). Uribe Uribe, who said that his principal qualification as an engineer lay in the *"arte de madrugar"* (the art of early rising), became a leading builder of roads and railroads in the Cauca.[23]

Western engineers in general and the *antioqueños* in particular differed somewhat from those in the capital in their attitudes toward foreign technical experts. The hostility to the use of foreign engineers expressed by the Society of Engineers in Bogotá did not find an echo in Antioquia. Unlike the *bogotanos*, the *antioqueños* rarely campaigned to displace foreigners. Foreign professors were sought avidly by Medellín's School of Mines between 1905 and 1935, decades after Bogotá's engineers began to resist vigorously government employment of foreigners where nationals might be used.[24]

These divergent attitudes may be attributable in part to the different experiences that the two regions had with foreign experts in the nineteenth century. In Bogotá, while various ordinary immigrants who settled contributed much to the region, most foreigners with formal scientific training stayed only for the duration of a brief contract and made no lasting contribution to the economy. Antioquia, however, possessed one natural attraction for foreign technicians. Its gold mines from the 1820s on lured British, French, Swedish, German, and American mining experts, many of whom settled in Antioquia for decades or married and founded families. Antioqueños freely recognized that such men as Tyrell Moore or Carlos Segismundo de Greiff had introduced fundamental improvements that had revolutionized gold mining in the province, substantially increasing its productivity. Some of the foreigners drawn by the mining economy played critical roles in scientific and technical instruction, teaching in the state *colegio* or the craft school when the *antioqueños* lacked adequate native professors. Thus *antioqueños* were conditioned to expect good from foreigners. One might say that to the *antioqueño* the European technicians represented the "good foreigner"; Bogotá was the external threat, *bogotanos* the resented competitors.

Such attitudes were confirmed with the efflorescence of Colombia's railroad era after 1875, when *antioqueños* could obtain lower-level technical jobs with the Cuban-American railroad entrepreneur Francisco Javier Cisneros but could expect nothing from Bogotá. Contracted in 1874 by the state of Antioquia to build the railway connecting the Magdalena River with Medellín, Cisneros used Cubans or North Americans as his chief engineers, but he did hire *antioqueños* as assistants. Some *antioqueños* worked their way up as engineers on the railway, and others were employed by Cisneros on the Cauca railway after 1879. Both in Antioquia and in the Cauca *antioqueños* also served as subcontractors to the main enterprise.[25] It is not surprising, therefore, that the *antioqueños* in general, including local engineers, viewed Cisneros as another in a succession of foreign benefactors.

Bogotá's political engineers had a less happy experience with Cisneros and he with them. On occasion they would attack Cisneros's work on technical grounds. In 1881, for example, Manuel Ponce de León, a generally esteemed Bogotá engineer, carried on a polemic with Cisneros over the advisability of using broad or narrow gauges.[26] Such attacks might have been variously motivated—by a desire to discredit Cisneros in order to replace him with a construction enterprise under the national government, by a desire to celebrate native technical competence, or by a genuine patriotic or technical concern. Whatever the case, by the early 1880's Cisneros was beginning to run into trouble with Bogotá's homegrown engineers.

A second and more dramatic case of such conflict occurred when Cisneros refused to hire a Colombian politician-engineer as his chief engineer on the Girardot railway. From his first activities in Antioquia in 1874 to his work on the Cauca railroad beginning in 1879 and the beginning of construction on the railroad from Girardot to Bogotá in 1881, Cisneros increasingly employed Colombian engineers in places of responsibility. In 1881 his chief engineer on the Girardot route was Rafael Arboleda Mosquera of Popayán, who had been trained in France and had some European railroad construction experience. Arboleda's appointment, however, marked the zenith of Colombian engineers' participation in Cisneros's many enterprises. When Arboleda died of yellow fever soon after beginning his labors, Cisneros replaced him as chief engineer with a long-time collaborator, the North American J. B. Dougherty. In doing so, Cisneros passed over a Colombian assistant engineer already on the job, Modesto Garcés, who, in Cisneros's opinion, "knew nothing about railroads." The disappointed Garcés was an engineer of the political stripe—educated at Bogotá's engineering school (1866–1870), he had served as the Liberal president of his native Cauca state—and he chose to fight. Garcés intrigued among the other Colombian employees against the new American chief engineer. The resulting conflict, including a free-for-all between partisans of the two engineers, forced Cisneros to dismiss many of those involved and strained Cisneros's relations with his principal Colombian backers. Reacting strongly to these events, Cisneros concluded that he could no longer trust Colombian engineers in positions of responsibility. In his subsequent work, he swung back to heavy reliance upon his Cuban and North American associates.[27]

While hostility to the use of foreign technicians emanated most strongly from Bogotá, it was not confined entirely to the engineers in the eastern zone. In other parts of the country political engineers, often men employed by the departmental governments, sought to keep construction projects under state administration, rather than under contract to foreign companies. This occurred even in Antioquia. In 1892, after seven dismal years of state-administered construction of the Antioquia railway, the department's official engineer sought to avoid contracting the job to a British company.[28] In this case as in others, the criticisms of the Colombian engineers may have had some technical and economic merit. But professional self-protection as well as the personal desire to figure as technical experts surely entered in.

Though some engineers in Antioquia depended upon government jobs, engineering there was less politicized than in Bogotá. In Antioquia, mining, railroad construction, and, after 1890, the beginnings of manufacturing, were keeping most local engineers occupied. *Antioqueño* engineers lived in an environment in which economic enterprise was the center of attention. As a group they were much less politically involved than their peers in Bogotá. This apolitical and entrepreneurial orientation, welling out of Antioquia's circumstances, found expression in and was reinforced by the dominant spirit at Medellín's Escuela de Minas. The long-time rector of the school, Tulio Ospina, echoing the themes of his father, Mariano, insistently preached the virtues of work, discipline, and practicality. Having given the school the motto "Trabajo y Rectitud," Ospina in 1912 elaborated on its meaning: the school's program and purpose were to be less scientific than moral, its aim not to form learned men but honorable, hardworking ones. Ospina insistently held before his students the model of the orderly, energetic, persevering Anglo-Saxon, urging them to overcome any temptation of Hispanic inconstancy and disorder. Tulio Ospina and his successors as rector of the mining school encouraged Antioquia's engineers to be different from those in Bogotá—they should be practical men rather than bookish academics, industrialists rather than politicians. This conception, substantially founded upon Antioquian reality and regional attitudes, long remained the most prominent feature in the self-image of the *antioqueño* engineer.[29]

As residents of the capital, Bogotá's politically sensitive engineers could readily conceive of professional organization and journalistic agitation as a means of opening up new opportunities. The Bogotá engineers in their organ, the *Anales de Ingeniería* (1887–), tended to indulge in hyperbole when discussing the plight of the Colombian engineer. Abelardo Ramos, one of the country's most successful engineers, protested that the railroads undertaken with the government's money had been under the exclusive dominion of foreigners, and that native nonprofessionals were usually employed in other projects. He claimed that in 1887 of more than two hundred Colombian engineers and surveyors 80 percent lived "more than discouraged, forgotten," without "bread or position," and with their "virile nature—in which one day the country placed great hope . . . eaten away inexorably by the worm of pessimism."[30]

While the Sociedad Colombiana de Ingenieros often exaggerated the case, it does appear that native engineers were far from fully employed in their profession. Notices in the *Anales de Ingeniería* for the years 1887 to 1891 mention fewer than sixty Colombian engineers working in some fashion on public works. And most of these were sporadically employed. Only a few of the more eminent—such as Manuel H. Peña, Juan Nepomuceno González Vásquez, Abelardo Ramos, and Enrique Morales—are mentioned as working on more than a few substantial projects. The rest, able to pick up only scattered surveying jobs, had to support themselves by teaching, if indeed they were not forced to move entirely outside the profession. Those who did commit themselves to teaching had to contend with the job insecurity created by Colombia's mercurial politics and the consequent vicissitudes of its educational institutions.[31]

In defending the interests and status of the Colombian engineer, the Sociedad Colombiana de Ingenieros stressed professionalism and a mild sort of nationalism. They emphasized several themes—the need to expand and strengthen Colombia's technical education, the necessity of using national rather than foreign engineers on public works, and the desirability of creating a truly national style in engineering.

To support using native technicians, the *Anales de Ingeniería* constantly pointed to Colombian achievements, first to the Cúcuta railways and then to the railways built in the vicinity of Bogotá in the 1880s.[32] In emphasizing the good works of Colombian engineers the *Anales* did not systematically denigrate foreigners. Some foreign experts were not only respected but also venerated by Colombian engineers who had received valuable practical training in the field under their supervision.[33] Still, the Bogotá engineers could be remarkably niggardly in their praise of the foreigner. The Cuban engineer-entrepreneur Francisco J. Cisneros without doubt contributed more than any single individual building Colombia's railroads in the nineteenth century. Yet his obituary in the *Anales de Ingeniería* was short and not at all effusive; in fact, it emphasized the exploits of the Colombians who had worked under Cisneros.[34]

When construction disasters occurred, the engineering society in Bogotá took care to place the blame, whenever possible, on the miscalculations of foreigners. The collapse of an iron bridge over the Río Negro was attributed more to the errors of the American engineer who had ordered the superstructure from the United States than to the subsequent mistakes of Juan Nepomuceno González Vásquez, who erected it. Another article on this fiasco omitted mention of any technical deficiencies, attributing the bridge's failure simply to the vibrations set up by the passage of a "disorderly" herd of cattle. Similarly, when the government in 1891 sought a North American hydraulic engineer to reconstruct the defective Bogotá aqueduct, the *Anales* hastened to point out that the original constructor of the faulty aqueduct had been a Venezuelan; it was "*not the work of any of the Colombian engineers.*" Even when foreigners could not be blamed, the Bogotá society was ever ready to sally forth to defend the oeuvre of its members, whether it was attacked in government inspection reports or, more embarrassingly, when it was exposed by the elements.[35]

In their anxiety to prove their competence, many Colombian engineers put a markedly higher value on solidity of construction than on economy. They tended to take a craftsman's view of their work, in contrast with foreigners, who performed their tasks in a capitalistic and businesslike spirit, emphasizing cost-cutting rather than quality. There was a continuing tendency for Colombian engineers to criticize the shoddiness of the creations of foreigners, praising the soundness of native constructions by comparison. By the same token, in the opinion of some foreign experts, Colombians, in their concern for quality, sometimes built at unnecessarily high cost.[36]

Some of Bogotá's engineers advocated not merely the use of Colombian personnel but also the development of a spirit of national autonomy in the practice of their profession. Carlos Téllez, just after returning from study at Lafayette College, criticized his contemporaries for their tendency to think of engineering only in grandiose terms and to depend too much on the elaborate and expensive technologies of the more advanced countries. Colombian engineers were underemployed, he suggested, in part because they tended to conceive of their mission as involving only such obvious tasks as building railroads. Few of them thought of using their technical knowledge in more pedestrian ways. He pointed out that the many Colombian engineers who were not engaged in public works rarely thought of applying their talents to such "simple" things as agricultural improvements, or the modernization of sugar and flour mills, or better design and construction of peasant huts. Similarly, in the execution of public works, Colombian engineers were thinking too big. They seemed to assume that everything had to be done according to the latest technical modes developed in the United States and Europe. Colombians were building railroads at great cost, when they might have been better advised, given the country's limited financial resources, to concentrate on canals, cart roads, or even good mule paths. Nor was the country rich enough to import custom-made iron bridges for all its rivers, as was the tendency of the time. Rather than procuring expensive foreign materials, Colombian engineers should devote themselves to discovering and adapting native resources. Colombians in short should provide distinctively national solutions for national problems. "In a word, let us move in the direction of progress, having as our vehicle our generous profession, and as our motto the wise English counsel *Paddle your own canoe.*"[37]

Bogotá's engineers recognized the superiority of research and instruction in Europe and the United States; no one suggested that engineers ought to be educated at home if they could afford to go abroad. At least by the 1880s, those who studied abroad were warmly welcomed into the fraternity on their return to Bogotá.[38] At the same time the Bogotá engineers wanted to develop a more autonomous, more national scientific community. Occasionally the editors of the *Anales de Ingeniería* lamented that "our science is copied [*de copia o de compilación*]" and called for "the creation of our own science . . . and the resolution of our own problems." In the teaching of science and technology they sought to develop institutions and approaches adapted to Colombia's limited resources and its peculiar needs. The rector of Bogotá's engineering school emphasized that the best professors were those who "take the trouble to eliminate from the foreign texts that which is *too big for us* [*lo que nos viene grande*]" and to add to them what is needed to *"nationalize them."*[39]

Some Colombian engineers practiced this doctrine of self-reliance. José María Villa of Antioquia, trained at the Stevens Institute in the 1870s, allegedly was inspired to take up bridge building by the erection of the Brooklyn Bridge at the time of his studies in the United States. Yet, while Villa was stimulated by a foreign model, he also was known for his passion for using native materials, employing foreign ones only if there was absolutely no alternative.[40] Villa undoubtedly was exceptional in his independence. But other native engineers gave thought to autochthonous solutions for Colombian problems—inventing machines to process *fique* ("agave fiber") or suggesting ways of using bamboo for building bridges. *Antioqueños* took pride in the fact that their region was able to produce improved coffee-processing machinery, which came into use in that region and elsewhere. Whenever a Colombian engineer made shift with what was locally available, the *Anales de Ingeniería* celebrated the fact.[41]

Making shift with native materials or locally adapted mechanical devices was most characteristic of the provinces. Bogotá's engineers displayed their greatest originality in pure mathematics, which offered the delights of unalloyed intellectuality. Judging from the lore that has been handed down, much of their inventiveness was expended in mathematical games. And when they ventured into mechanical invention, it was to perfect scientific instruments that were about as relevant to Colombian economic needs as parlor toys. Some innovations were not stimulated by local technical needs, and others were not supported by local technical skills. The two Colombian inventions of the latter part of the nineteenth century of which Bogotá's engineers were most proud were Rafael Nieto Paris's electric clock and his tachometer constructed to specifications in London.[42] It is of course easy to see in the mathematical parlor games the Latin American dilettante as he is usually pictured. But one must consider the particular atmosphere of Bogotá with its community of politicians, educators, and literati and an economy that did not offer challenges compelling the attention of the scientifically skilled. It is also probably true that a lack of research equipment made mathematics the only field in which scientifically trained Colombians might hope to make some notable progress.

Aside from those associated with mathematics, Colombian innovations were quite limited. While some Colombian engineers considered local solutions to problems peculiar to their mountainous, tropical, capital-short land, most of them, whether in Bogotá or in Medellín, assumed that the answers were to be found abroad. For them, the only question involved choosing the most appropriate foreign-developed technology. This course is hardly surprising. In civil, mining, mechanical, electrical, and industrial engineering, the industrial nations were pushing back most of the relevant technical frontiers long before the Colombian economy approached them. Thus the developed countries offered many technologies that could be adapted. Given the limited number of Colombia's technical elite and the fact that the country's weak economy could hardly stimulate or support much scientific research, it was inevitable and rational for its scarce technical resources to be devoted to the appropriation and utilization of foreign models.

The one area in which peculiar Colombian circumstances might permit substantial innovation in advance of the industrial powers was that of tropical agriculture. But this was precisely the area the Colombian government neglected except for the years from 1878 to 1885. The failure to develop tropical agronomy may seem surprising in an economy heavily dependent upon the export of tropical products. To the Colombian elite, however, the primary problem of the export economy was poor transportation; thus, they focused on appropriating the relevant techniques of civil engineering. Moreover, the neglect of tropical agronomy is in keeping with the tendency of export economies to allow the industrialized nations to decide the direction of change. Just as the upper classes in Colombia and elsewhere in Latin America were bent on emulating the consumption patterns of the European bourgeoisie, they also let the industrial powers shape the character of local technical advance. They generally addressed themselves most resolutely to those national problems for which the outside world had created some solutions, neglecting those that were more purely local in character. Thus, although their rhetoric was nationalistic, Bogotá's technical elite remained effectively dependent upon the technology of foreign powers.

In their diagnoses of the plight of the Colombian engineer, the Bogotá group tended to blame everyone but their own fraternity. The government had betrayed them by hiring foreigners and amateurs and by providing insufficient support for technical schools and the engineering society. Similarly, the engineers had been failed by Colombian private enterprise, which, either because of *"la raza"* or a "limited spirit of association," had not mounted projects large enough to require professional engineers.[43]

It seems rarely to have occurred to the Bogotá clique that Colombian engineers might create employment for themselves by playing an entrepreneurial role. Although they were quite willing to administer already-established enterprises, rather few engineers attempted to organize ventures themselves.[44] Bogotá's leading national entrepreneurs, even in activities requiring technical expertise, were businessmen without any professional training—such as Camilo Carrizosa in bridge construction, electricity, and telephone service (1876–1889); Carlos Tanco in railroads (1886–1908); and Santiago Samper in electric power.[45] Engineers possibly had less access to capital than ordinary businessmen. But this seems unlikely: their technical knowledge ought to have put them in a relatively favorable position.

In the opinion of some Colombians, it was actually the character of the Bogotá engineers' training that inhibited enterprise among them. Echoing the Bourbon reformers, these critics complained that the engineering school in Bogotá overemphasized mathematical theory and paid insufficient attention to practical applications. The establishment engineers in the capital, who had staffed the institution off and on for three decades, protested that this was not the case. The engineering school found it necessary to emphasize mathematics and scientific principles because entering students were badly prepared; but, within the limitations imposed by inadequate laboratory equipment, the faculty always stressed the practical.[46] Given the emphasis on the practical in the articles they wrote and in the announced curricula during the 1880s, these protestations seem plausible.[47]

The engineers' lack of enterprise seems ascribable rather to their tendency to think of themselves as professionals and to define their functions narrowly and in accord with prevailing social values. The engineers in Bogotá conceived of themselves as public servants, scholars, and technical experts, but, for the most part, not even potentially as entrepreneurs. (This seems to have been less true in the provinces where men were necessarily thrown back upon their own resources.)

As the engineers in the capital developed into a self-conscious professional fraternity, these attitudes became stronger. Toward the end of the century the *Anales de Ingeniería* was taking pains to distinguish engineers from mechanics and skilled workmen. To the criticism that the engineering school in Bogotá was not producing manufacturers and tradesmen, the *Anales* replied that this was not its function. If such men were to be trained, they ought to come from separate schools of mechanical arts, agriculture, and commerce.[48]

At the beginning of the twentieth century engineers were beginning to play significant roles in political leadership, some of them emerging as cabinet ministers. As they came to the fore politically, their attitudes and actions approximated those long standard among lawyer-politicians.[49] In the same years the *Anales de Ingeniería* began to refer to some members of the fraternity using the title of *doctor*.[50] The ambiguities in neo-Bourbon values had been carried to a logical conclusion. Bogotá now had a corps of technically knowledgeable men in its upper class, but it still had too many *doctores*.

While Bogotá's engineers became incorporated into the dominant political patterns of the national capital, their peers in Medellín remained apart. Defining themselves professionally in accord with the dominant tendencies of their region, *antioqueño* engineers thought of themselves primarily as industrial entrepreneurs rather than agents of state policy. Although some, such as Pedro Nel Ospina and Mariano Ospina Pérez, became highly successful in national politics, *antioqueño* engineers continued to nurture the self-image of the apolitical, economically practical, hardworking *paisa*.

At the end of the nineteenth century some factors were working for the creation of an active Colombian technical community, or rather several technical communities. In both Bogotá and Medellín there was at least the beginning of an economic and technical base. There existed national organisms for scientific and professional communication. And some Colombians with technical training were seeking to create identifiably national works. On the other hand, dominant social values still inhibited direct involvement with mechanical processes. And Colombian engineers in fact did little of note in the way of innovation. They took little interest in tropical agriculture, a field in which they might have made some contribution. And in other areas the country's lagging economy posed few problems for which some kind of solution could not be found in the more advanced countries. The Colombian technical elite, therefore, remained consumers rather than creators of technology. Nevertheless, they did serve their country's development as mediators in the adaptation and application of foreign techniques.

Epilogue

THE ideal of technical development was a continuing preoccupation of the Colombian elite from the end of the colonial period onward. Some of Colombia's most important leaders, influenced by the Spanish Bourbon tradition as well as by contemporary developments in the more developed Western nations, actively sought to embrace the technical advances of the era. But the Colombian milieu could not easily incorporate these advances. Neither the country's static economy nor its system of social values provided a basis for the assimilation of Western technology, much less for the growth of technical creativity. Colombian leaders recognized these obstacles. They hoped that technical education would serve as a means of breaking through them, that in an otherwise hopeless situation it might provide the cutting edge of development. Events proved, however, that technical training could not be implanted until something approaching an appropriate economic environment existed.

Between 1821 and 1850 the efforts of the Colombian elite failed almost completely, and they were only marginally successful in the balance of the nineteenth century. By the last quarter of the century a corps of several hundred native engineers existed, though there were still five times as many lawyers and three times as many physicians. At the lower level, less than 7 percent of the male population described themselves as artisans or as engaged in manufacturing,[1] and, with very few exceptions, these Colombians were not engaging in technical innovation; at best they were rather capable executors of borrowed technology.

At every stage in Colombia's halting development of a technical elite one can perceive obstacles posed by the country's social structure and prevailing values. At every point, however, it is also clear that the mission of science and technology was thwarted as much or more by its inapplicability in the context of nineteenth-century political disruption and economic constriction.

The clear division between a small aristocracy and a subservient work force in many parts of Colombia placed a curse upon manual labor, weakened interest in technical improvements, and thus, in different ways, kept both classes from securing mechanical experience. Mechanization was also deterred, however, by the country's geographic configuration. Its mountainous terrain isolated Colombians from each other and from the outside world, inhibiting the development of a substantial national market or of foreign ones that would have provided incentives for engagement with the process of production and for technical innovation.

Similarly, the implantation of science was impeded in the nineteenth century in part by a strong orientation toward political and legal-bureaucratic careers that originated in the Spanish tradition of service to the crown. But, as the impact of Mutis and the Botanical Expedition shows, this orientation was not clearly detrimental to the development of science in the colonial era. Even though a number of creole lawyers held government positions under Spanish rule, as long as New Granada remained firmly under monarchical control, the life of public office did not detract from the mission of science. Indeed, for at least a few creoles the Botanical Expedition joined scientific research and the honor of service to the crown. The republican era brought a sadly weakened government and the elimination of effective patronage; it also multiplied political opportunities, and the resulting agitation of partisan politics beat down the cultivation of science. At the same time an economy constantly disrupted by political warfare provided few prospects for economic enterprise and almost none for technical careers. While the character and the control of the country's political structure remained major issues and the economy remained stagnant, the pursuit of the scientific and the technical receded into irrelevance.

The neo-Bourbon elite was eager to alter both prevailing attitudes toward manual labor and the upper-class orientation toward politics. But in the political and economic circumstances of the nineteenth century, the practicality of "practical" careers was not at all evident. Colombia's economy did not support many individuals who could have served as appropriate models. Some of the foreign engineers who came to New Granada in the 1840s were held up as examples of titanic industry, persistence, and creativity. But as foreigners they were exceptional and more-or-less outside the system. The best national models of entrepreneurial endeavor in this period were merchant-capitalists like Francisco Montoya, Raimundo Santamaría, and Juan de Francisco Martín. But such men, while practiced in the ways of commerce, had no formal technical training. Their relative success served as an object lesson in the practical, but also in the unimportance of technical training.

In any case, for New Granadan youths, the most compelling models were neo-Bourbon leaders. And their careers exemplified the dominant values. As models, these servant-tended aristocrats and political leaders tended to reinforce the very attitudes they condemned. Thus, they resorted to exhortation and even to feeble efforts at coercion to turn the country's youth of all classes in a new direction. But, as their actions spoke louder than their words, these gestures proved futile.

The hortatory-coercive style, however, was not simply an indication of the obstruction of new values by the prevailing system. It also typifies the reaction of upper-class leadership to a stagnant economy. Even in the United States moralistic exhortation and at least the thought of coercion were likely to be found in places not yet completely integrated into the national economy. In 1818 Dewitt Clinton and other aristocratic New Yorkers were agitating for an agricultural college, supporting the idea as a means of steering upper-class children away from prestigious but useless legal, medical, and ministerial careers and into more practical endeavors. And some members of the local elite in upstate New York at about this time were attempting to "compel the people of this State to improve themselves in useful knowledge, whether they would consent to it or not." Soon afterward the completion of the Erie Canal brought a boom to upstate New York, and with it came a local reorientation toward the technical that neither exhortation nor coercion could have obtained.[2] In general, as economic development proceeded in Western countries, the use of overtly coercive mechanisms became unnecessary; it became possible to rely on the incentives and disciplines of the free market.

At a remove of several paces in the process of development, much the same thing occurred in Colombia. During the export expansion of the 1840s and 1850s Colombian leaders gave up explicit coercion of the lower classes in favor of market disciplines. First they dropped the pursuit of vagrants; then in 1850 they completed the abolition of Negro slavery. Similarly, after 1847 the Bogotá elite abandoned the attempt to coerce the sons of the upper class into the study of science; after that time policy makers relied, first, on positive incentives and, after the 1870s, on the opportunities offered by the economy to draw youths into careers in science and technology.

The first use of positive incentives, the military school of 1848–1854, proved a significant breakthrough. It proffered elite identification and held out the illusion of socially desirable public positions, of a new bureaucratic profession. At the same time it defined the mission of science in attractive and obviously consequential terms: graduates would not merely teach science in *colegios*; they would be the heroes whose roads would bind the nation together. In a sense Mosquera's military school, with its corollary of government employment of engineers, brought together again some of the elements of the Botanical Expedition—public patronage and position in the service of national scientific and technical development.

These symbolic considerations were undoubtedly important to the success of the short-lived military school. But the careers limned for the cadets of the military academy had meaning only in the context of the large-scale road-building projects of the 1840s and the growth of foreign commerce in the subsequent decade. Similarly, the more continuous instruction in science and engineering of the years after 1866 obviously found some support in that era's elaborate plans for, but somewhat less notable activity in, road and railroad construction.

The behavior of the neo-Bourbons and later Colombian leaders interested in technical improvement suggests a certain ambiguity in their values, a limit to their commitment to their stated goal. Their passion for political life set a poor example for their countrymen. It is difficult to believe that such men as José Manuel Restrepo or Lino de Pombo could have pursued their aims without occupying high public posts, despite the self-contradictions this involved. Their refusal to accept an office would simply have meant that men who were less able and less dedicated to technical advance might have determined the direction of policy. But some of Colombia's most vocal promoters of progress went beyond fulfilling the obligations of public service, revealing political ambitions and an appetite for partisan conflict that contrasted with their professions of concern for the practical. Mariano Ospina and General Mosquera, among the most notable proponents of technical improvement, were also among the most disruptive of politicians. As leaders of the contending parties in 1859 the intransigent, intensely partisan Ospina and the recklessly ambitious Mosquera were largely responsible for one of the country's most disastrous civil wars. Their example, furthermore, helped to perpetuate among succeeding generations a clannish, destructive style in politics. What one hand built up with enlightened policy, the other devastated with the sword or undermined with political machinations.

The political irresponsibility of the elite extended beyond the country's many civil wars. There was a marked tendency even among relatively pacific politicians to take up projects one year and then to neglect them the next. While the discontinuities in the evolution of Colombia's educational institutions may be ascribed in part to civil war and frequent fiscal crisis, it is also true that Colombian policy was much affected by the vagaries of a few individual politicians. One strong individual, like an Ospina or a Mosquera or a Camacho Roldán, would set a machine in motion, but after he left the government it would be left untended and break down. In each case—Ospina's university reform, Mosquera's military school, Camacho Roldán's Department of Agriculture—a year or two of vigorous activity by one man would give the institution enough momentum to carry it a few years before it ground to a halt. The succeeding administration would have taken up a new hobby.

Both the violent conflicts and the policy discontinuities of the nineteenth century suggest something about the order of commitments of many of the country's salient political leaders. Those who were most politically active gave their first priorities variously to their personal vanity, their ideological convictions in noneconomic matters, and their particular political friends. With the threat of class revolution, as in 1854, they could find the common tie of maintaining the upper class. But in general, while they found material development desirable, it was not at the quick of their concern.

The political conduct of the Colombian elite can be seen not merely as the expression of a particular system of values but also as a response to the economic environment. Given the constricted economic opportunities in most regions of the country, the goal of technical progress tended to have a certain phantasmic unreality. In the context of nineteenth-century Colombia, material improvement was an ideal abstraction, like so many others imported from the advanced countries. Colombian leaders did in some way believe in this abstraction, but in their economic milieu it represented a formal value rather than a behavioral reality.

Politics and political aspirations, particularly during the first half of the century and outside Antioquia, were much more palpable than the possibility of economic achievement or technical progress. Thus Generals Obando and Mosquera and lesser caudillos, especially in such economically restricted areas as the Cauca and Santander, turned easily to military-political enterprise. Even after the growth of exports brought more economic life to some areas of the country, the changeable external market caused frustrations that played a part in turning some leaders to violent political activity.

Fluctuations in Colombia's export economy can also be linked to some of the discontinuities in nineteenth-century policy. Roads and railroads that were built to transport one area's commodity were often abandoned when that region's product lost its external market. Similarly, Salvador Camacho Roldán's Department of Agriculture, created in response to the crises in tobacco and cinchona at the end of the 1870s, wilted in the 1880s as these products waned in significance. More generally, as the government was heavily dependent upon customs duties, any marked drop in foreign trade resulted immediately in a weaker fisc and the curtailment of schemes initiated in relatively prosperous years.

Twentieth-Century Development

If economic and political instability interacted to obstruct technical development in the second half of the nineteenth century, political stability and a booming export economy provided the basis for relatively rapid growth during the first decades of the twentieth. About 1904 the pieces began to come together. The War of the Thousand Days (1899–1903) and the loss of Panamá (1903) shocked the Colombian elite into the realization that they could no longer afford the luxury of partisan conflict. The bipartisan and undictatorial dictatorship of Gen. Rafael Reyes (1904–1909) responded to the emergency with decision and some success, laying the groundwork for a period of political peace that lasted until the 1930s and remained substantially intact until 1948. Reyes's government and subsequent administrations were aided by the dynamic expansion of Colombia's coffee exports. Colombia's exports to the United States were 80 percent higher in the Reyes years than they had been in the preceding five. The country's total exports almost doubled between 1910 and 1915 and again between 1915 and 1920. From 1911 through 1922 Colombia enjoyed an almost continuously favorable trade balance, a distinct novelty in the country's history.[3] In an atmosphere of unprecedented prosperity the upper class turned its attention from politics to the planting of coffee.

Colombia's greater internal political and economic strength facilitated an increased flow of foreign capital. With the growing coffee economy providing more substantial freight, some of the major railroad lines not far from completion, and Reyes's 1905 settlement of the foreign debt question, British capital was, for the first time, invested in Colombian railways in substantial amounts. Now when foreign railroad companies, mostly British, showed a renewed interest in concessions, it proved possible to float the London loans required to finance construction. Between 1905 and the outbreak of World War I, the Colombian government was able to contract more than three million pounds sterling in new loans for railway building. Under these favorable circumstances railroad construction surged forward. Between 1905 and 1914 track was laid at a rate of about fifty kilometers per year, more than twice that of the 1880s and 1890s.[4]

By 1909 Bogotá was connected to the Magdalena River; by 1915 Cali was linked to the Pacific, and Medellín was not far from blasting its way through the central cordillera to finish its line to the Magdalena. In 1930 Colombia still did not have an integrated transportation system. Its two largest cities, Bogotá and Medellín, lacked direct rail connections, although both were linked by rail to the Magdalena River. During the 1920s and 1930s Colombia was also developing the beginnings of a highway network that helped to link unconnected railway lines.[5] And SCADTA, a pioneer in commercial aviation, supplied constantly expanding service from its inception in 1920. The invention and introduction of automotive and air transportation, as complements as well as competitors to the railroad, made possible the development of a kind of national market that this awkward nineteenth-century transportation device alone could not obtain in the abrupt Colombian Andes.

As the transportation improvements of 1904 to 1940 began to knit together a national market, significant innovations occurred in other economic sectors. Banking and commerce expanded and became more organized. Pedro Nel Ospina, as president of the republic between 1922 and 1926, secured the creation of a modern central bank, and in 1928 the Bogotá stock exchange was organized. During the 1920s commercial banking expanded rapidly and became more concentrated. In the same period business interests became more organized and increasingly influential. Most notably, the National Federation of Coffee Growers, founded in 1927, soon became a powerful special interest, almost a second government. Meanwhile, manufacturing, for the most part of light consumer goods, came to be founded on a permanent basis. These industrial developments began to occur before World War I, most notably in the environs of Medellín and Bogotá; but, subsequently, manufacturing spread to other urban centers. With the Depression of the 1930s, as Colombia's capacity to import suddenly collapsed with the coffee market, national manufacturing became firmly implanted in a protected market.[6]

The industrial and urban development that took place after 1904 provided Colombian engineers with many more opportunities than they had known in the 1880s. Before World War I a significant minority of Colombian engineers were engaged as administrators, and in some cases as entrepreneurs, of mining, manufacturing, and urban construction enterprises. The majority continued to hold public or semipublic jobs—that is, jobs in which political connections were likely to be an important element—but the kinds of public employment available had multiplied. The building and administration of railroads and highways still provided the most jobs, but now there were also positions for municipal engineers, administrators of utilities, and, especially, public administrators operating in a variety of nonengineering fields.[7]

The expansion of opportunities for both public and private employment did not eliminate the concern of Bogotá's engineers for the "defense of the profession." Often Bogotá's political engineers undertook this defense in the late nineteenth-century style. In 1904 the Sociedad Colombiana de Ingenieros, after a campaign of more than a decade, succeeded in having itself named an official consulting body; much of its effort in subsequent years was devoted to attempting to get the government to use its services.[8] Complaints about the employment of foreign scientists and engineers also surfaced from time to time. When Pres. Marco Fidel Suárez appointed a foreigner to operate the national observatory in 1920, the Bogotá circle, for whom mathematics and astronomy were a principal point of pride, summoned up a rage that lasted for a decade.[9]

During the Depression and World War II, when foreign involvement in Colombia slackened, concern about foreign competition apparently receded somewhat. But immediately upon conclusion of World War II, Bogotá's political engineers voiced alarm at the prospective influx of foreign technicians along with foreign capital during the postwar era. Leaders of the engineering fraternity raised the spectre of foreign loan contracts stipulating the use of foreign engineers on government projects.[10]

While continuing the traditional approach of soliciting government favor, Colombia's engineers in the twentieth century also began to take up more effective, less merely rhetorical, tactics. They began to enter more notably into politics, using leadership positions to advocate policies favorable to *criollo* engineering interests. Colombian engineers, for example, played a particularly important role in the movements to nationalize and rationalize the country's various railroads.

The nationalization of Colombia's railways, it should be noted, followed predictable economic and political patterns. The Colombian political elite in general found it possible in the first decades of the century to begin to think of nationalization because several of the major roads were nearly finished and because increased inflows of capital tended to reduce the country's dependency upon foreign companies. The theme of nationalizing the railways was first sounded by a few politicians in the Reyes administration, but it began to gain support in the Colombian Congress after 1911. The nationalist tendency carried the day when the United States' 25-million-dollar indemnity for its 1903 intervention in Panama began to arrive in 1922. This windfall encouraged even conservative leaders to work to liberate Colombia completely from foreign capital in the construction of new track as well as to buy up some stretches of track already constructed. The movement for national control culminated in 1931 with the establishment of the beginnings of a national system.[11]

But while Colombia's capital position had much to do with the movement for national control, the Sociedad Colombiana de Ingenieros also played an important part as a pressure group. The engineering fraternity had a double interest. Government control rather than foreign, private control of the railways would surely mean more jobs for *criollo* engineers. On another level, as engineers they had an interest (reminiscent of Thorstein Veblen) in government control as a means of rationalizing the railway system. In 1915 the first comprehensive plan for unifying the railways under national control was presented in the Colombian Senate by an engineer, Felipe S. Escobar, with the backing of the Bogotá engineering society. Escobar's plan, like later ones presented by members of the engineering fraternity, called for the employment of engineers in national planning (in a Corps of Engineers) in order to create a less wasteful transportation policy. Vocal spokesmen for the engineers increasingly favored the removal of policy decisions from the hands of a Congress susceptible to political influences and their transfer to a technocracy in the executive branch.[12]

As Columbia's urban industrial economy grew, Colombian engineers confronted the problem of specialization. Before 1935 Colombian technical schools offered practically none. The standard curriculum of the National University and elsewhere provided a basic single-degree course in mathematics and civil engineering. Only the Escuela de Minas offered a program in mining engineering along with its civil engineering program. While Colombian engineers did develop specialties they found it necessary to go abroad to do so.[13]

During the 1930s interest in specialized training began to build. While much work in standard civil engineering—for example, transportation development and urban construction—remained to be done, the expanding industrial economy was making new claims on engineers' services, and some educational leaders were beginning to see the need for degree programs in such fields as industrial, petroleum, and chemical engineering. In this movement Bogotá's National University did not provide the leadership that might have been anticipated. In 1936 the university attempted to establish new programs in industrial and military engineering and astronomy and geodetics. The first of these two efforts failed, however, for lack of funds and adequate faculty. Subsequently, leaders at the National University tended to take a dim view of specialization. Initiative in the new fields came from the provinces—the Universidad Católica Bolivariana in Medellín and, more surprisingly, the Universidad del Cauca in Popayán offered specialties in industrial engineering; the Escuela de Minas in Medellín provided a specialized degree in petroleum engineering; and the universities in Bucaramanga and Cali initiated specialized work in electrical and mechanical engineering. The Escuela de Minas also sought in 1941 to create a program in chemical engineering, but permission was denied by authorities in the National University in Bogotá.[14]

Bogotá's engineers took a more active interest in specialization, however, when the end of World War II resurrected the threat of competition from foreign experts. At this point they became more clearly aware that failure to create specialized training would simply make Colombia more dependent upon foreign expertise.[15] It was also evident by the latter part of the 1940s that much of the work in transportation development had already been accomplished and that industry, along with urban development, represented the probable areas of growth. Increasing numbers of engineering graduates were likely to be employed not as engineers but as business managers or national economic planners. From 1947 through the 1960s, therefore, the Colombian engineering schools moved to introduce more extensive training in such fields as economics and administration and to develop more specialized technical programs. This was an international effort, with Colombian engineering students and faculty going abroad for advanced training and international development agencies sending foreign experts to help implant specialized programs in Colombia.[16] By the middle of the 1960s Colombian institutions were granting degrees in fifteen engineering fields. While civil engineering remained the largest single field by a ratio of more than two to one, the recently expanded specialties of chemical, mechanical, electrical, electronic, industrial, and petroleum engineering were together attracting more students than the standard civil engineering course (see Table 11).[17]

This development of specialties was apparently further encouraged by the increasing demand for engineering services as Colombia carried forward its efforts at industrialization. At the beginning of the 1960s Colombian universities were producing about 210 engineers per year, and Pres. Alberto Lleras Camargo claimed the country needed twice that many. In 1961 the Faculty of Engineering in the National University more than doubled the number of students it admitted and planned continued expansion through the 1960s.[18] By 1960 it seemed that the Colombian engineer-

TABLE 11. *Engineering Students by Field, 1965*

Field[a]	Number Enrolled	Graduates
Civil	4,040	218
Transport	229	—
Sanitary	39	—
Chemical	1,482	106
Electrical	669	68
Electronic	1,170	34
Electro-mechanical	116	13
Industrial	239	36
Mechanical	1,430	72
Mines and metallurgy	467	19
Petroleum	159	12

Source: República de Colombia, Departamento Administrativo Nacional de Estadística, *Anuario general de estadística, 1965, culturales*, II, 159, 163.

[a]Agriculture, forestry, geographical engineering, and mathematics are not included.

ing profession had moved beyond its earlier defensiveness to a new period of optimism and self-confidence.

While the economic defense of the profession for some time remained a preoccupation of spokesmen for Colombian technicians, their position—in terms of political power and social prestige—has long been secure. In the nineteenth century, Colombia's agents of the practical—substantial merchants, the handful of men who attempted industrial enterprise, and the country's most notable engineers—enjoyed the respect of their fellow citizens. But, with the economic developments of the twentieth century, representatives of business, industry, and engineering have come to the center of national attention, and Colombia's lawyers increasingly have had to share their near monopoly of politics with representatives of the newer technical elites.

Since the last decade of the nineteenth century, engineers have served frequently in cabinet posts—first, almost routinely as directors of the Ministry of Public Works and then in other ministries whose functions most nearly deal with economic questions (Finance, Development, Agriculture). By the 1950s there were occasions when as many as four engineers served in a single cabinet.[19] More recently, Colombia's latest technical field—economics—has been strongly represented in national administration.

The currently high status of technical professions is also indicated by the appearance of members of the technical elite as national political leaders. Since 1910 businessmen and engineers have been prominent among the presidents of the republic. Carlos E. Restrepo, who succeeded General Reyes in the presidency, emerged from the business community of Medellín, as did Pedro Nel Ospina, who was a Berkeley-trained mining engineer and an industrial entrepreneur as well as a large-scale agriculturalist. His nephew, Mariano Ospina Pérez, who studied engineering at the Escuela de Minas and Louisiana State University, served as the executive administrator of the National Federation of Coffee Growers and was a prominent businessman in other sectors before becoming president in 1946. His successor as president, Laureano Gómez, also educated as an engineer, dominated the Conservative party from 1930 until the emergence of Ospina Pérez in the 1940s, after which the two vied for leadership of Colombian conservatism. A third significant Conservative leader, Gen. Gustavo Rojas Pinilla, chief of the military government of 1954 to 1957 and later leader of a significant third party, also had an engineering background. Some more recent presidents, though not engineers, have been strongly identified with the business community—most notably Carlos Lleras Restrepo for the Liberals and Misael Pastrana Borrero for the Conservatives. Other men educated as engineers, like Carlos Sanz de Santamaría and Virgilio Barco, while not yet elected to the presidency, have figured in the first rank of midcentury political notables.

The prominence of businessmen and engineers in political leadership in part reflects the fact that, during the twentieth century, a substantial proportion of the upper class has received technical training or has enjoyed notable business success. Thus, simply as a matter of statistical probability, one might expect a number of the country's leaders to be found in the technical-economic sphere. But the selection of businessmen and technicians for political leadership seems more than a random process. To some degree it is an expression of the intensified aspirations for and concern about economic development among Colombia's urban sectors. In the struggle to develop, men with some claim to technical and economic competence not surprisingly have been viewed as appropriate leaders toward as well as symbols of current national goals. Politicians of the old forensic type have tended to fall into discard. Significantly, whenever a man who failed to fit the mold of technical competence was selected for (more than elected to) the presidency, many members of the urban elites were moved to despair. Guillermo León Valencia, president from 1962 to 1966, a poet's son from seigniorial Popayán and a politician with an antiquated, florid style, provoked qualms because he had neither the economic or technical training nor the practical business experience deemed necessary for a man leading the country toward economic development.

Even without formally entering the political world, Colombia's technical and business elites have enjoyed immense prestige. Industrialists like the Echavarría family have been compelling symbols to all levels of the country's urban society. In quite a different manner the Canadian-born economist Lauchlin Currie was greatly admired by younger members of the urban sectors during the 1950s and 1960s, serving as a kind of talisman of development. Thus, the country's larger merchants and businessmen-in-politics, long esteemed in the society, have since World War II been joined at its apex by industrialists and university-educated technicians. These men, much more than the traditional landowning element and perhaps as much now as lawyers, are the power holders in the society.

The emergence of the technical elites may be viewed in functional as well as symbolic terms. The more complex, industrial economy of the twentieth century increasingly requires administration and regulation by technically trained bureaucracies. Thus engineers and other technicians have found not only positions of prominence but also places of power less in the public eye. In the period before 1930 railroad administration occupied many. With the creation of the Banco de la República and the National Federation of Coffee Growers in the 1920s, other technical bureaucracies sprouted. The push for industrialization since 1930 has implied the development of government ministries serving as well as regulating the new industrial interests. More recently the need to plan and coordinate the development of the industrial economy brought the creation of substantial agencies for gathering national statistics and planning. With the development of these administrative organisms dealing with the complex problems of industrial development, the exercise of real power in the government has shifted markedly from the Congress to the executive branch and to such autonomous bodies as the Banco de la República and the regional development corporations. The increasingly marginal role of Congress is reflected in the widely criticized frivolity and irresponsibility of its members. The decline of the old politics of representative government and the emergence of technocratic administrative power has necessarily had some impact on the relative prestige of the various professions. The law degree is still sought by many as a Colombian equivalent of a liberal arts degree. But the study of law is now widely recognized as less of a key to power than the study of technical subjects, particularly economics or business administration.

One instrument and expression of this shift in power and prestige is the University of the Andes in Bogotá, founded in 1949 after the model of the American private university by Mario Laserna, a young Conservative landowner and ideologue, educated in mathematics at Columbia and in Germany. In the spirit of Mariano Ospina, Laserna conceived of the University of the Andes as an institution completely removed from the influence of national or student politics and thus presumably able to offer technical training of a higher standard than was possible in the National University. To this end Laserna and his collaborators created a university with a strong program in engineering, including two years of study in institutions in the United States. They purposely excluded a school of law. In its early years the Andes had strong support from the Colombian political and business elite, American corporations, and the Rockefeller Foundation. United States oil companies provided scholarships, permitting even some students from the lower sectors of the upper class to fulfill the Andes' costly program. *Andino* engineers and economists have found rapid advancement in business and government economic administration. The University of the Andes thus has become, as intended, a seminary of a new technical elite, originating from various levels of the upper and middle sectors but emerging to be completely integrated into the top of the existing social structure. The *andino* style has, at least until recently, been distinctly one of technical proficiency and political quietism. In many respects, the University of the Andes has represented the fulfillment of the dreams of nineteenth-century neo-Bourbons.

The University of the Andes stands as a symbol of Colombia's practical oligarchy, but contemporary statistics show that it is not representative of the educational structure as a whole. While Colombian education is markedly oriented toward the technical and practical, it remains feeble in quantitative terms. Even among Latin American nations, Colombia's expenditures on education, in relation to national income, have been relatively low. It is one of those countries whose economy, as reflected in its gross national product, is stronger than its educational system. At the beginning of the 1960s Colombia's primary school enrollment ratios were among the low ones in Latin America, lower even than those of Ecuador and Peru. And secondary education remained a bottleneck: private schools accounted for 65 to 75 percent of secondary instruction.[20] As in many less-developed countries, the educational structure is weak at the base.

On the other hand, the system serves a people who apparently are now notably directed toward the practical, at least in terms of formal educational aspirations. During the early 1960s almost a third of the students in higher education were in science and technology, a larger proportion than in almost any other country in Latin America and than in all but a few countries at any level of development.[21] As of 1965 students in engineering and agronomic sciences accounted for more than half the university enrollment. Together with those in economics and business administration they constituted more than two-thirds of the total. In enrollment and in number of graduates there were more than four times as many university students in these practical careers as there were studying the law.[22]

Secondary education similarly places a relatively strong emphasis on the technical. An unusually high proportion of secondary instruction is of a practical character. Almost a quarter of Colombia's secondary school enrollment in the early 1960s was in commercial, industrial, or agricultural schools. There is also a somewhat effective worker training program that is financed and controlled by employers. But, in technical education as in the system as a whole, the lower strata of the pyramid are rather narrow in relation to the top levels. In 1965 almost as many students were studying agronomy at the university level as at lower levels. Only half as many students were learning urban industrial skills as were studying engineering in universities.[23]

The upper classes in Colombia have embraced technical careers, at least as measured in aspirations for degrees. But the system remains weak at the middle level and at that of the mechanic or skilled workman. This result follows logically from the goals and attitudes of Lino de Pombo, Mariano Ospina, and other neo-Bourbons. They wanted the Colombian lower classes to become more proficient and productive. But they were more concerned with employing technical training to sustain the position of their families, their friends, and their class in an economically changing but traditionally ordered society. As their first goal was the nurture and maintenance of the elite, training at lower levels, while not ignored by any means, received less consistent and less effective attention.

Colombian values have shifted as the country has moved toward industrialization, but they have not changed fundamentally. Industry has become much more important in the economy and in Colombian conceptions of the nation's future. For the threadbare white-collar class the goal of industrial development has become a projection of their own largely unrealizable social aspirations. The country's growing urban population both admires and envies the men who command the country's industrial destinies—its substantial manufacturers, engineers, and economic planners.

But while industrialists and university-educated technical experts are highly respected, they continue to operate in a society marked by deep class cleavages. Lower-level technicians and manual workers still lack status. Consequently, the high-level experts remain rather distant from the processes of production. Higher-level technical education and industrial practice are still rather formally related. Many manufacturing enterprises are weakened by lack of close direction from their elegant administrators, who form part of a bureaucratic culture rather than a shop culture. And it is doubtful that any member of the upper class or of the struggling white-collar group would consider overhauling a motor even as a hobby. As mandarinism persists, so too does its corollary, technical weakness at the middle and lower levels. Much of Colombia's upper class is now technically trained but still affected by aristocratic values.

Appendixes

APPENDIX 1. *Prominent Public Figures Who Promoted Technical Education, 1821–1864*

INDIVIDUALS WHOSE HIGHER EDUCATION OCCURRED PRIMARILY IN THE LATE COLONIAL PERIOD

Name and Vital Data	Antecedents	Higher Education	Travel	Principal Non-political Activities	Most Important Civil Posts
José Manuel Restrepo (b. 1781, Envigado, Antioquia; d. 1863, Bogotá)	Father *hacendado* and gold-mining entrepreneur, Antioquia	*Filosofía*, Bogotá, 1799–1802; law, San Bartolomé, Bogotá, 1802–1806; informal studies with Caldas and Mutis (astronomy, geodesics, botany)	Jamaica and U.S., 1816–1819	Speculator in gold-bearing properties in Antioquia; ironworks	Gov., Antioquia, 1819–1820; sec. of interior, 1821–1830; Council of Government, 1831–1832; dir., Casa de Moneda, Bogotá, 1828–1860; dir., tobacco monopoly, 1833, 1836
Alejandro Osorio (b. 1790, Bogotá; d. 1863, Bogotá)	Don Domingo Osorio and doña Juana Josefa Uribe; occupation unknown	Law, El Rosario, Bogotá, *abogado*, 1811	?	Jurist; public officeholder; ironworks, textile mill	Sec. of government and war, 1819–1821; Supreme Court, 1821–1825; senator, 1827–1828; sec. of interior, 1830; sec. of government, 1847–1849
Francisco de Paula Santander (b. 1792, Rosario de Cúcuta; d. 1840, Bogotá)	Father substantial landowner (cacao), Cúcuta	Law, San Bartolomé, Bogotá; studies interrupted 1810	Europe and U.S., 1829–1832	Military officer; large landowner	Vice-pres. (in charge of government), 1819–1828; pres., 1832–1837

Name	Family	Education	Travel	Occupation	Career
Alejandro Vélez (b. 1794, Envigado, Antioquia)	?	*Filosofía*, Medellín, with José Félix Restrepo and Liborio Mejía; math and military engineering (military engineer, 1815–1821)	Europe, ca. 1822–1824; U.S., 1826–1829	?	Con. gen. and chargé, U.S., 1826–1829; prefect, Antioquia, 1829–1830; sec. of interior and foreign relations, 1831–1833, 1839–1841; coun. of state, 1833–1839
Lino de Pombo (b. 1796 or 1797, Cartagena; d. 1862, Bogotá)	Grandfather Spaniard; father colonial administrator (treas., Consulado, Cartagena; super., Casa de Moneda, Bogotá); uncle prominent merchant & head of Consulado, Cartagena	*Filosofía*, El Rosario, Bogotá; math and military engineering with Caldas (military engineer, 1815); further study in math, Alcalá de Henares, Spain, 1816–1819	Spain, 1816–1820; England, 1820–1825; Caracas, 1842	Educator (math)	Sec. of interior and foreign relations, 1833–1838; dir. of national credit, 1838–1839; envoy to Venezuela, 1842; sec. of finance, 1845–1846; sec. of foreign relations, 1855–1857
Juan de Dios Aranzazu (b. 1798, Le Ceja, Antioquia; d. 1845, Bogotá)	Grandfather Spanish merchant, Honda; father Spanish, large landowner, Antioquia	San Bartolomé, Bogotá; studies interrupted, 1810	Mexico, Antilles, between 1810 and 1815; Venezuela, 1830	Large landowner	Chamber of Deputies, 1823–1826; gov., Antioquia, 1832–1836; sec. of finance, 1837–1840; pres., Council of State, 1841–1843; in charge of presidency of republic, 1841

Name and Vital Data	Antecedents	Higher Education	Travel	Principal Non-political Activities	Most Important Civil Posts
Tomás Cipriano de Mosquera (b. 1798, Popayán; d. 1878, hacienda Coconuco, Popayán)	Father & mother of rich landowning families, leaders in Popayán; father *sargento mayor de milicias, alcalde ordinario, regidor perpetuo,* Popayán; gov., Popayán, 1814; uncle Joaquín Mosquera *oidor* in Bogotá and Mexico, min. on Council of the Indies, and pres. of Junta de Regencia in Spain, 1812	Studied privately	Jamaica, 1817–1818; U.S. and Europe, 1831–1833; Peru and Chile, 1842–1845); U.S., 1851–1854; Peru, 1867–?	Large landowner; professional military officer; commission merchant in New York, 1851–1854	Intendent, Guayaquil, and then Cauca, 1826; min. to Peru, 1829; sec. of war and in charge of interior and foreign relations, 1838–1840; gen.-in-chief of army, 1841–1842; min. to Peru and Chile, 1842–1845; pres. of republic, 1845–1849, 1861–1864, 1866–1867; pres., Cauca, 1858–1863, 1871–1873
Joaquín Acosta (b. 1800, Guaduas, Cundinamarca; d. 1852, Guaduas)	Father Spanish merchant, Honda; large landowner and *corregidor,* Guaduas	Franciscans, Bogotá; law, El Rosario, Bogotá (incomplete); chemistry and other sciences, Paris, 1825–1830	U.S. and Europe, 1825–1830; Europe, 1845–1849	Large landowner; professional military officer; science professor	Min. in Washington, 1842; sec. of foreign relations, 1843–1845
Pedro Alcántara Herrán (b. 1800, Bogotá; d. 1872, Bogotá)	Father Spanish captain of infantry, *guarda almacen,* and medium-scale merchant dealing in imported goods bought in Cartagena and	Law, San Bartolomé, Bogotá, 1813, one semester; after this in military service	U.S. and Europe, 1830–1834; U.S., 1847–1849, 1850–1854, 1855–1860, 1861–1863; Peru, 1864–1865; Europe and U.S., 1868	Landowner; professional military officer; commission merchant in New York, 1851–1854	Prefect, Cundinamarca, 1828–1830; sec. of war, 1830; gov., Bogotá, 1837–1838; sec. of interior and foreign relations, 1838–1839;

Individuals Whose Higher Education Occurred Primarily in the Republican Era

Rufino Cuervo (b. 1801, Tibirita; d. 1853, Bogotá)	Great grandfather Portuguese mining entrepreneur; father provincial lawyer-merchant; uncle guardian priest, professor at San Bartolomé, gov. of arch-bishopric	San Bartolomé, Bogotá, 1814–1817; law, El Rosario, Bogotá, 1817–1819	Europe, 1835–1836; Ecuador, 1840–1842; Europe, 1843–1844	Lawyer; landowner; educator (law)	Prefect, Bogotá prov., 1831–1835; rector, central university, 1836–1837; dir., tobacco monopoly, 1837; negotiator of div. of foreign debt, 1838–1839; dir. of national credit, 1839; min. to Ecuador, 1840–1842; sec. of finance, 1843; Supreme Court justice, 1845–1847; *designado*, 1846; vice-pres. of republic, 1847–1851

1855–1856, 1861–1862; sec. of war, 1854–1855; sen. for Tolima, 1870–1871; pres., Asamblea, Antioquia, 1871; sen. for Antioquia, 1872

Name and Vital Data	Antecedents	Higher Education	Travel	Principal Non-political Activities	Most Important Civil Posts
Mariano Ospina (b. 1805, Guasca, Cundinamarca; d. 1885, Medellín)	Father "modest" or medium-sized *hacendado*	*Filsofía* with José Félix Restrepo, San Bartolomé, Bogotá, 1823–1825; law, San Bartolomé, Bogotá, 1825–1827	Guatemala, 1863–1871	Educator (law, *filosofía*, history); agriculturalist	Leader in prov. of Antioquia, 1832–1840 (pres. of prov. chamber, rector of *colegio*, deputy to national Chamber of Representatives); sec. of interior and foreign relations, 1841–1845; gov., Antioquia, 1845–1847; pres., Chamber of Representatives, 1849; gov., prov. of Medellín, 1853–1854; pres. of Senate, 1856; pres. of republic, 1857–1861
Anselmo Pineda (b. 1805, Marinilla, Antioquia; d. 1880, Bogotá)	?	*Filosofía* with José Félix Restrepo, ca. 1822–1824, San Bartolomé, Bogotá	?	Military officer; bibliophile	Prov. treas., Antioquia, 1835?; gov., Pasto, ca. 1840; gov., Panamá, 1842–1843; rep. of Antioquia in Congress, 1843

Bogotá; d. 1877)	Sabana de Bogotá; father lawyer and merchant, Síndico Procurador de la Real Audiencia (Bogotá), patriot leader; executed 1816	1826 doctorado in law, Universidad de Santo Tomás	1864		*oficial mayor,* Hacienda, 1837–1838; dir., national credit, and dir., public instruction, 1839–1840; sec. of finance, 1842; dir. gen. tobacco monopoly, 1843–1848; sec. of finance, 1857–1861; *designado,* 1861; gov., state of Cundinamarca, 1868
José María Galavis (b. 1808, Bogotá; d. 1851, La Mesa)	Father-by-adoption, *oidor* Dr. Eustaquio Galavis	*Filosofía* with José Félix Restrepo, 1823; law, San Bartolomé, 1825–1826	?	Bureaucrat; journalist; jurist; educator	Archivist, chief of section, *oficial mayor,* Dept. of Interior and Foreign Relations; gov., Cauca, Neiva, Popayán; sec. of war, 1847; sec. of foreign relations, 1848; Chamber of Representatives; *fiscal,* Tribunal de Cundinamarca

Name and Vital Data	Antecedents	Higher Education	Travel	Principal Non-political Activities	Most Important Civil Posts
Pastor Ospina (b. 1809, Guasca, Cundinamarca; d. 1873, Guatemala)	Father "modest" or medium-sized *hacendado*	Graduated in medicine, Bogotá	Guatemala, 1861–1873	Agriculture; education	Gov., Mariquita, 1842; gov., Cartagena, 1844; gov., Bogotá, 1846; consul, Lima, 1847–1849; sen. & gov., Bogotá, 1853; sec. of government, 1854
Lorenzo María Lleras (b. 1811, Bogotá; d. 1868, Bogotá)	Father rather unsuccessful Catalan merchant; mother from Panamá	Graduated in law, El Rosario	U.S., Jamaica, 1828–1832	Educator (prof. languages and educational administrator-entrepreneur, rector, El Rosario, 1842–1846; private school entrepreneur, Colegio del Espíritu Santo, 1846–1852); journalist; theatrical entrepreneur	Sec. of Senate, 1833–1834; clerk, Dept. of Interior and Foreign Relations, 1836–1837; Chamber of Representatives, 1850–1851; sec. of foreign relations and internal improvements, 1853
Manuel Ancízar (b. 1812, hacienda Fontibón, Cundinamarca; d. 1882, Bogotá)	Father Basque merchant, Bogotá, 1805–1810; *hacendado*, 1810–1812; *corregidor*, Zipaquirá, 1816–?; *hacendado*, 1819...	Graduated in law, Havana	Lived in Cuba, 1820–1837?; in U.S., 1838?; in Venezuela 1840–1846; in Ecuador, Peru, Chile, 1852–1855	Journalism; education (rector, National University, 1870–?; and Colegio Mayor del Rosario)	Sec. of foreign relations and internal improvements, 1847–1848, 1861–1862, 1876, 1879; New Granadan

| José Eusebio Caro (b. 1817, Ocaña; d. 1853, Santa Marta) | Grandfather *oficial mayor* in viceregal govt.; father *oficial mayor* in viceregal govt.; uncle employee in viceregal govt.; mother of notable patriot family | Law, Universidad Central and San Bartolomé | U.S., 1850–1852 | Journalism | Clerk, Office of Public Credit, 1838–1839; chief clerk, Dept. of Foreign Relations, 1842–1845; Chamber of Representatives, 1843–1844; sub-dir. of treasury, 1846–1848; sec. of finance, 1848; chief accountant of republic, 1848–1849 | revol. gov. of Gen. Mosquera, 1860 |

APPENDIX 2. *Students in the Care of Gen. Pedro Alcántara Herrán, 1848–1863*

Father or Guardian	Occupation and Place of Residence of Father or Guardian	Name of Student	Time and Place of Study	Subjects Studied	Adult Life
José Domingo Pumarejo (uncle)	Landowner and politician, Valledupar (Senate, representing Santa Marta, 1842–1843)	Manuel Pumarejo	1848–July 1853, place unknown	Surveying	?
Manuel Antonio Arrubla (father)	Merchant-capitalist (importing, construction); landowner; politician, Bogotá and city of Antioquia	Juan Pablo Arrubla	1848–? Charles Bartlett; College Hill, Poughkeepsie	Preparatory (a problem child)	?
José Ignacio Márquez (father)	Lawyer; jurist; law professor; politician, Bogotá (sec'y. of finance, 1830–1831; vice-pres., 1832–?; pres., 1837–1841)	Gregorio Márquez	1849–? St. John's (Fordham) (1850–1851); Phippen, Peekskill	English and grammar level	1859, married in Medellín
Valentín Ferro (father)	Military officer[?], Bogotá	Joaquín Ferro	1850–1851, St. John's; Feb. 1851, West Cornwall; Stamford	Grammar level	?

tions (11 or 14 yrs.); dir. of public instruction; subordinate posts; language instructor secondary schools and Nat'l. Univ.; author of dictionaries, grammars, translations, readers, poetry (*Lecciones prácticas del francés, Curso de inglés, Compendio de gramática castellana, Rudimentos de historia universal,* trans. Samuel Smiles's *Character and Duty*)

training

skill; North Cornwall; Guilford, Conn.; Colegio de Rojas, N.Y.

gotá, 1836; d. Bogotá, 1889)

Applied chemistry, 1852; civil engineering, 1853

1850, E. Hall, Ellington; W. A. Benedict, Plainfield; 1850, briefly, Brown Univ.; 1852 and 1853, Yale; B.Ph. degree, Sheffield special school

Rafael Espinosa Escallón

Bonifacio Espinosa (father)

Military officer, *jefe de sección,* Guerra y Marina, 1842, Bogotá

English; bookkeeping and other commercial training

Interned in insane asylum, New York

1850–1851, St. John's

Pedro Pablo Mosquera

Dr. Joaquín Mosquera (father)

Civil engineer (Canal del Dique, Cartagena, 1855; roads to Magdalena Santander region); dean of faculty of math, 1887

Landowner, lawyer, politician, Popayán; pres., 1830; vicepres., 1833–1835

Father or Guardian	Occupation and Place of Residence of Father or Guardian	Name of Student	Time and Place of Study	Subjects Studied	Adult Life
Jose Ramón Borda (Romero) (father)	Merchant, Bogotá	Ricardo Borda	1850–1851, St. John's; Mr. Robinson, Guilford, Conn.	Herrán urged mechanical engineering	?
Antonio Malo (father)	Lawyer-politician, Bogotá; sen. from Tunja 1840–1842, 1845–1848; residence Bogotá until death in 1857	Jesus Malo Blanco	1851–1852, Hall, Ellington; Rutherford, Hempstead	Problem child	1859, murdered his brother, gov. of Cundinamarca; execution delayed because of apparent insanity; escaped; traveled to New York; returned to Bogotá after inclusion in 1863 post–civil war amnesty
Dr. Miguel Macaya (guardian?)	Lawyer-politician-journalist, Cartagena, Riohacho; Chamber of Representatives in Bogotá, 1842–1845; 1848 in Riohacha	Manuel Cotes	1852–1854, Colegio de Rojas, Guilford, Conn.	?	?
?	? Panamá?	Hannibal Arce	1852–?, A. Bernard, New York	?	?

Name	Father	U.S. education	Subjects	Career
Alejandro Borda	José Rodrigo Borda (Romero) ? Bogotá	1852–1854, Hempstead Institute; Tarrytown; Mystic River; 1853, Yale, dropped out, Dec. 1853; private instruction, New York	Bookkeeping, arithmetic, ...ogy, agriculture, French, commercial accounting; mercantile practice in Herrán's commercial house	1858, applied for patent for use of steam engine in agriculture (denied); *alcalde*, Bogotá, 1870s; ...tives, 1876
Dario Calvo	Mariano Calvo (father) Merchant-capitalist, politician, Bogotá (Sec'y. of finance, 1831, 1841; Chamber of Rep., 1846–1847)	Fall 1852–1854, Colegio de Rojas; 1853–1854, Yale (did not graduate)	Applied chemistry, experimental physics, mineralogy, agriculture	?

Father or Guardian	Occupation and Place of Residence of Father or Guardian	Name of Student	Time and Place of Study	Subjects Studied	Adult Life
Vicenta de B. Galavis (guardian); maintained by Fernando Caicedo Camacho	Father, Dr. José María Galavis? lawyer-military, politician, Bogotá; gov.,, Popayán, 1841; Chamber of Representatives, 1842, 1845; gov.,, Tunja, 1845; sec'y. of war, 1846; sec'y of foreign relations, 1848; d. September 1851. (Caicedo Camacho–Conservative politician, Cali-Bogotá; Chamber of Representatives, representing Buenaventura prov. Cali, 1852–1854	Urbano [Galavis?]	Fall 1852–Fall 1854, Hempstead; Barnard; Jamaica, N.Y.	?	?
José Ramón Duran	Landowner, Gigante (Huila)	Fructuoso Durán	Summer, 1852–Sept. 1853, Hempstead; 1853, New Haven prep.	Prep. for engineering at Yale	Involved in civil war of 1859–1862 as a supporter of Mosquera; 1860, imprisoned by conservatives in Antioquia

			ford; Hempstead; 1853–1854, St. John's	ing, Yale	
Juan Francisco Jaramillo	? Medellín	Tulio Jaramillo	July 1853 through 1853, Rojas; Essex, Conn.	Prep. for civil engineering	?
Diego Uribe	Conservative, merchant-capitalist, Bogotá	Juan de Dios Uribe	July 1853–?, Rojas; Essex, Conn.	Prep. for civil engineering	?
Gil Ricaurte (father)	? Bogotá	Fructuoso Ricaurte	?	?	?
Luciano Restrepo (brother b. 1812)	Merchant-capitalist, Medellín	Félix Antonio Restrepo	July 1853–1856, Rojas; 1853–1856, St. John's	?	Jesuit?
Victoriano Restrepo (father)	Merchant-capitalist, Medellín	Manuel A. Restrepo	Fall 1853–?, Jamaica (N.Y.?)	?	?
?	?	Eugenio Gómez	Fall 1853–?, New Haven	?	Engineer; contributor to *Anales de Ingeniería*
?	?	Francisco Romero	Fall 1853–1854, St. John's	?	Imprisoned by Liberals in Cartagena, 1861–1863

Father or Guardian	Occupation and Place of Residence of Father or Guardian	Name of Student	Time and Place of Study	Subjects Studied	Adult Life
Francisco Fábrega	Conservative politician, Veraguas (Panamá); Chamber of Representatives, 1843–1844; gov., Veraguas, 1850, 1853–1854; Senate, 1853, 1859; vice-gov., Panamá, 1856	Francisco Fábrega	Fall 1853–Fall, 1854 ?	?	?
Julio Arboleda	Landowner, politician, Popayán	Rafael Arboleda (b. Popayán, 1842; d. Girardot, 1882)	1853–1854, St. John's; later to Europe; ca. 1859, Dresden	English; ultimately became engineer	Civil engineer, Spain, Portugal, Colombia; conservative politician in Chamber of Representatives, 1869; dir. of works, Ferrocarril de Girardot, 1882
Julio Arboleda	Landowner, politician, Popayán	Julian Arboleda	1853–1854, St. John's; ca. 1859, Dresden; 1862, Paris	English	?
Petronila Rojas de Tamayo (mother)	? Bogotá	Genaro Tamayo	April 1854–?, Colegio de Rojas, N.Y.	?	?

Europe)

Vicente B. Villa	Merchant-capitalist, Medellín	Eduardo Villa	?	?	?
Lázaro María Herrera	Merchant, Santa Marta; d. Bogotá, 1859	Tomás Herrera	1853–1854, St. John's	?	?
Lázaro María Herrera	Merchant, Santa Marta; d. Bogotá, 1859	Juan Herrera	1854–?	?	Juan David Herrera? physician, Bogotá, 1870s–1920s; prof. anatomy, Nat'l. Univ., Bogotá, 1880–?
José Pablo Rodríguez de la Torre	Conservative politician, Cartagena; 1843, Chamber of Representatives; 1855, vice-gov., Cartagena; 1857, Senate	?	Jan. 1855–?	?	?
Gregoria Castillo de Guerra (mother)	? Bogotá	Policarpo Guerra Castillo	1855–1857, went to Europe; returned to New Granada, June 1858	?	Imprisoned ca. 1866 in Paris as accomplice in fraud in a gaming house
Tomasa Ramón de Arango (mother)	? Panamá	Ricardo Arango	July 1855–?, Fort Edward	?	Gov., Panamá, 1886–1890

Father or Guardian	Occupation and Place of Residence of Father or Guardian	Name of Student	Time and Place of Study	Subjects Studied	Adult Life
Manuel María Mallarino	Cali-Bogotá; gov., Buenaventura (Cali), 1842–1844, 1853–1855; rep., Buenaventura, 1840–1842, 1850–1851; sen., 1845, 1854; sec'y. of foreign relations, 1846–1848; vice-pres., 1855–1857.	Victor Mallarino (b. Cali, 1840; d. 1921)	July 1855–Jan. 1857; went on to England	?	Life dedicated to secondary instruction
Lino de Pombo	Educator-politician, Bogotá; sec'y. of interior and foreign relations, 1833–1838; sec'y. of *hacienda*, 1845–1846; sec'y. of foreign relations, 1855–1857	Fidel Pombo (b. 1837; d. 1901)	July 1855–1858, Yale, B.Ph. Sheffield special school; 1858–1861, Paris; 1861, certificate in assaying	Engineering, natural science, assaying	Prof. mineralogy, zoology, Nat'l. Univ., 1862–1872; founder of Sociedad Colombiana de Ingenieros; contributed to *Anales de Ingeniería*; wrote on math, geology, paleontology; manager, Bogotá gaslight co.; store-owner (books and stationery)
José María Botero Arango	Merchant-capitalist, city of Antioquia	Pedro Luis Botero	1855–1856, St. John's; May 1858,	?	?

Arango	city of Antioquia				
?	?	José León Reyes	Nov. 1853–?, New Haven	?	?
Antonio G. Manrique	? Bogotá	Mariano Manrique (b. Bogotá, 1829; d. Bogotá, 1870)	Nov. 1855–?	?	Poet
Manuel María Mallarino	Politician, Cali-Bogotá (see above)	José María Mallarino	Jan. 1856–June 1857, Guilford; Hempstead; New Haven; June 1857 to Europe	English, accounting & other commercial	1860, involved in civil war as Conservative; taken prisoner; narrowly escaped being shot; 1878–1879, wrote for Conservative political newspapers
Blas Arosemena (grandfather)	Lawyer, judge, politician, Panamá	Blas Paredes	Fall 1856–?	?	?
Justo Arosemena (father?)	Lawyer-politician, Panamá (and Bogotá); 1848, sec'y. of rels. exts; 1855–1857, Senate; 1863, pres. state of Panamá	Demetrio Tomás Arosemena?	Jan. 1857–? New Haven, Yale, B.Ph.; 1858, Sheffield Special School	Engineering	?

Father or Guardian	Occupation and Place of Residence of Father or Guardian	Name of Student	Time and Place of Study	Subjects Studied	Adult Life
Pastor Ospina	Politician, Bogotá; gov., Mariquita, 1842, Cartagena, 1843–1844, Bogotá, 1845–1857, 1854; Senate, 1854; Chamber of Representatives, 1842; sec'y. of finance & government, 1854–1855; gov., Bogotá, 1858; sen., 1859; 1862–1868, in exile in Guatemala	Sebastián Ospina (b. Bogotá, 1846)	Feb. 1862–1863, worked in machine shop, Paterson, N.J.; 1868, attended Georgetown (did not graduate)	Math, natural sciences, mechanical engineering	1863–1868, in Guatemala, forming and running scientific and tech. school; to Colombia 1872?; refused rectorship, Univ. de Antioquia, to engage in agri. in Llanos; 1876, led conservative insurrectionists; 1877, killed.
Gen. Pedro Alcántara Herrán	Conservative, military politician, Bogotá; pres. 1841–1843; ambass. to U.S., 1847–1849, 1855–1860, 1861–1862	Tomás Herrán (b. Bogotá, 1846; d. Liberty, N.Y., 1904)	Georgetown; A.B. with high honors, 1863; M.A., 1868		1868–1880, prof., Antioquia; 1880, Escuela Militar & Nat'l. Univ.; rector, Univ. of Antioquia; dir. of public instruction, Antioquia; Nat'l. Min. of Public Instruction, 1898; consul, Hamburg; chargé, Washington, 1901–1904

vice-consul, Mede-
llín

tended 1864, did not
graduate

tary pontifical, Bo-
gotá; pres. 1841–
1843; ambass. to
U. S., 1847–1849,
1855–1860, 1861–
1862

candia Herran

APPENDIX 3. *Careers of Prominent Alumni of Colegio Militar, 1848–1854 (for whom data are available)*

Members of Class Entering in 1848	Antecedents	Principal Careers	Technical and Engineering Work	Educational Services
Joaquín B. Barriga (b. Bogotá, 1830; d. Chapinero, 1905)	Conservative family; father Gen. Joaquín María Barriga, gov., Panamá, ca. 1845; sec'y. of war, 1846–1849; dir., Colegio Militar, 1849–?	Engineering	1857, private practice as surveyor; 1866, official ass't. engineer, state of Boyacá; 1874–1876, chief of second section, construction, Ferrocarril del Norte; 1882–1885, chief of section, construction, Ferrocarril de la Sabana; 1896, railroad in Zipaquirá saltmines	?
José Cornelio Borda Sarmiento (b. hacienda near Facatativá, 1829 or 1830; d. Callao, 1866)	Father *hacendado*; conservative family	Engineering (in France ca. 1850–1858); politics (fought in civil war, 1860–1863; 1866, killed by explosion in defense of Callao, Peru)	1857–1858, asked to examine Codazzi route to Magdalena; 1858, official assayer; 1858–1860, dir., national observatory, Bogotá	1863, taught physics in Colegio del Estado, Medellín
Ignacio Ortega	Bogotá military-political elite; Conservative	?	1866, official engineer; state of Cundinamarca	?
Rafael Pombo (b. Bogotá, 1833; d. 1912)	Respected aristocratic family entrenched and influential in Cartagena, Popayán, Bogotá; Conservatives; father Lino de Pombo, educator, poli-	Poet and general literatus; diplomat; educational functionary	?	1851–1854 prof. math, Colegio de San Buenaventura, Bogotá; 1873–? functionary in Dirección nacional de Instrucción Pública: published in *La*

Name	Family background	Profession	Career	Academic positions
D'Elhuyar (b. hacienda near Bogotá 1833; d. 1904)	largest landowning families in New Granada; Conservatives; father graduate of El Rosario and military officer in Independence, *jefe politico* of Bogotá, ca. 1845–1849; maternal grandfather Juan José D'Elhuyar, royal mineralogist, 1785–1796.		state of Antioquia; 1874–1876, chief of third section, construction, Ferrocarril del Norte; 1879–1880, on commission studying Girardot railroad route; 1881, report for national government on Puerto Wilches railroad	
Antonio Dussán Manrique (b. Villavieja [Neiva]; d. 1876)	Father José María Dussán, *hacendado*, provincial upper class; probably Liberal	Military; politician (became *gen. de brigada* in civil war of 1860; died in battle, 1876)	1866, ass't. engineer, state of Santander; ca. 1868–1875, surveyor, state of Tolima	1866–1867, rector of Escuela Militar i Politécnica, Bogotá
Juan Nepomuceno González Vásquez (b. Zipaquirá 1838; d. Bogotá 1910)	Provincial upper class; politics unclear, probably Liberal	Engineering of roads & railroads	Ca. 1861–1863, built bridges, Italy; 1863–1865, studied Poncet route to Magdalena River; 1864, "Engineer of the Republic"; 1866, official engineer, state of Santander; 1865–1869, built Cúcuta cartroad; 1869, worked on Cambao cartroad; 1869, studied route from Cúcuta to Magdalena; 1871, built mulepath to Villavicencio; 1872–1874, explorations for Ferrocarril del Norte; 1874–1876, chief of technical corps, same	1870, prof. geodesics and machinery, Nat'l. Univ.

Members of Class Entering in 1848	Antecedents	Principal Careers	Technical and Engineering Work	Educational Services
Manuel Ponce de León (b. Bogotá, 1829; d. Bogotá, 1899)	Respected Bogotá family; descended from Gen. Francisco de P. Vélez.	Engineering; teaching; gov't. posts—dir. of public works; 1891, subsec'y. of *fomento*; 1896, min. of treasury	1856, studied camino del Chocó, road to Amba-lema, other roads; 1858, maps and plans for salt-works, Zipaquirá, etc.; 1861–1866, publication of Codazzi maps; 1866–1867, chief engineer, state of Cundinamarca; worked on construction of cartroads of Cambao and Agualarga, Ferrocarril de la Sabana, bridges in Bo-gotá; 1874–1876, chief of first section, construc-tion, Ferrocarril del Norte; manager, Fe-rrocarril de la Sabana	1852–1853, taught math, Colegio Militar; prof. cal-culus, mechanics, con-struction, school of en-gineering, Nat'l Univ.; rector, faculty of math, Nat'l. Univ.
Juan Francisco Urrutia	Member of distinguished Popayán family; Con-servatives	?	1857, report on road from el Socorro to the Magda-lena River	?
Juan Estéban Zamarra (b. 1828; d. 1871)	Extremely poor, born in hut; protected and edu-cated by Bishop of Antio-quia; first education in seminary; seemingly Conservative	Lawyer (after Colegio Militar, studied law in Bogotá); 1855, at age 27, justice of Supreme Court	?	?

Bogotá)

Name	Politics/Background	Field	Activities
	elite; Conservatives; nephew of Gen. José María Ortega Nariño, dir. Colegio Militar, 1847–1849		state of Magdalena; 1872–1874; plotted route for railroad connecting Cúcuta with Magdalena River; 1879–1885, constructed Cúcuta railroad; 1887–1889, worked on Ferrocarril de la Sabana; 1889–1892, dir., Ferrocarril de la Sabana; 1898, inspected del Norte, Girardot, and Cauca railroads for natl. gov.
Indalecio Liévano (b. Carmen de Apicala, Tolima, 1834; d. Bogotá, 1913)	Politics unclear, probably Liberal	Engineering, scientific and technical instruction	1858, plan for railroad, Zipaquirá–Nemocón; 1859, appointed to Comisión Corográfica; 1863–1865, studied Poncet route to Magdalena River; 1866, nat'l. chief of engineers; 1879–1880, explored Girardot route for national government; 1884–1889, contract for construction of muleroad over Poncet route. 1850s, private instruction in surveying and engineering; 1866, prof. math, Colegio Militar y Escuela Politécnica and San Bartolomé; 1872, prof., Instituto de artes y Oficios; dir., National Observatory; published arithmetic and algebra texts; *Investigaciones científicas*; *Instrucción popular sobre meteorología agrícola* (special reference to indigo and coffee)

Members of Class Entering in 1848	Antecedents	Principal Careers	Technical and Engineering Work	Educational Services
Manuel H. Peña (b. Zipaquirá, 1836; d. New York, 1900)	Provincial upper class, definitely Liberal	Engineering; scientific and technical instruction	1864, private practice as surveyor; 1865–1866, surveys of disamortized church lands; 1866, official engineer, state of Boyacá; 1874, subchief, first section, construction, Ferrocarril del Norte; 1879–1880, on commission to study Girardot route; construction, Cambao road and mulepath from Huila to Cauca; 1882, engineer-in-chief, Ferrocarril de la Sabana; 1886–1889, construction, Girardot railroad; technical director, Bogotá aqueduct; studies of Samacá ironworks, draining of Lake Fuquene, and Medellín aqueduct; 1890s, government representative, Ferrocarril del Pacifico; 1898, inspected Ferrocarril de la Sabana; 1898–1899 director, construction, Ferrocarril de Girardot	1856–1867, directed private *colegio*, Zipaquirá; 1866, math, el Rosario; surveying, San Bartolomé; 1870, math, School of Engineering, Nat'l. Univ.

1837; d. Bogotá, 1901)

family in Cartagena, Popayán, Bogotá; Conservative; father Lino de Pombo, educator, politician, sec'y. of interior and foreign relations, 1833–1838; sec'y. of finance, 1845–1846; sec'y. of foreign relations, 1855–1857; many other posts

science

dinamarca *en diversas épocas"*

ogy, geology, metallurgy, zoology, Nat'l. Univ.; published works on geology and paleontology; treatise on infinitesimal calculus; wrote for *Anales de Ingeniería*

Notes

Abbreviations Used

AH   Archivo Herrán, Academia de Historia, Bogotá
ANCR   Archivo Nacional de Colombia, República, Bogotá
B.A.E.   Biblioteca de Autores Españoles
BHA   *Boletín de Historia y Antigüedades*
CN   *Codificación nacional de todas las leyes de Colombia desde el año de 1821, hecha conforme a la ley 13 de 1912, por la Sala de Negocios Generales del Consejo de Estado* (34 vols. [to 1884], Bogotá: Imprenta Nacional, 1924–1955)
DO   *Diario Oficial*, Bogotá
GNG   *Gaceta de la Nueva Granada*, Bogotá
GO   *Gaceta Oficial*, Bogotá
Memorias   The annual reports of Colombian ministers of state to the national congress (These reports have long and varying titles. Following the custom of Colombian scholars, this study cites these reports simply as Memorias, with the years [e.g., Memoria de Hacienda, 1835].)
Vargas Cartas   Commercial letters of Inocencio Vargas é Hijos (later Francisco Vargas y Hermanos), Bogotá

Introduction

1. A common view of Latin American values as they relate to development is summarized in Seymour Martin Lipset, "Values, Education, and Entrepreneurship," in *Elites in Latin America*, ed. Seymour Lipset and Aldo Solari, particularly pp. 5–21.

2. Aldo Solari, "Secondary Education and the Development of Elites," in *Elites in Latin America*, ed. Lipset and Solari, pp. 477–478.

3. William J. Callahan, *Honor, Commerce and Industry in Eighteenth-Century Spain*, pp. 1–6.

4. John Tate Lanning, *Academic Culture in the Spanish Colonies*, p. 9.

5. The importance of evenly distributed income in creating a demand for standardized factory-produced goods in England is discussed by David S. Landes in *The Unbound Prometheus*, pp. 47–52; for a discussion of the same phenomenon in the United States, see George H. Daniels, "The Big Questions in the History of American Technology," *Technology and Culture* 11, no. 1 (January 1970): 21; Nathan Rosenberg, *Technology and American Economic Growth*, p. 48.

6. Landes, *Unbound Prometheus*, pp. 66–72; Joseph Wickham Roe, *English and American Tool Builders*;

Eugene S. Ferguson, ed., *Early Engineering Reminiscences (1815–1840) of George Escol Sellers*; Monte A. Calvert, *The Mechanical Engineer in America, 1830–1910*, pp. 3–14.

7. Hugh Kearney, *Scholars and Gentlemen*; A. E. Musson and Eric Robinson, *Science and Technology in the Industrial Revolution*.

8. Jean Sarrailh, *L'Espagne éclairée de la seconde moitié du XVIIᵉ siècle*, pp. 165–184; Richard Herr, *The Eighteenth-Century Revolution in Spain*, pp. 33–34, 37–52, 387.

9. Callahan, *Honor, Commerce and Industry*.

10. Jaime Jaramillo Uribe, *El pensamiento colombiano en el siglo XIX*, pp. 22–24, 36–40, passim.

11. Of the letters received by Francisco de Paula Santander from Colombians traveling abroad (1825–1838), technical education was discussed in one of fourteen from Domingo Acosta, one of three from Joaquín Acosta, none of six from Pedro Alcántara Herrán, and none of eight from Alejandro Vélez (Roberto H. Cortázar, comp., *Correspondencia dirigida al General Francisco de Paula Santander*, I, 30–80; VI, 320–342; XIII, 457–467; XIV, 7–10). Of sixty-one of Santander's own letters written while in Europe and the United States (1829–1832), two made reference to European scientists, one to foreign education, and one to primary education (Roberto H. Cortázar, comp., *Cartas y mensajes del General Francisco de Paula Santander*, VIII, 31–208). Other useful sources on the attitudes and interests of these men while traveling abroad are José Manuel Restrepo, *Autobiografía*, pp. 24–27,

101–153, passim; *Diario del General Francisco de Paula Santander en Europa y los EE. UU., 1829–1832*; J. León Helguera and Robert H. Davis, eds., *Archivo epistolar del General Mosquera*, vol. 1; Soledad Acosta de Samper, *Biografía del General Joaquín Acosta*, pp. 107–315; Luis Augusto Cuervo, ed., *Espistolario del doctor Rufino Cuervo*, I, 320–346, passim; Ignacio Gutiérrez Ponce, *Vida de don Ignacio Gutiérrez Vergara y episodios históricos de su tiempo*, pp. 230–242.

1. Opportunities and Incentives

1. Robert Louis Gilmore and John Parker Harrison, "Juan Bernardo Elbers and the Introduction of Steam Navigation on the Magdalena River," *Hispanic American Historical Review* 28, no. 3 (August 1948): 336–338; Robert Louis Gilmore, "Federalism in Colombia, 1810–1858" (Ph.D. dissertation), p. 2.

2. Argentina's population did not exceed Colombia's until the 1890s. See J. de D. Higuita, "Estudio histórico analítico de la población colombiana en 170 años," *Anales de Economía y Estadística*, April 24, 1940, Suplemento, pp. 3–6; James R. Scobie, *Argentina*, p. 32.

3. Francisco Silvestre, *Descripción del Reyno de Santa Fe de Bogotá escrita en 1789 por D. Francisco Silvestre, secretario que fué del virreinato y antiguo gobernador de la provincia de Antioquia*, p. 40, passim; José Gaviria Toro, *Monografía de Medellín*, p. 11; *Guía oficial i descriptiva de Bogotá*; "Noticias estadísticas de la provincia de

Bogotá en el año de 1844," in Provincia de Bogotá, *Colección de todos los decretos de interés jeneral espedidas por la honorable cámara de la Provincia de Bogotá, desde 1832 . . . hasta 1843; Anuario estadístico de Colombia 1875*, pp. 28–46.

4. Miguel María Lisboa, *Relaçao de uma viagem a Venezuela, Nova Granada e Equador*, pp. 227–229. Other enthusiastic descriptions are in William Duane, *A Visit to Colombia*, pp. 460–477; William D. Robinson, *A Description of the Valley of Bogotá in the Republic of Colombia*, pp. 5–8.

5. Report of Henry Tracy on road from el Socorro to the Magdalena River, March 15, 1848, in *El Neo-Granadino*, September 16, 1848; "Camino de Honda," *El Neo-Granadino*, July 14, 1849; Ramón Guerra Azuola, "Apuntamientos de viaje" [1855], *BHA* 4 (January 1907): 430–443.

6. Frank Robinson Safford, "Commerce and Enterprise in Central Colombia, 1821–1870" (Ph.D. dissertation), Table 1, pp. 460–463.

7. Estanislao Gómez Barrientos, *Don Mariano Ospina y su época*, I, 47–48; Joaquín de Finestrad, "El vasallo instruido en el estado del Nuevo Reino de Granada y en sus respectivas obligaciones" [1783], in *Los comuneros*, ed. Eduardo Posada, p. 119; Basilio Vicente de Oviedo, *Cualidades y riquezas del Nuevo Reino de Granada*, pp. 49–50, 120–140; Pedro Fermín de Vargas, *Pensamientos políticos y memorias sobre la población del Nuevo Reino de Granada*, pp. 50–51.

8. Gabriel Giraldo Jaramillo, ed., *Relaciones de mando de los virreyes de la Nueva Granada*, pp. 35, 49–50, 61, 71–72, 123–126, 151, 162, 174–175; *The Present State of Colombia*, pp. 286–287; Henry Birchall, in *New Granada*, by John Diston Powles, p. 23.

9. Vargas, *Pensamientos políticos*, pp. 18–19, 24–30, 39–40; Rensselaer Van Rensselaer to Gen. Solomon Van Rensselaer, May 13, 1829, in *A Legacy of Historical Gleanings*, ed. Catherina V. R. Bonney, I, 483; Luis Ospina Vásquez, *Industria y protección en Colombia, 1810–1930*, p. 72.

10. On the spread of *polvillo*, see Francisco José de Caldas, "Memoria sobre la nivelación de las plantas . . . ," in *Obras de Caldas*, ed. Eduardo Posada, pp. 88–90; José Manuel Restrepo, *Diario político y militar*, II, 304, and IV, 528. On English plows, see *GNG*, October 27, 1833; on experiments with seed, see *GNG*, November 29, 1835, and José Manuel Restrepo, "Trigo chileno," *GNG*, January 29, 1837.

11. Safford, "Commerce and Enterprise," pp. 170–186.

12. Ibid.

13. These communities are presented as archetypes. There was considerable variation within each of these regions. Other parts of the country are not discussed here in order not to burden the reader.

14. In the 1760s, Oviedo, *Cualidades*, pp. 96–98, 100–110, 120–170, described most highland communities to the north of Bogotá as having considerably fewer Indians than "whites." Many of the people he classified as white were in reality mestizos.

15. Gaspard Theodore Mollien, *Travels in the Republic of Colombia in*

the Years 1822 and 1823, p. 77; *Present State of Colombia*, p. 291.

16. Oviedo, *Cualidades*, pp. 174–182; Finestrad, "El vasallo instruido," pp. 118–120; Vargas, *Pensamientos políticos*, pp. 83–84.

17. James J. Parsons, *Antioqueño Colonization in Western Colombia*, pp. 36–42, 60–95, passim. Silvestre, *Descripción del Reyno de Santa Fé de Bogotá*, pp. 187–193, 217–218, gives a very mixed picture of the state of Antioquia's economy and society in the latter part of the eighteenth century. Finestrad, "El vasallo instruido," pp. 135–136, emphasizes the concentration of wealth in the hands of merchants.

18. Ramón Zapata, *Dámaso Zapata ó La reforma educacionista en Colombia*, pp. 174–200.

19. In 1870 servants made up 10.5 percent of the population of Santander, 13 percent of Cundinamarca, and less than 5 percent of Antioquia, Bolívar, Boyacá, and the Cauca. Santander and Cundinamarca also had large numbers of vagrants; each counted more than six thousand or close to 1.5 percent of their populations. Vagrants made up more than 1 percent of the enumerated population of the eastern region as a whole, closer to 0.1 percent elsewhere (*Anuario estadístico . . . 1875*, pp. 22–27).

20. Vargas, *Pensamientos políticos*, p. 78; Eduardo Posada and Pedro M. Ibáñez, eds., *Relaciones de mando*, pp. 238–239, 456–459, 474–477.

21. Some liberals during the 1860s began to see that the land system tended to deter effective production but were not led by this conclusion to a wholesale attack on large holdings (S. S. [Silvestre Samper], "Cultivo del

tabaco," *La Opinión*, January 13, 1964; Felipe Pérez, *Jeografía de Tolima*, p. 56 [in his *Jeografía física i política de los Estados Unidos de Colombia*].

22. Manuel Ancízar, *Peregrinación de Alpha por las provincias del Norte de la Nueva Granada, en 1850–1851*, pp. 83, 92, 152.

23. For example, see *El Tiempo*, May 18, June 8, June 15, 1858.

24. In the newly founded town of Barichara, one late-eighteenth-century marriage was delayed for more than four years as both parties carried on protracted searches in Spain for documents certifying legitimate Spanish descent (Federico Vargas de la Rosa, "Arbol genealógico de la familia de Vargas de Barichara," manuscript in possession of Don Pedro Vargas, Bogotá).

25. Ignacio Gutiérrez Ponce, *Vida de Don Ignacio Gutiérrez Vergara y episodios históricos de su tiempo (1806–1877)*, pp. 29–34; Eduardo Posada, ed., *Cartas de Caldas*, pp. 1, 5.

26. Augusto Le Moyne, *Viajes y estancias en America del Sur*, p. 128.

27. The best example is Samuel Sayer, who moved through blacksmithing and brewing into a position of great respectability. Many others could be adduced.

28. Hugo Latorre Cabal, *Mi novela*, pp. 56–178, 207–208, 212–214.

29. Ignacio Gutiérrez Vergara to Rufino Cuervo, January 12, 1841, in *Epistolario del Doctor Rufino Cuervo*, ed. Luis Augusto Cuervo, II, 182.

30. See *Dote* of 9,000 pesos to Mauricio Rizo by José María Portocarrero and Josefa Ricaurte, January 9, 1837, Notaría 3ª Bogotá, 1837, v. 388, fols. 6, 8. Five percent on the value of land seems to have been the expected

income of Sabana landowners ("Don Simón o el usurero," *El Día*, December 15, 1844; *El Agricultor*, May 21, 1868). See a sneering account of Bogotá's capital resources in John Steuart, *Bogotá in 1836–7*, pp. 249–252.

31. José Eusebio Caro considered less than 1,500 pesos sufficient to maintain his wife and three children for two years, and his brother Diego's fondest dream was to combine two government salaries into an income of less than 2,500 pesos (José Eusebio Caro, *Epistolario*,. pp. 135, 280).

32. *Letters written from Colombia during a Journey from Caracas to Bogota, and thence to Santa Martha in 1823*, p. 152; Mollien, *Travels*, pp. 120–121, 199–201; Le Moyne, *Viajes*, p. 147. For a fuller exposition of this theme, see Safford, "Commerce and Enterprise," pp. 45–48.

33. Steuart, *Bogotá*, p. 152.

34. Lisboa, *Relaçao*, p. 241.

35. Leland H. Jenks, *The Migration of British Capital to 1875*, pp. 44–49, 63–64; Vicente Restrepo, *Estudio sobre las minas de oro y plata de Colombia*, pp. 135–137; Robert Arthur Humphreys, ed., *British Consular Reports on the Trade and Politics of Latin America, 1824–1826*, pp. 252–271.

36. Aníbal Galindo, "Historia de la deuda extranjera," *Anales de la Universidad* 5 (1871): 264–288; *GNG*, September 12, 1841; Clímaco Calderón, *Elementos de hacienda pública*, pp. 260–290.

37. In 1851, 377 of the 827 Europeans and North Americans in New Granada were residents of Panamá ("Noticias estadísticas de la provincia de Bogotá en el año de 1844," p. 7; "Cuadro de los estranjeros existentes en la República al

tiempo de levantar el censo de población de 1851," ANCR, Ministerio de Gobierno, Sección 3a, 1848–1855, tomo 556, fol. 677).

38. Francis Hall, *Colombia*, pp. 75–82, 91–93, 112–115, *Present State of Colombia*, pp. 171–181; José Manuel Restrepo, Memoria de lo Interior, 1827, p. 17; Steuart, *Bogotá*, pp. 165–171, 176–182, passim.

39. Frank Safford, "Significación de los antioqueños en el desarrollo económico colombiano," *Anuario Colombiano de Historia Social y de la Cultura*, no. 3 (1967), pp. 49–69.

40. Mollien, *Travels*, pp. 207, 434, purports to make an estimate for all of Gran Colombia (including Venezuela and Ecuador), but his calculation of domestic agricultural production seems to have been extrapolated from the *diezmo* ("tithe") figures for Antioquia, 1800–1804. Antioquia was not representative, as its economy was weighted heavily to mining. But *diezmo* figures for other parts of the country in later years produce about the same result (see, for example, Mariano Calvo, Memoria de Hacienda, 1841, pp. 30–31). *Diezmo* returns undoubtedly understate real production, because of home consumption of the product and rather considerable slippages in collection, but it is hard to know precisely how much. The relationship of cattle to crop production is suggested by fragmentary figures in *Anuario estadístico de Colombia, 1875*, pp. 124–147.

41. Richard Swainson Fisher, "General Statistics of South American States, exhibiting their area, population, commerce, revenue, debts, etc., for the official year 1855," *Hunt's Merchant's Magazine* 39 (October 1858): 487; *El*

Tiempo, February 10, 1857, May 18, 1858, and February 24, 1860; *La Opinión*, May 25, 1864, and June 8, 1864; Memoria de Hacienda i Fomento, 1868, Cuadro G; Memoria de Hacienda i Fomento, 1870, pp. li–lii.

42. During the colonial period customs duties accounted for less than 10 percent of total revenue collected. But, as colonial taxes were abolished, the proportion rose. In the years before 1850, customs duties tended to be about one-third of total revenues. In 1850, however, one major source of national revenue, the tobacco monopoly, was abolished, and some minor revenues were ceded to the provincial governments. As a result, customs duties climbed to one-half of the national total in the 1850s and amounted to two-thirds and sometimes three-quarters of the total in the 1870s (Felipe Pérez, *Geografía general de los Estados Unidos de Colombia*, pp. 192–199; Juan de Dios Aranzazu, Memoria de Hacienda, 1840, Cuadro no. 1; Rufino Cuervo, Memoria de Hacienda, 1843, Cuadro no. 1; Juan Clímaco Ordóñez, Memoria de Hacienda, 1845, Sección 2a; *Diario Oficial*, February 1, 1866, February 1, 1869, February 1, 1874, February 8, 1875, June 5, 1878, February 3, 1879; *El Tradicionista*, February 2, 1875).

43. For military expenditures 1832–1844, see Gustavo Arboleda, *Historia contemporánea de Colombia*, II, 228. These figures correspond with those in the annual Memorias de Hacienda and Memorias de Guerra. For budgets of later years, see Pérez, *Geografía general*, pp. 196–199. *Anuario estadístico . . . 1875*, pp. 211–212, 221, shows that national mili-

tary expenditures for 1873–1874 were less than 10 percent, and those of the states were about 12.5 percent.

44. Safford, "Commerce and Enterprise," Table 3, pp. 470–474.

45. George Rogers Taylor, *The Transportation Revolution, 1815–1860*, pp. 32–54, 74–102; Daniel Hovey Calhoun, *The American Civil Engineer*, pp. 8–22, 39–50, passim.

2. Learning to Work

1. Frederick Harbison and Charles A. Myers, *Education, Manpower, and Economic Growth*, pp. 81–83, 90–97.

2. Seymour Martin Lipset, "Values, Education, and Entrepreneurship," in *Elites in Latin America*, ed. Seymour Lipset and Aldo Solari, p. 19; Jane Meyer Loy, "Modernization and Educational Reform in Colombia, 1863–1886" (Ph.D. dissertation), pp. 38–41.

3. David Bushnell, *The Santander Regime in Gran Colombia*, pp. 183–188, provides a good account of developments in primary education between 1819 and 1827.

4. *CN*, I, 25, 27. Also quoted in Bushnell, *Santander Regime*, pp. 183–184, and Alexander Walker, *Colombia*, I, 413–425.

5. *CN*, II, 226. The Santander administration apparently remained somewhat more concerned about the political function of education than did the Congress. Article 8 of the reglamentary decree of October 3, 1826, required each school to have a banner modeled after the national flag and bearing the inscription "*educación gratuita en*

. . . [here the name of the parish]" (*CN*, VII, 404).

6. Bushnell, *Santander Regime*, pp. 183–184; Law of August 6, 1821, *CN*, I, 27–30; Law of March 18, 1826, *CN*, II, 230; Decree of October 3, 1826, *CN*, VII, 401.

7. Decree of October 3, 1826, *CN*, VII, 406.

8. Bushnell, *Santander Regime*, pp. 184–186.

9. The 1837 enrollment figure of 25,577 is in Gustavo Arboleda, *Historia contemporánea de Colombia*, I, 314. In my calculations I used an adjusted total population 1.75 million and assumed that children of school age made up one-sixth of the total population.

10. Articles 10 and 11, Decree of October 3, 1826, *CN*, VII, 404–405.

11. *GNG*, October 6, 1833, and November 2, 1834; Memoria de Guerra, 1834, p. 12; Memoria de Guerra, 1835, pp. 8–9; Memoria de Guerra, 1838, pp. 6–7.

12. "Asociación para instrucción primaria," *Constitución del Cauca*, August 10, 24, 31, September 7, 14, October 5, 12, 26, November 16, December, 1833; *Estatutos de la Sociedad de Educación Primaria de Bogotá, establecidos por la Cámara Provincial en 4 de Octubre de 1834*.

13. The Popayán society, in fact, had a ladies' auxiliary, formed of the most distinguished *damas* of that haughty town.

14. *Anuario . . . estadístico*, 1875, pp. 49, 78, 79.

15. It is difficult to determine precisely what happened during much of the Liberal period from 1849 to 1854. Administrative disorder was so great that statistics are extremely incomplete.

16. On peasant resistance to schooling, see Manuel Ancízar, *Peregrinación de Alpha por las provincias del Norte de la Nueva Granada, en 1850–1851*, pp. 83, 152, passim.

17. The compulsory character of the Spanish *hospicios* and Spanish social resistance to them are ably discussed in William J. Callahan, "The Problem of Confinement," *Hispanic American Historical Review* 51, no. 1 (February 1971): 1–24. Other basic sources are Pedro Rodríguez de Campomanes, *Discurso sobre el fomento de la industria popular* and *Discurso sobre la educación popular de los artesanos y su fomento*; Jean Sarrailh, *L'Espagne éclairée de la seconde moitié du XVIIe siècle*, pp. 27–28, 68–72, 262–268; Richard Herr, *The Eighteenth-Century Revolution in Spain*, pp. 33–34, 50–51, 155–164.

18. Eduardo Posada and Pedro M. Ibáñez, eds., *Relaciones de mando*, pp. 155–156, 248, 477–479; José Manuel Groot, *Historia eclesiástica y civil de Nueva Granada*, II, 230–231, 386–389; José Antonio de Plaza, *Memorias para la historia de la Nueva Granada desde su descubrimiento hasta el 20 de julio de 1810*, pp. 249, 351–352, 370, 386.

19. Posada and Ibáñez, eds., *Relaciones de mando*, pp. 248, 329, 477–479; *Papel Periódico de la Ciudad de Santa Fe*, June 10, 1791; Groot, *Historia eclesiástica y civil*, II, 230–231, 386–389.

20. For the background and development of the houses of refuge in the United States, England, and Prussia, see Bradford Kinney Peirce, *A Half-Century with Juvenile Delinquents*, pp. 3–20; and Blake McKelvey, *American Prisons*, pp. 3–20.

21. Francisco de Paula Santander, *Diario de General Francisco de Paula Santander en Europa y los EE. UU., 1829–1832*, pp. 361, 372.

22. Gustavo Arboleda views the Casa de Refugio as purely a resurrection of the colonial institution (*Historia contemporánea*, I, 232). Santander's proposal emphasizing foreign models is in *GNG*, September 22, 1833. Decree of provincial legislature of Bogotá, September 26, 1833, in Bogotá, province of, *Colección de todos los decretos de interés jeneral espedidos por la honorable cámara de la provincia de Bogotá, desde 1832 . . . hasta 1843, formada por el gobernador de la provincia Alfonso Acevedo Tejada*, pp. 17–22.

23. *GNG*, September 22, 1833.

24. Bogotá, province of, *Colección de todos los decretos . . . Bogotá, desde 1832 . . . hasta 1843*, p. 18

25. José María Mantilla, *Esposición del gobernador de la provincia de Bogotá . . . 1835*, p. 7.

26. Report of Rufino Cuervo in *GNG*, January 25, 1835; Mantilla, *Esposición . . . Gobernador . . . Bogotá . . . 1835*, p. 7; Lino de Pombo, Memoria de lo Interior y Relaciones Exteriores, 1836, p. 25; Alfonso Acevedo, "Informe," June 13, 1839, *GNG*, June 30, 1839; Luis Augusto Cuervo, "Elogio de don José Ignacio París," *BHA* 33, nos. 377–379 (March–April–May 1946): 230; José María Mantilla, *Informe . . . Gobernador . . . Bogotá, 1850*, pp. 11–12.

27. Posada and Ibáñez, eds., *Relaciones de mando*, pp. 248, 478; Mantilla, *Esposición . . . Gobernador . . . Bogotá . . . 1835*, p. 6; Lino de Pombo, Memoria de lo Interior y Relaciones Exteriores, 1836, p. 25;

Acevedo, "Informe," June 13, 1839, *GNG*, June 30, 1839; Vicente Lombana, *Informe . . . Gobernador . . . Bogotá, 1849*, p. 10; José María Mantilla, *Informe . . . Gobernador . . . Bogotá, 1850*, pages unnumbered; Patrocinio Cuellar, *Informe . . . Gobernador . . . Bogotá, 1851*, Cuadro 5; Patrocinio Cuellar, *Informe . . . Gobernador . . . Bogotá, 1853*, Cuadro 4.

28. Cuellar, *Informe . . . Gobernador . . . Bogotá, 1851*, pp. 20–21; idem, *Informe . . . Gobernador . . . Bogotá, 1853*, p. 6.

29. *El Neo-Granadino*, November 3, 1853; *El Tiempo*, September 18, 1855; Senén del Castillo, "Informe . . . contador personero . . . Bogotá," in *Informe . . . Gobernador . . . Bogotá, 1855*, by Pedro Gutiérrez Lee, p. 71; Gutiérrez Lee, *Informe . . . Gobernador . . . Bogotá, 1856*, p. 18.

30. Gutiérrez Lee, *Informe . . . Gobernador . . . Bogotá, 1856*, pp. 52–53; Placido Morales, report to governor, in Pedro Gutiérrez Lee, *Esposición . . . Gobernador de Bogotá . . . 1857*, pp. 51–52 and appendix.

31. Acevedo, "Informe," June 13, 1839, *GNG*, June 30, 1839. Some of the disadvantages of heaping too many functions on one *hospicio* had been recognized in Seville more than sixty years before by Gaspar Melchor de Jovellanos, who was also concerned about the counterproductivity of mingling idle, but uncorrupted, youths with hardened professional beggars and prostitutes. But, while Jovellanos realized that specialized institutions might be desirable, he was aware that such an elaborate system of social correction was not within the resources of most cities ("Discurso sobre la situación y división

interior de los hospicios con respecto a su salubridad," B.A.E., L, 431–435).

32. "Proyecto de lei que autoriza el concierto por escritura pública de los jóvenes que deben dedicarse a aprender algún oficio," *GNG*, February 18, 1838.

33. "Proyecto de lei sobre concierto de jóvenes," *El Argos*, April 28, 1839.

34. *CN*, VI, 28–31.

35. In 1842 the law was amended to permit swifter and more arbitrary condemnations for vagrancy. In 1836 the law had required that condemnations be made by a judicial process that might last a month or more. This came to be considered too cumbersome, and the 1842 law gave the *jefes de policía* the power to make immediate condemnations (Law of June 14, 1842, *CN*, IX, 419–420).

36. Sarrailh, *L'Espagne éclairée*, pp. 129, 359–363; Herr, *Eighteenth-Century Revolution*, pp. 34, 387.

37. Guillermo Hernández de Alba, *Aspectos de la cultura en Colombia*, pp. 236–237; *Constitucional de Cundinamarca*, November 6 and December 6, 1831.

38. Adolfo Dollero, *Cultura colombiana*, pp. 99, 658, 733; obituary note on Fray Pablo Ampudia, *El Día*, March 31, 1846; *El Nuevo Tiempo*, October 7, 1907; Ancízar, *Peregrinación de Alpha*, pp. 366, 438.

39. Robert Henry Davis, "Acosta, Caro, and Lleras" (Ph.D. dissertation), pp. 422–448, provides useful data on several types of philanthropic organization. On membership selection for the 1832 National Academy, ANCR, Instrucción pública, tomo 110, fols. 316–317, 675.

40. Joseph Leon Helguera and Robert Henry Davis, eds., *Archivo*

espistolar del General Mosquera— correspondencia . . . Herran, I, 189, 191–192, 194–195, 197, 201.

41. *GNG*, June 25, 1834, May 8, 1836; ANCR, Instrucción pública, tomo 110, fols. 196, 362–373.

42. Santander to Vicente Azuero, New York, January 4, 1832: "I do not say that these societies are bad. [But] I prefer the grain to the husk . . . I first want to lay the foundations of a building rather than decorating its salons" (Francisco de Paula Santander, *Cartas y mensajes del General Francisco de Paula Santander*, comp. Roberto H. Cortázar, VIII, 186). Lombana to Ignacio Gutiérrez Vergara, Bogotá, June 25, 1835: "General Cipriano Benvenuto de Mosquera [has] promoted the institution of a Society . . . with the object of attacking the vices of gaming and drunkenness. The templars, as they are called by the *Cachacos* [Bogotá dandies], are obligated not to drink spiritous liquors, not to play games of chance and not to give their daughters, their votes or bond to those who [do] . . . I, as I do not gamble, nor have anything to drink, nor the money to give bond, nor daughters to give in matrimony, have turned out to be a templar in the highest degree. Don Lino Pombo proposed . . . that they attack luxury, so that ladies may go to two functions in the same dress. Don Bruno Espinosa, Fray Tiburcio Pieschacón and other ecclesiastics who attended, proposed that they attack heresy, and other small things relative to the other world. . . . other no less respectable citizens are writing a manifesto, in which they promise to make clear the disadvantages of sobriety and temperance" (Academia Colombiana de Historia, Papers of Ignacio Gutiérrez Vergara, 1835–1837).

43. Ignacio Gutiérrez Ponce, *Vida de Don Ignacio Gutiérrez Vergara*, pp. 3–166, 219–220.

44. Ibid., pp. 35–51.

45. Ignacio Gutiérrez Vergara published *El hombre de bien* in 1841. This included sections on "moral thoughts on work," "domestic economy: duties of the husband and wife," "physical education in infancy," "the moral education of children," and "professors of arts and crafts." In 1842 José Eusebio Caro and José María Galavis published *El hombre honrado y laborioso*, with sections on "honor and credit," the passions, vice and virtue, gaming, egoism, philanthropy, idleness and work, and luxury (Gustavo Otero Muñoz, *Semblanzas colombianas*, II, 67–68).

46. Arboleda, *Historia contemporánea*, II, 111–112.

47. Conservative politicians in the Bogotá society were Ignacio Gutiérrez Vergara, president; Col. Anselmo Pineda; Juan Antonio Marroquín; Gen. Pedro Alcántara Herrán; Gen. Domingo Caicedo; Gen. José Acevedo Tejada; Dr. Rufino Cuervo; Dr. Mariano Ospina Rodríguez; Simón Burgos; Dr. Eusebio María Canabal; José Eusebio Caro; Dr. José Maria Galavis; and Juan de Dios Aranzazu. The church was represented by the archbishop of Bogotá, Manuel José Mosquera, and two other priests, one of whom was rector of the national university. The merchant-capitalists were Raimundo Santamaría, Luis M. Silvestre, Francisco Montoya, and Juan Manuel Arrubla (ibid., 112–113). Mariano Ospina, Memoria de lo Interior, 1843, pp. 54–55; Lombana, *Informe . . . Gobernador . . . Bogotá, 1849*, pp. 13–14.

48. Arboleda, *Historia contemporánea*, II, 113.

49. Ibid., p. 192.

50. Juan B. Sosa and Enrique I. Arce, *Compendio de la historia de Panamá*, p. 225, quoted by Adolfo León Gómez in "Anselmo Pineda," in *Colombianos ilustres*, ed. Rafael M. Mesa Ortiz, III, 384–385.

51. Gustavo Otero Muñoz, "Cien cancilleres colombianos," in *Historia de la Cancillería de San Carlos*, pp. 176–178; idem, *Semblanzas colombianas*, II, 232—233.

52. *GNG*, January 2, 1848, and March 5, 1848; Joseph Leon Helguera, "The First Mosquera Administration in New Granada, 1845–1849" (Ph.D. dissertation), pp. 517–518.

53. Decree of December 22, 1847, *CN*, XII, 481, 483.

54. Conservative politicians in the Instituto included Alejandro Osorio, José Manuel Restrepo, Pedro Fernández Madrid, Joaquín José Gori, Urbano Pradilla, Rufino Cuervo, Mariano Ospina, Lino de Pombo, José Eusebio Caro and Juan Antonio Marroquín. The liberals were represented by Lorenzo María Lleras, Justo Arosemena, Florentino González, and Vicente Lombana (see membership list in Arboleda, *Historia contemporánea*, II, 339). On the Instituto in Bogotá, see *GO*, February 3, 1848. On its spread to Medellín, Tunja, the Chocó, Mompós, Santa Marta, Popayán, Buenaventura, Neiva, Cartagena, Socorro, Riohacha, see *GO*, March 2, 26, April 16, 23, 27, May 11, June 1, 11, 1848.

55. *GO*, March 12, April 27, 1848; Arboleda, *Historia contemporánea*, II,

340; Ancízar, *Peregrinación de Alpha*, p. 150; *El Neo-Granadino*, November 5, 1851.

56. Even in the more egalitarian atmosphere of the United States during the Jacksonian era efforts of the upper class to introduce scientific agriculture were rejected by small farmers as the irrelevancies of rich gentlemen farmers (Sidney L. Jackson, *America's Struggle for Free Schools*, pp. 92, 108–109, 129–131).

57. Herr, *Eighteenth-Century Revolution*, p. 159.

58. Ancízar, *Peregrinación de Alpha*, pp. 83, 150, 152, 154.

59. Miguel María Lisboa, *Relaçao de uma viagem a Venezuela, Nova Granada e Equador*, pp. 94–109.

60. Agustín Rodríguez, *Informe que presenta a la Sociedad Democrática el director de ella*, pp. 2, 8.

61. José María Samper, *Historia de una alma, 1834 a 1881*, I, 217–220.

62. *GO*, May 3, 1851, and May 7, 1853. President López and his Secretario de Gobierno Francisco Javier Zaldúa in 1850 did recommend the creation of training shops for artisans (*talleres industriales*), but these had an entirely voluntary character. Liberals continued to sponsor voluntary artisan instruction in subsequent years (Arboleda, *Historia contemporánea*, III, 60).

63. *GO*, May 3, 1851.

64. Mariano Arosemena to Excelentísimo Sr. Presidente de la República Gen. Pedro Alcántara Herrán, August 9, 1843, AH, Correspondencia, Letra A. In 1848 Francisco J. Zaldúa as governor of Vélez province was pushing sons of "the most notable families" to become artisans' apprentices and claimed their parents' approval (*GO*, March 5, 1848). Gen. T. C. Mosquera once tried his hand at blacksmithing (to the extent of making some nails)—though only to prove that he could do it (M. Leonidas Scarpetta and Saturnino Vergara, *Diccionario biográfico de los campeones de la libertad de Nueva Granada, Venezuela, Ecuador i Peru*, p. 369).

65. Acosta de Samper, *Biografía del General Joaquín Acosta*, pp. 17–18.

66. Decree of November 15, 1847, *CN*, XII, 476–477; Helguera, "The First Mosquera Administration," p. 180; ANCR, Instrucción pública, tomo 132, fol. 860.

67. *GO*, March 5, 1848.

68. ANCR, Instrucción pública, tomo 132, fols. 513, 858–859.

69. Decree of November 15, 1847, in *CN*, XII, 476–477.

70. Helguera, "The First Mosquera Administration," pp. 180–181.

71. The names of the apprentices give little clue to their social position. See ANCR, Instrucción pública, tomo 132, fol. 860, and *GO*, March 5, 12, 19, 23, April 6, 16, 23, 1848.

72. Helguera, "The First Mosquera Administration," p. 181; ANCR, Instrucción pública, tomo 132, fols. 858–860. A few of Reed's students appear to have been affected by his construction course. Francisco Olaya became a locally notable architect. And Ramón Guerra Azuola, possibly influenced by his association with Reed, as well as by the creation of a military school in Bogotá, turned from a traditional career in law to one as a teacher of engineers (Helguera, "The First Mos-

quera Administration," p. 181; *Anales de Ingeniería* 1, no. 9 [April 1888]: 260, and 13, no. 149 [July 1905]: 1, 3, 10–11).

73. ANCR, Instrucción pública, tomo 132, fol. 861.

74. Domingo Saiz to Señor Gen. Pedro A. Herrán, September 23, 1859, AH, Correspondencia, varios de letra S., fols. 16–17. The Quaker establishment of Philadelphia (1830–1860) also apprenticed its sons in machine shops, but probably more to instruct than to correct them (Monte A. Calvert, *The Mechanical Engineer in America, 1830–1910*, pp. 3–15).

75. Manuel Murillo Toro, who became the most important Liberal leader between 1850 and 1875, was born in the town of Chaparral (in present-day Tolima) of rather poor parents. Through the special protection of a local priest, he was able to study in the *colegio* in Ibagué, and in the university in Bogotá he supported himself by working as a clerk. Aquileo Parra, who became a very influential Liberal leader in the 1870s and 1880s, was born in the small town of Barichara in Socorro province; after brief studies in two local *colegios*, he had to abandon his education to undertake commercial perambulations with his brother. Similarly, José María Rojas Garrido, a leader of the Mosquera wing of the party, was born in Agrado in present-day Huila, a town so small that during most of his youth it did not even have parish status. Rojas Garrido's social origins are further suggested by the fact that he did not reach the university in Bogotá until the advanced age of twenty-one, at which point he had already practiced *la abogacia empírica* (without formal training) in the small towns of the province.

The origins of some other liberals were more clearly upper class, albeit also of provincial families. But many of these liberals from relatively notable families were placed in straitened circumstances when they lost fortunes and sometimes fathers in the civil war of 1839–1842. Salvador Camacho Roldán's father, the liberal senator from the *llanos* province of Casanare, was a highly respected man. But he was not wealthy, and his fortunes were diminished when as a result of the civil war the conservatives sent him into exile in 1841. In this period and afterward Salvador Camacho Roldán interrupted his university studies to support his family by working in a hardware and spice shop. Similarly, while the Samper family was not wealthy, it was highly respected in the Honda region; José María Samper the elder served as a senator in the latter part of the 1840s. But, in order for all seven Samper brothers to be educated, particularly after financial losses incurred in the war of 1839–1842, all of them had to work hard in the family's commercial and agricultural enterprises (Otero Muñoz, "Cien cancilleres colombianos," in *Historia de la Cancillería*, pp. 185–187, 241–243; Aquileo Parra, *Memorias de Aquileo Parra, presidente de Colombia de 1876 á 1878*, Felipe Pérez, *Jeografía física i política de los Estados Unidos de Colombia*, II, 57; Samper, *Historia de una alma*, I, 64–95, 137, 159–163, 197–212; Salvador Camacho Roldán to Director general de Instrucción pública, November 24, 1845, ANCR, Instrucción pública, tomo 118, fols. 512–514).

76. Medardo Rivas, *Los trabajadores de tierra caliente.*

Academic Science for the Upper Class: Bourbons and Neo-Bourbons

1. In his model for the diffusion of European science, George Basalla sees a first, or "nonscientific," phase, in which European collectors of botanical, geological, or other lore introduce conceptions of modern science to the heathen lands they explore. In a second, or "colonial," phase the heathens have become interested in modern science but are still totally dependent upon Europe for scientific ideas and institutional support. The two phases obviously overlap. In New Granada the first phase is most evident between 1760 and 1830; the second phase runs through the entire nineteenth century, with some attenuation of scientific and technical dependency after 1880. The Basalla model is presented in "The Spread of Western Science," *Science*, May 5, 1967, pp. 611–622.

3. The Enlightenment in New Granada

1. The pre-1750 histories of these institutions—unnecessary to this study—are treated at length in José Abel Salazar, *Los estudios eclesiásticos superiores en el Nuevo Reino de Granada (1563–1810)*, and more briefly in Gabriel Porras Troconis, *Historia de la cultura en el Nuevo Reino de Granada*, pp. 15–216, and Luis Antonio Bohórquez Casallas, *La evolución educativa en Colombia*, pp. 74–138. See also such studies of individual institutions as Guillermo Hernández de Alba, *Crónica del muy ilustre Colegio Mayor de Nuestra Señora del Rosario de Santa Fé de Bogotá*; Daniel Restrepo, S.J., and Guillermo and Alfonso Hernández de Alba, *El Colegio de San Bartolomé*; Pedro Vargas Sáez, C.M., *Historia del Real Colegio Seminario de S. Francisco de Asis de Popayán*.

2. The colonial curriculum is described in colorful and slightly exaggerated terms in José Antonio de Plaza, *Memorias para la historia de la Nueva Granada desde su descubrimiento hasta el 20 de Julio de 1810*. His much-quoted description is probably more accurately applied to 1760 than to the end of the colonial period, to which it refers. For other nineteenth-century variations on Plaza see José María Vergara y Vergara, *Historia de la literatura en Nueva Granada desde la Conquista hasta la Independencia (1538–1820)*, II, 33–34, and Mariano Ospina [Rodríguez], *El Doctor José Félix de Restrepo y su época*, pp. 61–62.

3. Vargas Sáez, *Historia . . . Seminario . . . Popayán*, pp. 462–463, 548–549; Francisco Antonio Moreno y Escandón, "Método provisional é interino de los estudios que han de observar los colegios de Santa Fé, por ahora, y hasta tanto que se erige universidad pública, o Su Majestad dispone otra cosa," *BHA* 23, nos. 264–265 (September and October 1936): 644, 649, 651.

4. Richard Herr, *The Eighteenth-Century Revolution in Spain*, pp. 24–25, 38–43, 163–165.

5. Ibid., pp. 165–172, passim; John Tate Lanning, *The Eighteenth-Century Enlightenment in the University of San Carlos de Guatemala*, p. xx, passim.

6. A. Federico Gredilla, *Biografía de José Celestino Mutis, con la relación de*

su viaje y estudios practicados en el Nuevo Reino de Granada, pp. 11–33, 62–65, 96–97, 104–105, 142–146, 166–171.

7. Hernández de Alba, *Crónica*, 91–96; Gredilla, *Biografía de Mutis*, pp. 18, 47–49, 166–168; Carlos Restrepo Canal, "Incidentes que dieron origen al plan de estudios de Moreno y Escandón," *BHA* 23, no. 266 (November 1936): 730–734.

8. John Tate Lanning has suggested that the Dominicans were less concerned about Copernicanism than about the university reform being proposed by Moreno and Guirior; the attack on Mutis, under this construction, was supposed to throw the modernists on the defensive ("El sistema de Copérnico en Bogotá," *Revista de Historia de América*, no. 18 [December 1944], pp. 279–306). For somewhat different accounts, see Carlos Cortés Vargas, "Un pleito santafereño y Moreno y Escandón," *BHA* 18, no. 207 (March 1930): 200–208; José Manuel Marroquín, "Biografía de don Francisco Antonio Moreno y Escandón," *BHA* 23, nos. 264–265 (September–October 1936): 529–550; Restrepo Canal, "Incidentes," pp. 730–733. On degree standards and the excess of lawyers, see Francisco Antonio Moreno y Escandón, "Copia de un documento sobre exceso de abogados," Santafé, 1771, manuscript collection, Biblioteca Luis Angel Arango, Bogotá.

9. Moreno y Escandón, "Método," pp. 644–646, 648, 650–652. At least one of the texts prescribed by Moreno, the mathematics of Christian von Wolff (1679–1754), had already been used in San Bartolomé.

10. "Representación dirigida al Rey por los padres franciscanos," *BHA* 24,

no. 272 (June 1937): 333–337; "Arbitrios para el establecimiento de universidad pública," ibid., pp. 340–343; "Compendio de lo actuado sobre estudios públicos," ibid., pp. 344–345; Salazar, *Estudios eclesiásticos*, pp. 450–451.

11. Nineteenth-century authors and later writers who followed their accounts assumed that the Moreno plan was vetoed by authorities in Spain (Plaza, *Memorias*, p. 327; Vergara y Vergara, *Historia*, II, 40–41). Twentieth-century research indicates, however, that the plan met its ultimate downfall in Bogotá. The junta of October, 1779, included the Visitador Juan Francisco Gutiérrez de Piñeres, the archbishop of Santa Fe, the rectors of the Universidad de Santo Tomás and of San Bartolomé, and the vice-rector of Rosario, among others ("Compendio de lo actuado," p. 262; Hernández de Alba, *Crónica*, II, 186–188).

12. Eduardo Posada and Pedro M. Ibáñez, eds., *Relaciones de mando*, p. 252.

13. José Manuel Pérez Ayala, *Antonio Caballero y Góngora*, pp. 166–168, 179–181. The plan of 1787 is printed in Guillermo Hernández de Alba, *Aspectos de la cultura*, pp. 136–165. With Mutis's advice, Caballero y Góngora prescribed more current texts than those previously suggested by Moreno; his list included Nollet's experimental physics, Linnaeus on botany, and Buffon on natural history.

14. "Avisos de Hebephilo a los jóvenes de los colegios sobre la inutilidad de sus estudios presentes . . . ," *Papel Periódico de la Ciudad de Santafé de Bogotá*, April 1 and 8, 1791. Vergara y Vergara, *Historia*, II, 41–42, asserted

that this was written by the creole Francisco Antonio Zea, and this judgment is followed, with some inaccuracies, in Roberto Botero Saldarriaga, *Francisco Antonio Zea*, pp. 45–57. On the *Papel Periódico* and its editor, see Rolando René Frágola [J. Torre Rebello], "Manuel del Socorro Rodrigues," *BHA* 15, no. 169 (August 1925): 46–48.

15. Florentino Vezga, *La Expedición Botánica*, pp. 33–88; Vergara y Vergara, *Historia*, II, 20–21, 42, 150.

16. Restrepo's course was not very advanced, but it did include notions of arithmetic, astronomy, mechanics, hydraulics, statics, and optics (Botero Saldarriaga, *Zea*, p. 30).

17. On Popayán, see Guillermo Hernández de Alba, *Vida y escritos del doctor José Félix de Restrepo*, pp. 137–138; see also pp. 14–21, 38–41. The account of Vargas Sáez, *Historia . . . Colegio Seminario . . . Popayán*, pp. 521–523, 546–558, varies from Hernández de Alba on a number of important details. See also Eduardo Posada, ed., *Cartas de Caldas*, pp. 32, 34–35, 58, 71–72; Gustavo Arboleda, *Diccionario biográfico y genealógico del antiguo departamento del Cauca*, pp. 10–11, 30, 64–65, 81–85, 90, 213, 357, 391–392, 429. On Bogotá, see "La astronomía en Santafé," *BHA* 1, no. 6 (February 1903): 303–306; Guillermo Hernández de Alba, ed., *Archivo epistolar del sabio naturalista Don José Celestino Mutis*, II, 145–155.

18. Gredilla, *Biografía de Mutis*, pp. 142–159; Bernardo J. Caycedo, *D'Elhuyar y el siglo XVIII neogranadino*, pp. 17–77, 110–171, 206–214, passim; Domingo de la Peña, "Biografía de Don Jacob Benjamín Wiesner, *BHA* 16, no. 192 (December

1927): 730–740; Julio César García, "Historia de la Escuela Nacional de Minas," *Anales de la Escuela Nacional de Minas*, no. 42 (October 1937), p. 8.

19. Alfredo D. Bateman, "Historia de la matemática y la ingeniería," in *Apuntes para la historia de la ciencia en Colombia*, ed. Jaime Jaramillo Uribe, pp. 8–10; Pedro María Ibáñez, *Crónicas de Bogotá*, II, 59, 67, 95, 118, 182, and III, 388; Alfredo D. Bateman, *Páginas para la historia de la ingeniería colombiana*, pp. 9–18; Alfredo D. Bateman, *Los ingenieros de Cartagena*, pp. 5–37.

20. The work of the Botanical Expedition falls into two stages. The first, from 1783 to 1791, centered on Mariquita, where Mutis as chief botanist and then D'Elhuyar as chief of mines both held forth and provided each other with reinforcement. From 1791 until his death in 1808, Santa Fe de Bogotá was Mutis's residence and thus the headquarters of the Expedition (Vezga, *La Expedición Botánica*, pp. 31–82; Gredilla, *Biografía de Mutis*, pp. 165–177, 192, 197–207).

21. In the Mariquita stage the most notable *criollo* assistants were Fray Diego García of Cartagena; Fr. Eloy Valenzuela, a secular priest from the Bucaramanga region; and Pedro Fermín de Vargas, a lawyer-administrator. García discovered a variety of cinchona and other plants with medicinal properties in Valledupar. Valenzuela, after withdrawing from the expedition, continued an active pursuit of botany as a parish priest in Bucaramanga. Vargas never made any scientific contributions. But his *Pensamientos políticos sobre la agricultura, comercio y minas del Virreinato de Santafé de Bogotá* is the most

substantial colonial writing promoting national economic development, ranging widely in its suggestions for the development of communications, export agriculture, manufacturing, and mining. Another economic writer affected by the Expedition was José Ignacio de Pombo of the Consulado of Cartagena. After 1791, in the Bogotá stage, the principal assistants were Francisco Antonio Zea of Medellín, a recent graduate in law of San Bartolomé; Mutis's nephews, José and Sinforoso; Francisco José de Caldas; and Jorge Tadeo Lozano. At least three other men have been listed as investigators from the Expedition: Bruno Landete, Jose Camblor, and Juan Bautista Aguiar (Vezga, *La Expedición Botánica*, pp. 40–49; Vargas Sáez, *Historia . . . Colegio Seminario . . . Popayán*, p. 547, Gredilla, *Biografía de Mutis*, pp. 178–188, 206–211).

22. It is sometimes assumed that Lozano, having offered to give a chemistry course, actually taught it (e.g., Fabio Lozano y Lozano, "Biografía de don Jorge Tadeo Lozano," *BHA* 10, nos. 119–120 [September–October 1916]: 695–698; Adolfo Dollero, *Cultura colombiana*, p. 59). But Guillermo Hernández de Alba indicates that the plan for such a course was blocked by an official of the *audiencia* of New Granada (*Crónica*, II, 329–335). It appears that chemistry was not taught in New Granada before the Independence era. In Caldas's description of scientific instruction as of December, 1807, chemistry and mineralogy are not mentioned. And a later article by José María Salazar laments the lack of such courses (Francisco José de Caldas, "Estado de la geografía del vireinato de Santa Fé de

Bogotá," and José María Salazar, "Memoria descriptiva del pais de Santa Fé de Bogotá," in *Semanario de la Nueva Granada*, ed. Joaquín Acosta, pp. 32, 408 n. 2. See also Francisco José de Caldas, "Descripción del Observatorio astronómico de Santa Fé de Bogotá, situado en el jardín de la real Expedición botánica," in *Semanario de la Nueva Granada* p. 44). Anillo had studied in Madrid with Benito Bails. It is not clear when his school began to function; but, as Anillo was sent by order of Charles III, it may have begun operations in the 1790s (José Manuel Groot, *Historia eclesiástica y civil de Nueva Granada*, II, 480).

23. Lino de Pombo, "Memoria histórica sobre la vida, carácter, trabajos científicos y literarios, y servicios patrióticos de Francisco José de Caldas," first printed 1852, reprinted in *Anales de Ingeniería* 8, nos. 98, 99, 100 (October–November–December 1896): 328–357; Vezga, *La Expedición Botánica*, pp. 62–66, 74–79; Vergara y Vergara, *Historia de la literatura*, II, 149–169; Eduardo Posada, ed., *Obras de Caldas*, pp. xix–xx, passim; Groot, *Historia eclesiástica y civil*, II, 451–455, 458–461, 468; Arboleda, *Diccionario*, pp. 81–85; Dollero, *Cultura colombiana*, pp. 105–112.

24. José María Salazar, "Memoria descriptiva del pais de Santa Fé de Bogotá," in *Semanario de la Nueva Granada*, p. 408.

25. Based on two surviving lists, one for the end of January, 1810 (*Semanario de la Nueva Granada*, pp. 545–546), the other a continuation dated March 31, 1810 (in *Semanario del Nuevo Reyno de Granada*, pp. 29–31, in Colección Pineda, Biblioteca Nacional, Bogotá). It

is quite possible that there were additional subscribers. The best represented towns were Santa Fe de Bogotá (14), Cartagena (13), Tunja and Cali (each 9), Antioquia (7), Cartago (6), Popayán and Medellín (each 5), and Nóvita and Ibagué (each 3). Surprisingly, San Martín in the eastern plains had 9 subscribers, and such out-of-the-way places as Chire and Pore, in the Casanare region, and Carnicerías, in the upper reaches of the Magdalena River, were also represented. The viceregally sponsored *Papel Periódico*, which was more rhetorical and less seriously scientific than the *Semanario*, had at least 147 subscribers in its first year, many of them royal officials. (*Papel Periódico*, March 4 and June 24, 1791).

26. Quoted in Arcesio Aragón, *La Universidad del Cauca*, pp. 17–18.

27. Plaza, *Memorias*, p. 387.

28. Ibid., pp. 125–154; Mariano Ospina, *El Doctor José Félix de Restrepo y su época*, pp. 83–96.

29. *Semanario de la Nueva Granada*, pp. 156–161, 229–242, 421–425, 428; Arboleda, *Diccionario*, pp. 64–66, 359, 433–434; Dollero, *Cultura colombiana*, pp. 41, 44, 50–51, 54, 92, 100–103, 724; Bohórquez Casallas, *La evolución educativa*, p. 175.

30. Vezga, *La Expedición Botánica*, pp. 177, 182–186; P.M.I. [Pedro María Ibáñez], "Centenario del Observatorio de Bogotá," *BHA* 1, no. 12 (August 1903): 648; Pedro María Ibáñez, "Benedicto Domínguez," *BHA* 12, no. 142 (December 1919): 631–634.

31. Botero Saldarriaga, *Zea*, passim; Andrés Posada Arango, "Zea," *BHA* 8, no. 87 (August 1912): 174–177; F. Mutis Durán, "Don Sinforoso Mutis," *BHA* 8, no. 88 (September 1912): 193–235;

Ospina, *José Félix de Restrepo*, pp. 67–109; Guillermo Hernández de Alba, *Vida y escritos del doctor José Félix de Restrepo*, pp. 20–31; Bohórquez Casallas, *La evolución educativa*, p. 185.

4. Academic Science: The Neo-Bourbons, 1821–1845

1. The republican era also brought a quickening of interest in the law in the United States. Among graduates of Harvard College, the proportion who took up careers in law went from 13 percent (1771–1775) to 20 percent (1776–1780) to 30 percent (1786–1790) to 37 percent (1796–1800). The same pattern applies to most of the other American institutions existing then. At Harvard and other schools the law remained overwhelmingly the dominant choice, even outranking courses in "commercial pursuits," until at least 1875 (Bailey B. Burritt, *Professional Distribution of College and University Graduates*, pp. 14–19, 26, 29–34, 39–40, 55, 80–144).

2. There were, however, isolated cases of clerical resistance. Salvador Jiménez de Enciso, bishop of Popayán (1816 [effectively 1818]–1840), attempted to obstruct the teaching of mathematics and the general functioning of the university in Popayán in the early republican period (Joaquín Mosquera to Francisco de Paula Santander, Popayán, August 27, 1833, Francisco de Paula Santander, *Correspondencia dirigida al General Francisco de Paula Santander*, comp. Roberto H. Cortázar, VIII, 341–343).

3. Restrepo's early meteorological and other scientific studies are in the

private archive of the late Monsignor José Restrepo Posada, Bogotá. For his public services, as well as those of Pombo and Ospina, see Appendix 1.

4. Francisco de Paula Santander, *Cartas y mensajes del General Francisco de Paula Santander*, X, 339–340, and *Correspondencia . . . Santander*, XIV, 171–172.

5. Rivero had studied at mining schools in France, Spain, and Freiberg during the Independence era; among his discoveries was a new metal, humboldtine. The two technicians were Justine-Marie Goudot and Jacques Bourdon (Florentino Vezga, *La Expedición Botánica*, pp. 178–180; Roberto Botero Saldarriaga, *Francisco Antonio Zea*, pp. 66–68, 297–298; Margarita Combes, *Roulin y sus amigos*, pp. 5–30; *La Grande Encyclopédie*, VII, 839–840; *Enciclopedia Universal Ilustrada Europeo-Americana*, LI, 901. These accounts vary on the details, but I have placed most faith in Vezga, who knew some of the participants and appears to have had trustworthy documents in hand).

6. As finally worked out by José Manuel Restrepo, the minister of the interior, all the courses in the mining school were to be given by three professors; plans for the museum were cut back even more (*CN*, VII, 171, 175; David Bushnell, *The Santander Regime in Gran Colombia*, p. 189).

7. José Manuel Restrepo, Memoria de lo Interior, 1824, p. 13; Combes, *Roulin*, p. 29; Evelyn Jeanne Goggin Ahern, "The Development of Education in Colombia, 1820–1850" (M.A. thesis), p. 37; Jean-Baptiste Boussingault, *Memoires de J. B. Boussingault*, IV, 39–45, 64–93, 191–196, 218, and V,

1–17; Pedro Nisser, *Sketch of the Different Mining and Mechanical Operations employed in . . . South American Goldworks . . . particularly those of . . . Antioquia*, pp. 39, 43–44.

8. *Enciclopedia Universal Europeo-Americana*, LI, 901; Soledad Acosta de Samper, *Biografía del General Joaquín Acosta*, p. 233 n.; Boussingault, *Memoires*, passim.; Carlos E. Chardón, *Boussingault*, p. 92.

9. Vezga, *La Expedición Botánica*, p. 182; ANCR, Instrucción pública, tomo 110, fols. 200, 393.

10. Combes, *Roulin*, pp. 21–28, 54–59. It is not clear whether the low salaries for science professors set by the Colombian government in 1827 affected the foreign scientists' decision to leave or represented the government's reaction to decisions they had already made. The 1827 decree provided 600 pesos for the director of the museum of natural history, 800 for the professors of botany and agriculture, 400 for a professor of chemistry. Boussingault and Roulin had allegedly been promised salaries in the neighborhood of 7,000 and 2,000 pesos, respectively (Decree of June 15, 1827, *CN*, VII, 474–475; Chardón, *Boussingault*, p. 20; Combes, *Roulin*, p. 28). The salaries stipulated in the 1827 decree were not much lower than those in the United States. Frederick Rudolph cites 600 to 700 dollars as common at the better colleges between 1805 and 1835, with only a few places (e.g., University of Virginia, Harvard) paying 1,500 dollars or more ("Who Paid the Bills?" *Harvard Educational Review* 21, no. 2 [Spring 1961]: 153). The United States' larger and more developed scientific community enabled it to appropriate the scientifically trained

at lower cost. On the one hand, the greater availability of native scientists made colleges less dependent upon foreigners and helped to hold down salary costs. On the other hand, foreign scientists in the United States enjoyed the reinforcement of a scientific community, greater access to basic equipment, and many opportunities for extra-academic income in the dynamic North American economy. On the extent and sophistication of the American scientific community, see George H. Daniels, *American Science in the Age of Jackson*, pp. 13–40, 229–232.

11. Botero Saldarriaga, *Zea*, p. 298.

12. Some Colombians suggest the mission failed because of its association with Zea, whose mishandling of foreign loans became a scandal in 1822–1823 (Tomás Rueda Vargas, *Escritos*, I, 177–178, and Alfredo D. Bateman, *El Observatorio Astronómico de Bogotá*, p. 64). In fact, the mission was warmly endorsed after the Zea scandal broke and was enthusiastically supported by José Manuel Restrepo, the secretary of the interior, whose prestige and influence were considerable.

13. According to Boussingault, the Colombian experience played an important part in redirecting his career from mining and mineralogy to agricultural chemistry. The agricultural problems of Antioquia first drew his attention to agronomy as a field for serious research (Boussingault, *Memoires*, IV, 196). Rivero and Boussingault almost immediately took advantage of the research opportunities in Colombia, publishing scientific memoirs as early as 1823, sometimes in Bogotá but more frequently in France. For the Bogotá publications of 1823–1824 (on the milk

of the cow-tree, iron meteorites, etc.), see Eduardo Posada, *Bibliografía bogotana*, II, 39, 63, 88. These and other works appeared simultaneously in the *Annales de chimie* and other leading European journals, where they were read with approval by Joseph Gay-Lussac among other notables (Boussingault, *Memoires*, II, 288). François Roulin later published his *Histoire naturelle et souvenirs de voyage* and various other works on New Granada. Other works are cited in Ignacio Gutiérrez Ponce, *Vida de Don Ignacio Gutiérrez Vergara y episodios históricos de su tiempo*, p. 238 n. 1.

14. Vezga, *La Expedición Botánica*, p. 182.

15. Because he lacked a university education, Matís was unwilling to undergo the usual semipublic competition for a university chair. He therefore served only as a substitute for Céspedes, with less than a third of the professor's salary. Whether because he lacked social status or because he was incompetent, students left his classes in droves (ANCR, Instrucción pública, tomo 110, fols. 354–355, 389–391, 509–510, 756; tomo 113, fols. 76, 92, 94, 150, 167).

16. J. J. O., "Noticia biográfica del Doctor Juan María Céspedes," *GO*, March 5, 1848; Vezga, *La Expedición Botánica*, pp. 182–187; Boussingault, *Memoires*, II, 134; Céspedes's report, July 29, 1842, ANCR, Instrucción pública, tomo 115, fols. 668–669.

17. On Bogotá, see Robert Henry Davis, "Acosta, Caro, and Lleras" (Ph.D. dissertation); *GNG*, December 9, 1832, May 26, 1833, November 30, 1834; ANCR, Instrucción pública, tomo 110, fols. 116, 127, 130, 139, 140, 152,

198, 210, 270, 312, 353, 354, 389–391, 509–510, 756, 760, 764, 781; tomo 112, fol. 539; tomo 113, fol. 195; tomo 114, fols. 23, 840–845, 953–954; tomo 115, fols. 294, 300, 496–497, 541; tomo 126, fols. 220, 260, 615. Acosta's accounts as director of the National Museum to 1837 reveal no laboratory expenses; in a period of two years (1837–1839), Osorio spent only ninety-six pesos on chemicals, fuel, etc. (ANCR, Instrucción pública, tomo 126, fols. 2–60). On Cartagena, see ANCR, Instrucción pública, tomo 128, fol. 697. On Popayán, see Arcesio Aragón, *La Universidad del Cauca*, pp. 129–133. Pombo's ideas on technical education at this time are in *Constitución del Cauca*, December 29, 1832. See also Certámenes, *Constitución del Cauca*, July 27, 1833; ANCR, Instrucción pública, tomo 112, fols. 629–632; tomo 113, fols. 529–557; tomo 115, fols. 119–146.

18. Certámenes, Pamplona, 1836, Medellín, 1837, and Tunja, 1837, in ANCR, Instrucción pública, tomo 112, fols. 83–98, 578–586, 720–732; Tunja, 1838, Mompox, 1837, tomo 113, fols. 596–597, 765–770; Santa Marta, 1838, Pamplona, 1839, tomo 114, fols. 552–562, 859–874; Socorro, 1839, Ibagué, 1840, tomo 115, fols. 20, 467–473; Vélez, 1836, tomo 125, fols. 515–530; Santa Marta, 1839, Panamá 1839, tomo 126, fols. 672–682, 910–921; Pasto, 1840, Santa Rosa de Viterbo, 1841, Antioquia, 1841, tomo 127, fols. 144, 325, 500–502.

19. ANCR, Instrucción pública, tomo 114, fol. 696; tomo 115, fols. 322, 332, 429; tomo 125, fol. 722; tomo 126, fols. 745–896.

20. The most notable instigators were Juan de Dios Aranzazu, a large land-owner in the environs of Rionegro who was governor in 1833; his secretary, Mariano Ospina, who may have conceived the idea; Col. Juan María Gómez, who contracted the chemistry professor in Paris; Francisco A. Obregón, Aranzazu's successor as governor; and a priest, Dr. Estanislao Gómez, who undertook the subscription of private donations. Among the sources of public funds that the province attempted to use were a new tax on gold presented for founding (at first blocked by Antioquia's own senators in Bogotá) and monies originally designated for scholarships and roadbuilding. See Gabriel Henao Mejía, *Juan de Dios Aranzazu*, pp. 24, 33–50, 229–233; Decree of May 4, 1835, *CN*, V, 441–442; Juan de Dios Aranzazu to Francisco de Paula Santander, Medellín, January 1, 1834 and September 7, 1836, Santander, *Correspondencia . . . Santander*, I, 164, 181; Francisco A. Obregón, *Esposición . . . Gobernador . . . Antioquia . . . 1836*; *GNG*, May 7, 1837; Emilio Robledo, *La Universidad de Antioquia, 1882–1922*, pp. 58, 63, 67–68, 71–73, 255–259.

21. Robledo, *La Universidad de Antioquia*, pp. 76–77, 81–82; ANCR, Instrucción pública, tomo 126, fol. 715 vta.; Luciano Brugnelly, Medellín, to Ignacio Gutiérrez, Bogotá, September 1 [?], 1837, in Archivo, Academia de Historia, Bogotá, Ignacio Gutiérrez Vergara papers, 1837.

22. In the 1820s and 1830s salaries for professors of philosophy and letters and jurisprudence ranged from 200 to 500 pesos per year. In contrast, in 1823 a salary of 800 pesos was allotted for a chair in botany, and in 1837 a salary of 1,000 pesos for one in chemistry and

mineralogy (*CN*, V, 650, 662–663, 691, 710, 768, 781–782, 791; VI, 313; VII, 135–137, 145, 171, 196, 200, 204, 226–227, 233–234, 239–240, 382, 474–475). In 1847 2,000 reales (or 250 pesos) per course were allotted in philosophy and literature and 2,400 reales (or 300 pesos) in jurisprudence and medicine. Pay for mathematics, botany, and physics professors was about at the same levels; they received 4,000 to 4,800 reales (500 to 600 pesos) per year for teaching duties usually involving two courses. Several professors of chemistry and mineralogy, however, were authorized salaries of 8,000 to 9,600 reales (1,000 to 1,200 pesos) per year (*CN*, XII, 457–467). Brugnelly received 1,200 (Robledo, *Universidad de Antioquia*, pp. 76–77).

23. *El Argos*, November 25, 1838; *GNG*, January 13 and April 7, 1839.

24. *CN*, I, 25–26.

25. José Manuel Restrepo, Memoria de lo Interior, 1823, pp. 24–25, and Memoria de lo Interior, 1824, pp. 9–13.

26. Provision for these chairs seems to have been little more than a pious gesture. In the *colegio* in Cali the chair in mineralogy was to be paid no more than 200 pesos; in Ibagué a salary of 250 pesos was authorized (Decrees of October 9 and December 21, 1822, and January 29, 1823, in *CN*, VII, 119–121, 136–137, 144–146; Articles 133–143, 148–162, *CN*, VII, 429–435).

27. Articles 20, 21, 22, 23, Decree of October 3, 1826, *CN*, VII, 407–408; John L. Young, "University Reform in New Granada, 1820–1850" (Ph.D. dissertation), p. 39.

28. Decree of November 17, 1827, *CN*, VII, 499–501.

29. Decree of March 31, 1832, Article 5, cited in Decree of March 1, 1834, establishing a chair of jurisprudence in the *colegio* in Vélez, *CN*, VII, 649.

30. Pedro Alcántara Herrán, Memoria de lo Interior y Relaciones Exteriores, 1839, p. 38.

31. Decrees of September 4, 1832, March 1, 1834, July 31, 1834, February 20, 1835, June 15, 1835, June 27, 1835, July 22, 1835, August 31, 1835, September 30, 1835, October 9, 1835, November 14, 1835, November 21, 1835, January 12, 1836, January 18, 1836, October 15, 1836, October 29, 1836, November 7, 1836, November 26, 1836, January 12, 1837, March 20, 1837, March 30, 1837, April 27, 1837, May 1, 1837, November 4, 1837, January 11, 1838, October 25, 1838, October 31, 1838, December 6, 1838, December 7, 1838, December 19, 1838, September 5, 1839, in *CN*, V–VIII. ANCR, Instrucción Pública, tomo 114, fol. 475, 501, 643–649.

32. Gustavo Arboleda, *Historia contemporánea de Colombia*, I, 315.

33. Lino de Pombo's paternal grandfather, a Spaniard, had married into the Valencia family of Popayán, owners of vast landed estates and rich gold mines in the Cauca region. Lino de Pombo's father, Manuel, after graduating in law in Bogotá, went to Spain; there, in the royal chapel of Aranjuez, he married Beatriz O'Donnell, daughter of an Irish colonel and Mariana de Anethan y Mareshal of Luxembourg. Manuel Pombo then joined his brother in Cartagena, where he served as treasurer of the Consulado. Later he was appointed superintendent of the royal mint in Bogotá, a post he held at the beginning of the Independence era (Gustavo Ar-

boleda, *Diccionario biográfico y genealógico del antiguo departamento del Cauca*, pp. 356–358, 447–448).

34. Among the many improvements José Ignacio de Pombo advocated was the establishment of a School of Drawing, Mathematics, Mineralogy, Botany, Zoology, and Chemistry, as well as improved medical instruction, including an anatomical theater. In the smallpox vaccination campaign of the first decade of the nineteenth century, when the vaccine sent to Cartagena was thought to be unusable, he prepared vaccine by a method recently discovered in Edinburgh. Lino de Pombo's second cousin, Miguel de Pombo, one of those executed in 1816, was secretary of the vaccination junta in Bogotá and as such contributed to Caldas's *Semanario* ("Informe de Don José Ignacio de Pombo [del Consulado de Cartagena] sobre asuntos económicos y fiscales," *BHA* 13, no. 154 [1921]: 688–697; *Semanario de la Nueva Granada*, pp. 157–161; Arboleda, *Diccionario*, pp. 356, 359).

35. Pombo's biography of Caldas (first published in *La Siesta*, Bogotá, 1852) is reprinted in *Anales de Ingeniería* 8, nos. 98, 99, 100 (October, November, December 1896): 327–367, and in part in Francisco José de Caldas, *Viajes*, pp. 6–39. See also José Manuel Groot, *Historia eclesiástica y civil de Nueva Granada*, II, 461; Ramón Guerra Azuola, "Don Lino de Pombo," *Anales de Ingeniería* 9, nos. 101 and 102 (January–February 1897): 1–18.

36. Gustavo Otero Muñoz, "Cien cancilleres colombianos," in *Historia de la Cancillería de San Carlos*, pp. 142–143.

37. *Discurso de apertura de estudios pronunciado en la Universidad Depar-tamental del Cauca el día primero de octubre de 1830 por el catedrático de matemáticas*, in Biblioteca Nacional, Bogotá.

38. Pombo served as secretary of the interior and foreign relations (1833–1838, 1840), governor of the province of Bogotá (1840–1841), envoy to Venezuela (1841–1842), senator from Cartagena (1844–1849), secretary of finance (1846), director of national credit on various occasions, procurador general (attorney-general) (1854–1855), secretary of foreign relations (1855–1857), and, as José Manuel Restrepo's successor, director of the national mint (1860–1861). With Santander and José Ignacio de Márquez he wrote the Penal Code of 1837. He is better known as the compiler of the first important collection of laws made in the republic, the *Recopilación Granadina* (1843–1845) (Gustavo Otero Muñoz, *Semblanzas colombianas*, II, 118–121; Otero Muñoz, "Cien cancilleres colombianos," pp. 142–143; Arboleda, *Historia contemporánea*, II, 7, 14, 107, 149–150, 166, 201, 232, 238, 250, 291–292, 295, 343, 418; IV, 21–22, 269, 279; José Manuel Restrepo, *Autobiografía*, p. 51).

39. In addition to teaching in the university in Popayán in the early 1830s, Pombo served as professor of mathematics in the Colegio Militar in Bogotá (1848–1854), in the Colegio de la Independencia in Bogotá (1853–1854, 1855, and perhaps afterward), and in the Colegio San Bartolomé (1857–1858). His texts were *Lecciones de geometría analítica* (1851) and *Lecciones de aritmética y algebra* (1858) (Otero Muñoz, *Semblanzas colombianas*, II, 118–121; Arboleda, *Historia*

contemporánea, II, 338; III, 366; IV, 247; V, 355).

40. Arboleda, *Historia contemporánea*, II, 232, 241–242, 246, 248, 250; *El Día*, October 26 and December 21, 1845; October 4, 8, December 6, 1846; *GNG*, January 28, 1847; *El Neo-Granadino*, November 23, 1848, November 30, 1849, April 4, 1851; Caja de ahorros de la Provincia de Bogotá. *Cuarto informe anual de la Junta de Inversión i Superintendencia*; *El Tiempo*, December 25, 1855; Caja de ahorros de Bogotá, *13°Informe anual de la Junta de Inversión i Superintendencia*.

41. "Instrucción pública," *Constitucional del Cauca*, November 24, December 8, 22, 29, 1832. These articles are unsigned, but Pombo in 1842 described himself as their author (ANCR, Instrucción pública, tomo 115, fol. 567).

42. Pombo, Memoria de lo Interior y Relaciones Exteriores, 1836, p. 32. See ANCR, Instrucción pública, tomo 125, fols. 61, 70–73, for the law of May 30, 1835, and Pombo's subsequent efforts to limit its effects through administrative dispositions.

43. Aside from Restrepo, who served to June, 1839, and again in 1840–1841, the directors general in the 1839–1841 period included Alejandro Vélez, Ignacio Gutiérrez Vergara, Gutiérrez Vergara's close friend Rufino Cuervo, and Eusebio María Canabal. Cuervo and Canabal were former rectors of national universities. The rectors of the three national universities formed part of the centralizing establishment, among other reasons because they acted as agents of the national government supervising the provincial *colegios* in their

respective regions. See, for example, Cuervo as rector of the central university on the *colegio* in Ibagué, 1837, ANCR, Instrucción pública, tomo 126, fol. 122. The liberal Lorenzo María Lleras, as well as such conservatives as Joaquin Acosta and José Eusebio Caro, expounded these neo-Bourbon doctrines (Davis, "Acosta, Caro, and Lleras," pp. 393–395).

44. Herrán, Memoria de lo Interior y Relaciones Exteriores, 1839, p. 38; ANCR, Instrucción pública, tomo 126, fols. 244, 489–514, 936–949.

45. Duque Gómez as rector of the Colegio del Rosario in 1837 had urged a new philosophy program, including more emphasis on higher mathematics than was then common, as well as the study of agriculture, veterinary medicine, chemistry, and botany. In 1840 the vice-rector of the central university, Vicente Lombana, also emphasized the natural sciences. A less technical orientation can be seen in Eusebio María Canabal, September 15, 1842 (ANCR, Instrucción pública, tomo 126, fols. 244, 489–502, 504–514, 673–683).

46. Manuel Briceño, "Doctor Mariano Ospina," in Mariano Ospina Rodríguez, *El Doctor José Félix de Restrepo y su época*; Estanislao Gómez Barrientos, *Don Mariano Ospina y su época*, I, 11–24.

47. Gómez Barrientos, *Don Mariano Ospina*, I, 18–28; Carlos E. Restrepo, "Doctor Mariano Ospina," *BHA* 8, no. 87 (August 1912): 129–156. Ospina's descriptions of his plans of 1826 and 1827 were his recollections to various *antioqueño* friends many years afterward. Nevertheless, it may be assumed that the basic outlines were as he later presented them.

48. Juan de Dios Aranzazu to Francisco de Paula Santander, Medellín, September 7, 1836, in Francisco de Paula Santander, *Correspondencia . . . Santander*, comp. Cortázar, I, 181; Robledo, *Universidad de Antioquia*, pp. 58, 63, 67.

49. Unos alumnos de Santa Librada, "Instrucción pública," Cali, May 9, 1845, broadside in Colección Pineda; Ospina, Memoria de lo Interior i Relaciones Exteriores, 1842, pp. 45–46.

50. "Instrucción pública," *El Día*, January 30, 1842.

51. Pombo, Memoria de lo Interior, 1836, p. 32.

52. Law of May 16, 1840, *CN*, VIII, 568–569.

53. Article 3 of the law of May 15, 1841, declared that professional courses to be creditable toward degrees "must be taken in the universities; but not on this account is their teaching prohibited" in provincial *colegios* if they provided instruction in the "preferred subjects" (*CN*, IX, 214).

54. Articles 16, 17, Decree of December 1, 1842, *CN*, IX, 595.

55. The university of the second district (Cartagena), while theoretically well endowed, underwent a financial crisis in the 1840s because of the economic decline of the port of Cartagena, which made income on its properties hard to collect. In addition the university in Cartagena found it difficult to collect its debts because the law of *juicios ejecutivos* of June 22, 1842, denied schools special privileges in judicial action on bankruptcies. The university could not press debtors for payment for fear they might declare bankruptcy (Manuel del Río to Pres. Pedro A. Herrán, Cartagena, July 19, 1844, AH,

Correspondencia, letra R). Lack of funds played an important part in Cartagena's failure to establish scientific instruction according to Ospina's prescriptions (Ospina, Memoria de lo Interior, 1845, p. 56).

56. The income of the central university varied from 4,000 to 7,500 pesos in the 1830s and 1840s. With the revenues of el Rosario and San Bartolomé added, the total funds available for public higher education in the capital amounted to slightly more than 15,000 pesos. In Cartagena the total was under 12,000 pesos, and in Popayán somewhat more than 6,000 pesos (ANCR, Instrucción pública, tomo 115, fols. 279, 358–366, 535, 648–649; tomo 126, fols. 232, 450–470, 632. On the revenues of *colegios*, an accessible source is "Cuadro de las rentas de los Seminarios i Colejios provinciales existentes en la República, en el año económico contado de 1° de septiembre de 1846 a 31 de agosto de 1847," in República de Nueva Granada, Departamento de Relaciones Exteriores, *Estadística general de la Nueva Granada, conforme al decreto ejecutivo de 18 de diciembre de 1846 . . . Parte primera*, p. 195).

57. Articles 115, 123, 124, 129–133, 183, 244–256, 302, Decree of December 1, 1842, *CN*, IX, 610–614, 619, 629–631, 637. There were two significant exceptions to these prescriptions —students could enroll in professional courses in natural sciences or theology without the *bachiller* if they came from provinces more than twenty leagues from the capital (Articles 303, 304, 306, *CN*, IX, 637–638).

58. ANCR, Instrucción pública, tomo 117, fols. 432, 437–438.

59. Ospina, Memoria de lo Interior y

Relaciones Exteriores, 1843, pp. 50–52. In provinces like Mariquita and Neiva, the war wreaked havoc on provincial revenues that supported the *colegios*. In the fighting, some provincial officials absconded with government funds, while rebel forces seized others; everywhere tax collection broke down. In some cases funds belonging to the *colegios* were used for the war. Even institutions that were not directly in the line of fire found it difficult to collect their rents and principals lent at interest during and after the civil war. Because of its own wartime losses of revenue and accumulated debts, the national government was in no position to come to the aid of higher education ("Estracto de la memoria del Gobernador de Mariquita . . . 1841," *GNG*, May 1, 1842; "Estracto de la memoria presentada por el Gobernador de Neiva . . . 1841," *GNG*, May 1, 1842; Ospina, Memoria de lo Interior y Relaciones Exteriores, 1844, pp. 3–34).

60. Juan de Dios Aranzazu to Col. Juan María Gómez, August 25, 1843, and June, 1844, in Henao Mejía, *Aranzazu*, pp. 361, 386–387. Gómez as governor proposed Aranzazu's idea to the provincial legislature, but the liberals in this body were able to defeat the plan (Robledo, *Universidad de Antioquia*, pp. 88–89).

61. Mariano Ospina to Gen. Pedro A. Herrán, Medellín, September 5, 1845, in AH, Correspondencia, Ospina.

62. The Jesuit *colegio*'s public examinations of October, 1846, covered reading, writing, Christian doctrine, Spanish grammar, Latin, French, principles of geography and history, notions of mathematics, and declamation. The report on the examinations noted that the students did best in Latin and declamation ("Colejio privado de la Compañía de Jesús en Medellín," *El Antioqueño Constitucional*, November 8, 1846).

63. Young, "University Reform," p. 85.

64. Ospina, Memoria de lo Interior, 1845, p. 50.

65. "Informe que presenta el Gobernador de Tunja al Sr. Director General de Instrucción Pública sobre el Colegio de Boyacá," July 8, 1845, ANCR, Instrucción pública, tomo 117, fols. 533, 539–541.

66. Young concludes from the fragmentary information available that the number of university degrees awarded annually in Bogotá and Popayán dropped in the first half of the 1840s. In Popayán ten doctorates were awarded in 1839, five in 1846 ("University Reform," p. 78).

67. Unos alumnos de Santa Librada, "Instrucción pública," Cali, May 9, 1845, broadside in Colección Pineda, Biblioteca Nacional, Bogotá.

68. Daniels, *American Science in the Age of Jackson*, p. 35; Stanley Martin Guralnick, "Science and the American College" (Ph.D. dissertation), pp. 6–7, 60, 62, 65, 71, 73, 74, 79, 80, 119–125, 128, 151, 158, 168, 171–174, 195, 214–215, passim. The cramming of new courses into the old curriculum is well illustrated in Dartmouth's curricula in the years 1822 and 1860. See Leon Burr Richardson, *History of Dartmouth College*, I, 376–377, II, 430–431.

69. Guralnick, "Science and the American College," pp. 168–173.

70. Samuel Rezneck, *Education for a Technological Society*, pp. 11–14, 35–39, 53–54, 67, 87–90, 139–140;

Eugene S. Ferguson, ed., *Early Engineering Reminiscences (1815–1840) of George Escol Sellers*, passim.; Bruce Sinclair, *Early Research at the Franklin Institute*, pp. 3–15; Monte A. Calvert, *The Mechanical Engineer in America, 1830–1910*, pp. 3–14, 43–49; Russell H. Chittenden, *History of the Sheffield Scientific School of Yale University, 1846–1922*, I, 70–74; *DAB*, VI, 165–166, XX, 379; *Appleton's Cyclopaedia of American Biography*, IV, 727.

71. Daniels, *American Science in the Age of Jackson*, p. 36; Guralnick, "Science and the American College," pp. 225–226.

72. Articles 144–148, 152, Decree of December 1, 1842, *CN*, IX, 614–615.

73. Amos Eaton at the Rensselaer School also first envisioned his institution as a seminary for science teachers. Despite the growth of civil engineering in the United States in the 1820s and Eaton's own technical orientation, Rensselaer did not offer a degree in civil engineering until 1835 (Rezneck, *Education for a Technological Society*, pp. 23–25, 43–60).

74. Sinforniano Villa, June 19, 1844, ANCR, Instrucción pública, tomo 115, 606 v. This quotation, discovered by Young, is translated somewhat differently in his "University Reform," p. 97.

5. The Decline of Neo-Bourbonism

1. Joseph Leon Helguera, "The First Mosquera Administration in New Granada, 1845–1849" (Ph.D. dissertation), pp. 171–174, 177–179. Further details in ANCR, Instrucción pública, tomo 117, fol. 783; tomo 118, fol. 628; tomo 119, fols. 104, 194–195, 197, 282–283, 759; tomo 120, fols. 418, 471, 497–498; tomo 132, fols. 917–922.

2. ANCR, Instrucción pública, tomo 130, fols. 567–574, 588.

3. Ibid., tomo 130, fol. 613; tomo 132, fols. 867–903, 917–921; tomo 133, fol. 17. See also Helguera, "The First Mosquera Administration," p. 173.

4. Urrutia's father, Manuel José, had taught humanities in the Popayán Seminary and figured as an important leader in the city and provincial governments. Manuel José's brother, Mariano, had taught Latin in the Seminary and later in the university in Popayán. Mariano had also served as vice-rector and *rector encargado* and represented Popayán in the national Chamber of Deputies and Senate (Gustavo Arboleda, *Diccionario biográfico y genealógico del antiguo departamento del Cauca*, pp. 437–438).

5. This depiction of the Urrutia-Eboli controversy is based primarily on the account of the rector of the university (Juan A. Castro, "Contestación al papel intitulado 'Una negra injusticia,'" Popayán, December 1, 1849). The students' side of the story is presented in Manuel José Urrutia, "Una negra injusticia," Popayán, November 28, 1849, and "Vergüenza pública," signed by "Unos amigos de la verdad i del jóven Eustaquio Urrutia," Popayán, December 2, 1849 (all broadsides in Colección Pineda, Biblioteca Nacional, Bogotá). See also ANCR, Instrucción pública, tomo 129, fols. 422–427. Próspero Pereira Gamba, *Biografía del Professore Giuseppe Eboli, Napolitano*, pp. 16–17, omits mention of the Popayán fight, claiming he left simply because Peru offered more money.

6. John Lane Young, "University Reform in New Granada" (Ph.D. dissertation).

7. Arcesio Aragón, *Universidad del Cauca*, p. 231; ANCR, Instrucción pública, tomo 132, fols. 925, 940. On the role of lawyers in university administration, see Young, "University Reform," pp. 113–114.

8. ANCR, Instrucción pública, tomo 132, fols. 917–921.

9. Ibid., tomo 132, fols. 917–922, 924, 941–943 v.

10. Ibid., tomo 120, fols. 153, 167–169, 442–445, 486–489, 497–498, 549–551, 625, 677–690, 704, 706, 723–724; Luis Augusto Cuervo, ed., *Epistolario del Doctor Rufino Cuervo*, III, 240–244 n.

11. ANCR, Instrucción pública, tomo 132, fols. 925–940, 947–956.

12. Márquez had advocated the importation of foreign science teachers in his presidential address of 1839 (*GNG*, March 3, 1839). His only notable excursion into another part of the country occurred in the fall of 1840, when fear that the capital city would be seized by rebel forces drove him from Bogotá to the safety of Popayán. He did not travel overseas until 1850, after his attitudes had long been formed and his period of leadership over (Carlos Cuervo Márquez, *Vida del Doctor José Ignacio Márquez*, passim).

13. Aragón, *Universidad del Cauca*, pp. 227–228, 231, 232, 238–239, 243; Young, "University Reform," pp. 85, 90–91. Eboli is also credited with technical contributions that aided exports of quinine sulphate (Pereira Gamba, *Eboli*, p. 16).

14. Zenón Caicedo, apparently with no training other than that he received at the Colegio de Santa Librada, became a notable builder of bridges over the Cauca River. Liborio Vergara, after studying with Chassard took an engineering degree in Europe; later he played a leading role in road and railroad construction in the Cauca and served as a science instructor (Arboleda, *Diccionario*, 71, 79, 447, 468; Joaquín Ospina, *Diccionario biográfico y bibliográfico de Colombia*, I, 388–389; "Puente colgante de Aganche," *Anales de Ingeniería* 5, no. 57 [August 1892]: 277–279; "Puentes baratos," *Anales de Ingeniería* 6, no. 68 [August 1893]: 255; "Zenón Caicedo," *Anales de Ingeniería* 12, no. 140 [November 1901]: 101–102).

15. Bergeron received his annual salary of 1,250 pesos (1,000 dollars) for nearly four years. He went unpaid from April 1852, until at least August, 1853 (ANCR, Instrucción pública, tomo 133, fols. 7–9, 91, 107–108, 174, 192, 203).

16. Lino de Pombo, Memoria de lo Interior y Relaciones Exteriores, 1836, cuadro 3; Pedro Alcántara Herrán, Memoria de lo Interior y Relaciones Exteriores, cuadro 10; Mariano Ospina, Memoria de lo Interior y Relaciones Exteriores, 1843, cuadro 16; Ospina, Memoria de lo Interior y Relaciones Exteriores, 1844, cuadro 36; Ospina, Memoria de lo Interior y Relaciones Exteriores, 1845, cuadro 24; José Ignacio Márquez, Memoria de Gobierno, 1846, cuadros 1 and 3; Alejandro Osorio, Memoria de Gobierno, 1847, cuadros 5 and 6; Osorio, Memoria de Gobierno, 1848, cuadros 4 and 7.

17. In Popayán nearly 85 percent of the doctoral degrees (1839–1850) were in law. In Bogotá fragmentary figures suggest proportions of about 60 percent law, 30 percent medicine, 10 percent

theology degrees. In Cartagena, medicine accounted for a larger proportion of the degrees awarded (Young, "University Reform," pp. 75–77, and Aragón, *Universidad del Cauca*, pp. 227, 635–637).

18. Decree of June 13, 1846, according to ANCR, Instrucción pública, tomo 129, fol. 422.

19. The right of provincial *colegios* to give certified academic or professional courses, even though they lacked a full faculty, was reaffirmed as a general policy incorporated in the organic decree on university education (Articles 20, 25, 43, Decree of September 10, 1845, *CN*, XI, 177–178, 180, 183).

20. ANCR, Instrucción pública, tomo 117, fols. 432, 437–438, and tomo 119, fols. 206–208.

21. Ezéquiel Rojas, for the Consejo de la Facultad de Jurisprudencia, to Rector de la Universidad del primer distrito, Bogotá, August 9, 1845, ANCR, Instrucción pública, tomo 118, fols. 247–248.

22. "Informe que el Sr. Rector del Colegio de Santa Librada ha pasado . . . 12 de noviembre del año de 1846" and "Representación," July 15, 1846, ANCR, Instrucción pública, tomo 130, fols. 623–628, 634–635. Osorio had a number of other objections to the Cali program, including the rather trifling one that the librarian was being paid too high a salary ("Continúa la cuestión del Colejio de Cali," September 3, 1846, ANCR, Instrucción pública, tomo 130, fol. 638). The removal of the chair in theology originally had been suggested by Cenón Pombo, younger brother of Lino, who as rector of the university in Popayán had jurisdiction over the

colegio in Cali. Before a *colegio* could have its courses accredited as being of university status, the rector of the national university in its region had to report to the central government on the *colegio*'s capacity to support university courses. As the rectors of the universities had an interest in promoting their own institutions, they generally took a rather stiff position toward the aspiring *colegios* in their regions. Usually they urged the central government to require the *colegios* to maintain the full complements of professors required by existing educational plans (in 1845 this meant six professors in the introductory courses alone). Although the rectors' recommendations undoubtedly conditioned decisions in Bogotá, during the Mosquera administration the central authorities sometimes took a more liberal view and permitted accreditation with fewer professors than the university rectors recommended. For example, Pablo Calderón, rector of the university in Bogotá, recommended six chairs in *literatura y filosofía* for the Colegio de Floridablanca in the province of Pamplona. But the Secretario de Gobierno ultimately required only three professors (ANCR, Instrucción pública, tomo 118, fol. 32; tomo 119, fols. 235–237, 241–242).

23. Juan Nepomuceno Núñez Conto, Rector, Colegio Nacional de Santa Librada, to Gobernación, provincia de Buenaventura, Cali, September 9, 1845 (ANCR, Instrucción pública, tomo 129, fol. 677 v.), favors the development of scientific careers. His increasingly jaundiced views were expressed in "Continúa la cuestión del Colejio de Cali," September 1, 1846, and in re-

ports of October 7, 1846, and November 12, 1846, ANCR, Instrucción pública, tomo 130, fols. 623–628, 630, 638.

24. On Cali, see sources in note 22. On Tunja, see ANCR, Instrucción pública, tomo 116, fols. 206–209; tomo 117, fols. 533–541.

25. ANCR, Instrucción pública, tomo 116, fols. 151–153.

26. Lleras's increasing irritation, beginning in the middle of 1847, is documented in ANCR, Instrucción pública, tomo 132, fols. 2–84; for his activity in Congress, see Archivo del Congreso, Senado, 1848, VIII, Proyectos de ley aprobados en tercer debate, fols. 67–71, and Archivo del Congreso, Camara, 1850, X, Proyectos de ley, 81–99. Young's excellent account exaggerates perhaps in representing Lleras's activities as those of a "private school interest" ("University Reform," p. 166). See also Robert Henry Davis, "Acosta, Caro, and Lleras" (Ph.D. dissertation), pp. 212–213.

27. Archivo del Congreso, Senado, 1848, VIII, Proyectos de ley aprobados en tercer debate, fol. 38.

28. José María Samper, *Historia de una alma*, I, 120–122.

29. Young, "University Reform," pp. 165–166.

30. Archivo del Congreso, Senado, 1848, VIII, Proyectos de ley aprobados en tercer debate, fols. 32–38, 51, 53–55; Gustavo Arboleda, *Historia contemporánea de Colombia*, II, 361–362; Estanislao Gómez Barrientos, "Mariano Ospina R.," in *Colombianos ilustres*, ed. Rafael Mesa Ortiz, IV, 55–56.

31. *CN*, XIII, 71–73; Young, "University Reform," pp. 167–168.

32. *CN*, XIV, 52–55.

33. Rafael Rivas, "El Colejio del Rosario i la clase de química," 1851, Fondo Pineda, Biblioteca Nacional; Informe, Governor of Bogotá province, *GO*, October 18, 1852.

34. P.M.I. [Pedro María Ibáñez], "Centenario del Observatorio de Bogotá," *BHA* 1, no. 12 (August 1903): 649; Alfredo D. Bateman, *El Observatorio Astronómico de Bogotá*, p. 86.

35. Law of June 8, 1850, and Decree of August 25, 1850, *CN*, XIV, 143–144, 238–264. On priorities of instruction, see articles 16 and 17, p. 241. In 1853 Juan Nepomuceno Gómez, secretary of finance, proposed agricultural schools (*GO*, April 26, 1853).

36. ANCR, Instrucción pública, tomo 133, fols. 12, 29, 37–39, 40, 114–115, 137, 178, 220, 225–226, 230–233.

37. ANCR, Instrucción pública, tomo 133, fols. 326–327, 346–347, 385; Aragón, *Universidad del Cauca*, pp. 231–243.

38. ANCR, Instrucción pública, tomo 133, fols. 292–297, 575–584.

39. *GO*, January 2, February 2, 16, March 16, 20, April 13, May 28, 1851; October 14, 21, 1852; January 11, 15, 18, 22, 27, 28, February 15, 22, 1853; January 3, 1854. ANCR, Instrucción pública, tomo 133, fols. 254, 263–265, 554, 555. *Crónica del Colejio de Boyacá en 1856* and *Programa de exámenes públicos de los alumnos del Colejio de San José de Guanentá en 1863*, Fondo Pineda, Biblioteca Nacional.

40. *El Pueblo*, April 25, May 15, 1858; Emilio Robledo, *La Universidad de Antioquia 1882–1922*, pp. 125–127.

41. Among the outstanding schools and their faculty: Colegio de la Independencia, Bogotá, 1853, with

mathematics taught by Isidro Arroyo and Lino de Pombo; Colegio del Sagrado Corazón de Jesús, Bogotá, 1855, with mathematics through calculus taught by Indalecio Liévano, astronomy and physics by Venancio Restrepo, chemistry by Dr. Antonio Vargas, mineralogy and geology by Pastor Ospina, botany and zoology by José G. Triana; the Santamaría *colegio* in Nemocón (north of Bogotá), 1860, with Nepomuceno Santamaría teaching mathematics through calculus and Eustacio Santamaría teaching chemistry and agriculture; Colegio del Rosario, 1865–1867, with chemistry taught by Ezequiel Uricoechea (*GO*, February 20, 1851; January 8, February 9, 1853. *Prospectos del Colejio i Escuela del Sagrado Corazón de Jesús . . .* , 1855; *Programas . . . del establecimiento de educación de Paredes é Hijos . . .* Piedecuesta, 1859; *Certámenes del Colejio de Pérez en . . . 1864; Certámenes en el Colejio del Rosario . . .* 1865 and 1867 [all Fondo Pineda, Biblioteca Nacional]. *Almanaque curioso para el año de 1861*, p. 29).
    42. *GO*, February 20, 1851; *Prospectos del Colejio . . . del Sagrado Corazón . . .*
    43. Robledo, *Universidad de Antioquia*, pp. 125–127.
    44. *GO*, February 23, 1851; Davis, "Acosta, Caro, and Lleras," pp. 214–224; Andrés Soriano Lleras, *Lorenzo María Lleras*, p. 42; Lorenzo María Lleras, "Ultima plumada del Doctor Lorenzo María Lleras," Bogotá, 1868. José Manuel Restrepo, *Diario político y militar*, IV, 184, gives the 1850 enrollment as 170.
    45. ANCR, Instrucción pública, tomo 133, fols. 223, 340–343, 575–584;

Miguel María Lisboa, *Relaçao de uma viagem a Venezuela, Nova Granada e Equador*, pp. 251–254, 283–284.
    46. *GO*, March 8, 1853.
    47. ANCR, Instrucción pública, tomo 133, fols. 46, 51, 52, 81, 86, 89, 531, 543.
    48. Robledo, *Universidad de Antioquia*, pp. 113, 129, 131–133, 140, 164–165, 178; Aragón, *Universidad del Cauca*, pp. 247–248; Francisco de P. Borda, "Colejio universitario de Paredes é hijos," *BHA* 11, no. 131 (September 1917): 642–649.

The Origins of a Colombian Engineering Profession

    1. *Constitucional del Cauca*, October 5, 1833; Eloy B. de Castro, "Datos sobre la historia del estudio de las matemáticas en Colombia," *Anales de Ingeniería* 10, nos. 113–114 (January–February 1898): 14.
    2. *GNG*, June 23, 1833, August 17, 1834, August 21, 1836, February 19, 1837; *CN*, IV, 336–337, V, 7–8, 84–85, 172–173, VI, 56, 291–293.
    3. *GNG*, September 17, 1837, April 28, 1839, August 18, 1839; *El Argos*, August 12, 1838; Pedro Alcántara Herrán, Memoria de lo Interior y Relaciones Exteriores, 1839, p. 16.
    4. Lino de Pombo, Memoria de lo Interior y Relaciones Exteriores, 1837, pp. 50–51; José Ignacio de Márquez, presidential message, *GNG*, March 4, 1838; Herrán, Memoria de lo Interior y Relaciones Exteriores, 1839, pp. 45–47; L. de P., "Derecho de caminos," *El Argos*, April 21, 1839.
    5. Decree of May 27, 1842, *GNG*, June 5, 1842, and *CN*, IX, 378–380;

GNG, September 4, 1842; Jorge Hoyos to Gen. Pedro Alcántara Herrán, October 21, 1842, AH, Correspondencia, Hoyos; Vicente de la Roche to Gen. Pedro Alcántara Herrán, July 4, 1844, AH, Correspondencia, de la Roche.

6. Joseph Leon Helguera, "The First Mosquera Administration in New Granada, 1845–1849" (Ph.D. dissertation), pp. 462–481, passim.

6. Study Abroad

1. Joaquín Acosta to Francisco de Paula Santander, September 19, 1825, and Domingo Acosta to Francisco de Paula Santander, April 19, 1835, in Francisco de Paula Santander, *Correspondencia . . . Santander*, comp. Roberto H. Cortázar, I, 52–55, 76; ANCR, Instrucción pública, tomo 125, fol. 39; "Sociedades agrícolas," *Constitucional del Cauca*, November 17, 1832; *GNG*, March 6, 1836; Archivo del Congreso, Cámara, 1837, tomo XIV, Proyectos pendientes para primer debate, fol. 258; Francisco A. Obregón, *Esposición que el Gobernador de Antioquia dirije a la cámara de la provincia en sus sesiones ordinarias de 1836*.

2. On Julio Arboleda and Pedro Fernández Madrid (England, 1830s), see *Papel Periódico Ilustrado*, November 20, 1883, pp. 82–87, and April 1, 1883, p. 215. See also ANCR, Instrucción pública, tomo 130, fol. 563; Gustavo Arboleda, *Diccionario biográfico y genealógico del antiguo departamento del Cauca*, pp. 14, 214; Joseph Leon Helguera, "The First Mosquera Administration in New Granada 1845–1849" (Ph.D. dissertation), p. 473; Joseph Leon Helguera and

Robert H. Davis, eds., *Archivo epistolar del General Mosquera: Correspondencia con . . . Herrán*, I, 115–116, 120, 138.

3. Samuel Rezneck, *Education for a Technological Society*, pp. 43–44, 57–60, 78–86, 97–99.

4. Calculated from data in *Semicentennial Catalogue—Officers and Students of the Rensselaer Polytechnic Institute 1824–1874*, bound with *Proceedings of the Semi-Centennial Celebration of the Rensselaer Polytechnic Institute*, pp. 14–66, 83; and Henry B. Nason, ed., *Biographical Record of the Officers and Graduates of the Rensselaer Polytechnic Institute, 1824–1886*, pp. 448–458, 574–582. The totals include two Spaniards as well as six alumni with Spanish or Portuguese surnames whose origins are unknown (see Table 6).

5. On the Japanese, see Rezneck, *Education for a Technological Society*, p. 179. Material on Latins tabulated in Table 6.

6. This statement assumes the accuracy of the upward revision of export figures in William Paul McGreevey, *An Economic History of Colombia, 1845–1930*, pp. 35–37, 99, 102.

7. See, for example, *Gaceta Mercantil*, 1847–1850, 1859–1860; *El Neo-Granadino*, 1848–1857; *El Vapor*, 1857–1858; and *El Tiempo*, 1855–1860.

8. In addition to the sons of the more notable Conservative leaders, some others who studied with the Jesuits and followed them abroad after 1850 were Diego Fallón (b. Santa Ana, Tolima, 1834) and Belisario Peña (b. Zipaquirá, 1834) (Guillermo and Alfonso Hernández de Alba, "Galería de hijos insignes de nuestra historia," in Daniel

Restrepo, *El Colegio de San Bartolomé*, pp. 228–229; Luis Orjuela, *Minuta histórica zipaquireña*, p. 188).

9. As quoted in Estanislao Gómez Barrientos, *Don Mariano Ospina y su época*, II, 179.

10. Ibid., pp. 549–553; Joaquín Ospina, *Diccionario biográfico y bibliográfico de Colombia*, III, 180–182.

11. Pedro de la Herrán, "Cartas dirigidas a su esposa Matea durante los años de 1795 a 1803," seventeen manuscript letters in Biblioteca Luis Angel Arango, manuscript collection.

12. When the Liberals gained power in 1849, Herrán came back to New Granada. In 1851 he returned to New York, where he formed a mercantile partnership with his father-in-law, General Mosquera. In 1855 Herrán was reappointed minister to the United States and left the partnership. He served as minister until 1860, when he left his post to aid the Conservative government against the revolutionary hosts led by General Mosquera. In 1861 Mosquera reappointed Herrán minister in Washington, only to dismiss him in 1862 when he found that Herrán was acting as representative of the defunct Conservative government. Because of Herrán's excellent relations in Washington, however, the United States continued to recognize him as New Granada's representative until the middle of 1863, after which time he finally left the country (Eduardo Posada and Pedro M. Ibáñez, *Vida de Herrán*, pp. 133–214; AH, Rejistro de correspondencia, 1850–1853, and Copiador de cartas, no. 1, 1854–1855).

13. The problem of determining the occupations of members of the upper class in the nineteenth century is difficult, not only because of the sparseness of data on some individuals, but also because there was little specialization of function. In any part of the country, including Bogotá, one man was likely to play three or more different roles. The men are categorized here according to their dominant occupations. Thus, most of the lawyers, politicians, and merchants owned some land. But only those who did not practice law or trade (or practiced them infrequently) and who were thought of by their contemporaries as landowners are so considered.

14. As in the case of occupation, some individuals' places of residence are hard to specify. Many of the people listed as provincials spent some time in the Congress in Bogotá. On the other hand, Manuel María Mallarino of Cali is considered a resident of Bogotá because after 1840 he was holding office in the capital more than half the time. Similarly, Manuel Antonio Arrubla is classified as a resident of Bogotá. Although he came from the city of Antioquia and retained some economic interests there, he normally lived in the capital.

15. J. Domingo Pumarejo to Pedro Alcántara Herrán, Valledupar, December 21, 1847, and Riohacha, July 16, 1848, AH, Correspondencia, letra P.

16. Mariano Ospina Rodríguez, Medellín, to Tulio Ospina, July 11, 1877, quoted in Estanislao Gómez Barrientos, "Mariano Ospina R.," in *Colombianos ilustres*, ed. Rafael M. Mesa Ortiz, IV, 176.

17. Ibid., p. 177.

18. In a letter of February 27, 1877,

Mariano Ospina commented to Pedro Nel: "In infancy and in youth there is an irresistible propensity to take seriously the dreams of the imagination which make one look with disdain . . . upon the prosaic realities of life. . . . I reiterate to you my counsels of modesty, of benevolence for all, of tolerance, of punctuality in the fulfillment of all your duties." And the following March 13, he added, "I have noted with very much pleasure . . . that you are occupied now much more with ideas and facts than with phrases, which is a great progress. It did not seem strange to me that at your age you should exert yourself to *make style*, as the French say, looking for new phrases and subtle allusions, which is a dominant vice and has been always since literature reached a high degree of perfection. . . . I expected that on reaching the age of good sense you would correct your style, striving for that noble simplicity of expression which produces thought with clarity and precision, and constitutes the best merit of style; and I see with satisfaction that you are taking this road before I expected" (ibid., pp. 174–175).

19. Pastor Ospina, Cartagena, to Señor Gen. Pedro A. Herrán, New York, February 27, 1862, and July 31, 1862, AH, correspondencia, Ospina to Herrán, II, typescript, pp. 135–136, 143. Pastor Ospina, brother of Mariano Ospina Rodríguez, the president of Colombia whose government had just been overthrown by General Mosquera, wrote these letters from prison in Cartagena. On October 22, 1862, Herrán placed Sebastian in a large plant manufacturing machinery in Paterson, New Jersey (Pedro A. Herrán, New York, to Pastor Ospina, October 17, 1862, and October 26, 1862, AH, correspondencia, Pastor Ospina, typescript, pp. 40–41).

20. "It is not a very easy thing to place a foreign youth in a respectable house in this country, if one is to impose the condition, which seems to me indispensable, that the work with which he be occupied be beneficial" (Pedro A. Herrán, New York, to Ciudno. Manl. M. Mallarino, September 3, 1855, in AH, Libro copiador, no. 1, 1854–1855, fol. 429). See Adolfo Harker Mutis, *Mis recuerdos*, pp. 15–23, for his contrasting experience in England in the 1840s.

21. Inocencio Vargas, Bogotá, to Santamaría & Cía., Liverpool, September 25, 1857, in Vargas Cartas, Bogotá, 1856–1857, fol. 443; José Eusebio Caro, *Epistolario*, pp. 159, 441–442.

22. Angel and Rufino José Cuervo, *Vida de Rufino Cuervo y noticias de su época*, II, 164; Pedro A. Herrán to M. M. Mallarino, September 3, 1855, AH, Libro copiador, no. 1, 1854–1855, fol. 429. Among the aristocrats who sent sons to Herrán for commercial training were Antonio Manrique and José Rodrigo Borda.

23. José Manuel Restrepo, *Autobiografía*, p. 42.

24. See J. Domingo Pumarejo, to Pedro A. Herrán, Valledupar, December 21, 1847, AH, correspondencia, Letra P.

25. In 1852 Herrán found it necessary to withdraw a young *antioqueño* from a school in Stamford, Connecticut, because the master forced him to attend Protestant services (AH, Registro de correspondencia, 1850–1853, letters to

R. E. Rice, Stamford, August 10 and 25, 1852, and to Eugenio Uribe, Medellín, November 21, 1852).

26. Pedro A. Herrán to Rafael Espinosa, March 8, March 24, and November 6, 1852, in AH, Rejistro de correspondencia, 1850–1853. On William A. Norton and John A. Porter at Brown and Yale, see Russell H. Chittenden, *History of the Sheffield Scientific School of Yale University, 1846–1922*, I, 55–61.

27. Yale had benefited from the services of the country's leading academic chemist and geologist, Benjamin Silliman, for more than half a century (1802–1853) and of an outstanding astronomer, meteorologist, and teacher of physics, Denison Olmsted, for more than a quarter century (1825–1859). The Yale Scientific School had been developed between 1847 and 1852 by the agricultural chemist John P. Norton, and after his death it was carried on by the two scientists who had decamped from Brown. By 1856 the Yale Scientific School boasted four professors of technical subjects, plus the services of professors of physics, geology, and the other sciences in Yale College. Its instruction was marked by heavy emphasis on student-conducted laboratory experiments (Chittenden, *History of the Sheffield Scientific School*, I, 28–69).

28. Luis M. Silvestre to Ciudadano Jral. Pedro A. Herrán, Honda, January 9, 1856, AH, correspondencia, letra S, fols. 35–36. The celebrated Benjamin Silliman, Sr., had retired, and both he and his son, who was teaching at Yale in 1856, taught chemistry and geology, not math or engineering (Chittenden, *History of the Sheffield Scientific School*, I, 28–30, 45–46, 63).

29. Herrán offered little hope to Mallarino and Arosemena that their sons would be accepted at West Point. The son of Venezuelan Gen. José Antonio Páez had been permitted to attend at an earlier period, but the unfavorable impression he left made it doubtful that the academy would repeat the experiment (Pedro Alcántara Herrán, New York, to Ciudno. Manl. M. Mallarino, February 5 and 22, 1856, and to Justo Arosemena, December 19, 1856, in AH, Libro copiador, no. 2, 1856–1857, fols. 74–76, 120–122, 549). According to academy records, Julián A. D. Páez attended West Point from July, 1823, to June, 1827, when he was "dropped." Foreign cadets were not again admitted to the academy until 1884 when two Guatemalans were admitted by joint resolution of the U.S. Congress (personal communication from Mary Piccone, archives assistant, U.S. Military Academy, April 15, 1969).

30. *Semi-Centennial Catalogue . . . Rensselaer*, p. 31, passim; Nason, ed., *Biographical Record*, pp. 394, 448–548, 574–583; Joaquín Ospina, *Diccionario biográfico y bibliográfico de Colombia*, III, 430–431, 965–966; personal communication from Linda Cusanelli, reference assistant, Stevens Institute of Technology, April 16, 1970; Monte A. Calvert, *The Mechanical Engineer in America, 1830–1910*, p. 49; Emilio Robledo, *La vida del General Pedro Nel Ospina*, pp. 33, 45–47; *Anales de Ingeniería* 5, no. 57 (April 1892): 279–283, and no. 58 (May 1892): 320; personal communications from reference librarian at Stevens Institute of Technology and university archivists at Columbia University and University of California, Berkeley.

31. Advertisement, in Julio A. Garavito, *Almanaque de "El Bogotano" histórico, eclesiástico y literario para el año de 1883*, p. 102. See also Abelardo Ramos, "Astronomía y geodesia," *Anales de Ingeniería* 1, no. 8 (March 1888): 225; "Elias Loomis," ibid. 3, no. 28 (November 1889): 99–100; "Variedades," ibid. 3, no. 28 (November 1889): 127; "Instituto de Ingenieros Mecánicos," ibid. 3, no. 36 (July 1890): 403; "La Universidad de Purdue," ibid. 5, no. 57 (April 1892): 284–286.

32. Pedro A. Herrán to Eugenio M. Uribe, September 3, 1855, and to Ciudno. Manl. M. Mallarino, October 4, 1855, in AH, Libro copiador, no. 1, 1854–1855, fols. 431, 483; and Pedro A. Herrán to M. M. Mallarino, October 1, 1856, AH, Libro copiador, no. 2, 1856–1857, fol. 238 vta.

33. For example, José María Davison visited the United States in 1858 and 1875 to study salt-making processes in Syracuse as well as other industrial sites. In 1876–1877 two of Colombia's most promising young engineers, Enrique Morales R. and Abelardo Ramos, spent a year on an extended study tour in the United States and became converts to the "American school" of engineering (Luis Orjuela, "José María Davison," *Anales de Ingeniería* 12, no. 140 [November 1901]: 98–99; 13, no. 158 [April 1906]: 292).

34. James S. Easby-Smith, *Georgetown University in the District of Columbia, 1789–1907*, II, 190–191; personal communication from Ann C. Clark, assistant reference librarian, Georgetown University Library, March 20, 1969.

35. Acosta's studies were only partly scientific. He also took lessons in fencing and elocution, and he seems to have displayed as much (or more) interest in politics and the humanities as in science (Soledad Acosta de Samper, *Biografía del General Joaquín Acosta*, pp. 205–229, 436–456).

36. Adolfo Dollero, *Cultura colombiana*, pp. 118–120; ANCR, Instrucción pública, tomo 133, fol. 127. *Papel Periódico Ilustrado*, January 1, 15, 1884, April 22, 1884, and *Colombia Ilustrada*, October 22, 1890, give data on such physicians as Antonio Vargas Reyes (Paris, 1840–1843), Manuel Uribe Angel (U.S. and Europe, 1849–1852), Manuel Plata·Azuero (U.S., England, Paris, 1854–1857), José Vicente Uribe (Europe and U.S., 1850s), and Andrés Posada Quijano (Paris, 1878–1882).

37. The Colombian government appointed Peña consul in Bordeaux and then secretary of the Colombian legation in Paris in order to facilitate his studies (Abelardo Ramos, "Manuel H. Peña," *Anales de Ingeniería* 12, no. 139 [October 1901]: 69; Diódoro Sánchez, "Biografía del Dr. José María González Benito," ibid. 14, nos. 165–166 [November–December 1906]: 135; Enrique Morales R. "Juan N. González Vásquez," ibid. 18, nos. 211–212 [September–October 1910]: 119).

38. Emiro Kastos, "Estudios industriales," *El Pueblo*, September 6, 1855. Moore, who had come to the mining regions of Antioquia and the Cauca in 1829, revolutionized *antioqueño* mining techniques by introducing the first mechanically operated ore crushers. He later introduced a variety of other hydraulically driven machines and established the first large smelting furnaces in Antioquia (Gabriel Henao Mejía,

Juan de Dios Aranzazu, pp. 221–225).

39. Gómez Barrientos, *Don Mariano Ospina*, II, 423, 425.

40. Otero Muñoz, "Cien cancilleres colombianos," in *Historia de la cancillería de San Carlos*, p. 295; Emilio Robledo, *Vida del General Pedro Nel Ospina*, pp. 46–47.

41. Alfredro D. Bateman, *Páginas para la historia de la ingeniería colombiana*, pp. 217–226, 327, 559–562.

42. Arboleda, *Diccionario*, pp. 278–279, 295; Marco A. Pizano, "Una amistad de colegio," *Papel Periódico Ilustrado*, October 1, 1882, pp. 62–63; Arturo D. Malo O'Leary, "El Colegio de Stonyhurst," *El Repertorio Colombiano*, September, 1878, pp. 222–232; Bateman, *Páginas*, pp. 332–335, 536–537.

43. Personal communications from reference librarians at Fordham, Yale, and Georgetown university libraries.

44. In 1834 one of the best *colegios* in Bogotá, that run by José Triana, cost about 200 pesos for boys under fourteen. The Instituto Benedeti in Cartagena in 1846 cost about 200 pesos for boys under thirteen, about 240 for those over sixteen. Some lesser *colegios* were even cheaper (*GNG*, September 28, 1834; flyers in Colección Pineda, Biblioteca Nacional, Bogotá, and in ANCR, Instrucción pública, tomo 119, fols. 625–626; *El Vapor*, January 27, 1858).

45. In the early stages some fathers expected an education in the United States to cost no more than 200 dollars a year (J. D. Pumarejo, Valledupar, to Pedro A. Herrán, December 21, 1847, in AH, correspondencia, letra P.). Herrán initially estimated annual costs at 300 to 350 dollars. By 1851 his esti-

mate for boys aged seven to ten had risen to 480 dollars, and for older youths costs tended to be from 625 to 720 dollars per year. See Pedro A. Herrán to J. Domingo Pumarejo, November 19, 1848, ibid. Also Herrán to Manuel María Velasco, February 12, 1851; to Bonifacio Espinosa, October 12 and November 20, 1851; to Manuel M. Mosquera, May 14, 1852; to Alejandro McDowall, August 19, 1852; and to Pedro Vásquez, November 2, 1852 (all in AH "Rejistro de correspondencia, 1850–53"). See also Herrán to José R. Borda, January 5, 1853; to Mariano Calvo, December 15, 1853; to José Ramón Durán, December 16, 1853; to Fernando Caicedo Camacho, December 16, 1853; to Diego Uribe, December 16, 1853; to Francisco A. Jaramillo, December 16, 1853 (all in AH, "Rejistro de cartas escritas a los jóvenes que están a mi cargo y a sus padres," 1853).

46. See table on p. 307.

47. Malo's performance in New Granada is described in José María Cordóvez Moure, *Reminiscencias de Santafé y Bogotá*, pp. 1435–1440. Herrán's troubles with him are suggested in letters to Jesús Malo Blanco, June 3, 1851; to José Ignacio de Márquez, June 8, 1851; to Antonio Malo, June 9, 1851; to J. I. Márquez, September 14, 1851; to Jesús Malo Blanco, September 17, 1851; to J. I. Márquez, September 14, 1851; to Antonio Malo, June 13, 1851 (all in AH, "Rejistro de correspondencia, 1850–1853"). Other difficult cases were Pedro Pablo Mosquera, who had to be sent home to Popayán after a series of nervous breakdowns, and Juan Pablo Arrubla, who (in Herrán's view) had

Latin American students at Rensselaer (1850–1874).

Caribbean and Mezo-American Students			South American Students		
	Degree	No Degree		Degree	No Degree
Cubans	16	38	Brazilians	7	6
Puerto Ricans	2	4	New Granadans	2	0
Mexicans	0	4	Ecuadorians	0	1
Costa Ricans	0	1	Peruvians	2	3
			Chileans	1	0
Total	18	47		12	10

Source: Based on data in *Proceedings of the Semi-Centennial . . . Rensselaer*, pp. 14–66, 83. The low rate of finishing for Cubans and Mexicans is possibly attributable to political events at home. Greater difficulty and cost of transportation may have been factors selecting more qualified students. Or parents in distant lands, considering the greater psychological effort and cost involved in sending their sons, may have been more likely to demand a higher return on their investment, namely the degree.

been spoiled by the indulgences of his rich *antioqueño* father (ibid., passim).

48. Cases of Luis G. Rivas, Nicolás Osorio, Carlos Tanco, Joaquín Antonio de Mier, Wenceslao Campuzano, Nicolás Tanco Armero (*Papel Periódico Ilustrado*, May 5, 1883, p. 251, and May 25, 1883, pp. 293–294; *Colombia Ilustrada*, July 20, 1889, p. 94, October 15, 1889, p. 134, February 15, 1890, p. 157, January 31, 1891, pp. 322–327). One exception was José María Quijano Otero, who studied medicine in Bogotá and commerce in Europe but dropped both professions for a career in literature and politics (*Papel Periódico Ilustrado*, September 30, 1883, pp. 34–35).

49. *Papel Periódico Ilustrado*, January 1, 1884, pp. 118–121; January 15, 1884, p. 134; April 22, 1884, pp. 246–249; *Colombia Ilustrada*, October 22, 1890, pp. 258–259, 264–267.

50. Otero Muñoz, "Cien cancilleres colombianos," in *Historia de la cancillería de San Carlos*, pp. 295–298; *Anales de Ingeniería* 11, no. 127 (March 1899): 67–77; Bateman, *Páginas*, pp. 463–467.

51. Dollero, *Cultura colombiana*, pp. 127, 131, 138, 505; Ospina, *Diccionario*, I, 153.

52. The students associated with General Herrán who later played important roles in Colombian education were Juan David Herrera, who served for fifty years as professor of medicine in the National University; Víctor Mallarino, a life-long secondary school teacher; Venancio González Manrique, professor of Spanish, English, and French in the National University, author of texts in language and history, director of public education, and "national interpreter" in the 1870s and 1880s; Fidel Pombo, professor of math

in the Colegio de San Bartolomé in the 1860s and of natural sciences in the National University after 1868; Rafael Espinosa Escallón, dean of the faculty of mathematics in the 1880s; and Tomás Herrán, professor of English and mathematics in the National University, rector of the University of Antioquia, director of public education in Antioquia, national minister of public instruction, and ultimately Colombian minister in Washington (Ospina, *Diccionario*, II, 620–621, 627–628; Dollero, *Cultura colombiana*, pp. 81, 127, 138, 341; *Anales de la Universidad* 3, no. 13 [January 1870]: 179–184, and 5, no. 25 [January–March 1871]: 13–26; *Anales de la Instrucción Pública* 1, no. 1 [September 1880]: 52–54, 63, 67, 72; *Anales de Ingeniería* 1, no. 1 [August 1887]: 27; Gómez Barrientos, *Don Mariano Ospina* I, 236).

53. Dollero, *Cultura colombiana*, pp. 118–119, 120–121.

54. These include Rafael Arboleda (Paris, Spain), Alejandro Manrique C. (Spain), Fidel Pombo (Yale, Paris, England), Juan Nepomuceno González Vásquez (Paris, England, Spain, Italy), Pedro Sosa (Rensselaer Polytechnic, U.S., Mexico) (Ospina, *Diccionario*, I, 153, 300–301; *Anales de Ingeniería* 2, no. 19 [February 1889]; 10, no. 121 [September 1898]: 256–279; 12, no. 137 [August 1901]: 4–8; 18, nos. 211–212 [September, October 1910]: 119–126).

55. The Cuban engineers who graduated from Rensselaer, in contrast with the first Brazilians, were constantly employed in railroad construction and as municipal engineers from 1857, when the first Cuban graduated, to the end of the 1860s. Apparently the outbreak of civil war in Cuba in 1868 caused some of

the Cuban engineers to emigrate (*Semi-Centennial Catalogue . . . Rensselaer*, pp. 22–23; Nason, ed., *Biographical Record*, pp. 281, 295, 307–308, 310, 322, 328–329, 332–333, 350, 356, 362, 371, 376–377, 383–384, 414, 418).

56. Arboleda, *Diccionario*, p. 295. Another early overseas student could not teach chemistry in Cartagena (1839–1842) because the university lacked the funds to pay him (ANCR, Instrucción pública, tomo 114, fols. 475, 643–649).

57. Pedro A. Herrán, to José González Carazo, Macía é hijo, Francisco de Zubiría, and others, November 4, 1855, AH, Libro copiador, no. 1, 1854–1855, fol. 538; Pedro A. Herrán to Rafael Espinosa, December 19, 1856, AH, Libro copiador, no. 2, 1856–1857, fol. 553; "Boletín industrial," *El Tiempo*, August 11 and November 3, 1857; *Anales de Ingeniería* 1, no. 1 (August 1887): 27.

58. Cordóvez Moure, *Reminiscencias*, pp. 782, 1055.

59. They included Ricardo Arango, who served as governor of Panamá in the 1880s; José María Mallarino, who was an active Conservative political writer in the latter part of the 1870s; Juan de Dios Uribe, another political writer; and Rafael Arboleda Mosquera.

60. Robledo, *Vida del general Pedro Nel Ospina*, p. 43; Ospina, *Diccionario*, III, 180–182.

61. Ospina, *Diccionario*, I, 300–301; Enrique Naranjo M., "José Cornelio Borda y la defensa del Callao en 1866," *BHA* 7, no. 82 (March 1912): 647–649; "José Cornelio Borda," *BHA* 32, nos. 363–364 (January–February 1945): 19–62. The last of these sources, a re-

print of a memorial released at the time of his death, seems the most trustworthy; unlike the others it indicates that Borda was appointed but did not actually serve as a chief engineer in France.

62. Ospina, *Diccionario*, I, 153.
63. "Bienvenida," *Anales de Ingeniería* 2, no. 19 (February 1889): 207.

7. The Colegio Militar

1. The evolution of a sister institution, the nautical school in Cartagena, for the education of river pilots and naval officers, will not be treated here in detail. Pieces of its history from 1824 to 1850 can be found in Humberto Triana y Antorveza, "La Escuela Náutica de Cartagena," *Boletín cultural y bibliográfico* 7, no. 8 (1964): 1372–1376, and in John Lane Young, "University Reform in New Granada" (Ph.D. dissertation), pp. 103–105.
2. Frederick B. Artz, *The Development of Technical Education in France, 1500–1850*, pp. 47–48, 55–59, 82–86, 91–101, 151–155; *La Grande Encyclopédie*, XV, 399–413, 421.
3. Sidney Forman, *West Point*, pp. 15–38, 74–88; Daniel Hovey Calhoun, *The American Civil Engineer*, p. 40.
4. Artz, *Development of Technical Education in France*, pp. 167–172, 231; Forman, *West Point*, pp. 61–66, 72; Calhoun, *American Civil Engineer*, pp. 40–42, 164–166.
5. Francisco José de Caldas, "Plan razonado de un Cuerpo militar de Ingenieros mineralógicos en el Nuevo Reino de Granada," in Diego Mendoza, *Expedición botánica de José Celestino Mutis al Nuevo Reino de Granada y*

memorias inéditas de Francisco José de Caldas, pp. 93–130.
6. Lino de Pombo, "Memoria histórica sobre la vida, carácter, trabajos científicos y literarios, y servicios patrióticos de Francisco José de Caldas," *Anales de Ingeniería* 8, nos. 98, 99, 100 (October, November, December 1896): 358–364.
7. David Bushnell, *The Santander Regime in Gran Colombia*, p. 189; ANCR, Instrucción pública, tomo 115, fols. 694–700 v.
8. Pleas for action on the military school appear in José Hilario López, Memoria de Guerra, 1834, pp. 12–13; Antonio Obando, Memoria de Guerra, 1836, pp. 7–8.
9. "Instrucción pública," *Constitución del Cauca*, December 29, 1832. Pombo describes himself as author of this article in ANCR, Instrucción pública, tomo 115, fol. 567. See also *Constitución del Cauca*, November 16, 1833.
10. The law of April 29, 1836 is in *CN*, III, 311–317. On military instruction in Bogotá from 1837 to 1839, see ANCR, Instrucción pública, tomo 112, fols. 250, 458–462; tomo 113, fol. 171; tomo 114, fols. 45, 949–952; tomo 115, fols. 285–287.
11. ANCR, Guerra, tomo 770, fols. 601–602; José Hilario López, Memoria de Guerra, 1838, pp. 2–4; Tomás Cipriano de Mosquera, Memoria de Guerra, 1838, pp. 22–23; José Acevedo, Memoria de Guerra, 1842, pp. 13–15. See also *GNG*, August 13 and September 3, 1837.
12. López, Memoria de Guerra, 1838, p. 3–4; Tomás Cipriano de Mosquera, Memoria de Guerra, 1839, p. 22–23; Tomás Cipriano de Mosquera,

Memoria de Guerra, 1840, pp. 7–8; José Acevedo, Memoria de Guerra, 1841, pp. 13–14; José Acevedo, Memoria de Guerra, 1844, pp. 7–8; José Acevedo, Memoria de Guerra, 1845, pp. 29–30.

13. ANCR, Instrucción pública, tomo 115, fols. 607 r-v.

14. Laws of May 2 and 7, 1845, *CN*, XI, 69–71, 89–91; *GNG*, November 9, 1845; law of June 9, 1846, *CN*, XI, 400–402; Joseph Leon Helguera, "The First Mosquera Administration in New Granada, 1845–1849" (Ph.D. dissertation), pp. 483–487; "Canal de Cartajena," *El Día*, May 24, 1845.

15. Zawadsky offered the people of New Granada a text on civil engineering, to which the Colegio Militar subscribed.

16. *GNG*, February 21, 1847.

17. Law of June 1, 1847 and Decree of July 20, 1847, *CN*, XII, 111, 326–336.

18. Those most committed to military training probably were Gen. José María Ortega, director; Col. Santiago Fraser, a Scot who had fought in the Wars of Independence, inspector; and Dr. José María Galavis, professor of military legislation. Another member of the faculty in its first two years was Miguel Bracho, a Venezuelan liberal-in-exile, who served as professor of drawing and instructor of the preparatory class.

19. ANCR, Guerra, tomo 715, fols. 868–869; tomo 763, fol. 661.

20. The original curriculum for the third year was extended to cover two years, so that a whole course might be devoted to calculus, the following year to principles of mechanics, road and bridge building, architecture, and so forth (ibid., tomo 748, fols. 38–43, 109–110, 133 v., 174; tomo 761, fols. 691–693).

21. Pombo's severity and meticulousness are evident in the periodic reports that the faculty rendered on class performance and examinations. The form of Pombo's elaborate reports was ultimately followed by the other faculty members (see ibid., tomo 747, fols. 989–991; tomo 748, fols. 49–51, 88–90, 128–129, 216–220, 228–229; tomo 768, fols. 350, 408–410, 527–528; tomo 793, fol. 43; tomo 1410, fols. 53–59, 113–119).

22. Ibid., tomo 793, fol. 208 v. Tomás Rueda Vargas believes only two of the 1848–1854 graduates became *militares* (*Escritos*, III, 238–239).

23. Most viewed the Colegio Militar simply as a cheap way to get a good education; beyond this, career aims were a bit vague. For specific statements of career goals, civil and military, see ANCR, Guerra, tomo 748, fol. 17; tomo 770, fols. 483, 489, 521, 598, 660, 681, 779; tomo 811, fol. 456.

24. Alejandro Osorio, Memoria de Gobierno, 1848, p. 32; Mosquera presidential message of 1849; ANCR, Guerra, tomo 761, fols. 688–690.

25. Joaquín M. Barriga, Memoria de Guerra, 1849, p. 10; Tomás Herrera, Memoria de Guerra, 1850, pp. 22–25; Valerio F. Barriga, Memoria de Guerra, 1851, p. 17; Valerio F. Barriga, Memoria de Guerra, 1852, p. 42; Valerio F. Barriga, Memoria de Guerra, 1853, pp. 24–25.

26. *GO*, December 9, 1852; October 24, 26, 27, 1853.

27. Herrera, Memoria de Guerra, 1850, pp. 22–23; Barriga, Memoria de Guerra, 1853, pp. 23–27.

28. Helguera, "The First Mosquera Administration," p. 184. The first students are listed in Joaquín M. Barriga,

Memoria de Guerra, 1848, Cuadro 2.

29. Juan Estéban Zamarra was protected, educated, and presumably nominated for the Colegio Militar by the Bishop of Antioquia. His travel expenses to Bogotá were paid through alms collections (Joaquín Ospina, *Diccionario biográfico y bibliográfico de Colombia*, III, 997–999).

30. Of thirty students in the first preparatory class, at least twelve were either of the Bogotá upper class or sons of high-ranking officers, six were upper-stratum provincials, and one (Cayo Mendoza) was a tailor or the son of a tailor (ANCR, Guerra, tomo 715, fols. 894, 932; tomo 747, fols. 896, 917–952, 980; tomo 748, fol. 52, 88, 112, 132–133, 181 v).

31. ANCR, Guerra, tomo 761, fols. 680–682; tomo 768, fol. 545.

32. Reports on students' performances are in ANCR, Guerra, tomo 747, fols. 989–991; tomo 748, fols. 49–51, 88–90, 128–129, 216–220, 228–229; tomo 768, fols. 350, 408–409, 527–528; tomo 793, fols. 43, 135–137, 205–208; tomo 811, fols. 253–255, 319–326, 361, 430–434; tomo 1410, fols. 53–59, 113–119, 166–168, 188.

33. Cf. Tables in Memorias de Guerra, previously cited. Of the eleven who graduated or came closest to graduating between 1851 and 1854, the first eight were from Bogotá, the last three from the adjacent provinces of Zipaquirá and Tequendama.

34. 1848–1849: 189,200 reals; 1851–1852: 76,748 reals (Laws of May 28, 1848, and June 4, 1851, *CN*, XIII, 200, and XIV, 478. First noted by Young, "University Reform," p. 103).

35. *GO*, March 17, 29, April 2, 15, 1853. Liberal suspicion of the military

school may have surfaced earlier, during the Conservative rebellion that began in July, 1851. José Manuel Restrepo, a Conservative, claimed the school's temporary suspension during the rebellion was prompted by cadet hostility to the government. War Department documents, however, indicate that some cadets actively supported the government and that government officials at the time took a favorable view of the school (Restrepo, *Diario*, IV, 189; ANCR, Guerra, tomo 1410, fol. 108; Arboleda, *Historia contemporánea*, III, 236; V. F. Barriga, Memoria de Guerra, 1852, p. 40).

36. The course of the bill to abolish the academy, presented by Estanislao Silva, can be traced in Archivo del Congreso, Cámara, 1854, III, Proyectos de ley suspendidos, fols. 103–106, and in *GO*, February 16, 18, 22, 23, 27, 1854. A substitute bill by Alipio Mantilla and Rito Antonio Martínez called for schools of mathematics and physical sciences, engineering, and natural history (Museo Nacional) in Bogotá, mining in Medellín, agriculture in Cali, commerce in Panamá, navigation in Cartagena, and manufacturing in Socorro. Popayán, traditionally an educational center, was conspicuously absent (*GO*, April 7, 1854).

37. Rito Antonio Martínez report on proyecto of Estanislao Silva, Archivo del Congreso, Cámara, 1854, III, Proyectos de ley suspendidos, fol. 103.

38. ANCR, Guerra, tomo 747, fols. 222–223; Pedro A. Herrán, Memoria de Guerra, 1855, p. 23; Gustavo Arboleda, *Historia contemporánea de Colombia*, IV, 31, 260, 266, 419.

39. Mosquera decree of August 24, 1861, *CN*, XIX, 328–330. On Lleras's

312 Notes to Pages 179–182

administration and standards, see
ANCR, Guerra, tomo 867, fols.
114–116, 119–120, 124, 249, 281, 398,
408, 417, 419, 468. On January 12,
1867, there were 109 students; the maximum was 130 (ibid., tomo 867, fols.
718, 793, 816).

40. Valerio F. Barriga, Memoria de
Guerra, 1866, pp. 12–13; Rudecindo
López, Memoria de Guerra, 1867, p.
14; José María Baraya, Memoria de
Guerra, 1868, pp. 27–28; José María
Vergara y Vergara and J. B. Gaitán,
*Almanaque de Bogotá i guia de foras-
teros para 1867*, p. 313; Enrique Otero
D'Costa, "El Coronel Santiago Fraser,"
BHA 15, no. 176 (June 1926): 482; Os-
pina, *Diccionario*, I, 699.

41. Decree of February 21, 1883, *El
Ingeniero*, no. 1, pp. 4–9. See also ibid.,
December 15, 1883, pp. 502–514.

42. Various of the elements of prestige and the practical in the appeal of
the military school are suggested in
Ramon Guerra Azuola's later comment
that young men of his generation had
been enticed by "the allure of the
novelty of the scientific career which the
government opened to us, and of the
honorific place which was offered us in
the army" (quoted in Diódoro Sánchez,
"Instituto Central de Matemáticas,"
Anales de Ingeniería 5, no. 53
[December 1891]: 129).

43. The 277,000 dollars includes
160,000 budgeted for government investments in steamboat navigation on
the country's rivers (*GNG*, April 25,
1847; Decree of December 23, 1847,
CN, XII, 492–493; Helguera, "The First
Mosquera Administration," pp.
462–481).

44. *GO*, February 17 and 23, 1850,
and June 23, 1850; *El Día*, March 2,

1850; Victoriano de Diego Paredes,
Memoria de Relaciones Exteriores,
1851, pp. 13–15; José María Plata,
Memoria de Relaciones Exteriores,
1852, pp. 18–21; *El Neo-Granadino*,
September 3, 1852; José María Plata,
Memoria de Relaciones Exteriores,
1853, p. 36; Cerbeleón Pinzón,
Memoria de Relaciones Exteriores,
1854, Appendix.

45. On Manuel Ponce de León, see
Anales de Ingeniería 11, no. 127 (March
1899): 81–108. On Indalecio Liévano,
see Próspero Pereira Gamba and Sal-
vador Camacho Roldán i. Cía., *Revista
Comercial*, April 20, 1863; *La Opinión*,
April 13, July 27, and August 10, 1864;
"Camino de Poncet," *El Comercio*,
November 26, 1884; and *Anales de
Ingeniería* 22, nos. 257–258
(July–August 1914): 2–16. On Manuel
H. Peña, see *Anales de Ingeniería* 12,
no. 139 (October 1901): 67–71; on
Joaquín B. Barriga, ibid. no. 148 (June
1905): 355–356; on Juan N. González
Vásquez, ibid. 18, nos. 211–212
(September–October 1910): 119–126.
See also Alfredo Ortega Díaz,
*Ferrocarriles colombianos: Resumen
histórico*, pp. 29, 364–365, 426–428,
533–534, 558–578; Juan Francisco Ur-
rutia, report on Socorro road, *El
Tiempo*, February 3, 1857; ad, *El
Tiempo*, February 13, 1857; José A.
Currea, *Informe . . . Secretario de
Hacienda . . . al Gobernador del Estado de Cundinamarca, 1858*, p. 47;
José Manuel Restrepo, *Diario político y
militar*, IV, 739; Ospina, *Diccionario*, I,
300–301, 699, II, 505–506; Adolfo Dollero, *Cultura colombiana*, pp. 113–114,
129–130, 138.

46. In 1866 eight of the ten best-
paying posts in the national corps of en-

gineers created by Mosquera were filled by former students of the military school of the 1848–1854 period; these positions provided salaries of 1,800 pesos. Two others held subordinate posts with salaries of 840 pesos. In the same period national ministers were paid 2,500 pesos and colonels in the army 1,680. (Vergara y Vergara and Gaitán, *Almanaque de Bogotá . . . 1867*, pp. 311–317). On Mosquera's attentions in 1866–1867, see also Diódoro Sánchez, "Biografía del Dr. José María González Benito," *Anales de Ingeniería* 14, nos. 165–166 (November–December 1906): 136, and Enrique Morales R., "Juan N. González Vásquez," ibid. 18, nos. 211–212 (September–October 1910): 119–126.

47. Based on sources listed in note 45.

48. Luis Antonio Bohórquez Casallas, *La evolución educativa en Colombia*, pp. 410–411; Barriga, Memoria de Guerra, 1853, Cuadro 13; *La Opinión*, April 13, 1864; Vergara y Vergara and Gaitán, *Almanaque de Bogotá . . . 1867*, pp. 313, 330–333; "Personal de la Universidad Nacional, 1870," *Anales de la Universidad* 3 (1870): 179–183; "Instituto de artes i oficios," *La Ilustración*, June 27, 1872.

49. In the 1860s the common salary for New Granadan professors of technical subjects was 140 to 160 pesos per course per year. In an exceptional case, the annual salary was 480 pesos. As late as the 1880s Colombian professors of natural sciences in the national university were still paid only 480 pesos (Vergara y Vergara and Gaitán, *Almanaque de Bogotá . . . 1867*, pp. 313, 330–333; *Anales de la Instrucción pública* 2, no. 7 [April 1881]: 118).

50. This comparison is between the most successful students in both groups. The two groups as a whole may not have been equivalent in aptitudes, but it is hard to say precisely how much they differed. The factors selecting youths for study abroad were solely wealth and their parents' desire to send them. While many parents sent boys in whom they placed a good deal of hope, at least some sent their sons abroad for disciplinary or remedial reasons. One might assume that the Colegio Militar group was selected to a greater degree on the basis of apparent aptitude—many of the cadets were being educated at the expense of the government, which also had made a long-range commitment to employ them. It appears, however, that some of the youths enrolled in the military academy were also sent there for remedial purposes.

51. *Anales de Ingeniería* 12, no. 139 (October 1901): 67–71; 18, nos. 211–212 (September–October 1910): 119–126.

52. The Peñas and some of the Gonzálezes were leading Liberals in Zipaquirá (Luis Orjuela, *Minuta histórica zipaquireña*, pp. 85–86, 152–154, 433; Ospina, *Diccionario*, III, 255–256). Indalecio Liévano's father, Félix José, was a liberal, as was a more remote but more renowned antecedent, Romualdo Liévano (ANCR, Guerra, tomo 770, fol. 618; José María Baraya, *Biografías militares ó historia militar del pais en medio siglo*, p. 164; *Cartas y mensajes de Santander*, VII, 363–364; VIII, 61, 95, 150, 191).

53. This is not to say that there was no foreign interest in the eastern cordillera. Abortive contracts were made with British companies for railroads from Bogotá through Santander to the

Magdalena (1872–1874 and again 1876–1879) and with an American company for a railroad running more directly from Bogotá to the Magdalena (1874–1879). But all these efforts suffered from feeble (and sometimes virtually nonexistent) financial backing. Ultimately, in 1881 the Cuban-American Francisco Javier Cisneros, who constructed much of the Antioquia railway, also took on the Girardot route in the western cordillera. Nevertheless, the foreign role in this region was clearly weaker than it was in Antioquia or the Caribbean coast (Ortega, *Resumen histórico*, pp. 390–393, 420–429, 531–539, 562–568, 572–576. J. Fred Rippy, "Dawn of the Railway Era in Colombia," *Hispanic American Historical Review* 23 [November 1943]: 650–663, provides a brief summary, based on Ortega but selectively emphasizing the contributions of foreigners).

8. Stumbling Progress, 1863–1903

1. Antonio Pérez Aguirre, *25 años de historia colombiana, 1853 a 1878*, pp. 216–221; Felipe Pérez, *Geografía general de los Estados Unidos de Colombia*, pp. 173–178.

2. Miguel Samper, "La miseria en Bogotá," in Miguel Samper, *Escritos político-económicos*, I, 56.

3. Pérez Aguirre, *25 años*, pp. 218–219, 348, passim, tends to emphasize the positive, while giving much evidence of disorder. The number of revolutions in this period varies with the counter and his definition. A conservative text by Jesús María Henao and Gerardo Arrubla (*History of Colombia*, p. 487), states that the number of "struggles" was "over forty." Another conservative source, José de la Vega (*La federación en Colombia*), is more restrained.

4. Pérez Aguirre, *25 años*, p. 257; "Instrucción pública," *El Tiempo*, February 24, 1864; P. P. S. "Vías de comunicación," *La Opinión*, June 29, 1864.

5. Luis Ospina Vásquez, *Industria y protección en Colombia, 1910–1930*, p. 237; Alfredo Ortega Díaz, *Ferrocarriles colombianos: Resumen histórico*, pp. 18–25.

6. Figures for the first half of the century are based on Memoria de Hacienda i Fomento, 1868, Cuadro G, which gives the official totals from 1832 to 1867. The official Colombian figures substantially understate the amount of trade, whether because of contraband or incomplete or lost records. For an upward revision of the figures for the period 1845–1885, based on United States and British data, see William Paul McGreevey, *An Economic History of Colombia, 1845–1930*, pp. 99, 102.

7. Gustavo Otero Muñoz, *La vida azarosa de Rafael Núñez*, p. 196.

8. Robert Carlyle Beyer, "Transportation and the Coffee Industry in Colombia," *Inter-American Economic Affairs* 2, no. 3 (1948): 17–30.

9. National revenues between 1832 and 1842 generally amounted to considerably less than 2.5 million pesos, or roughly 2 million dollars. Between 1842 and 1850 they were closer to 2.9 million pesos, or 2.32 million dollars. Total provincial revenues in these years (including provincial, communal, and municipal taxes) appear to have amounted to

somewhere between 200,000 and 400,000 dollars per annum. In the 1850s, after the fiscal decentralization of 1850, national revenues dropped again to 2 million dollars or less, while provincial ones did not rise above 700,000 dollars. (For national data on the period see Juan de Dios Aranzazu, Memoria de Hacienda, 1840, p. 1; Mariano Calvo, Memoria de Hacienda, 1841, p. 3; Jorje J. Hoyos, Memoria de Hacienda, 1842, Cuadro no. 2; Rufino Cuervo, Memoria de Hacienda, 1843, Cuadro no. 1; Juan Climaco Ordóñez, Memoria de Hacienda, 1844, p. 12; Juan Climaco Ordóñez, Memoria de Hacienda, 1845, Seccion 2a.; Memoria de Hacienda, 1859, p. 8. Provincial revenues from 1832 to 1850 are calculated on the basis of scattered data, which show that most provinces collected 10,000 to 20,000 pesos. [In 1832 there were 15 provinces and in 1843 the number had increased to 20.] Data on provinces are in Francisco A. Obregón, *Esposición . . . Gobernador de Antioquia . . . 1839*, pp. 23–24; Gobernador de Mariquita . . . , 1841, *GNG*, May 1, 1842; Gobernador de Neiva . . . 1842, ibid.; Neiva, 1844, Pamplona, 1844, Popayán, 1844, Santa Marta, 1844, ibid., January 26, 1845; Gobernador de Neiva, 1846, ibid., October 25, 1846; Gobernador de Mariquita, ibid., December 13, 1846; re: Bogotá province, 1847 and 1848, ibid., October 14, 1847 and December 24, 1848. On the changes brought by decentralization see *GO*, November 28, 1850, February 24, April 14, 18, 20, 1855; *Gaceta de Cundinamarca*, December 7, 1857.)

10. National figures for 1850–1851, 1869–1870, 1879–1880 in Pérez, *Geografía general* (1833), pp. 196–199.

State data for the 1870s based on 1873–1874 figures in *Anuario estadístico . . . 1875*, p. 221.

11. Pérez, *Geografía general*, pp. 196–199, 207–208; Ortega, *Resumen histórico*, pp. 258–563; Ospina Vásquez, *Industria y protección*, pp. 233–238; Jane Meyer Loy, "Modernization and Educational Reform" (Ph.D. dissertation), pp. 9, 16, 19–20.

12. Ortega, *Resumen histórico*, pp. 26–28; Ospina Vásquez, *Industria y protección*, pp. 234, 280; Pérez, *Geografía general*, pp. 198–199, 205–206.

13. The 206 kilometers excludes the 80 kilometers of track built across the Isthmus of Panama in the 1850s (Ortega, *Resumen histórico*, pp. 27, 276, 484–486, 572; E. R. Esmond to Hon. James D. Porter, assistant secretary of state, Medellín, September 9, 1885, Despatches of U.S. Consuls, Medellín 1859–1902; Nepomuceno Santamaría, "Ferrocarril de La Dorada," *Anales de Ingeniería*, September 1, 1889, p. 49).

14. A remarkably well informed discussion of prospective railroad costs based on the experience of other countries can be found in Salvador Camacho Roldán to Medardo Rivas April 25, 1872, in "Correspondence of Medardo Rivas" (2 vols. property of José Manuel Rivas Sacconi, Bogotá), I, fol. 114. Later confirmation of Camacho Roldán's suspicions and a general discussion of the various difficulties appears in Ortega, *Resumen histórico*, pp. 73–76. See also J. Fred Rippy, "Dawn of the Railway Era in Colombia," *Hispanic American Historical Review* 23 (November 1943): 456–458.

15. Rippy, "Dawn of the Railway Era in Colombia," pp. 456–458; Ospina

Vásquez, *Industria y protección*, pp. 234, 237–240, 278; Ortega, *Resumen histórico*, p. 28; "Contrato sobre construcción de obras públicas," *Anales de Ingeniería* 4, no. 39 (October 1890): 66–67.

16. Ortega, *Resumen histórico*, pp. 43, 402; James J. Parsons, *Antioqueño Colonization in Western Colombia*, p. 169.

17. Eugenio Díaz, *Manuela, novela de costumbres colombianas*, I, 157; *El Tiempo*, November 23, 1858; ad, *El Tiempo*, August 9, 1865; "El país progresa en lo material," *El Tiempo*, October 4, 1865; ad, *El Tiempo*, February 14, 1866; Aníbal Galindo, *Estudios económicos y fiscales*, p. 102; William Scruggs, "Colombia and Its People," July, 1883, United States, Bureau of Foreign Commerce, *Reports from the Consuls of the United States on the Commerce, Manufactures, etc., of their Consular Districts*, no. 31, pp. 111–114.

18. Frank Robinson Safford, "Commerce and Enterprise in Central Colombia, 1821–1870" (Ph.D. dissertation), pp. 157–186; Ospina Vásquez, *Industria y protección*, pp. 274; Nestor Castro to W. Hunter, Esq., second assistant secretary of state, May 4, 1882, Despatches of U.S. Consul, Medellín, 1859–1902.

19. Ospina Vásquez, *Industria y protección*, pp. 267–275, 316–317.

20. William Scruggs, "Colombia and Its People," December 20, 1882, United States, Bureau of Foreign Commerce; *Reports from the Consuls of the United States on the Commerce, Manufactures, etc., of their Consular Districts*, no. 32, pp. 223–226; *Anales de Ingeniería* 3, no. 29 (December 1889): 127–134.

21. "Instrucción pública," *El Tiempo*, March 2, 1864. See also ibid., July 13, 1864. The law of September 22, 1867, and other documents on the foundation of the university appear in *Anales de la Universidad Nacional* 1, (September 1868–September 1869): 7–16.

22. The national government provided scholarships for thirty-six or seventy-two students (4 or 8 from each state), depending upon fiscal circumstances (*CN*, XXIV, 111–112; XXVI, 186; XXVIII, 38–41).

23. Bailey B. Burritt, *Professional Distribution of College and University Graduates*, Table 69, p. 144, passim. Burritt's sample of thirty-seven institutions, as previously noted, does not include such technical schools as West Point, Rensselaer, M.I.T., or the land-grant colleges. On the other hand, it does include such notable general universities as Harvard, Yale, Pennsylvania, Columbia, Brown, Vermont, Michigan, Bucknell, Syracuse, Rochester, New York University, Wisconsin, Northwestern, Chicago, California at Berkeley, Minnesota, Nebraska, Colorado, and Vanderbilt. These make up more than half the institutions surveyed and the overwhelming preponderance of the students. Therefore, while the sample is somewhat biased in favor of liberal arts colleges and against purely technical schools, its results can be taken as at least suggestive of a dominant tendency in American higher education.

24. Article 2, Law 4 of 1874 (March 7), *CN*, XXVII, 17.

25. Pérez, *Geografía general* (1883),

p. 288, represents enrollments as roughly 80 in engineering, 100 in law, and 120 each in natural sciences and medicine—an exaggeration in the case of engineering and a gross one for the time he published. After the restoration of engineering to civil control, enrollment figures were 1887, 40 plus; 1888, 43; 1890, 32; 1891, 22; 1892, 48; 1893, 37; 1894, 52. (Memoria de Instrucción Pública, 1888, Documentos, pp. 21–22; Memoria de Instrucción Pública, 1890, p. lxi; Memoria de Instrucción Pública, 1892, p. 101; Memoria de Instrucción Pública, 1894, pp. lxxii, 45).

26. Manuel Briceño, *La Revolución (1876–77)*, pp. 41–77; Pérez Aguirre, *25 años*, pp. 348–391; Law 23 of 1876 (May 17) and Law 26 of 1876 (May 22), *CN*, XXVIII, 35, 38–41.

27. Law 69 of 1877 (June 1), *CN*, XXVIII, 443–445; Decree 504 of 1879 (November 26), *CN*, XXIX, 443–449; "Informe del Consejo Académico," Memoria de Instrucción Pública, 1884, Documentos, pp. 7, 10–19.

28. Memoria de Instrucción Pública, 1880 (published 1881), Documentos, pp. 35–41.

29. "Informe del Consejo Académico," Memoria de Instrucción Pública, 1884, pp. 7–20; Memoria de Instrucción Pública, 1885, pp. 4–5; Law 23 of 1884 (July 26), *CN*, XXIV, 40–46; Decree 854 of 1884 (October 21), *CN*, XXIV, 264–266.

30. "Discurso del Señor Abelardo Ramos," *Anales de Ingeniería* 1, no. 1 (August 1887): 6.

31. In 1886 and 1887, Facultad de Matemáticas; 1888, Instituto Central de Matemáticas; 1891, Instituto Central de Matemáticas e Ingeniería.

32. *Anales de Ingeniería* 1, no. 1 (August 1887): 27; 1, no. 11 (June 1888): 324–327; 1, no. 37 (August 1890): 10–11; 4, no. 47 (June 1891): 322–323; 9, nos. 111–112 (November–December 1897): 321–326; 11, no. 128 (April 1899): 110–115.

33. Memoria de Instrucción Pública, 1892, p. 101; Memoria de Instrucción Pública, 1894, pp. 45; Memoria de Instrucción Pública, 1898, pp. 30–32; Documentos, pp. 20–23; Alfredo D. Bateman, *Páginas para la historia de la ingeniería colombiana*, pp. 220–221, 358.

34. Gregorio Obregón in Memoria de Fomento, 1881, pp. 84, 87; *El Relator*, March 29, 1878; Salvador Camacho Roldán, *Artículos escogidos*, pp. 16–40 passim; Memoria de Fomento, 1880 (published 1881), Parte Tercera, 25–129.

35. Law 63 of 1878 (July 5), Decree 337 of 1878 (August 6), and Decree 514 of 1879 (November 29), *CN*, XXIX, 164, 219–222, 449–455; Decree 284 of 1880 (May 15), *CN*, XXX, 339–341. Juan de Dios Carrasquilla, "Segundo informe que presenta el Comisario de la Agricultura Nacional. [1880]," quoted in Memoria de Fomento, 1890, pp. 152–155.

36. Ramón Zapata, *Dámaso Zapata; ó La reforma educacionista en Colombia*, p. 220; *La Reforma*, December 31, 1878, January 7, 17, and 28, 1879, November 14, 1879, and June 26, 1880; Gustavo Otero Muñoz, *Wilches y su época*, pp. 357–358; Decree number 636 of 1878 (December 17), *CN*, XXIX, 265–267.

37. Memoria de Fomento, 1884, pp. 114–115, discusses the failure of E.

Hambursin. José M. Gutiérrez de Alba, though admired, apparently did not last long (Memoria de Fomento, 1885, Documentos, p. 198).

38. Carlos Michelsen Uribe, "Tercer Informe del Comisario Nacional de Agricultura," in Memoria de Fomento, 1880 (published 1881), Parte Tercera, pp. 2–25; Memoria de Fomento, 1881, pp. 85, 135.

39. In addition to sources cited in note 38, see Memoria de Fomento, 1884, pp. 112–115; Memoria de Fomento, 1885, pp. xli–xlv, 175–185; R. F. [Ruperto Ferreira], "Sociedad de Ciencias Agronómicas," *Anales de Ingeniería* 12, no. 147 (May 1905): 321–323; Víctor Manuel Patiño, "Historia de la técnica agropecuaria en Colombia," in *Apuntes para la historia de la ciencia en Colombia*, ed. Jaime Uribe Jaramillo, p. 188.

40. Memoria de Fomento, 1885, Documentos, pp. 216–223; Memoria de Instrucción Pública, 1888, p. xxxix; Memoria de Instrucción Pública, 1890, pp. lxix–lxxx; Memoria de Instrucción Pública, 1892, Documentos, p. 115; Memoria de Instrucción Pública, 1898, pp. 30–31, Documentos, pp. 19–20.

41. Memoria de Fomento, 1880 [1881], Tercera Parte, p. 493; Memoria de Fomento, 1881, p. 88; Memoria de Fomento, 1885, Documentos, pp. 176, 187, 201.

42. Memoria de Fomento, 1890, pp. 152–155; Memoria de Fomento, 1880 [1881], Tercera Parte, pp. 146–148; Memoria de Fomento, 1884, pp. 116–118; Memoria de Fomento, 1885, Documentos, pp. 190–199; Memoria de Fomento, 1894, pp. 157–158.

43. Decree 333 of 1881 (May 25), *CN*,

XXXI, 262–286; Law 43 of 1882 (July 27) and Law 85 of 1882 (September 20), *CN*, XXXII, 75, 255–256; *El Comercio*, November 28, 1884; Tulio Ospina, "Informe del Rector de la Escuela Nacional de Minas," *Anales de la Escuela Nacional de Minas* 1, no. 3 (July 1912): 126.

44. Ospina, "Informe," pp. 126–128; Memoria de Instrucción Pública, 1892, pp. 117–119; Julio César García, "Historia de la Escuela Nacional de Minas," *Anales de la Escuela Nacional de Minas*, no. 42 (October 1937), pp. 13, 15, 16.

45. Tulio Ospina, "Informe."

46. Ibid., pp. 129–145; Juan de la C. Posada, "Profesor Samuel B. Christy," *Boletín de la Sociedad Antioqueña de Ingenieros*, no. 1 (February 1915), pp. 10–11; Memoria de Instrucción Pública, 1892, pp. xxxv–xxxvi, 118–119; Memoria de Instrucción Pública, 1894, pp. lxxxii–lxxxiii.

47. Analysis based on data in Ospina, "Informe," pp. 130–133. Alumni who worked in several fields are counted under each category.

48. One interesting suggestion, apparently never implemented, was that engineering courses be given in one-year modules (to use a current term), for example, hydraulics and architecture; roads and bridges; geology, mineralogy, metallurgy, and mining. A student would take as many of these as his time, inclinations, and financial resources might permit ("Escuela de ingeniería civil," *Anales de Ingeniería* 1, no. 4 [November 1887]: 97–100). Circular of Fortunato Pereira Gamba and Pedro de Francisco, ibid. 10, nos. 115–116 (March–April 1878): 96.

49. Informe del Director Jeneral de Instrucción Primaria de la Union, 1876, pp. 4–97; Memoria de Instrucción

Pública, 1880 [1881], pp. 38–101; Memoria de Instrucción Pública, 1884 [1885], p. 16.

50. *Anales de la Instrucción Pública* 11 (1887): 268–270; Memoria de Instrucción Pública, 1890, p. cxlvi; Memoria de Instrucción Pública, 1880 [1881], pp. 71–73.

51. "Actos lejislativos," *La Ilustración*, May 16, 1872; "Instituto de artes i oficios," ibid., June 27, 1872; *Anuario estadístico de Colombia. 1875*, p. 81.

52. Alfonso Mejía Robledo, *Vidas y empresas de Antioquia*, pp. 29, 69–70.

53. "Revista de los Estados: Antioquia," *La Ilustración*, June 1, 1870, November 14 and December 3, 1872, August 16, October 7, and December 30, 1873. See also *Boletín Oficial de Antioquia*, August 8, 1870, and *El Pueblo*, May 7, 1871. I am indebted to Roger Brew for useful information on the Medellín school in this and subsequent paragraphs.

54. Decree 571 of 1872 (December 27), *CN*, XXVII, 296–299; *Diario de Cundinamarca*, January 5, 1875; Briceño, *La Revolución*, p. 77; "Informe del Consejo Académico," Memoria de Instrucción Pública, 1884, Documentos, pp. 6–7; Decree 854 of 1884 (October 21), *CN*, XXXIV, 265.

55. *Boletín Industrial*, February 29, 1876, and December 19, 1878.

56. *La Ilustración*, June 17 and December 3, 1870, October 29, 1872; *Boletín Industrial*, December 5, 1878; *La Reforma*, November 14, 1879.

57. Memoria de Fomento, 1881, pp. 61–68, 120–121; Memoria de Instrucción Pública, 1880 [1881], pp. 71–72; Memoria de Instrucción Pública, 1881 [1882], p. 48.

58. Decree 592 of 1881 (August 9), *CN*, XXXI, 356–357; Memoria de Instrucción Pública, 1892, pp. xlvi–xlvii; Memoria de Instrucción Pública, 1898, pp. 39–40, and Documentos, pp. 34–37.

59. Memoria de Instrucción Pública, 1890, pp. cli–clii; Memoria de Instrucción Pública, 1894, pp. lx–lxiii.

60. Decree 376 of 1881 (June 15), *CN*, XXXI, 305–310; Law 23 of 1884 (July 26), *CN*, XXXIV, 40–46.

61. Memoria de Instrucción Pública, 1890, pp. xxxiii–xxxvi, lxxxviii–xc, xcix; Memoria de Instrucción Pública, 1892, pp. xxiii–xxix, 122–127; Memoria de Instrucción Pública, 1898, pp. 38–39.

62. *Anales de la Instrucción Pública*, November 30, 1880, pp. 306–314.

63. Copious material on their studies can be found in ibid., vols. 1–5 (1880–1883).

9. A Place for Engineers

1. Of the 275 men listed as engineers in the 1870s, half were on the Isthmus of Panama and for the most part were foreigners (*Anuario estadístico . . . 1875*, pp. 22–28). See also "Discurso del Señor Abelardo Ramos, pronunciado en la instalación de la Sociedad," *Anales de Ingeniería* 1, no. 1 (August 1887): 7–9.

2. Abelardo Ramos, "Manuel H. Peña," *Anales de Ingeniería* 12, no. 139 (October 1901): 68; José María González B., "Biografía de Manuel Ponce de León," ibid. 11, no. 127 (March 1899): 87; Diódoro Sánchez, "Biografía del Dr. José María González Benito," ibid. 14, nos. 165–166 (November–December 1906): 135–136; José María Vergara y Vergara and J. B. Gaitán, *Almanaque de Bogotá . . . 1867*, pp. 313, 330–333.

3. Some examples: The first section of the Bolívar railway, constructed at Barranquilla in 1869–1871, was started with London capital and British engineers and finished by Bremen capital and German engineers. In the Cauca valley a British-financed railroad construction company first used an American engineer (1863–1865), turning to local talent, a Polish immigrant, only when the American died. Similarly, in 1872–1873, a British company seeking to build a railroad north from Bogotá naturally entrusted its surveys, plans, and other engineering work to Englishmen, though seven of Colombia's leading engineers were employed as assistants (Hoenigsberg, Wessels y Compañía, *Cuestión Jimeno-Hoenigsberg, en su parte moral*, pp. 8–13; J. Fred Rippy, "Dawn of the Railway Era in Colombia," *Hispanic American Historical Review* 23, no. 4 (November 1943): 651, passim; Alfredo Ortega Díaz, *Ferrocarriles colombianos: Resumen histórico*, pp. 257, 393–395, 419–424, 454–458, 463; *Anales de Ingeniería* 1, no. 11 (June 1888): 322–323, and III, no. 26 (September 1889): 53–54.

4. In 1883–1884 Cisneros was constructing four railroads. On two of them (Girardot and La Dorada) virtually the entire technical staff was foreign, generally American or Cuban. On the Antioquia and Cauca railways Americans held the top posts, but some Colombians worked at the construction and operations level, often as subcontractors. Cisneros employed many influential Colombians (e.g., Dámaso Zapata, José María Samper, Carlos Sáenz) as administrators or agents. Nicolás Tanco

Armero, another administrator, was an influential Colombian and had spent many years in business in Cuba (*La Industria*, March 1, 8, 22, 29, May 10, June 21, August 23, 30, September 11, 20, October 11, December 4, 1883; January 19, February 13, May 24, 31, July 5, 26, September 5, 20, 1884. *Colombia Ilustrada*, January 31, 1891, pp. 322–327, 300).

5. Salvador Camacho Roldán, *Notas de viaje*, p. 215.

6. *La Industria*, numbers cited in note 4; also August 2, 1883.

7. "Discurso del Señor Abelardo Ramos," *Anales de Ingeniería* 1, no. 1 (August 1887): 7–9; "Carreteras," ibid. 13, no. 157 (March 1906): 261.

8. "El año nuevo," ibid. 2, no. 18 (January 1889): 161–162.

9. "Boletín industrial," *El Tiempo*, February 2, 1858, and April 20 and June 22, 1864; "Santander," *La Opinión*, May 31, 1864, and June 29, July 27, August 3, 1864.

10. The route to Peñon del Conejo, traced by the French engineer Antoine Poncet in 1848 and retraced and revised by Indalecio Liévano in 1863–1865; the Occidente route, from Bogotá to Honda, being promoted by an American, Charles Brown; various routes following the Bogotá or Apulo river basins to the port of Girardot on the Magdalena; and the Ferrocarril del Norte to link Bogotá, the population centers of Boyacá and Santander, and the lower Magdalena.

11. The Girardot route was the cheapest and most easily constructed and would serve to connect the Tolima region to the capital; but its terminus lay above the head of practicable steam

navigation on the Magdalena River. The Occidente and Poncet routes came closer to the head of navigation, but they would have been more costly to construct. And, while they would have facilitated the foreign trade of Cundinamarca, they would not have helped to tie the eastern region together. The Ferrocarril del Norte would integrate the whole eastern cordillera while at the same time expanding its foreign trade; on the other hand, it was expected to cost three times as much as the other projects. Some of the various considerations are presented by Aníbal Galindo, in articles written between 1874 and 1880, in his *Estudios económicos y fiscales*, pp. 99–168. See also Salvador Camacho Roldán's attacks on the Ferrocarril del Norte in the *Diario de Cundinamarca*, June 12–July 10, 1874, and in *El Tradicionista*, June 23–June 30, 1874. They are reprinted in his *Escritos varios*, tercera serie, pp. 31–90.

12. Salvador Camacho Roldán, secretary of finance (1870–1872) and of the treasury (1878–1879), was a vigorous proponent of the Girardot railway, along the route of which he owned a hacienda by 1874. Aquileo Parra, secretary of finance (1872–1876) and simultaneously president of the state of Santander (1874–1875), promoted the Ferrocarril del Norte (Carare route). The Occidente road to Honda was officially adopted by the state of Cundinamarca and its president in 1874–1876, Gen. Eustorgio Salgar, who had been the national president in 1870–1872 (*Boletín Industrial*, April 8 and 15, 1875; Otero Muñoz, *Wilches y su época*, pp. 165–166, 403; Aquileo Parra, *Memorias*

de Aquileo Parra, pp. 625–650, 667–671, 679–683; *Diario de Cundinamarca*, October 19, 1875, contains Salgar's criticisms of the Ferrocarril del Norte).

13. Three of the four directors of the Ferrocarril del Norte in January, 1875 (Vicente Lafaurie, José María Saravia Ferro, and Silvestre Samper), turned up shortly afterward as founders of and large stockholders in Camacho Roldán's Compañía del Camino de Carriles del Suroeste ("Crónica local," *El Tradicionista*, January 19, 1875; *Boletín Industrial*, April 8 and 15, 1875).

14. Ortega Díaz, *Resumen histórico*, pp. 364–365, 426–428, 533–534, 558–578.

15. [Modesto Garcés], "Un viaje a Venezuela," *Anales de Ingeniería* 1, no. 1 (August 1887): 11–12; "Mejoras materiales de Boyacá," ibid. 1, no. 1 (August 1887): 15–16; "Vía de Cambao," ibid. 1, no. 5 (December 1887): 129–138; Diódoro Sánchez, "Carlos Téllez," ibid. 1, no. 7 (February 1888): 194; Abelardo Ramos, "Puente de fierro sobre el Río Negro," ibid. 1, no. 9 (April 1888): 257–260; "Puente sobre el Río Plata," ibid. 2, no. 13 (August 1888): 1–8; ibid. 3, no. 27 (October 1889) 76; Diódoro Sánchez, "Camilo A. Carrizosa," ibid. 3, no. 29 (December 1889): 127–135; ibid. 3, no. 29 (December 1889): 135–136; ibid. 3, no. 34 (May 1890): 333–334.

16. "Discurso del Señor Abelardo Ramos," ibid. 1, no. 1 (August 1887): 6–9.

17. The subscribing members presumably did not represent the total membership, as there were eighty-three members in 1888 and ninety-six in

1890 but only sixty-five subscribing *socios de número* in 1898 (*Anales de Ingeniería* 1, no. 6 [January 1888]: 162, 192; 4, no. 37 [August 1890]: 3–4; 10, nos. 113–114 [January–February 1898]: 15–25).

18. *Anuario estadístico . . . 1875*, pp. 2–28.

19. Everett E. Hagen, *On the Theory of Social Change*, pp. 353–384; Frank Safford, "Significación de los antioqueños en el desarrollo económico colombiano," in *Anuario Colombiano de Historia Social y de la Cultura*, pp. 49–69; Gabriel García Márquez, *Cien años de soledad*, pp. 177–186.

20. *Anales de Ingeniería* 6, no. 68 (August 1893): 255, and 10, nos. 113–114 (January–February 1898): 30–45.

21. For example, see Abelardo Ramos, *"ingeniero interventor"* in "Ferrocarril del Cauca," *Anales de Ingeniería* 10, nos. 119–120 (July–August 1898): 238–240, and Manuel H. Peña as government representative in negotiations regarding the same enterprise in ibid. 10, nos. 115–116 (March–April 1898): 92–105. See also Ortega, *Resumen histórico*, pp. 478, 483, 495–496, for other mention of Bogotá engineers with government appointments in the Cauca.

22. Two notable exceptions were Modesto Garcés of Cali and Luis María Tisnés of Sonsón, Antioquia, both of whom graduated from the National University in 1870. Garcés gravitated into the Bogotá group, but Tisnés returned to Medellín, where he became a mainstay of the Escuela de Minas (Alfredo D. Bateman, *Páginas para la historia de la ingeniería colombiana*, pp. 65, 547–558).

23. Julián Uribe Uribe was given to saying that "any man on the street knows more than I, but . . . few can compete with me in quantity of work." Of *antioqueño* origin, he was famous for his prolonged labors in the wilderness, allegedly working as long as two years at a time without coming into town (Joaquín Ospina, *Diccionario biográfico y bibliográfico de Colombia*, I, 388–389; III, 809–810).

24. Three of eighteen professors in the Medellín school in 1914 were foreign; later there were as many as six foreigners (*Anales de la Escuela Nacional de Minas* 1, no. 1 [March 1912]: 7–31; 1, no. 8 [April 1914]: 426–439; 1, no. 42 [October 1937]: 18, 19, 23–24).

25. Hernan Horna, "Francisco Javier Cisneros" (Ph.D. dissertation), pp. 96, 103, 110, 125, 151, 166, 207, 252.

26. Ibid., pp. 223–224.

27. Ibid., pp. 229–232. Horna relates the facts but does not note the pattern portrayed here.

28. Ibid., p. 287.

29. *Anales de la Escuela Nacional de Minas* 1, no. 2 (April 1912): 63; 1, no. 5 (March 1913): 234–240; 1, no. 8 (April 1914): 406–408. I have derived further information on the attitudes of *antioqueño* engineers in the twentieth century from interviews with Luis Ospina Vásquez, Dario Suescún, and Peter Santamaría (Medellín, July 9–14, 1972).

30. *Anales de Ingeniería* 1, no. 1 (August 1887): 6–9.

31. Ibid.; also 1, no. 2 (September 1887): 41–42; 2, no. 18 (January 1889): 161–162.

32. Ibid. 1, no. 1 (August 1887); and 2, no. 18 (January 1889): 161–162.

33. Ibid. 1, no. 11 (June 1888):

322–323; 3, no. 26 (September 1889): 53–54; 6, no. 61 (January 1893): 3–5. Other positive comments in ibid. 7, nos. 82–84 (October–December 1894): 307–319.

34. Diódoro Sánchez, "Francisco Javier Cisneros," *Anales de Ingeniería* 10, nos. 119–120 (July–August 1898): 200–201.

35. Abelardo Ramos, "Puente de fierro sobre el Rio Negro," *Anales de Ingeniería* 1, no. 9 (April 1888): 257–260; [Modesto Garcés?], "Un viaje a Venezuela," ibid. 1, no. 1 (August 1887): 11–12; "El Acueducto," ibid. 4, no. 46 (May 1891): 294; "Puente sobre el Rio Plata," ibid. 2, no. 13 (August 1888): 1–8. See also Diódoro Sánchez, "Instituto Central de Matemáticas," ibid. 5, no. 53 (December 1891): 129–130.

36. Cf. judgment of French engineer Raymond Le Brun on the Colombian-built Ferrocarril de la Sabana and Colombian reaction in *Anales de Ingeniería* 2, no. 24 (July 1889): 353–362, and Ortega Díaz, *Resumen histórico*, p. 576. The same contrast between foreign shoddiness and national quality is emphasized by Ortega in his discussions of the Ferrocarril del Pacífico (*Resumen histórico*, pp. 483–501). The theme of solid national works versus frail foreign works appeared as early as 1858 (cf. Alfredo D. Bateman, *El Observatorio Astronómico de Bogotá*, p. 89).

37. "Labores para el ingeniero en Colombia," *Anales de Ingeniería* 1, no. 2 (September 1887): 41–43. Téllez graduated as a civil engineer from Lafayette College (Pennsylvania) in 1884. He died several months after penning this manifesto (Diódoro

Sánchez, "Carlos Téllez," ibid. 1, no. 7 [February 1888]: 194).

38. "Bienvenida," *Anales de Ingeniería* 2, no. 19 (February 1889): 207. In the mechanical arts they looked to the industrial schools of France. Other admired institutions were West Point, Rensselaer, Stevens, and the Ecole Centrale in Paris (M. A. R. [Manuel Antonio Rueda], "La ley 121 de 1887," ibid. 1, no. 3 [October 1887]: 68–69; Modesto Garcés, "El Conservatorio de Artes y Oficios de Paris," ibid. 1, no. 9 [April 1888]: 264–267; "Discurso del Señor Abelardo Ramos," ibid. 1, no. 1 [August 1887]:6; Abelardo Ramos, "Astronomía y geodesia," ibid. 1, no. 8 [March 1888]: 225).

39. "La actividad científica en Bogotá," *Anales de Ingeniería* 7, no. 81 (September 1894): 257–259; Ramón Guerra Azuola, "Juicio histórico-crítico de nuestras ciencias matemáticas en el pasado y el presente, y su probable futuro," ibid., 10, nos. 113–114 (January–February 1898): 7.

40. Ospina, *Diccionario*, III, 965.

41. Ramón Guerra Azuola, "La guadua," *Anales de Ingeniería* 1, no. 3 (October 1887): 76–79, and 1, no. 7 (February 1888): 205–207; "Puentes baratos," ibid. 6, no. 68 (August 1893): 255; "Máquinas para extraer el fique," ibid. 7, nos. 76–77 (April–May 1894): 99–102; F. S. Escobar, "Notable obra de arte," ibid. 13, nos. 150–151 (August–September 1905): 39–43.

42. Bateman, *El Observatorio*, pp. 97–111, 123–157.

43. "La ingeniería en Colombia," *Anales de Ingeniería* 11, nos. 125–126 (January–February 1899): 34–35.

44. Some exceptions included Indalecio Liévano's road to the Magdalena

River (1884–1889) and his urban development enterprises; Abelardo
Ramos at times played an entrepreneurial role in bridge construction, and
Lorenzo Codazzi in ironworks. Also
Juan Nepomuceno González Vásquez
and Fortunato Pereira Gamba were at
least willing to take part in companies in
which landowners and merchants were
also involved ("El Ferrocarril de Girardot," Anales de Ingeniería 6, nos. 82–84
[October–December 1894]: 289–307;
"Ingeniería municipal: Tranvía de San
Cristóbal," ibid. 10, no. 118 [June
1898]: 176–185; Diódoro Sánchez,
"Muerte del eminente ingeniero y presidente fundador de la Sociedad Colombiana de Ingenieros," ibid. 13, no. 158
[April 1906]: 292; Julio Garavito A.,
"Indalecio Liévano," ibid. 22, nos.
257–258 [July–August 1914]: 2–16).

45. Diódoro Sánchez, "Camilo A.
Carrizosa," Anales de Ingeniería 3, no.
29 (December 1889): 127–135; Enrique
Morales R., "Santiago Samper," ibid.,
13, no. 155 (January 1906): 193–194. Between 1886 and his death in 1908, Carlos Tanco took on contracts for four
different railways—the Sabana
(1886–1898), Girardot (1893–1894), Sur
(1893–1895), and Tolima (1893–1908)
(Ortega, Resumen histórico, pp.
392–393, 572–578, 611–612, 626–634).

46. Julio Garavito, "Ignorancia industrial," Anales de Ingeniería 10, no.
121 (September 1898): 293–297; Ramón
Guerra Azuola, "Informe anual del Rector de la Facultad de Matemáticas e
Ingeniería," ibid. 11, no. 128 (April
1899): 110–115.

47. M[iguel] Triana, "Estudio de la
ingeniería," Anales de Ingeniería 1, no.
1 (August 1887): 13–15, and 1, no. 2

(September 1887): 43–45; M. A. R.
[Manuel Antonio Rueda], "La ley 121
de 1887," ibid. 1, no. 2 (September
1887): 33–36, and 1, no. 3 (October
1887): 65–70; M. A. R., "Escuela de Ingeniería Civil," ibid. 1, no. 4 (November
1887): 97–100; Rafael Espinosa Escallón,
"Instituto Central de Matemáticas,"
ibid. 1, no. 11 (June 1888): 324–327;
"Instituto Central de Matemáticas e
Ingeniería," ibid. 4, no. 47 (June 1891):
322–323.

48. Julio Garavito, "Ignorancia industrial," Anales de Ingeniería 10, no.
121 (September 1898): 293; Ruperto
Ferreira, "Las enseñanzas en la Facultad de Matemáticas," ibid. 11, no. 128
(April 1899): 110–115.

49. In 1909 professors and students of
the Facultad de Ingeniería in Bogotá
provided the first leadership for rebellion against the administration of Gen.
Rafael Reyes (Bateman, Páginas, p.
223).

50. Anales de Ingeniería 12, no. 137
(August 1901): 2; 12, no. 137 (August
1901): 10–15; 13, nos. 150–151
(August–September 1905): 39; 13, no.
158 (April 1906): 290–302; 13, no. 159
(May 1906): 322–323; 14, nos. 165–166
(November–December 1906): 129–194.

Epilogue

1. Anuario estadístico . . . 1875, p.
28.

2. Samuel Rezneck, Education for a
Technological Society, quotations on
pp. 12, 21; see also pp. 6–14, 23–42,
59–60.

3. Luis Ospina Vásquez, Industria y

protección en Colombia, 1810–1930, pp. 322–325, 357.

4. Alfredo Ortega Díaz, *Ferrocarriles colombianos: Resumen histórico,* I, 27, 43, 113–122.

5. H. Theodore Hoffman, "A History of Railway Concessions and Railway Development Policy in Colombia to 1943" (Ph.D. dissertation), pp. 64, 120–124, 153–155; Ospina Vásquez, *Industria y protección,* p. 352.

6. Ospina Vásquez, *Industria y protección,* pp. 326–348, 387–404, passim.

7. *Anales de la Escuela Nacional de Minas* 1, no. 3 (July 1912): 130–134.

8. "Actividades profesionales," *Ingeniería y Arquitectura* 7, no. 76 (July–August 1947): 34.

9. "Un triste capítulo en la historia del Observatorio Astronómico Nacional," from *Anales de Ingeniería,* no. 455 (March 1931), reprinted in Alfredo D. Bateman, *El Observatorio Astronómico de Bogotá,* pp. 159–165.

10. *Ingeniería y Arquitectura* 6, no. 63 (May–June 1945): 2; 10, nos. 100–102 (July–December 1951): 60; 11, no. 121 (January–February 1955): 2.

11. Hoffman, "Railway Concessions," pp. 28–31, 267–277, and passim; W. Rodney Long, *Railways of South America,* Part Two, pp. 27–31.

12. Donald S. Barnhart, "Colombian Transport and the Reforms of 1931," *Hispanic American Historical Review* 38, no. 1 (February 1958): 1–24; Ortega, *Resumen histórico,* I, 70.

13. Until 1950 the engineering faculty in the National University in Bogotá granted only civil engineering degrees ("Algunos datos sobre estudios de ingeniería en Colombia" and "Lista de graduados . . ." in *Ingeniería y Arquitectura* 8, nos. 92–93 (March–June 1950): 7–16). For a standard curriculum, see ibid. 5, no. 60 (November–December 1944): 7–8.

14. "Nuevos pénsumes en la Facultad de Minas de Medellín," *Ingeniería y Arquitectura* 3, no. 32 (January 1942): 29–35. Some Bogotá engineers resisted specialized instruction in the fear that a new emphasis on specialties would dilute the basic preparation in mathematics that they considered both necessary and a particular strength of the Bogotá school.

15. "La Convención Nacional de Ingenieros Colombianos," *Ingeniería y Arquitectura* 9, nos. 100–102 (July–December 1951): 60–64.

16. *Anales de la Escuela Nacional de Minas,* no. 42 (October 1937), p. 25. *Ingeniería y Arquitectura* 5, no. 55 (January–February 1944): 23–24; 8, no. 87 (May–June 1949): 29; 10, nos. 97–98 (January–April 1951): 2; 11, no. 130 (July–August 1956): 2; 12, no. 133 (January–February 1957): 2; 12, no. 134 (March–April 1957): 2–14; 14, no. 158 (March–April 1961): 6; 14, no. 160 (July–August 1961): 20–22; 14, no. 168 (November–December 1962): 7; 15, no. 172 (November–December 1963): 6.

17. República de Colombia, Departamento Administrativo Nacional de Estadística, *Anuario general de estadística, 1965, culturales,* II, 159, 163.

18. *Ingeniería y Arquitectura* 14, no. 160 (July–August 1961): 9–10, 20–21.

19. *Ingeniería y Arquitectura* 10, no. 119 (September–October 1954): 3; 11, no. 121 (January–February 1955): 2; 12, no. 138 (November–December 1957): 12.

20. Frederick Harbison and Charles A. Myers, *Education, Manpower, and Economic Growth*, pp. 45–48, 84.

21. Ibid., p. 82.

22. Calculated from Departamento Administrativo Nacional de Estadística, *Anuario general de estadística, 1965, culturales*, II, 159, 163.

23. Ibid., II, 114, 131, 159, 163; Harbison and Myers, *Education, Manpower, and Economic Growth*, pp. 82, 91.

Glossary

aguardiente: sugar-cane liquor manufactured for mass consumption in Colombia.
alcaldes: in the colonial period officers in the *cabildos*, or city councils; in the
republican era the office became more detached from the *cabildo* but
retained many of the same functions, among them a low-level judicial role.
andino: reference to alumni of the Universidad de los Andes, Bogotá.
antioqueños: natives of the province of Antioquia, Colombia.
Archbishop-Viceroy: Antonio Caballero y Góngora (1723–1796), archbishop of the
archdiocese of Santa Fe, who served also as viceroy of New Granada from
1782 to 1788. Known in works on Colombian history as the Archbishop-
Viceroy, since he was the only individual to hold both posts in colonial New
Granada.
bachiller: individual who has graduated from *colegio* (secondary school).
bogotanos: natives of the city of Bogotá or its immediate environs.
Cauca valley: in this work "Cauca region" refers to the upper sectors of the Cauca
River valley, from Popayán in the south to Cartago in the north. "Cauca
valley" refers more particularly to the narrow, elongated valley running
from Cali in the south to Cartago in the north. As used in this work the term
does not apply to the lower reaches of the Cauca River passing through
Antioquia.
civilista: civilian opposing military power or dominance.
colegio: educational institution that, in the republican period, provided secondary-
level instruction. In the colonial era there were two classes of *colegios*:
colegios mayores, which gave instruction leading to professional degrees,
usually in civil or canonical law, and *colegios menores*, which were devoted
to work in Latin and other secondary subjects preparatory to enrollment in
colegios mayores, or universities. In the republican era the term *colegio*
gradually became identified exclusively with preparatory work.
colegio nacional: name given Colombia's three major universities (in Bogotá,
Cartagena, and Popayán) in 1850; this designation persisted until the National University was created in 1867.
Comisión Corográfica: scientific expedition established at the end of the first
Mosquera administration (1845–1849) and put into operation by the subsequent López administration (1849–1853). Under the direction of Col.
Agustín Codazzi, its mission was to map the country and to provide precise
descriptions of the economies and societies of the country's various regions.
The mission included artists, who sketched plant and animal life as well as
significant features of the country's geography and society.

cordillera: mountain range.

corregidor: local or provincial governor in the colonial period.

costeños: natives of Colombia's Caribbean coast.

criollo: native, born in the land.

cundinamarqués: native of Cundinamarca (region around Bogotá).

diezmo: tithe, collected by royal government in the colonial period and then by the republican government; a 10 percent tax on agricultural production.

empleomanía: mania for government jobs, considered to be deeply rooted in Spanish tradition.

facultades mayores: university faculties conducting studies leading to the professional or doctorate degree.

filosofía: in the late eighteenth and nineteenth centuries *filosofía* meant specifically "natural philosophy," or physics and allied natural sciences.

Gólgotas: young radical Liberals in Colombia of the years 1850–1854.

Guanentá: a mountainous region in southern Santander characterized by many small communities nestling in pockets in the broken terrain; the largest communities in the region were and are el Socorro and San Gil.

hospicio: poorhouse, house of correction, or orphan asylum.

latifundia: large landholdings.

letrado: man educated in the law.

minifundia: landholdings too small adequately to sustain a family.

ministeriales: politicians who controlled or participated in Colombia's national government between 1837 and 1845, almost all of whom became known as Conservatives after 1849.

moderados: Colombian politicians who opposed both military dictatorship and punitive actions against those who had participated in the dictatorships of 1826 through 1831; many *moderados* of 1831–1837 became the *ministeriales* of 1837–1845.

mosquerista: follower of Gen. Tomás Cipriano de Mosquera.

payanés: native of Popayán.

populacho: the masses or lower classes.

pordiosero: beggar.

posada: inn.

prócer: participant in the Independence movement, particularly in its early phases.

proyecto: plan or scheme; a *proyecto de ley* is equivalent to an American legislative bill.

pureza de sangre: "purity of blood," in Spain originally meant certification that all ancestors were of legitimate Christian descent; in the New World it was extended to mean certification that all ancestors were of Spanish, as opposed to Indian, Negro, or mestizo, origin.

"la raza": reference to the Spanish American heritage, usually used as a short-hand explanation for negative characteristics.

Reconquista: Christian reconquest of the Iberian peninsula after the Islamic conquest of A.D. 711. The Reconquista is variously dated: its focal period covered the eleventh through the thirteenth centuries, but it could be said to have begun long before the eleventh century and not to have terminated until the expulsion of Moslem power from Granada in 1492.

repartimiento: Spanish word for partition or distribution; it was applied to various institutions in the Spanish colonial period. In this work it refers only to the *repartimiento de indios*, or distribution of forced Indian labor.

santandereanos: natives of the Santander region.

santanderistas: adherents of Gen. Francisco de Paula Santander.

Siete Partidas: code of legal principles promulgated by Alfonso X of Castile (1252–1284).

Spanish Pacifiers: reference to Spanish military forces that subdued the Independence movement in Venezuela and Colombia between 1815 and 1819.

tertulias: regular social gatherings of a loosely constituted but identifiable upper-class group; a circle of friends.

toderos: Colombian term for generalist, or person who cannot confine his work to one specialty.

urbanidad: civility, good manners.

Bibliographic Note

THE research for this book has been most intensively concentrated on the neo-Bourbons, particularly in Bogotá and in the years between 1820 and 1870. In order to round out the theme, I carried out more limited research, essentially in printed materials, for the western provinces and for the periods preceding 1820 and following 1870. This book therefore must be viewed, particularly for the less thoroughly treated regions and periods, as an interpretive overview rather than as the definitive treatment. Much remains to be done. For leads into any aspect of the subject, an investigator can do no better than to consult the extensive works of Alfredo D. Bateman, a Bogotá engineer, much of whose life has been devoted to compiling data on the history of science and engineering in Colombia. The libraries of the Sociedad Colombiana de Ingenieros in Bogotá and the Sociedad Antioqueña de Ingenieros in Medellín also offer a wealth of materials.

For this work the most pertinent archival materials used were (1) documents in the Instrucción Pública and Guerra y Marina sections in the Archivo General de la Historia Nacional in the Biblioteca Nacional, Bogotá; (2) the personal papers of Pedro Alcántara Herrán (cited as Archivo Herrán) in the Academia Colombiana de Historia; and (3) the Archivo del Congreso, Bogotá. The commercial papers of Inocencio Vargas e Hijos, later Francisco Vargas y Hermanos, Bogotá, were of some use for the chapter on foreign study. I also consulted, but found less useful for this topic, papers of José Manuel Restrepo and Ignacio Gutiérrez Vergara, also in the Academia Colombiana de Historia, and those of Medardo Rivas, in the possession of José Manuel Rivas Sacconi, Bogotá. The most useful and illuminating materials of José Manuel Restrepo (particularly regarding the late colonial Enlightenment) were in the possession of the recently deceased Monsignor José Restrepo Posada, who graciously permitted me to roam through his archives. The materials in this archive, however, are overwhelmingly abundant, and I had time only to glimpse their richness.

Ample printed materials, particularly almanacs and other pamphlets, are deposited in various *fondos* of the Biblioteca Nacional (Fondo Pineda, Fondo Quijano de Otero), in the Biblioteca Luis Angel Arango, and in the library of the Academia Colombiana de Historia. I am indebted to Fray Alberto Lee López, O.F.M., archivist of the Academia Colombiana de Historia, and to Professor J. León Helguera for access to this library. Pamphlets listed below are those used and most pertinent for this topic which are to be found in the Fondo Pineda and the Fondo Quijano of the Biblioteca Nacional and in the Biblioteca Luis Angel Arango. The innumerable programs of *colegio certámenes* (demonstrations) to be found throughout the volumes on Instrucción Pública in the Archivo Nacional are not listed.

Newspapers, both the official gazettes (*Gaceta de Colombia*, *Gaceta de la Nueva Granada*, *Gaceta Oficial*, and *Diario Oficial*) and dozens of privately published ones, provided a substantial amount of information. The most extensive collections are in the Biblioteca Nacional and the Biblioteca Luis Angel Arango. The collections owned by the latter are more complete and more rationally organized; the Biblioteca Nacional, however, possesses more titles, including fragmentary collections of the principal journals of the late colonial period. Ministerial and other government reports, another fundamental source, are most amply collected and best organized in the Biblioteca Luis Angel Arango. The Biblioteca Nacional, however, can be used to fill in certain gaps in that collection.

For the period after 1870, the most useful contemporary publications for the history of education and the practice of science and technology in Colombia are *La Agricultura*, *Anales de Ingeniería*, *Boletín de la Sociedad Antioqueña de Ingenieros*, *Anales de la Escuela de Minas*, *Anales de la Universidad Nacional*, *Anales de la Instrucción Pública*, *La Industria*, *Papel Periódico Ilustrado*, and *Colombia Ilustrada*. Twentieth-century publications, offering articles with retrospective views on the subject, many of them from the pen of Ing. Alfredo Bateman, are *Anales de Ingeniería*, *Ingeniería y Arquitectura*, and *Revista de la Academia Colombiana de Ciencias Exactas, Físicas y Naturales*.

The following Bibliography lists only those materials actually cited or those that were particularly pertinent to the formulation of my conception of the topic. The Bibliography lists historical articles from scholarly journals but not articles from contemporary serials even though they are cited in the notes.

Bibliography

Archival Materials

Public

Academia Colombiana de Historia. Personal papers of Gen. Pedro Alcántara Herrán [cited as Archivo Herrán], José Manuel Restrepo, and Ignacio Gutiérrez Vergara.

Archivo del Congreso Nacional. Records of Senado and Cámara. [Used selectively for specific pieces of legislation, particularly in the 1847–1870 period.]

Archivo Nacional de Colombia—República. Records of Secretaría de Guerra y Marina, 1829–1897, and Secretaría de Instrucción Pública, 1823–1884.

Biblioteca Luis Angel Arango. Manuscript Collection.

Acosta, Joaquín. "Testamento del General Joaquín Acosta."

"Correspondencia dirigida al Coronel Anselmo Pineda, 1845 a 1854."

"Correspondencia dirigida al General Francisco de Paula Santander por diferentes personas, durante los años de 1812 a 1839."

Cuenca, Tomás. "Diario de mi vida."

Cuervo, Rufino. "Documentos de Rufino Cuervo, 1832–1847."

Gómez, Víctor. "Carta dirigida a Alejandro Vélez sobre renuncia de Mariano Ospina Rodríguez de la gobernación de Antioquia" [Medellín, 1831].

Herrán, Pedro Alcántara. "Cartas escritas por el General Herrán en el año de 1829."

Herrán, Pedro de la. "Cartas dirigidas a su esposa Matea durante los años de 1795 a 1803."

Moreno y Escandón. "Copia de un documento sobre exceso de abogados." Santafé, 1771.

Pradilla, Urbano. "Cartas dirigidas a don Lino de Pombo, 1840–1843."

Santander, Francisco de Paula. "Cartas, mensajes y documentos del General Santander, de 1819 a 1833."

Private

Restrepo, José Manuel. Papers. In archive of the late Monsignor José Restrepo, Bogotá.

Rivas, Medardo. Papers. In possession of Dr. José Manuel Rivas Sacconi, Bogotá.

Vargas é Hijos, Inocencio [later Francisco Vargas y Hermanos]. Commercial letters, Bogotá, 1850–1880. In possession of don Pedro Vargas, Bogotá. [Cited as Vargas Cartas.]

Theses and Dissertations

Ahern, Evelyn Jeanne Goggin. "The Development of Education in Colombia, 1820–1850." M.A. thesis, University of California, Berkeley, 1947.

Davis, Robert Henry. "Acosta, Caro, and Lleras: Three Essayists and Their Views of New Granada's National Problems, 1832–1853." Ph.D. dissertation, Vanderbilt University, 1969.

Gilmore, Robert Louis. "Federalism in Colombia, 1810–1858." Ph.D. dissertation, University of California, Berkeley, 1949.

Guralnick, Stanley Martin. "Science and the American College: 1828–1860." Ph.D. dissertation, University of Pennsylvania, 1969.

Helguera, Joseph Leon. "The First Mosquera Administration in New Granada, 1845–49." Ph.D. dissertation, University of North Carolina, 1958.

Hoffman, H. Theodore. "A History of Railway Concessions and Railway Development Policy in Colombia to 1943." Ph.D. dissertation, American University, 1947.

Horna, Hernan. "Francisco Javier Cisneros: A Pioneer in Transportation and Economic Development in Colombia." Ph.D. dissertation, Vanderbilt University, 1970.

Loy, Jane Meyer. "Modernization and Educational Reform in Colombia, 1863–1886." Ph.D. dissertation, University of Wisconsin, 1969.

Nichols, Theodore H. "The Caribbean Gateway to Colombia: Cartagena, Santa Marta, and Barranquilla, and the Connections with the Interior, 1820–1940." Ph.D. dissertation, University of California, Berkeley, 1951.

Safford, Frank Robinson. "Commerce and Enterprise in Central Colombia, 1821–1870." Ph.D. dissertation, Columbia University, 1965.

Young, John Lane. "University Reform in New Granada, 1820–1850." Ph.D. dissertation, Columbia University, 1970.

Official Publications

Bogotá, Province of. *Colección de todos los decretes de interés jeneral espedidos por la honorable cámara de la provincia de Bogotá, desde 1832 . . . hasta 1843, formada por el gobernador de la provincia Alfonso Acevedo Tejada.* Bogotá: Imprenta de Nicolás Gómez, 1844.

Colombia. Comisión Corográfica. *Jeografía física i política de las provincias de la Nueva Granada, por la Comisión Corográfica bajo la dirección de Agustín*

Codazzi. Bogotá: Imprenta del Estado, 1856. Reprint. (4 vols.) Archivo de la Economía Nacional. Bogotá: Banco de la República, 1957–1959.

————. Consejo de Estado. *Codificación nacional de todas las leyes de Colombia desde el año de 1821, hecha conforme a la ley 13 de 1912, por la Sala de Negocios Generales del Consejo de Estado*. 34 vols. [to 1884]. Bogotá: Imprenta Nacional, 1924–1955.

————. Ministerio de Educación Nacional. *Compilación de disposiciones sobre regime*[n.?] *de universidades, 1888–1952: Compilación elaborada por Miguel Tarayona Gutiérrez y Carlos Acosta Sarmiento, inspectores nacionales de universidades*. Bogotá: Imprenta Nacional, 1952.

————. Ministerio de Gobierno. *Archivo del Congreso Nacional: Indice alfabético, 1819–1935. Leyes, proyectos, rehabilitaciones, memoriales, telegramas, etc*. Prepared by Ernesto Esguerra Serrano. 2 vols. Bogotá, 1936–1942.

[————. Ministerio de Relaciones Exteriores]. Nueva Granada, República. Departamento de Relaciones Exteriores. *Estadística general de la Nueva Granada, que conforme al Decreto ejecutivo de 18 de diciembre de 1846 pública la Secretaría de Relaciones Exteriores. Parte Primera: Población e instituciones*. Bogotá: Imprenta de J. A. Cualla, 1848.

Cortés, Enrique. *Informe del director jeneral de instrucción primaria de la Union*. Bogotá: Imprenta de Medardo Rivas, 1876.

Cuellar, Patrocinio, *Informe del gobernador de la provincia de Bogotá a la honorable cámara de provincia*. Bogotá, 1851.

————. *Informe del gobernador de la provincia de Bogotá a la honorable cámara de provincia*. Bogotá, 1853.

Currea, José A. *Informe del secretario de hacienda al gobernador del Estado de Cundinamarca, 1858*. Bogotá, 1858.

Esposiciones de los gobernadores de Bogotá, Cundinamarca, i Zipaquirá, dirigidas por el de la provincia de Bogotá, reintegrada, a la Asamblea Constituyente en 1855. Bogotá, 1855.

Gutiérrez Lee, Pedro. *Esposición del gobernador de Bogotá*. Bogotá, 1855.

————. *Esposición del gobernador de Bogotá*. Bogotá, 1856.

————. *Esposición del gobernador de Bogotá a la Asamblea Constituyente del Estado de Cundinamarca*. Bogotá: Imprenta de Francisco Torres Amaya, 1857.

Informe. Director jeneral de la instrucción pública, 1870, 1876.

Lombana, Vicente. *Informe del gobernador de la provincia de Bogotá a la honorable cámara de provincia*. Bogotá, 1849.

Mallarino, Manuel María. *Memoria del gobernador de Buenaventura a la cámara provincial*. Cali, 1843.

Mantilla, José María. *Esposición que el General José María Mantilla, gobernador interino de la provincia de Bogotá, presenta a la cámara de la misma en sus sesiones de 1835*. Bogotá: Imprenta de Nicomedas Lora, 1835.

————. *Informe del gobernador de la provincia de Bogotá a la honorable cámara de provincia*. Bogotá, 1850.

Memorias de Fomento, 1880–1894. [Included agriculture, internal improvements, and various sorts of technical education.]
Memorias de Gobierno, 1846–1861. [Public instruction moved from Interior to Gobierno in 1846, as did internal improvements in 1855.]
Memorias de Guerra y Marina, 1823–1870.
Memorias de Hacienda, 1823–1863, 1880–1897.
Memorias de Hacienda y Fomento, 1864–1879. [Public instruction and internal improvements after 1864 were in the new department of Fomento.]
Memorias de Instrucción Pública, 1880–1898.
Memorias de lo Interior y Relaciones Exteriores, 1823–1845.
Mendoza, Rafael. *Informe del gobernador de la provincia de Bogotá a la provincia de Bogotá a la honorable cámara de la provincia.* Bogotá, 1852.
Obregón, Francisco A. *Esposición que el gobernador de Antioquia dirije a la cámara de la provincia en sus sesiones ordinarias de 1836.* Medellín: Imprenta de Manuel A. Balcázar, 1836.
————. *Esposición que el gobernador de Antioquia dirije a la cámara de la provincia en sus sesiones ordinarias de 1839.* Medellín: Imprenta de Manuel Antonio Balcázar, 1839.
[Pereira Gamba, Próspero.] Estado Soberano de Cundinamarca. *Memoria que el Secretario de Gobierno encargado del despacho de Fomento dirige al gobernador del estado para la asamblea legislativa de 1882.* Bogotá: Imprenta de Pizano, 1882.
Zaldúa, Manuel M. *Esposición del gobernador de la provincia de Vélez a la honorable cámara de 1847.* Bogotá: Imprenta de Nicolás Gómez, 1847.

Books, Pamphlets, and Articles

Acevedo Latorre, Eduardo. "Codazzi en Colombia." *Revista de la Academia Colombiana de Ciencias* 10, no. 41 (August 1959): xxv–xxxi.
Acosta de Samper, Soledad. *Biografía del General Joaquín Acosta.* Bogotá: Librería Colombiana, Camacho Roldán, 1901.
————. "Don Alejandro Vélez." *Boletín de Historia y Antigüedades* 2, no. 23 (July 1904): 675–683.
Acuña, Luis Alberto. "Esbozo biográfico de Agustín Codazzi." *Revista de la Academia Colombiana de Ciencias Exactas, Físicas y Naturales* 8, no. 29 (November 1950): 123–129.
Adams, Don. "The Study of Education and Social Development." *Comparative Education Review* 9, no. 3 (October 1965): 258–269.
Addy, George M. "Alcalá before Reform—the Decadence of a Spanish University." *Hispanic American Historical Review* 58, no. 4 (November 1968): 561–585.
————. *The Enlightenment in the University of Salamanca.* Durham, N.C.: Duke University Press, 1966.

Almanaque curioso para el año de 1861. Bogotá: Imprenta de "El Mosaico," 1860. [Pamphlet, Fondo Pineda.]

Alvarez Lleras, Jorge. "Alejandro de Humboldt—noticia biográfica y literaria." *Revista de la Academia Colombiana de Ciencias Exactas, Físicas y Naturales* 3, nos. 9–10 (March–September 1939): 182–187.

———. "Breve historia del Observatorio Astronómico Nacional." *Revista de la Academia Colombiana de Ciencias Exactas, Físicas y Naturales* 5, no. 20 (August 1944): 552–556.

Ancízar, Manuel. *Almanaque para el año de 1849*. Bogotá: Imprenta de Ancízar, 1849 [?].

———. *Peregrinación de Alpha por las provincias del Norte de la Nueva Granada en 1850–1851*. Biblioteca de la Presidencia de Colombia, vol. 24. Bogotá: Empresa Nacional de Publicaciones, 1956.

Anderson, C. Arnold, and Bowman, Mary Jean. *Education and Economic Development*. Chicago: Aldine Publishing Co., 1965.

Anuario estadístico de Colombia, 1875. Bogotá: Medardo Rivas, 1875. "Arbitrios para el establecimiento de universidad pública." *Boletín de Historia y Antigüedades* 24, no. 272 (June 1937): 341–343.

Aragón, Arcesio. *La Universidad del Cauca: Monografía histórica*. Popayán: Imprenta Oficial, 1925.

Arango Mejía, Gabriel. *Genealogías de Antioquia y Caldas*. 2d ed. 2 vols. Medellín: Imprenta Editorial Medellín, 1942.

Arboleda, Gustavo. *Diccionario biográfico y genealógico del antiguo departamento del Cauca*. Bogotá: Librería Horizontes, 1962.

———. *Historia contemporánea de Colombia (desde la disolución de la antigua república de ese nombre hasta la época presente)*. 6 vols. Bogotá: Librería Colombiana de Camacho Roldán y Tamayo, 1918–1919; Popayán: Imprenta del Departamento, 1930; Cali, 1933, 1935.

Arboleda, Sergio. *Las letras, las ciencias y las bellas artes en Colombia*. 3d. ed. Biblioteca Aldeana de Colombia, no. 51. Bogotá: Editorial Minerva, 1963.

Arias, Juan de Dios. "El Colegio de San José de Guanentá en San Gil, Primera Época, 1787–1824." *Boletín de Historia y Antigüedades* 30, nos. 342–343 (April–May 1943): 386–409.

Arias de Greiff, Jorge. "El diario inédito de Humboldt." *Revista de la Colombiana de Ciencias* 13, no. 51 (December 1969): 394–401.

Artz, Frederick B. *The Development of Technical Education in France, 1500–1850*. Cleveland: Society for the History of Technology, 1966.

"La astronomía en Santafé." *Boletín de Historia y Antigüedades* 1, no. 6 (February 1903): 303–306.

Atcon, Rudolph P. *The Latin American University: A Key for an Integrated Approach to the Coordinated Social, Economic and Educational Development of Latin America*. Bogotá: Eco: Revista de la Cultura de Occidente, 1966.

Atienza, Julio de. *Títulos nobiliarios hispanoamericanos*. Madrid: M. Aguilar, 1947.

"Avisos de Hebephilo a los jóvenes de los colegios sobre la inutilidad de sus estudios presentes." *Papel Periódico de la Ciudad de Santafé de Bogotá*, April 1 and 8, 1791.

Azevedo, Fernando de, ed. *As ciências no Brasil*. 2 vols. São Paulo: Edições Melhoramentos, 1955.

————. *A cultura brasileira: Introdução ao estudo da cultura no Brasil*. Instituto Brasileiro de Geografia e Estatística, Comissão Censitária Nacional. Rio de Janeiro: Serviço Gráfico do Instituto Brasileiro de Geografia e Estatística, 1943.

Banco de la República. *Atlas de economía colombiana: Primera entrega, aspectos físico y geográfico*. Bogotá: Imprenta del Banco de la República, 1959.

Baraya, José María. *Biografías militares ó historia militar del país en medio siglo*. Bogotá: Imprenta de Gaitán, 1874.

Barclay, W. S. "The Geography of South American Railways." *Geographical Journal* 49, no. 3 (March 1917): 161–201; 49, no. 4 (April 1917): 241–282.

Barnhart, Donald S. "Colombian Transport and the Reforms of 1931: An Evaluation." *Hispanic American Historical Review* 38, no. 1 (February 1958): 1–24.

Basalla, George. "The Spread of Western Science." *Science*, May 5 1967, pp. 611–622.

Bateman, Alfredo D. "Apuntamientos para la historia de la ingeniería colombiana: José Celestino Mutis." *Ingeniería y Arquitectura* 3, no. 25 (June 1941): 30–32.

————. "La Comisión Corográfica." *Ingeniería y Arquitectura* 7, no. 73 (January–February 1947): 35.

————. "Don Francisco José de Caldas." *Ingeniería Arquitectura* 3, no. 31 (December 1941): 35–37; 3, no. 32 (January 1942): 40.

————. "La Expedición Botánica." *Ingeniería y Arquitectura* 3, no. 26 (July 1941): 25, 28–29; 3, no. 27 (August 1941): 36–38; 3, no. 28 (September 1941): 39–40; 3, no. 29 (October 1941): 34–37.

————. "Las figuras de la Comisión Corográfica." *Revista de la Academia Colombiana de Ciencias* 10, no. 38 (March 1957): 413–417.

————. *Francisco Javier Cisneros*. Bogotá: Editorial Kelly, 1970.

————. *Francisco José de Caldas: Síntesis biográfica*. Bogotá: Editorial Kelly, 1969.

————. *Los ingenieros de Cartagena*. Bogotá: Seguros Colombia-Banco de Construcción, n.d. [1964?].

————. "Jorge Alvarez Lleras." *Revista de la Academia Colombiana de Ciencias Exactas, Físicas y Naturales* 8, no. 32 (June 1952): v–x.

————. "Misiones científicas del siglo XIX." *Ingeniería y Arquitectura* 6, no. 71 (September–October 1946): 40; 6, no. 72 (November–December 1946): 39.

[Many other historical and biographical articles by Alfredo Bateman appear in *Ingeniería y Arquitectura* from 1940 to 1961. Almost all these, however, have been reprinted and are more easily used in his books (listed above). When information from the articles is used in this text, these volumes are cited.]

————. *El Observatorio Astronómico de Bogotá: Mongrafía histórica con ocasión del 150° aniversario de su fundación.* Bogotá: Imprenta Nacional, 1954.

————. *Páginas para la historia de la ingeniería colombiana: Galería de ingenieros colombianos.* Biblioteca de Historia Nacional, vol. 114. Bogotá: Editorial Kelly, 1972.

————. "La reglamentación de la ingeniería." *Ingeniería y Arquitectura* 4, no. 51 (September 1943): 16–18.

————. "Una misión científica en los albores de la República." *Universidad Nacional de Colombia*, no. 17 (1953), pp. 207–213.

Becerra, Ricardo. "The Republic of Colombia." *Harper's New Monthly Magazine* 79, no. 474 (November 1889): 920–928.

Becker, Jerónimo, and Rivas Groot, José María. *El Nuevo Reino de Granada en el siglo XVIII*. Biblioteca de Historia Hispano-Americana. Madrid: Imprenta del Asilo de Huérfanos del S.C. de Jesús, 1921.

La Beneficencia de Cundinamarca, 1869–1969. [No publication data given.]

Bennett, Charles Alpheus. *History of Manual and Industrial Education up to 1870.* Peoria: Manual Arts Press, 1926.

Bertelson, David. *The Lazy South.* New York: Oxford University Press, 1967.

Beyer, Robert Carlyle. "Transportation and the Coffee Industry in Colombia." *Inter-American Economic Affairs* 2, no. 3 (Winter 1948): 17–30.

Bining, Arthur Cecil. *Pennsylvania Iron Manufacture in the Eighteenth Century.* Harrisburg: Pennsylvania Historical Commission, 1938.

Bishop, J. Leander. *A History of American Manufacture from 1608 to 1860.* 3 vols. Philadelphia: Edward Young & Co., 1868.

Bohórquez Casallas, Luis Antonio. *La evolución educativa en Colombia.* Bogotá: Publicaciones Cultural Colombiana, [1956].

Bonney, Catherina V. R., ed. *A Legacy of Historical Gleanings.* 2 vols. Albany, N.Y.: J. Munsell, 1875.

Borda, Francisco de P. "Colejio universitario de Paredes é hijos." *Boletín de Historia y Antigüedades* 11, no. 131 (September 1917): 642–649.

Botero Saldarriaga, R. *Francisco Antonio Zea*. Bogotá: Ediciones del Concejo, 1945.

Boussingault, Jean-Baptiste. *Memoires de J.-B. Boussingault.* 5 vols. Paris: Typographie Chamerot et Renouard, 1892–1903.

————. *Viajes científicos a los Andes Ecuatoriales ó colección de memorias sobre física, química e historia natural de la Nueva Granada, Ecuador y Venezuela, presentadas a la Academia de Ciencias de Francia por M. Boussingault, su actual presidente, y miembro del Consejo de Estado de la*

República y por el Sr. Dr. Roulin: Traducidas con anuencia de los autores por J. Acosta, y precedidas de algunas nociones de geología, por el mismo. Edited by Lasserre. Paris: Librería Castellana, 1849.

Briceño, Manuel. "Don Mariano Ospina." *Papel Periódico Ilustrado*, February 15, 1883, pp. 150–154.

———. *La Revolución (1867–77): Recuerdos para la historia.* 2d ed. Biblioteca de Historia Nacional, vol. 76. Bogotá: Imprenta Nacional, 1947.

Burritt, Bailey B. *Professional Distribution of College and University Graduates.* U.S. Bureau of Education Bulletin, no. 19. Washington, D.C.: Government Printing Office, 1912.

Bushnell, David. *The Santander Regime in Gran Colombia.* Newark: University of Delaware Press, 1954.

Caja de ahorros de Bogotá. *13° informe anual de la Junta de Inversión i Superintendencia.* Bogotá: Imprenta de Pizano i Pérez, 1859. [Pamphlet, Biblioteca Nacional.]

Caja de ahorros de la Provincia de Bogotá. *Cuarto informe anual de la Junta de Inversión i Superintendencia.* Bogotá: Imprenta de El Día, 1849. [Pamphlet, Biblioteca Nacional.]

Caldas y Tenorio, Francisco José de. *Cartas de Caldas.* Compiled and published by Eduardo Posada. Biblioteca de Historia Nacional, vol. 15. Bogotá: Imprenta Nacional, 1917.

———. *Estudios varios: Precedidos de la biografía del sabio por Lino de Pombo.* Biblioteca del Maestro, Section II: Educación, no. 1. Bogotá: Imprenta Nacional, 1941.

———. *Obras completas de Francisco José de Caldas.* Published by la Universidad Nacional de Colombia. Bogotá: Imprenta Nacional, 1966.

———. *Viajes.* Biblioteca Aldeana de Colombia, Ciencias y Educación, no. 41. Bogotá: Editorial Minerva, 1936.

Calderón, Clímaco. *Elementos de hacienda pública.* Bogotá: Imprenta de La Luz, 1911.

Calhoun, Daniel Hovey. *The American Civil Engineer: Origins and Conflict.* Cambridge, Mass.: Technology Press, 1960.

Callahan, William J. *Honor, Commerce and Industry in Eighteenth-Century Spain.* Kress Library of Business and Economics, no. 22. Boston: Harvard Graduate School of Business Administration, 1972.

———. "The Problem of Confinement: An Aspect of Poor Relief in Eighteenth-Century Spain." *Hispanic American Historical Review* 51, no. 1 (February 1971): 1–24.

Calvert, Monte A. *The Mechanical Engineer in America, 1830–1910: Professional Cultures in Conflict.* Baltimore: Johns Hopkins Press, 1967.

Camacho Roldán, Salvador. *Artículos escogidos.* Bogotá: Librería Colombiana, n.d.

———. *Escritos varios.* 3 vols. Bogotá: Librería Colombiana, 1892–1895.

————. *Notas de viaje (Colombia y Estados Unidos de América)*. Bogotá: Librería Colombiana, 1890.

Campomanes, Pedro Rodríguez de. *Discurso sobre el fomento de la industria popular*. Madrid: Imprenta de D. Antonio de Sancha, 1774.

————. *Discurso sobre la educación popular de los artesanos y su fomento*. Madrid: Imprenta de D. Antonio de Sancha, 1775.

Caro, José Eusebio. *Epistolario*. Prologue by Lucio Pabón Núñez. Biblioteca de Autores Colombianos, no. 62. Bogotá: Ministerio de Educación Nacional, Ediciones de la Revista Bolívar, 1953.

Carrasquilla, Juan de Dios. *Segundo informe anual que presenta el Comisario de la Agricultura Nacional al Poder Ejecutivo para el conocimiento del Congreso*. Bogotá: Imprenta de Rivas, 1880. [Also may be found, for this and other years, as appendix to annual reports of Ministerio de Fomento.]

Castro, Eloy B. de. "Datos sobre la historia del estudio de las matemáticas en Colombia." *Anales de Ingeniería* 10, nos. 113–114 (January–February 1898): 13–15.

Castro, Juan A. *Contestación al papel intitulado "Una negra injusticia."* Popayán, December 1, 1849. [Pamphlet, Fondo Pineda.]

"Catálogo general de la Biblioteca de la Sociedad Colombiana de Ingenieros." *Anales de Ingeniería* 42, no. 493 (1934): 800–845.

Catalogue of the Trustees, Officers and Students of the University of Pennsylvania. Philadelphia, 1852–1890.

Caycedo, Bernardo J. *D'Elhuyar y el siglo XVIII neogranadino*. Bogotá: Ediciones de la Revista Ximénez de Quesada, 1971.

Certámenes del Colejio de Pérez en Noviembre de 1864. Bogotá: Imprenta de la Nación, 1864. [Pamphlet, Fondo Pineda.]

Certámenes en el Colejio del Rosario: Año de 1865. Bogotá: Imprenta de Echeverría Hermanos, 1865. [Pamphlet, Fondo Pineda.]

Chardón, Carlos E. *Boussingault: Juicio crítico del eminente agrónomo del siglo XIX, su viaje a la Gran Colombia y sus relaciones con el Libertador y Manuelita Saénz*. Ciudad Trujillo: Editorial Montalvo, 1953.

Chittenden, Russell H. *History of the Sheffield Scientific School of Yale University, 1846–1922*. 2 vols. New Haven: Yale University Press, 1928.

Cifuentes Porras, Delio. "Francisco Javier Cisneros." *Boletín de Historia y Antigüedades* 2, no. 23 (July 1904): 685–688.

Clark, Victor S. *History of Manufactures in the United States, 1607–1860*. Washington, D.C.: Carnegie Institution of Washington, 1916.

Cohen, I. Bernard. *Some Early Tools of American Science*. Cambridge, Mass.: Harvard University Press, 1950.

Colegio de Cali. Cali: Impreso por Vicente Aragón, 1846. [Pamphlet, Fondo Pineda.]

Colegio Mayor y Seminario de San Bartolomé: La clase de filosofía. Bogotá: F. M. Stokes, 1826. [Pamphlet, Fondo Pineda.]

Colejio de Nuestra Señora del Rosario. Bogotá: Imprenta de Gaitán, 1867. [Pamphlet, Fondo Pineda.]

Combes, Margarita. *Roulin y sus amigos: Burguesía desvalida y arriesgada, 1796–1874*. Biblioteca Popular de Cultura Colombiana, no. 30. Bogotá: Editorial ABC, 1942.

"Compendio de lo actuado sobre estudios públicos." *Boletín de Historia y Antigüedades* 24, no. 272 (June 1937): 343–371.

Cordóvez Moure, José María. *Reminiscencias de Santafé y Bogotá*. Madrid: Aguilar, 1957.

Cortázar, Roberto H., comp. *Cartas y mensajes del General Francisco de Paula Santander*. 10 vols. Bogotá: Librería Voluntad, 1953–1956.

————. "El Colegio del Rosario en la Independencia." *Boletín de Historia y Antigüedades* 6, no. 66 (November 1910): 338–361.

————, comp. *Correspondencia dirigida al General Francisco de Paula Santander*. 14 vols. Bogotá: Librería Voluntad, 1965–1970.

Cortés Vargas, Carlos. "Un pleito santafereño y Moreno y Escandón." *Boletín de Historia y Antigüedades* 18, no. 207 (March 1930): 200–208.

Crónica del Colejio de Boyacá en 1856. Bogotá: Imprenta de Francisco Torres Amaya, n.d. [Pamphlet, Fondo Pineda.]

Cuervo, Angel and Rufino José. *Vida de Rufino Cuervo y noticias de su época*. 2d ed. 2 vols. Biblioteca Popular de Cultura Colombiana, nos. 84–85. Bogotá: Prensas de la Biblioteca Nacional, 1946.

Cuervo, Luis Augusto. "Elogio de don José Ignacio de París." *Boletín de Historia y Antigüedades* 33, nos. 377–379 (March, April, May 1946): 222–238.

————, ed. *Epistolario del Doctor Rufino Cuervo*. 3 vols. Biblioteca de Historia Nacional, vols. 22–24. Bogotá: Imprenta Nacional, 1918–1922.

Cuervo Márquez, Carlos. *Vida del Doctor José Ignacio Márquez*. 2 vols. Biblioteca de Historia Nacional, vols. 17–18. Bogotá: Imprenta Nacional, 1917.

Cuervo Márquez, Luis. "Carlos Cuervo Márquez." *Revista de la Academia Colombiana de Ciencias Exactas, Físicas y Naturales* 3, no. 11 (January–February, March, April 1940): 351–355.

Daniels, George H. *American Science in the Age of Jackson*. New York: Columbia University Press, 1968.

————. "The Big Questions in the History of American Technology." *Technology and Culture* 11, no. 1 (January 1970): 1–21.

Del Rio, Angel, ed. *Responsible Freedom in the Americas*. Garden City, N.J.: Doubleday & Co., 1955.

Deyrup, Felicia Johnson. *Arms Makers of the Connecticut Valley: A Regional Study of the Economic Development of the Small Arms Industry, 1798–1870*. Smith College Studies in History, vol. 33. Northampton, 1948.

Díaz, Eugenio. *Manuela, novela de costumbres colombianas*. 2 vols. Paris: Librería Española de Garnier Hermanos, 1889.

Dobbs, Archibald Edward. *Education and Social Movements, 1700–1850*. London: Longmans, Green & Co., 1919.

Dollero, Adolfo. *Cultura colombiana: Apuntaciones sobre el movimiento intelectual de Colombia, desde la conquista hasta la época actual*. Bogotá: Editorial Cromos, 1930.

Douglas, Paul H. *American Apprenticeship and Industrial Education*. New York: Columbia University, 1921.

Duane, William. *A Visit to Colombia*. Philadelphia: Thomas H. Palmer, 1826.

Durand, William Frederick. *Robert Henry Thurston, a Biography: The Record of a Life of Achievement as Engineer, Educator, and Author*. New York: American Society of Mechanical Engineers, 1929.

Easby-Smith, James S. *Georgetown University in the District of Columbia, 1789–1907*. 2 vols. New York: Lewis Publishing Co., 1907.

Ellis, William Arba. *Norwich University, 1819–1911: Her History, Her Graduates, Her Role of Honor*. 3 vols. Montpelier, Vt.: Capitol City Press, 1911.

————, ed. *Roster of the Graduates and Past Cadets of Norwich University: The Military College of the State of Vermont*. Bradford, Vt.: Opinion Press, 1907.

Enciclopedia Universal Ilustrada Europeo-Americana. 70 vols. Madrid: Espasa-Calpe, 1908–1930.

Estatutos de la Sociedad de Educación Primaria de Bogotá, establecidos por la Cámara Provincial en 4 de octubre de 1834. Bogotá: Imprenta de J. A. Cualla, 1834. [Pamphlet, Fondo Pineda.]

Estudios industriales sobre la minería antioqueña en 1856: Con varios cuadros estadísticos i la carta minerológica de la provincia. Medellín: Imprenta de Lince, n.d.

Etienne, C. P. *Nouvelle-Grenade: Aperçu général sur la Colombie et recits de voyages en Amérique*. Geneva: Imprimerie Maurice Richter, 1887.

Fals Borda, Orlando. "Bases for a Sociological Interpretation of Education in Colombia." In *The Caribbean: Contemporary Colombia*, edited by A. Curtis Wilgus, pp. 183–213. Gainesville: University of Florida Press, 1962.

Ferguson, Eugene S., ed. *Early Engineering Reminiscences (1815–40) of George Escol Sellers*. Washington, D.C.: Smithsonian Institution, 1965.

Fernandes, Florestan. *Educação e sociedade no Brasil*. São Paulo: Dominus Editora, 1966.

Finestrad, Joaquín de. "El vasallo instruido en el estado del Nuevo Reino de Granada y en sus respectivas obligaciones." In *Los comuneros*, edited by Eduardo Posada. Biblioteca de Historia Nacional, vol. 4. Bogotá: Imprenta Nacional, 1905.

Fisher, Berenice M. *Industrial Education: American Ideals and Institutions*. Madison: University of Wisconsin Press, 1967.

Fisher, Richard Swainson. "General Statistics of South American States, exhibiting their area, population, commerce, revenue, debts, etc. for the official year 1855." *Hunt's Merchant's Magazine* 39, no. 4 (October 1858): 487.

Forman, Sidney. *West Point: A History of the United States Military Academy*. New York: Columbia University Press, 1950.

Frágola, Rolando René [J. Torre Rebello]. "Manuel del Socorro Rodrigues." *Boletín de Historia y Antigüedades* 15, no. 169 (August 1925): 46–51.

Gale, Laurence. *Education and Development in Latin America: With Special Reference to Colombia and Some Comparison with Guyana, South America*. London: Routledge & Kegan Paul, 1969.

Galindo, Aníbal. *Estudios económicos y fiscales*. Bogotá: H. Andrade, 1880.

———. "Historia de la deuda extranjera." *Anales de la Universidad* 5 (1871): 264–288.

———. *Historia económica y estadística de la hacienda nacional desde la colonia hasta nuestros días*. Bogotá: Imprenta de Nicolás Pontón, 1874.

———. *Recuerdos historicos de Aníbal Galindo, 1840 a 1895*. Bogotá: Imprenta de La Luz, 1900.

Garavito, Julio A. *Almanaque de "El Bogotano" histórico, eclesiástico y literario para el año de 1883*. Bogotá: Imprenta de La Luz, 1882.

García, Juan Crisóstomo. "Noticia histórica de Boussingault." *Boletín de Historia y Antigüedades* 27, nos. 310–311 (August–September 1940): 684–687.

García, Julio César. "Historia de la Escuela Nacional de Minas." *Anales de la Escuela Nacional de Minas*, no. 42 (October 1937), pp. 7–25.

García Márquez, Gabriel. *Cien años de soledad*. Buenos Aires: Editorial Sudamericana, 1967.

Gaviria Toro, José. *Monografía de Medellín: 1675–1925*. Medellín: Imprenta Oficial, 1925.

Gilmore, Robert Louis, and Harrison, John Parker. "Juan Bernardo Elbers and the Introduction of Steam Navigation on the Magdalena River." *Hispanic American Historical Review* 23, no. 3 (August 1948): 335–359.

Giraldo Jaramillo, Gabriel. *Bibliografía colombiana de viajes*. Biblioteca de Bibliografía Colombiana, no. 2. Bogotá: Editorial ABC, 1957.

———. *Bibliografía de bibliografías colombianas*. Corrected and revised by Rubén Pérez Ortiz. 2d ed. Publicaciones del Instituto Caro y Cuervo, serie bibliográfica, vol. 1. Bogotá: Imprenta Patriótica del Instituto Caro y Cuervo, 1960.

———, ed. *Colombianos en Suiza: Suizos en Colombia. Breve antología de viajes*. Bogotá: Editorial Santafé, 1955.

———, ed. *Relaciones de mando de los virreyes de la Nueva Granada: Memorias económicas*. Archivo de la Economía Nacional, no. 13. Bogotá: Banco de la República, 1954.

———, ed. *Viajeros colombianos en Alemania*. Bogotá: Imprenta Nacional, 1955.

Gómez, Alfonso Javier. *Cisneros*. Medellín, 1915.

Gómez Barrientos, Estanislao. *Don Mariano Ospina y su época*. 2 vols. Medellín: Imprenta Editorial "Gaceta Antioqueña," 1913–1915.

———. *25 años a través del Estado de Antioquia (1863–1888)*. 2 vols. Medellín: Tipografía de San Antonio, 1918; Imprenta Oficial, 1927.

Gómez Restrepo, Antonio. *Historia de la literatura colombiana*. 3 vols. Biblioteca Nacional de Colombia. Bogotá: Imprenta Nacional, 1938–1943.

González Brun, Guillermo. *Gobernantes de Colombia*. Bogotá: Editorial Sur America, 1936.

González Suárez, Federico. *Memoria histórica sobre Mutis y la Expedición Botánica de Bogotá en el siglo décimo octavo, 1782–1808*. 2d ed. Quito: Imprenta del Clero, 1905.

La Grande Encyclopédie, inventaire raisonné des sciences, des lettres et des arts. 31 vols. Paris: Société anonyme de La Grande Encyclopédie, n.d.

Gredilla, A. Federico. *Biografía de José Celestino Mutis, con la relación de su viaje y estudios practicados en el Nuevo Reino de Granada*. Madrid: Establecimiento Tipográfico de Fortanet, 1911.

Groot, José Manuel. *Historia eclesiástica y civil de Nueva Granada*. 5 vols. Biblioteca de Autores Colombianos, vols. 57–61. Bogotá: Ministerio de Educación Nacional. Ediciones de la Revista Bolívar, 1953.

Guerra, José Joaquín. "La Comisión Corográfica." *Ingeniería y Arquitectura* 8, no. 91 (January–February 1950): 33–36.

Guerra Azuola, Ramón. "Apuntamientos de viaje." *Boletín de Historia y Antigüedades* 4 (January 1907): 430–443.

———. "Don Lino de Pombo: Tributo en su centenario." *Anales de Ingeniería* 9, nos. 101–102 (January–February 1897): 1–18.

Guía oficial i descriptiva de Bogotá. Bogotá: Imprenta de la Nación, 1858.

Gutiérrez Ponce, Ignacio. *Vida de don Ignacio Gutiérrez Vergara y episodios históricos de su tiempo (1806–1877)*. London: Bradbury, Agnew, 1900.

H. A. P. *El Señor Enrique Paris*. Bogotá: Imprenta de Echeverría Hermanos, 1864. [Pamphlet, Fondo Pineda.]

Habakkuk, H. J. *American and British Technology in the Nineteenth Century: The Search for Labour-Saving Inventions*. Cambridge: At the University Press, 1962.

Hagen, Everett E. *On the Theory of Social Change: How Economic Growth Begins*. Homewood, Ill.: Dorsey Press, 1962.

Hall, Francis. *Colombia: Its Present State, in respect of climate, soil, productions, population, government, commerce, revenue, manufactures, arts, literature, manners, education, etc*. London: Baldwin, Cradock and Joy, 1824.

Harbison, Frederick, and Myers, Charles A. *Education, Manpower, and Economic Growth: Strategies of Human Resource Development*. New York: McGraw-Hill, 1964.

———. *Manpower and Education: Country Studies in Economic Development*. New York: McGraw-Hill, 1965.

Harker Mutis, Adolfo. *Mis recuerdos*. Biblioteca Santander, vol. 23. Bogotá: Editorial Cosmos, 1954.

Harrison, John Fletcher Clews. *Learning and Living, 1790–1960: A Study in the History of the English Adult Education Movement*. London: Routledge & Kegan Paul, 1961.

Hartley, Edward Neal. *Ironworks on the Sangus*. Norman: University of Oklahoma Press, 1957.

Havighurst, Robert J., and Gouveia, Aparecida J. *Brazilian Secondary Education and Socio-Economic Development*. New York: Praeger, 1969.

Havighurst, Robert J., and Moreira, J. Roberto. *Society and Education in Brazil*. Pittsburgh: University of Pittsburgh Press, 1965.

Helguera, J. León. "La primera administración Mosquera, 1845–1849." *Economía Colombiana* 2, no. 4 (August 1954): 125–130.

————, and Davis, Robert H., eds. *Archivo epistolar del General Mosquera: Correspondencia con el General Pedro Alcántara Herrán*. Biblioteca de Historia Nacional, vols. 116, 117. 2 vols. of projected 3. Bogotá: Editorial Kelly, 1972.

————, eds. *Archivo epistolar del General Mosquera: Correspondencia con el General Ramón Espina, 1835–1866*. Biblioteca de Historia Nacional, vol. 108. Bogotá: Editorial Kelly, 1966.

Henao, Jesús María, and Arrubla, Gerardo. *History of Colombia*. Translated and edited by J. Fred Rippy. Chapel Hill: University of North Carolina Press, 1938.

Henao Mejía, Gabriel. *Juan de Dios Aranzazu*. Biblioteca de Autores Colombianos, vol. 55. Bogotá: Ministerio de Educación Nacional, Ediciones de la Revista Bolívar, 1953.

Hernández de Alba, Guillermo, ed. *Archivo epistolar del sabio naturalista Don José Celestino Mutis*. 2 vols. Instituto Colombiano de Cultura Hispánica, Colección José Celestino Mutis, vols. 3 and 4. Bogotá: Editorial Kelly, 1968.

————. *Aspectos de la cultura en Colombia*. Biblioteca Popular de Cultura Colombiana. Bogotá: Ministerio de Educación Pública, 1947.

————. "Breve historia de la Universidad de Colombia." *Boletín de Historia y Antigüedades* 28, nos. 323–324 (September–October 1941): 829–846.

————. *Crónica del muy ilustre Colegio Mayor de Nuestra Señora del Rosario de Santa Fe de Bogotá*. 2 vols. Bogotá: Editorial Centro, 1938–1940.

————, ed. *Diario de observaciones de José Celestino Mutis, 1760–1790*. 2 vols. Instituto Colombiano de Cultura Hispánica, Colección José Celestino Mutis, vols. 1 and 2. Bogotá: Editorial Minerva, 1957–1958.

————, ed. *Epistolario de Rufino José Cuervo con Luis María Lleras y otros amigos y familiares*. Instituto Caro y Cuervo, Archivo Epistolar Colombiano, vol. 3. Bogotá, 1969.

————, ed. *El plan de estudios del arzobispo-virrey: Contribución al estudio del desarrollo de las humanidades en Colombia*. Bogotá: Instituto Caro y Cuervo, 1946.

————. *Vida y escritos del doctor José Félix de Restrepo*. Bogotá: Imprenta Nacional, 1935.

Herr, Richard. *The Eighteenth-Century Revolution in Spain*. Princeton: Princeton University Press, 1958.

Higuita, J. de D. "Estudio histórico analítico de la población colombiana en 170 años." *Anales de Economía y Estadística*. April 24, 1940, Suplemento, pp. 1–23.

Hindle, Brooke. *The Pursuit of Science in Revolutionary America, 1735–1789*. Chapel Hill: University of North Carolina Press, 1956.

Hoenigsberg, Wessels y Compañía. *Cuestión Jimeno-Hoenigsberg, en su parte moral*. Cartagena, 1871. Reprint. Bogotá: Foción Mantilla, 1872. [Pamphlet, Biblioteca Luis Angel Arango.]

Hofstadter, Richard, and Hardy, C. DeWitt. *The Development and Scope of Higher Education in the United States*. New York: Columbia University Press, 1952.

Hofstadter, Richard, and Smith, Wilson. *American Higher Education: A Documentary History*. 2 vols. Chicago: University of Chicago Press, 1961.

Holguín y Caro, Margarita, ed. *Los Caros en Colombia de 1784 a 1925, su fe, su patriotismo, su amor*. 2d ed. Bogotá: Instituto Caro y Cuervo, 1953.

Holton, Isaac F. *New Granada: Twenty Months in the Andes*. New York: Harper & Brothers, 1857.

Howe, Walter. *The Mining Guild of New Spain and Its Tribunal General*. Cambridge, Mass.: Harvard University Press, 1949.

Humboldt, Alexander von. *Alejandro de Humboldt en Colombia; extractos de sus obras compilados . . . por Enrique Pérez Arbelaez*. Bogotá: Empresa Colombiana de Petroleos, 1959.

———. *Voyage aux régions équinoxiales du nouveau continent, fait en 1799, 1800, 1801, 1802, 1803 et 1804 pour Al. de Humboldt et A. Bonpland: Redigé par Alexandre de Humboldt . . .* 3 vols. Paris, G. Dufour et Comp., 1814–1819.

Humphreys, Robert Arthur, ed. *British Consular Reports on the Trade and Politics of Latin America, 1824–1826*. London: Offices of the Royal Historical Society, 1940.

Ibáñez, Pedro María. "Alejandro Osorio Uribe." *Boletín de Historia y Antigüedades* 10, nos. 119–120 (September–October 1916): 727–728.

———. "Benedicto Domínguez." *Boletín de Historia y Antigüedades* 12, no. 142 (December 1919): 631–634.

———. "Centenario del Observatorio de Bogotá." *Boletín de Historia y Antigüedades* 1, no. 12 (August 1903): 943–950.

———. *Crónicas de Bogotá*. 4 vols. Biblioteca de Historia Nacional, vols. 10–12, 32. Bogotá: Imprenta Nacional, 1913–1923.

———. *Memorias para la historia de la medicina en Santa Fe*. 2d ed. Universidad Nacional de Colombia. Bogotá: Imprenta Nacional, 1968.

"Informe de Don José Ignacio de Pombo (del Consulado de Cartagena) sobre asuntos económicos y fiscales." *Boletín de Historia y Antigüedades* 13, no. 154 (1921): 688–697.

J. J. O. "Noticia biográfica del Doctor Juan María Céspedes." *Gaceta Oficial*, March 5, 1848.

Jackson, Sidney L. *America's Struggle for Free Schools: Social Tension and Educa-*

tion in New England and New York, 1827–42. Washington, D.C.: American Council on Public Affairs, 1941.

James, Preston E. "The Transportation Problem of Highland Colombia." *The Journal of Geography* 22 (December 1923): 346–357.

Jaramillo Arango, Jaime. "Don José Celestino Mutis y las expediciones botánicas españolas del siglo XVII al Nuevo Mundo." *Revista de la Academia Colombiana de Ciencias Exactas, Físico-Químicas y Naturales* 9, nos. 33 and 34 (May 1953): 14–31.

Jaramillo Uribe, Jaime, ed. *Apuntes para la historia de la ciencia en Colombia*. Bogotá: Servicios Especiales de Prensa, n.d. [1971].

———. *Entre la historia y la filosofía*. Colección Populibro, vol. 22. Bogotá: Editorial Revista Colombiana, 1968.

———. *El pensamiento colombiano en el siglo XIX*. Bogotá. Editorial Temis, 1964.

Jefferson, Carter. "Worker Education in England and France, 1800–1914." *Comparative Studies in Society and History* 6, no. 3 (April 1964): 345–366.

Jenks, Leland H. *The Migration of British Capital to 1875*. New York: Alfred A. Knopf, 1927.

Jernegan, Marcus Wilson. *Laboring and Dependent Classes in Colonial America, 1607–1783: Studies of the Economic, Educational, and Social Significance of Slaves, Servants, Apprentices, and Poor Folk*. Chicago: University of Chicago Press, 1931.

Johnson, Thomas Cary, Jr. *Scientific Interests in the Old South*. New York and London: D. Appleton-Century Co., 1936.

"Jose Cornelio Borda." *Boletín de Historia y Antigüedades* 32, nos. 363–364 (January–February 1945): 19–62.

Jovellanos, Gaspar Melchor de. *Obras publicadas e inéditas*. Collection made and illustrated by Cándido Nacedal. 5 vols. Biblioteca de Autores Españoles, vols. 46, 50, 85–87. Madrid: Hermando, etc., 1933–.

Kastos, Emiro [Juan de Dios Restrepo]. *Artículos escogidos*. New edition. London: Juan M. Fonnegra, 1885.

Katz, Michael B. *The Irony of School Reform: Educational Innovation in Mid-Nineteenth Century Massachusetts*. Cambridge, Mass.: Harvard University Press, 1968.

Kearney, Hugh. *Scholars and Gentlemen: Universities and Society in Pre-industrial Britain, 1500–1700*. London: Faber & Faber, 1970.

Kelly, Thomas. *A History of Adult Education in Great Britain from the Middle Ages to the Twentieth Century*. Liverpool: Liverpool University Press, 1962.

Landes, David S. *The Unbound Prometheus: Technological Change and Industrial Development in Western Europe from 1750 to the Present*. Cambridge: At the University Press, 1969.

Lanning, John Tate. *Academic Culture in the Spanish Colonies*. New York: Oxford University Press, 1940.

———. *The Eighteenth-Century Enlightenment in the University of San Carlos de Guatemala*. Ithaca: Cornell University Press, 1956.

————. "El sistema de Copérnico en Bogotá." *Revista de Historia de América*, no. 18 (December 1944), pp. 259–306.

Latorre, Gabriel. *Francisco Javier Cisneros y el Ferrocarril de Antioquia: Reseña histórica*. Medellín: Tipografía Helios, 1924.

Latorre Cabal, Hugo. *Mi novela: Apuntes autobiográficos de Alfonso López*. Bogotá: Ediciones Mito, n.d.

Latorre Mendoza, Luis. *Historia é historias de Medellín, siglos XVII, XVIII, XIX*. Medellín: Ediciones de los Talleres de la Imprenta Departamental, 1934.

Laverde Amaya, Isidoro. *Apuntes sobre bibliografía colombiana, con muestras escogidas en prosa y en verso*. Bogotá: Imprenta de Zalamea Hermanos, 1882.

Le Moyne, August. *Viajes y estancias en América del Sur: La Nueva Granada, Santiago de Cuba, Jamaica y el istmo de Panamá*. Biblioteca Popular de Cultura Colombiana, vol. 59. Bogotá: Editorial Centro, 1945.

Letters written from Colombia during a Journey from Caracas to Bogotá, and thence to Santa Martha in 1823. London: G. Cowie & Co., 1824.

Liévano, Indalecio. *Instrucción popular sobre meteorolojía agrícola especialmente sobre el añil i el café*. Bogotá, 1868.

————. *Tratado de aljebra*. Bogotá: Imprenta de Medardo Rivas, 1875.

Lipset, Seymour Martin, and Solari, Aldo, eds. *Elites in Latin America*. New York: Oxford University Press, 1967.

Lisboa, Miguel María. *Relaçao de uma viagem a Venezuela, Nova Granada e Equador*. Brussels: A. Lacrois, Verbockhoven e Cía., Editores, 1866.

Lleras, Lorenzo María. *La República de Colombia*. Bogotá: Impreso por Nicomedes Lora, 1837.

————. *Ultima plumada del Doctor Lorenzo María Lleras*. Bogotá: Imprenta de Echeverría Hermanos, 1868. [Pamphlet, Biblioteca Luis Angel Arango.]

Long, W. Rodney. *Railways of South America*. Part II. Department of Commerce, Bureau of Foreign and Domestic Commerce, Trade Promotion Series, no. 39. Washington, D.C.: Government Printing Office, 1927.

López de Mesa, Luis. *Introducción a la historia de la cultura en Colombia: Sinopsis del desarrollo cultural de este país e interpretación de sus causas y dificultades. Datos sobre la orientación filosófica ibero-americana. Nómina de algunas publicaciones importantes. Ciudadanos extranjeros que han contribuido notablemente al progreso de esta república*. Bogotá: Published by author, 1930.

Lozano y Lozano, Fabio. "Biografía de don Jorge Tadeo Lozano." *Boletín de Historia y Antigüedades* 10, nos. 119–120 (September–October 1916): 695–698.

McGreevey, William Paul. *An Economic History of Colombia, 1845–1930*. Cambridge Latin American Studies, no. 9. Cambridge: At the University Press, 1971.

McKelvey, Blake. *American Prisons: A Study in American Social History prior to 1915*. Chicago: University of Chicago Press, 1936.

Malo O'Leary, Arturo D. "El Colegio de Stonyhurst." *El Repertorio Colombiano*, September 1878, pp. 222–232.

Mann, Charles Riborg. *A Study of Engineering Education prepared for the Joint Committee on Engineering Education for the National Engineering Societies*. Carnegie Foundation for the Advancement of Teaching Bulletin, no. 11. New York, 1918.

Marroquín, José Manuel. "Biografía de don Francisco Antonio Moreno y Escandón." *Boletín de Historia y Antigüedades* 23, nos. 264–265 (September–October 1936): 529–550.

Martínez Delgado, Luis. "Federico Lleras Acosta." *Revista de la Academia Colombiana de Ciencias* 12, no. 45 (November 1963): 119–120.

Mejía Robledo, Alfonso. *Vidas y empresas de Antioquia: Diccionario biográfico, bibliográfico y económico*. Medellín: Impresa Departamental de Antioquia, 1951.

Mendoza, Diego. *Expedición botánica de José Celestino Mutis al Nuevo Reino de Granada y memorias inéditas de Francisco José de Caldas*. Madrid: Librería General de Victoriano Suárez, 1909.

Merritt, Raymond E. *Engineering in American Society, 1850–1875*. Lexington: University Press of Kentucky, 1969.

Mesa Ortiz, Rafael M., ed. *Colombianos ilustres*. 5 vols. Bogotá and Ibagué: Imprenta de La República; Arboleda & Valencia, etc., 1916–1929.

Mollien, Gaspard Theodore. *Travels in the Republic of Colombia in the Years 1822 and 1823*. London: C. Knight, 1824.

Moreira, J. Roberto. "Some Social Aspects of Brazilian Education." *Comparative Education Review* 4, no. 2 (October 1960): 93–96.

Moreno y Escandón, Francisco Antonio. "Estado del Virreinato de Santafé, Nuevo Reino de Granada." *Boletín de Historia y Antigüedades* 23, nos. 264–265 (September–October 1936): 547–616.

————. "Método provisional e interino de los estudios que han de observar los colegios de Santa Fé, por ahora, y hasta tanto que se erige universidad pública, o Su Majestad dispone otra cosa." *Boletín de Historia y Antigüedades* 23, nos. 264–265 (September–October 1936): 644–672.

Musson, Albert Edward, and Robinson, Eric. *Science and Technology in the Industrial Revolution*. Manchester: Manchester University Press, 1969.

Mutis, José Celestino. *Archivo epistolar del sabio naturalista don José Celestino Mutis*. Compilation, prologue and notes by Guillermo Hernández de Alba. 2 vols. Instituto Colombiano de Cultura Hispánica, Colección José Celestino Mutis, vols. 3–4. Bogotá: Editorial Kelly, 1968.

————. *Diario de observaciones de José Celestino Mutis, 1760–1790*. Transcription, prologue and notes by Guillermo Hernández de Alba. 2 vols. Instituto Colombiano de Cultura Hispánica, Colección José Celestino Mutis, vols. 1–2. Bogotá: Editorial Minerva, 1957–1958.

Mutis Duran, F. "Don Sinforoso Mutis." *Boletín de Historia y Antigüedades* 8, no. 88 (September 1912): 193–235.

Naranjo M., Enrique. "José Cornelio Borda y la defensa del Callao en 1866."
  Boletín de Historia y Antigüedades 7, no. 82 (March 1912): 647–649.
Nariño, Antonio. *Informe sobre la decadencia de la agricultura i medios de su
  fomento, presentado a la prefectura de este departamento, como miembro
  de la comisión nombrada para este fin por la junta de comerciantes i
  agriculturas*. Bogotá, 1830. [Pamphlet, Fondo Pineda.]
Nason, Henry B., ed. *Biographical Record of the Officers and Graduates of the
  Rensselaer Polytechnic Institute, 1824–1886*. Troy, N.Y.: William H.
  Young, 1887.
Nelson, Richard R.; Schultz, T. Paul; and Slighton, Robert L. *Structural Change in
  a Developing Economy: Colombia's Problems and Prospects*. Rand Corpora-
  tion Research Study. Princeton: Princeton University Press, 1971.
Nisser, Pedro. *Sketch of the Different Mining and Mechanical Operations em-
  ployed in . . . South American Goldworks . . . particularly those of . . . .
  Antioquia*. Stockholm: P. A. Norstedt, 1834.
Oliver, John W. *History of American Technology*. New York: Ronald Press Co.,
  1956.
Orjuela, Luis. *Minuta histórica zipaquireña*. Bogotá: Imprenta de La Luz, 1909.
Ortega Díaz, Alfredo. *Ferrocarriles colombianos: Legislación ferroviaria*. Bib-
  lioteca de Historia Nacional, vol. 80. Bogotá: Imprenta Nacional, 1949.
———. *Ferrocarriles colombianos: Resumen histórico*. 2 vols. [Bound together,
  pages numbered consecutively.] Biblioteca de Historia Nacional, vol. 26.
  Bogotá: Imprenta Nacional, 1923.
———. *Ferrocarriles colombianos: La última experiencia ferroviaria del país,
  1920–1930*. Biblioteca de Historia Nacional, vol. 47. Bogotá: Imprenta
  Nacional, 1932.
Ortega Ricaurte, Daniel, ed. *Indice general del Boletín de Historia y Antigüedades,
  Volumenes I–XXXVIII, 1902–1952*. Academia Colombiana de Historia.
  Bogotá: Editorial Paz, 1953.
Ortega Torres, José J., ed. *Indice del "El Repertorio Colombiano."* Publicaciones
  del Instituto Caro y Cuervo, Serie Bibliográfica, vol. 3. Bogotá: Imprenta
  Patriótica del Instituto Caro y Cuervo, 1961.
———, ed. *Indice del "Papel Periódico Ilustrado" y de "Colombia Ilustrada."*
  Publicaciones del Instituto Caro y Cuervo, Serie Bibliográfica, vol. 4.
  Bogotá: Imprenta Patriótica del Instituto Caro y Cuervo, 1961.
Ortiz, Sergio Elías. *Del Colegio de la Compañia de Jesús a la Universidad de
  Nariño, 1712–1904*. Pasto: Imprenta del Departamento, 1956.
———, ed. *Escritos de dos economistas coloniales: Don Antonio de Narváez y la
  Torre y Don José Ignacio de Pombo*. Archivo de la Economía Nacional, vol.
  29. Bogotá: Banco de la República, 1965.
Osorio Racines, Felipe, ed. *Decretos del General Santander, 1819–1821*. Univer-
  sidad Nacional de Colombia. Bogotá: Imprenta Nacional, 1969.
Ospina, Joaquín. *Diccionario biográfico y bibliográfico de Colombia*. 3 vols.
  Bogotá: Editorial de Cromos, 1927; Editorial Aguila, 1937–1939.

[Ospina, Mariano.] *Mariano Ospina avisa que intenta abrir una escuela de niños en la ciudad de Medellín.* [Medellín?], 1834. [Pamphlet.]

Ospina Rodríguez, Mariano. *Artículos escogidos.* Medellín: Imprenta Republicana, 1884.

————. *El Doctor José Félix de Restrepo y su época.* Biblioteca Aldeana de Colombia, Ensayos, no. 55. Bogotá: Editorial Minerva, 1936.

Ospina Vásquez, Luis. *Industria y protección en Colombia, 1810–1930.* Medellín: Editorial Santa Fe, 1955.

Ossa V., Peregrino. "Coronel José María Gutiérrez, 'El Fogoso.'" *Ingeniería y Arquitectura* 13, no. 146 (March–April 1959): 36–37.

Otero D'Costa, Enrique. "El Coronel Santiago Fraser." *Boletín de Historia y Antigüedades* 15, no. 176 (June 1926): 475–483.

Otero Muñoz, Gustavo. "Cien cancilleres colombianos." In *Historia de la Cancillería de San Carlos.* Bogotá: Imprenta del Estado Mayor General, 1942.

————. *Historia del periodismo en Colombia (1791–1890).* Biblioteca Aldeana de Colombia, Periodismo, no. 6. Bogotá: Editorial Minerva, 1936.

————. *Semblanzas colombianas.* 2 vols. Bogotá: Editorial ABC, 1938.

————. *La vida azarosa de Rafael Núñez, un hombre y una época.* Biblioteca de Historia Nacional, vol. 83. Bogotá: Editorial ABC, 1951.

————. *Wilches y su época.* Biblioteca Santander, vol. 9. Bucaramanga: Imprenta del Departamento, 1936.

Ots Capdequi, José María. *Las instituciones del Nuevo Reino de Granada al tiempo de la independencia.* Madrid: Consejo Superior de Investigaciones Científicas, 1958.

Oviedo, Basilio Vicente de. *Cualidades y riquezas del Nuevo Reino de Granada.* Biblioteca de Historia Nacional, vol. 45. Bogotá: Imprenta Nacional, 1930.

Paredes, Jaime. *Caldas.* Bogotá and Medellín: Librería Siglo XX, 1946.

Parra, Aquileo. *Memorias de Aquileo Parra, presidente de Colombia de 1876 á 1878.* Bogotá: Librería Colombiana, 1912.

Parra, Caracciolo. *Filosofía universitaria venezolana, 1788–1821.* 2d ed. Caracas: Parra León Hermanos, 1934.

Parsons, James J. *Antioqueño Colonization in Western Colombia.* Rev. ed. Berkeley and Los Angeles: University of California Press, 1968.

Peirce, Bradford Kinney. *A Half-Century with Juvenile Delinquents; or, the New York House of Refuge and Its Times.* New York: D. Appleton and Co., 1869.

Peña, Domingo de la. "Biografía de Don Jacob Benjamín Wiesner." *Boletín de Historia y Antigüedades,* no. 192 (December 1927), pp. 730–739.

Pereira Gamba, Próspero. *Biografía del Professore Giuseppe Eboli, Napolitano.* Naples: Tiografía del Giornale di Napoli, 1871.

Pérez, Felipe. *Geografía general de los Estados Unidos de Colombia.* Bogotá: Imprenta de Echeverría Hermanos, 1883. [A completely different work from his 1862–1863 volume of the same title.]

————. *Jeografía física i política de los Estados Unidos de Colombia*. Bogotá: Imprenta de la Nación, 1862–1863.

Pérez Aguirre, Antonio. *25 años de historia colombiana, 1853 a 1878: Del Centralismo a la federación*. Bogotá: Editorial Sucre, 1959.

Pérez Arbeláez, Enrique. *José Celestino Mutis y la Real Expedición Botánica del Nuevo Reino de Granada*. Instituto Geográfico Agustín Codazzi. Bogotá: Antares, Tercer Mundo, 1967.

Pérez Ayala, José Manuel. *Antonio Caballero y Góngora: Virrey y arzobispo de Santa Fe, 1723–1796*. Bogotá: Imprenta Municipal, 1951.

Pizano, Marco A. "Una amistad de colegio." *Papel Periódico Ilustrado*, October 1, 1882, pp. 62–63.

Plaza, José Antonio de. *Memorias para la historia de la Nueva Granada desde su descubrimiento hasta el 20 de julio de 1810*. Bogotá: Imprenta del Neo-Grandino, 1850.

Pombo, Lino de. *Discurso de apertura de estudios pronunciado en la Universidad Departamental del Cauca el día primero de octubre de 1830 por el catedrático de matematicas*. Bogotá: Imprenta de B. Espinosa, 1830. [Pamphlet, Biblioteca Nacional.]

————. *Lecciones de jeometría analítica*. Bogotá: "El Día," 1850.

————. "Memoria histórica sobre la vida, carácter, trabajos científicos y literarios, y servicios patrióticos de Francisco José de Caldas." *La Siesta*, Bogotá, 1852. Reprinted in *Anales de Ingeniería* 8, nos. 98–100 (October–December 1896): 328–357.

————; Murillo, Luis María; and Bateman, Alfredo. *Francisco José de Caldas: Su vida, su personalidad y su obra*. Supplement to *Revista de la Academia Colombiana de Ciencias Exactas, Físicas y Naturales*. Bogotá: Librería Voluntad, 1958.

[Pontón Santander, Sista.] *Prospectos del Colejio i Escuela del Sagrado Corazón de Jesús, fundados en la capital de la Nueva Granada para la educación i enseñanza de los señoritos pensionistas i niños esternos*. Bogotá: Imprenta de Echeverría Hermanos, 1855. [Pamphlet, Fondo Pineda.]

Porras Troconis, Gabriel. *Historia de la cultura en el Nuevo Reino de Granada*. Seville: Escuela de Estudios Hispano-Americanos, 1952.

Posada, Eduardo. *Bibliografía bogotana*. 2 vols. Biblioteca de Historia Nacional, vols. 16, 36. Bogotá: Imprenta Nacional, 1917–1925.

————, ed. *Cartas de Caldas*. Biblioteca de Historia Nacional, vol. 15. Bogotá: Imprenta Nacional, 1917.

————, ed. *Obras de Caldas*. Biblioteca de Historia Nacional, vol. 9. Bogotá: Imprenta Nacional, 1912.

Posada, Eduardo, and Ibáñez, Pedro M., eds. *Relaciones de mando*. Biblioteca de Historia Nacional, vol. 13. Bogotá: Imprenta Nacional, 1910.

————. *Vida de Herrán*. Bogotá: Imprenta Nacional, 1903.

Posada Arango, Andrés. "Zea." *Boletín de Historia y Antigüedades* 8, no. 87 (August 1912): 174–177.

Powles, John Diston. *New Granada: Its Internal Resources*. London: A. H. Bailey and Co., 1864.

The Present State of Colombia. London: John Murray, 1827.

Programa de exámenes públicos de los alumnos del Colejio de San José de Guanentá en 1863. n.d. [Pamphlet.]

Programas para los exámenes del establecimiento de educación de Paredes é hijos, 1857. Piedecuesta: Imprenta de Paredes e Hijos por B. Bermúdez, 1857. [Pamphlet, Fondo Pineda.]

Programas para los exámenes del establecimiento de educación de Paredes é hijos que tendrán lugar en los días 20 a 31 de octubre de 1859. Piedecuesta: Imprenta de Paredes e Hijos, 1859. [Pamphlet, Fondo Pineda.]

Proyecto de código de instrucción pública para el Estado de la Nueva Granada acordado por el Consejo de Estado para presentarlo al Congreso de 1834. Bogotá: Imprenta de B. Espinosa, por José Ayarza, n.d. [Pamphlet.]

Pursell, Carroll W., ed. *Readings in Technology and American Life*. New York: Oxford University Press, 1969.

Quien es quién en Colombia. Bogotá: Editorial Kelly, [1945].

Reclús, Armando. *Exploraciones a los Istmos de Panamá y Darien en 1876, 1877 y 1878*. Madrid, 1881. Reprint. Panama City: Publicaciones de la Revista Loteria, 1957–1958.

Reclús, Elisée. *Colombia*. Translated and annotated by F. J. Vergara y Velasco. Biblioteca de la Presidencia de Colombia, vol. 47. Bogotá: Imprenta Nacional, 1958.

Reglamento del Liceo Granadino. N.d. [August, 1856]. [Pamphlet, Fondo Pineda.]

Rensselaer Polytechnic Institute. *Semicentennial Catalogue—Officers and Students of the Rensselaer Polytechnic Institute 1824–1874*. Bound with *Proceedings of the Semi-Centennial Celebration of the Rensselaer Polytechnic Institute*. Troy, N.Y.: Wm. H. Young, 1875.

"Representación dirigida al Rey por los padres franciscanos." *Boletín de Historia y Antigüedades* 24, no. 272 (June 1937): 333–337.

República de Colombia, Departamento Administrativo Nacional de Estadística. *Anuario general de estadística, 1965, culturales*. Vol. 2. Bogotá: Lithografía Colombiana, 1965.

Restrepo, Carlos E. "Doctor Mariano Ospina." *Boletín de Historia y Antigüedades* 7, no. 87 (August 1912): 129–156.

Restrepo, Daniel, S.J., and Hernández de Alba, Guillermo and Alfonso. *El Colegio de San Bartolomé*. Bogotá: Sociedad Editorial, 1928.

Restrepo, José Félix. *Lecciones de física para los jóvenes del Colegio Mayor Seminario de San Bartolomé de Bogotá*. Bogotá: F. M. Stokes, 1825.

———. *Publicación sobre instrucción pública*. Bogotá: Imprenta de la República, por N. Lora, 1825. [Pamphlet.]

Restrepo, José Manuel. *Autobiografía: Apuntamientos sobre la emigración de 1816, é indices del "Diario Político."* Biblioteca de la Presidencia de Colombia, vol. 30. Bogotá: Empresa Nacional de Publicaciones, 1957.

————. *Diario político y militar*. 4 vols. Biblioteca de la Presidencia de Colombia, vols. 1–4. Bogotá: Imprenta Nacional, 1954–1955.

————. *Historia de la Nueva Granada*. 2 vols. Bogotá: Editorial Cromos, 1952; Editorial El Catolicismo, 1963.

Restrepo, Vicente. *Estudio sobre las minas de oro y plata de Colombia*. Archivo de la Economía Nacional, vol. 7. Bogotá: Banco de la República, 1952.

Restrepo Canal, Carlos, ed. "Documentos del Archivo Nacional." *Boletín de Historia y Antigüedades* 24, no. 272 (June 1937): 331–371.

————. "Don José Félix de Restrepo." *Boletín de Historia y Antigüedades* 35, nos. 399–401 (January–March 1948): 163–184.

————. "Incidentes que dieron origen al Plan de Estudios de Moreno y Escandón." *Boletín de Historia y Antigüedades* 23, no. 266 (November 1936): 730–734.

————. *José Félix de Restrepo, jurisconsulto, humanista y hombre de estado, 1760–1832*. Bogotá: Editorial Kelly, 1970.

Restrepo Sáenz, José María, and Rivas, Raimundo. *Genealogías de Santa Fe de Bogotá*. Vol. 1. Bogotá: Librería Colombiana, n.d.

————. *Gobernadores y próceres de Neiva*. Biblioteca de Historia Nacional, vol. 63. Bogotá: Editorial ABC, 1941.

Rezneck, Samuel. *Education for a Technological Society: A sesquicentennial History of Rensselaer Polytechnic Institute*. Troy, N.Y.: Rensselaer Polytechnic Institute, 1968.

Richardson, Leon Burr. *History of Dartmouth College*. 2 vols. Hanover, N.H.: Dartmouth College Publications, 1932.

Ricketts, Palmer C. *Rensselaer Polytechnic Institute: A Short History*. Engineering Science Series, no. 29. Troy, N.Y.: Rensselaer Polytechnic Institute, 1930.

Rippy, J. Fred. "Dawn of the Railway Era in Colombia." *Hispanic American Historical Review* 23, no. 4 (November 1943): 650–663.

Rivas, Medardo. *Los trabajadores de tierra caliente*. Bogotá: Ministerio de Educación, 1946.

Rivas, Rafael. *El Colegio del Rosario i la clase de química*. Bogotá: Imprenta del Neo-Granadino por León Echeverría, 1851. [Pamphlet, Fondo Pineda.]

Rivas, Raimundo. "Informe sobre servicios del Doctor Alejandro Osorio." *Boletín de Historia y Antigüedades* 19, no. 223 (August 1932): 561–565.

Rivas Sacconi, José Manuel. "Panorama de la vida académica en el Nuevo Reino de Granada." *Boletín de Historia y Antigüedades* 37, nos. 423–425 (January–March 1950): 150–184.

Robinson, William D. *A Description of the Valley of Bogotá in the Republic of Colombia*. New York: J. W. Palmer & Co., 1824.

Robledo, Emilio. *Apuntaciones sobre la medicina en Colombia*. Cali: Biblioteca de la Universidad del Valle, 1959.

————. *Bosquejo biográfico del Señor Oidor Juan Antonio Mon y Velarde, Visitador de Antioquia, 1785–1788*. 2 vols. Archivo de la Economía Nacional, vols. 11–12. Bogotá: Banco de la República, 1954.

————. *La Universidad de Antioquia, 1882–1922*. Medellín: Imprenta Oficial, 1923.

————. *La vida del General Pedro Nel Ospina*. Medellín: Imprenta Departamental, 1959.

Rodríguez, Agustín. *Informe que presenta a la Sociedad Democrática el director de ella*. Bogotá: Imprenta de Nicolás Gómez, 1849. [Pamphlet, Fondo Pineda.]

Rodríguez, Jorge. "Sinopsis estadística de Antioquia." *Boletín de Estadística Departamental* [Antioquia, Dirección de Estadística Departamental], July 20, 1920.

Rodríguez Plata, Horacio. *La antigua provincia del Socorro y la Independencia*. Biblioteca de Historia Nacional, vol. 98. Bogotá: Publicaciones Editoriales Bogotá, 1963.

————. "Orígenes de la Universidad Nacional de Colombia." *Boletín de Historia y Antigüedades* 53, nos. 624–625 (October–November 1966): 609–622.

Rodríguez Rojas, José María. *Panorama de la educación colombiana*. Medellín: Editorial Bedout, 1963.

Roe, Joseph Wickham. *English and American Tool Builders*. New Haven: Yale University Press, 1916.

Rosenberg, Nathan. *Technology and American Economic Growth*. New York: Harper & Row, 1972.

Ross, Earle D. *Democracy's College: The Land Grant Movement in the Formative Stage*. Ames: Iowa State College Press, 1942.

Röthlisberger, Ernst. *El Dorado: Estampas de viaje y cultura de la Colombia suramericana*. Translated by Antonio de Zubiaurre. Archivo de la Economía Nacional. Bogotá: Banco de la República, 1963.

Roulin, François Désiré. *Histoire naturelle et souvenirs de voyage*. Paris: Hetzel, 1860.

Rudolph, Frederick. *The American College and University: A History*. New York: Alfred A. Knopf, 1962.

————. "Who Paid the Bills?" *Harvard Educational Review* 21, no. 2 (Spring 1961): 152–157.

Rueda Vargas, Tomás. *Escritos*. 3 vols. Bogotá: Antares, 1963.

Safford, Frank. "Significación de los antioqueños en el desarrollo económico colombiano: Un exámen crítico de las tesis de Everett Hagen." In *Anuario Colombiano de Historia Social y de la Cultura*, pp. 49–69. Bogotá: Universidad Nacional de Colombia, 1967.

Saffray, Charles. *Viaje a Nueva Granada*. Biblioteca Popular de Cultura Colombiana, vol. 110. Bogotá: Ministerio de Educación, 1948.

Salazar, José Abel. *Los estudios eclesiásticos superiores en el Nuevo Reino de Granada (1563–1810)*. Madrid: Consejo Superior de Investigaciones Científicas, Instituto Santo Toribio de Mogrovjo, 1946.

Samper, José María. *Historia de una alma, 1834 a 1881*. 2 vols. Biblioteca Popular de Cultura Colombiana, vols. 107–108. Bogotá: Ministerio de Educación Pública, 1946.

————. *Proyecto de ley sobre fomento de la instrucción pública presentado a la Cámara de Representantes por J. M. Samper.* Bogotá, 1864. [Pamphlet, Fondo Pineda.]

Samper, Miguel. *Escritos político-económicos.* 4 vols. Bogotá: Editorial de Cromos, 1925–1927.

Samper Ortega, Daniel. "Don Ezequiel Uricoechea." *Revista de la Academia Colombiana de Ciencias Exactas, Físicas y Naturales* 8, no. 32 (June 1952): 514–516.

Santander, Francisco de Paula. *Cartas y mensajes del General Francisco de Paula Santander.* Compiled by Roberto H. Cortázar. 10 vols. Bogotá: Librería Voluntad, 1953–1956.

————. *Correspondencia dirigida al General Francisco de Paula Santander.* Compiled by Roberto H. Cortázar. 14 vols. Bogotá: Librería Voluntad, 1965–1970.

————. *Diario del General Francisco de Paula Santander en Europa y los EE. UU., 1829–1832.* Transcription, notes, and commentary by Rafael Martínez Briceño. Bogotá: Imprenta del Banco de la República, 1963.

Sarrailh, Jean. *L'Espagne éclairée de la seconde moitié du XVIIe siècle.* Paris: Imprimerie Nationale, 1954.

Scarpetta, M. Leonídas, and Vergara, Saturnino. *Diccionario biográfico de los campeones de la libertad de Nueva Granada, Venezuela, Ecuador i Peru.* Bogotá: Imprenta de Zalamea, 1879.

Schenck, Ferdinand von. *Viajes por Antioquia en el año de 1880.* Archivo de la Economía Nacional, no. 9. Bogotá: Banco de la República, 1953.

Schmookler, Jacob. "Economic Sources of Inventive Activity." *Journal of Economic History* 22, no. 1 (March 1962): 1–20.

Schumacher, Herman Albert. *Biografía del General Agustín Codazzi.* Translated by Francisco Manrique. San Fernando de Apure: Tifografía Augusta, 1916.

Scientific American. *Technology and Development.* New York: Alfred A. Knopf, 1963.

Scobie, James R. *Argentina: A City and a Nation.* New York: Oxford University Press, 1964.

Scruggs, William. "Colombia and Its People" [December 20, 1882, and July 1883]. In United States, Bureau of Foreign Commerce, *Reports from the Consuls of the United States on the Commerce, Manufacturers, etc., of their Consular Districts,* vol. 10, nos. 31 and 32 (July 1883 and August 1883), pp. 111–114 and 223–226. Washington, D.C.: Government Printing Office, 1883.

Semanario de la Nueva Granada. Edited by Joaquín Acosta. Paris: Lasserre, 1849.

Shafer, Robert Jones. *The Economic Societies in the Spanish World (1763–1821).* Syracuse, N.Y.: Syracuse University Press, 1958.

Silvestre, Francisco. *Descripción del Reyno de Santa Fe de Bogotá escrita en 1789 por D. Francisco Silvestre, secretario que fué del virreinato y antiguo gobernador de la provincia de Antioquia.* Biblioteca Popular de Cultura Colombiana, vol. 121. Bogotá: Ministerio de Educación Nacional, 1950.

Silvestre, Luis Segundo de. *Proyecto sobre un instituto nacional de ciencias y bellas artes, presentado al ciudadano Presidente de la Nueva Granada, doctor Mariano Ospina R., por su secretario privado Señor Silvestre.* Bogotá: Imprenta de F. Torres Amaya, 1858. [Pamphlet, Fondo Pineda.]

Sinclair, Bruce. *Early Research at the Franklin Institute: The Investigation into the Causes of Steam Boiler Explosions, 1830–1837.* Philadelphia: Franklin Institute, 1966.

Soriano Lleras, Andrés. *Don José María y Don José Gerónimo Triana.* Bogotá: Editorial Kelly, 1971.

———. *Itinerario de la Comisión Corográfica y otros escritos.* Bogotá: Imprenta Nacional, 1968.

———. *Lorenzo María Lleras.* Biblioteca Eduardo Santos, vol. 14. Bogotá: Editorial Sucre, 1958.

———. *La medicina en el Nuevo Reino de Granada durante la conquista y la colonia.* Bogotá: Imprenta Nacional, 1966.

Steuart, John. *Bogotá in 1836–7.* New York: Harper and Brothers, 1838.

Struik, Dirk J. *The Origins of American Science (New England).* New York: Cameron Associates, 1948, 1957.

Tafur Garcés, L. "Expediciones y exploraciones científicos en territorios gran colombianos." *Boletín de Historia y Antigüedades* 42, nos. 485–486 (March–April 1955): 167–180.

Taylor, George Rogers. *The Transportation Revolution, 1815–1860.* The Economic History of the United States, vol. 4. New York: Holt, Rinehart and Winston, 1964.

Temin, Peter. "Labor Scarcity and the Problem of American Industrial Efficiency in the 1850s." *Journal of Economic History* 26, no. 3 (September 1966): 277–298.

Tewksbury, Donald G. *The Founding of American Colleges and Universities before the Civil War with Particular Reference to the Religion Influences Bearing Upon the College Movement.* New York: Teachers College, Columbia University, 1932.

Tisnes J., Roberto María, C.M.F. *Un precursor, Don Pedro Fermín de Vargas.* Bogotá: Editorial Kelly, 1969.

Triana y Antorveza. "La Escuela Náutica de Cartagena." *Boletín Cultural y Bibliográfico* [Banco de la República, Bogotá] 7, no. 8 (1964): 1372–1376.

True, Alfred Charles. *A History of Agricultural Education in the United States, 1785–1925.* U.S. Department of Agriculture, Miscellaneous Publications, no. 36. Washington, D.C.: Government Printing Office, 1929.

Tryon, Rolla Milton. *Household Manufactures in the United States, 1640–1860.* Chicago: University of Chicago Press, 1917.

Universidad de San Marcos, Lima. *Universidad de San Marcos de Lima, durante la colonización española (Datos para su historia).* With an introduction by David Rubio, O.S.A. Madrid: Juan Bravo, 1933.

University of Pennsylvania. *Biographical Catalogue of the Matriculates of the College (1749–1893)*. Philadelphia: Society of the Alumni, 1894.
Unos alumnos de Santa Librada. *Instrucción pública*. Cali, May 9, 1845. Cali: Impreso por Vicente Aragón, 1845. [Pamphlet, Fondo Pineda.]
Unos amigos de la educación. *Continua la cuestión del Colejio de Cali*. Cali: Impreso por Vicente Aragón, 1846. [Pamphlet.]
Unos amigos de la verdad i del jóven Eustaquio Urrutia. *Vergüenza pública*. Popayán, December 2, 1849. [Pamphlet, Fondo Pineda.]
Uribe, Joaquín Antonio. *Cuadros de la naturaleza*. Prologue by Emilio Robledo. Selección Samper Ortega de Literatura Colombiana, Ministerio de Educación Nacional. Bogotá: Editorial Minerva, 1936.
Uribe Angel, Manuel. *Geografía general y compendio histórico del Estado de Antioquia en Colombia*. Paris: Imprenta de Victor Goupy y Jourdan, 1885.
Uribe Uribe, Lorenzo, S.I. "La Expedición Botánica del Nuevo Reino de Granada: Su obra y sus pintores." *Revista de la Academia Colombiana de Ciencias Exactas, Físico-Químicas y Naturales* 9, nos. 33 and 34 (May 1953): 1–13.
———. "Francisco Javier Matís, el pintor botánico (en el segundo centenario de su nacimiento)." *Revista de la Academia Colombiana de Ciencias* 12, no. 45 (November 1963): 89–92.
Urrutia, Manuel José. *Una negra injusticia*. Popayán, November 28, 1849. Broadside. [Pamphlet, Fondo Pineda.]
Valle, Rafael Heliodoro. "Químicos mexicanos." *Historia Mexicana* 4, no. 1 (July–September 1954): 115–123.
Vargas, Pedro Fermín de. *Pensamientos políticos y memorias sobre la población de Nuevo Reino de Granada*. Archivo de la Economía Nacional, no. 10. Bogotá: Banco de la República, 1953.
Vargas Muñoz, Andrés. "Venancio González Manrique." *Boletín de Historia y Antigüedades* 2, no. 18 (February 1904): 364–368.
Vargas Reyes, Antonio. *El Dr. Rafael Rivas i la clase de química*. Bogotá, 1851. [Pamphlet, Fondo Pineda.]
Vargas Sáez, Pedro, C.M. *Historia del Real Colegio Seminario de S. Francisco de Asís de Popayán*. Biblioteca de Historia Nacional, vol. 75. Bogotá: Editorial ABC, 1945.
Vega, José de la. *La federación en Colombia (1810–1912)*. Bogotá: Imprenta de la Cruzada, 1912.
Vergara y Vergara, José María. *Historia de la literatura en Nueva Granada desde la Conquista hasta la Independencia (1538–1820)*. Notes by Antonio Gómez Restrepo and Gustavo Otero Muñoz. 3 vols. Biblioteca de la Presidencia de Colombia, vols. 48–50. Bogotá: Editorial ABC, 1958.
———, and Gaitán, J. B. *Almanaque de Bogotá i guia de forasteros para 1867*. Bogotá: Imprenta de Gaitán, 1866.
Vezga, Florentino. *La Expedición Botánica*. Biblioteca Aldeana de Colombia, Ciencias y Educación, no. 48. Bogotá: Editorial Minerva, 1936.

Walker, Alexander. *Colombia: Being a geographical, statistical, agricultural, commercial and political account of that country, adapted for the general reader, the merchant and the colonist*. 2 vols. London: Baldwin, Cradock and Joy, 1822.

Wilson, James Grant, and Fiske, John, eds. *Appleton's Cyclopaedia of American Biography*. 7 vols. New York: D. Appleton and Co., 1887–1900.

Zapata, Ramón. *Dámaso Zapata; ó La reforma educacionista en Colombia*. Bogotá: El Gráfico, 1961.

————. "Francisco José de Caldas." *Boletín de Historia y Antigüedades* 29, nos. 332–333 (June–July 1942): 555–579.

————. "Humboldt en Colombia." *Ingeniería y Arquitectura* 13, no. 147 (May–June 1959): 8–15.

Zerda, Liborio. "Jose Celestino Mutis." *Papel Periódico Ilustrado*, December 20, 1883, p. 103.

Periodicals

El Agricultor, Bogotá, 1868–1869, 1879, 1882–1884.

Anales de Ingeniería [Sociedad Colombiana de Ingenieros], Bogotá, 1887–1935.

Anales de la Escuela Nacional de Minas, Medellín, 1912–1937.

Anales de la Instrucción Pública en los Estados Unidos de Colombia [Ministerio de Educación Nacional], Bogotá, 1880–1889.

Anales de la Universidad Nacional de los Estados Unidos de Colombia [Universidad Nacional], Bogotá, 1868–1880.

El Antioqueño Constitucional, Medellín, 1846–1847.

El Argos, Bogotá, 1837–1839.

Boletín de la Sociedad Antioqueña de Ingenieros, 1915–1920.

Boletín Industrial, Barranquilla, 1872–1874, 1876.

Boletín Industrial [Pereira Gamba y Compañía], Bogotá, 1866–1875.

Boletín Industrial [Pereira Gamba y Compañía], Medellín, 1871, 1874–1879.

Boletín Oficial [Antioquia], Medellín, 1868–1879.

Colombia Ilustrada, Bogotá, 1889–1892.

El Comercio, Bogotá, 1883–1885.

El Constitucional del Cauca, Popayán, 1832–1834.

El Constitucional de Cundinamarca, Bogotá, 1831–1835, 1841–1842, 1844–1845, 1848, 1850–1852.

Correo Curioso de Santafé de Bogotá, Bogotá, 1801.

El Cultivador Cundinamarqués, Bogotá, 1832.

El Día, Bogotá, 1840–1851.

Diario de Cundinamarca, Bogotá, 1869–1876.

Diario Oficial, Bogotá, 1864–1880.

Economía Colombiana, 1954–1958.

Gaceta de Colombia, Bogotá, 1823–1831.
Gaceta de Cundinamarca, Bogotá, 1857–1860.
Gaceta de la Nueva Granada, Bogotá.
Gaceta Mercantil, Santa Marta, 1847–1850.
Gaceta Oficial, Bogotá, 1848–1861.
La Ilustración, Bogotá, 1870–1873, 1875–1876, 1882–1883.
La Industria, Bogotá, 1883–1889.
Ingeniería y Arquitectura [Universidad Nacional, Facultades de Ingeniería y Arquitectura; Asociación de Ingenieros], Bogotá, 1941–1963.
El Ingeniero [Organo de la Escuela de Ingeniería Civil y Militar], Bogotá, 1883–1884.
El Neo-Granadino, Bogotá, 1848–1857.
La Opinión, Bogotá, 1863–1865.
Papel Periódico de la Ciudad de Santa Fe, 1791–1797.
Papel Periódico Ilustrado, Bogotá, 1881–1888.
El Patriota, Bogotá, 1873.
El Pueblo, Medellín, 1855–1859, 1871.
La Reforma, Bogotá, 1878–1884.
Rejistro Oficial, Bogotá, 1861–1864.
El Relator, Bogotá, 1877–1879.
El Repertorio Colombiano, Bogotá, 1878–1899.
La Restauración, Medellín, 1865–1867.
Revista Comercial [Pereira Gamba, Camacho Roldán i Compañía], Bogotá, 1863.
Revista de la Academia Colombiana de Ciencias Exactas, Fisicas y Naturales, Bogotá, 1938–1967. [After 1957 entitled *Revista de la Academia Colombiana de Ciencias*.]
Semanario del Nuevo Reyno de Granada, 1808–1811. [Available in several incomplete runs in Fondo Pineda and Fondo Quijano Wallis, Biblioteca Nacional, Bogotá.]
El Tiempo, Bogotá, 1855–1860, 1861, 1864–1866.
El Tradicionista, Bogotá, 1871–1875.
El Vapor, Honda, 1857–1858.

Index

Abeja de Cartagena, La, 65
Acevedo Tejada, Gen. José, 169, 280 n.47
Acosta, Domingo, 147, 272 n.11
Acosta, Joaquín, 16, 75–76, 272 n.11, 292 n.43; foreign study of, 15, 147, 158, 305 n.35; as science professor, 103–105
Agricultor, El, 197
Agricultural production, 43, 275 n.40
Agricultural research, 197–200
Agricultural science, instruction in, 105, 138, 196, 198–199, 203
Agricultural technology, backwardness of, 26–27, 71–72, 191
Agriculture: National Department of, 197–199; National Institute of, 198; technical improvement of, 196–200; tropical, 43, 219–220, 223–224, 226
Agronomy, tropical, Colombian failure to develop, 223–224, 226
Anales de Ingeniería, 219–222, 225
Ancízar, Manuel, 68, 76, 125
Anillo, Bernardo, 94, 97, 286 n.22
Antioquia: rivalry of, with Bogotá, 203–205, 214–215; University of, 194
Aranzazu, Juan de Dios, 119, 280 n.47, 290 n.20
Araujo, Dr. José Dionisio, 106
Arboleda, Julio, 134
Arboleda Mosquera, Rafael, 165, 218, 308 nn.54 and 59
Architectural school, Bogotá, 76–77, 281 n.72
Arosemena, Mariano, 75
Arroyo, Isidro, 300 n.41
Artisan education. *See* Industrial education
Artisans: education of, in Colegio Militar, 176; organizations of, 72–74
Asylum of San José, Bogotá, 206

Banco de la República, 239. *See also* Bank, central
Bank, central, 233. *See also* Banco de la República
Banking, commercial, 188, 233. *See also* Credit institutions
Barco, Virgilio, 238
Bayón, Dr. Francisco, 103, 199
Barriga, Gen. Joaquín, 174
Barriga, Gen. Valerio F., 173
Basalla, George, 283 n.1
Bentham, Jeremy, 133
Bergeron, Aimé, 125, 172
Berrío, Pedro Justo, 204
Bolívar, Simón, 102, 109, 115
Bonpland, Aimé de, 94
Borda, José Cornelio, 164–165
Boston University, 162
Botanical Expedition, 93–94, 285 nn.20 and 21
Botany: instruction in, 104, 105, 198–199, 202, 204; study of, 87, 91, 93–94, 104, 153, 162–163
Bourbon administrators, Spanish: interest of, in scientific and technical knowledge, 83, 88–90, 92–93
Bourdon, Jacques, 102, 288 n.5
Boussingault, Jean-Baptiste, 101–103, 289 n.13
Bracho, Miguel, 310 n.18
Brain drain, 162–163, 183
Brown University, 155–156
Brugnelly, Luciano, 106–107
Brusual, Blas, 169
Buffon, Georges Louis Leclerc, Comte de, 284 n.13
Bureaucratic careers, 39–40
Bureaucratic orientation among Bogotá engineers, 215–216, 224–226
Bureaucratic tradition, Spanish, 6–7, 228

Bureaucratization of technical careers, 180–183, 215–216, 219–220, 224–226, 229–230
Business administration, instruction in, 206, 241. *See also* Commercial training

Cabal, José María, 91, 97
Caballero y Góngora, Antonio (archbishop and viceroy), 90, 93
Cabrera, Carlos Francisco, 93
Caicedo, Zenón, 216, 297
Caldas, Francisco José de, 63–64, 94, 96–97, 111, 167–168, 213
Callahan, William J., 14
Camacho Roldán, Salvador, 192, 282 n.75, 321 nn.12 and 13; as agricultural improver, 197–198, 230–231
Campomanes, Pedro Rodríguez de, 15
Canabal, Dr. Eusebio María, 280 n.47, 293 nn.43 and 45
Canal del Dique, 164, 170
Career orientation of university students, 99, 107, 109–110, 113, 120–121, 139, 193–194; compared to that in United States, 193, 287 n.1
Caro, José Eusebio, 66, 154, 280 nn.47 and 54, 293 n.43
Carrasquilla, Juan de Dios, 198–199
Carrizosa, Camilo, 224
Casa de Refugio: in Bogotá, 57–62; in Cartagena, 73
Caste designations, 34
Céspedes, Dr. Juan María, 103–104
Charles, Edmond, 126
Charles III, 86, 93
Chassard, François, 126, 129
Chemistry, study of, in colonial period, 91, 94, 97
Chemistry instruction: in artisans' schools, 204; in 1830s, 104–107, 110; in 1840s, 126–130; in 1850s, 135, 137–138; lack of, in colonial period, 95, 286 n.22; lack of laboratory, 289–290 n.17; in normal schools, 202–203
Cisneros, Francisco Javier, 165, 210, 217–218, 220, 314 n.53, 320 n.4
Civil conflicts, effects of, 44–45, 54–55, 208, 227; before 1850, 44–45, 54–55, 66, 115–116; 1850–1880, 54–55, 139–140, 164, 181, 185–186, 214; 1870–1900, 188, 189–190, 194–195, 199, 200–201, 204, 213; on primary education, 54–55; on public works, 189–190, 213; on technical education, 115–116, 139–140, 194–195, 196, 199, 200–201, 204, 208
Civil engineering, orientation of military training to, 166–168, 170–173, 310 nn.18 and 20
Clinton, Dewitt, 229
Codazzi, Col. Agustín, 126, 135, 182
Coffee Growers, National Federation of, 233, 239
Colegio del Espíritu Santo, Bogotá, 138
Colegio Militar, Bogotá, 143, 145, 158, 161, 166–167, 170–178, 180–184; academic standards in, 172–173, 175, 177; alumni of, compared to Colombians who studied abroad, 183; career appeal of, 180–182, 312 n.42; curriculum of, 171–173, 310 n.20; demise of, 167, 177–178; and development of bureaucratic technicians, 180–183, 215–216, 229–230; elitism of, 174–178, 184; employment of graduates of, 180–184, 209–210, 215–216, 230, 312–313 n.46; enrollment in, by region, 174–176; faculty of, 171–172, 310 n.20; motives for enrollment in, 172, 310 n.23; objections to, 173, 177–178; orientation of, to civil engineering, 166–167, 170–173; preparatory class in, 175–176; results of, 143, 145, 180–184, 229–230, 313 n.50; social origins of students of, 174–178, 311 n.30
Colegio Militar y Escuela Politécnica, Bogotá, 179
Colegios, financial resources of, 118, 137–138. *See also* Rosario, Colegio Mayor de Nuestra Señora de; San Bartolomé, Colegio Real Mayor y Seminario de; Santa Librada, Colegio de, Cali

Colegio-Seminario, Popayán, 91, 94

Columbia University, 156

Comisión Corográfica, 68, 173, 182

Commerce, School of, Barranquilla, 206

Commercial training: in England, 154–155; in United States, 154–155, 159, 303 nn.20 and 22

Concertaje. See Forced apprenticeship

Constitution of 1886, effects of, on public works, 190

Constitution of Rionegro, 185–186

Consumption standards, 38–39

Copernican system, dispute over, 87–88, 91

Correo Curioso, Erudito, Económico y Mercantil, El (Santa Fe de Bogotá), 94

Craft instruction. *See* Industrial education

Credit institutions, 45, 70–71

Cuellar, Patrocinio, 60–61, 139

Cuervo, Rufino, 64, 154, 280 nn.47 and 54, 293 n.43

Currie, Lauchlin, 239

Debt: foreign, 41–42; national, 41–42

De Francisco Martín, Juan, 228

De Greiff, Carlos Segismundo, 217

D'Elhuyar, Juan José, 92

Dirección General de Instrucción Pública, 109, 113, 293 n.43

Discontinuities in policy, 45, 163–164, 179–180, 190, 195–196, 199, 208, 230–232

Domestic Service, School of, 206

Domínguez, Benedicto, 97, 103

Dominican Order, opposition of, to Bourbon university reforms, 86–89

Dougherty, J. B., 218

Duque Gómez, José, 16, 113–114, 293 n.45

Eboli, Giuseppe, 125, 126, 129

Echavarría family, 239

Ecole centrale des arts et manufactures, 158, 323 n.38

Ecole des ponts et chaussées, 158

Ecole polytechnique, 166, 168

Economic opportunities, 40–41; and political behavior, 231

Education, higher, policy. *See* Higher education policy

Education, private, cost of, compared to foreign study, 306 nn. 44 and 45

Engineering, Colombian: compared to foreign, 221; criticized, 221–222; national spirit in, 221–222; specialization in, 201–202, 208, 235–237, 325 n.14

Engineering education: development of, in United States compared, 46; effects of politics on, 177–180, 194–195; before 1860, 101–102, 105, 126, 169, 170–172; 1865–1900, 179–180, 193–196, 198–199, 200–201, 204, 222, 224; enrollments in, 194–195, 198, 199, 237, 316–317 n.25; in military schools, 166–169, 170–173, 178–180, 194–195; in twentieth century, 235–237

Engineering profession, Colombian: defense of, 213, 216–221, 234, 236–237; development of, 143–145; development of, in Antioquia, 200–202, 204, 214–218, 225–226; 1864–1900, 193–197, 200–202, 209–226; role of Colegio Militar in development of, 181–184, 229–230; status of, 213, 237–240; in twentieth century, 237–240

Engineering science curricula: before 1860, 102, 105, 167–169, 170–172, 310 n.20; 1865–1900, 179, 195, 198–199, 200–202, 224, 318 n.48; in twentieth century, 235–236

Engineers, Colombian, employment opportunities for: of Colegio Militar alumni, 180–183, 210, 212, 312–313 n.46; of Colegio Militar alumni compared to foreign educated, 183, 210; before 1870, 45–46, 169–170, 209–210; 1870–1900, 201–202, 210–213, 215–218, 320 nn.3 and 4; of foreign educated, 163–165, 183, 210,

218; by region, 215–216; in twentieth century, 233–234, 239

Engineers, Colombian: as entrepreneurs, 224–225; regional differences of, 213–220, 225; salaries of, 312–313 n.46

Engineers and technicians in political leadership, 225, 238–239

Enlightenment, Spanish, 57

Escobar, Felipe S., 235

Escuela de Ingeniería Civil y Militar, Bogotá, 179–180

Escuela Nacional de Artes y Oficios, Bogotá, 206

Escuela Nacional de Minas, Medellín, 194, 200–202, 219; beginnings of specialization in, 235–236; employment of alumni of, 201

Escuela Náutica, Cartagena. *See* Nautical school, Cartagena

Escuelas de artes y oficios, 193, 204–205

Espinosa Escallón, Rafael, 164, 308 n.52

Espinosa Guzmán, Rafael, 207–208

Esquiaqui, Col. Domingo de, 93

Exports, 43–44, 187–188; as a source of policy discontinuities, 231. *See also* Foreign trade

Ezpeleta, José de (viceroy), 58, 90

Feijóo y Montenegro, Fray Benito Gerónimo, 10, 15, 86

Fellenberg, Philipp Emanuel von, 115

Fiscal resources, lack of, 199. *See also* Revenues, national and provincial

Forced apprenticeship, 56, 62–63

Fordham University. *See* St. John's College

Foreign engineers: attitudes toward, 216–221; importation of, in republican period, 101, 125, 170, 184; as models of industry, 170, 228; preference to, in employment, 170, 209, 210–213, 216–220, 320 nn.3 and 4

Foreign investment, 41–42

Foreign science professors: in Antioquia, 106–107, 137, 200, 204,

217, 322 n.24; attitudes of, 102–103, 127–128; in Colegio Militar, 172; effectiveness of, 126–129, 297 n.14; in 1820s and 1830s, 101–103, 106–107; in 1840s, 117, 119, 125–129; in 1850s, 137; after 1870, 198–199, 200, 202, 204, 322 n.24; salaries of, 101, 103, 118, 126–127, 297 n.14; salaries of, compared to those of Colombian professors, 107, 182

Foreign study, 147–165, 207–208; *antioqueño* interest in, 152, 156, 158; attitudes toward, 147–148, 149, 151, 152–155, 164–166, 222; and commercial training, 143, 154–156, 159, 161; cost of, 160, 306 n.45; in Europe, 147–149, 151, 157–159, 207–208; government supported, 147–148, 206–208, 305 n.37; of mechanical arts, 147, 153–154, 205–206; of medicine, 161; practical orientation of, 152–153, 158–160, 162, 207–208; results of, 159–165, 205, 306–307 nn.46 and 52, 313 n.50; of science and engineering, 15, 143, 145, 147–148, 153–154, 155–165, 205, 207–208, 218, 222, 236, 240; in United States, 148, 149, 151–157, 207–208, 305 n.33

Foreign trade, 43–44; expansion of, 148–149, 187–188. *See also* Exports

Freiberg, mining academy at, 158, 159

Galavis, José María, 66, 280 nn.47 and 54, 310 n.18

Gálvez, José de, 92

Garavito, Julio, 196

Garcés, Modesto, 218, 322 n.22

García Rovira, Custodio, 97

Geographic survey, national. *See* Comisión Corográfica

Georgetown University, 151, 159

Gólgotas, 173

Gómez, Col. Juan María, 290 n.20

Gómez, Dr. Estanislao, 290 n.20

Gómez, Laureano, 238

Gomila, Ignacio, 125

González, Florentino, 177, 280 n.54

González Vásquez, Juan Nepomuceno, 158, 161, 181, 220, 308 n.54, 313 n.52
Goudin, Fray Antonio, 89
Goudot, Justine-Marie, 102, 288 n.5
Guerra Azuola, Ramón, 281 n.72, 312 n.42
Guirior, Manuel de (viceroy), 87–89; viceregal government of, 57
Gutiérrez Vergara, Ignacio, 66, 280 n.47, 297 n.43

Harvard University. *See* Lawrence Scientific School
Herrán, Gen. Pedro Alcántara, 13, 75, 113, 144, 178, 272 n.11, 280 n.47; presidential administration of, 117, 124; as sponsor of Colombian students in United States, 151–157, 159–161, 164–165, 302 n.12, 303 nn.19, 20, and 25, 304 n.29
Herrán, Tomás, 308 n.52
Higher education policy: in colonial period, 86–91; 1821–1845, 99, 107–111, 116–119, 122–123, 168–169; 1845–1849, 124–125, 130, 133–134, 170–172; 1850–1863, 134–139, 177–178, 187; 1863–1900, 192–195, 196–198, 200
Holguín, Carlos, administrations of, 206–207
Hospicio. See Casa de Refugio
Houses of refuge, in United States, 58–59
Humboldt, Alexander von, 94, 95–96

Immigration, 42
Income levels, 35–38; of upper class, 275 n.31
Independence, effects of, 83–84
Industrial education: Caballero y Góngora plan for, 90; in Caracas, 71; of Colombians in United States, 77–78, 153–154; and conservatives, 57; 1830–1860, 49, 55–79; 1865–1900, 202–207; as instrument for social order, 49, 56–57; Liberal attitudes toward, 73–74, 281 n.62;

for lower classes, 55–74; in normal schools, 202; in twentieth century, 241; for upper class, 75–79, 115, 153–154; voluntarist efforts and, 63–69
Industrial expositions, 66–67
Industrial training. *See* Industrial education
Institute of Natural, Physical, and Mathematical Sciences, Bogotá, 125, 127
Instituto Caldas, 65, 68
Iron manufacture, 191–192
Irurita, José Rafael, 105

Jaramillo Uribe, Jaime, 14
Jesuit instruction, 85, 155; Conservative faith in, 119, 134, 149, 151; weakness in science in, 119, 295 n. 62
Jovellanos, Gaspar Melchor de, 13, 15, 278 n.31
Jussieu, Antoine Laurent de, 104

Lafayette College, 221
Lancaster, Joseph, 52
Lancasterian system, 52
Land distribution: effects of, 33; Liberals on, 274 n.21
Laneret, Louis, 92
Lanz, José María, 101
Laserna, Mario, 240
Law degrees, status of, 113
Lawrence Scientific School, Harvard University, 122, 157
Lawyers, excessive numbers of, 88, 112–113; and political turbulence, 116
Legal education: concern for standards in, 112–114, 116; efforts to restrict, 99, 107–110, 112–114; interest in, 99, 109–110, 120, 297–298 n.17; proliferation of, 109–111, 112; provincial reaction to restrictions of, 119–121
Legal profession, orientation to, in United States compared, 287 n.1
Lewy, Bernard, 125, 127–129

Liberal educational reforms, 134–136; effects of, 136–139
Liberal leaders, social origins of, 282 n.75
Liberal reforms, effects of, 136–139
Liévano, Indalecio, 300 n.41, 313 n.52, 320 n.10, 323–324 n.44
Linnaean system, 104
Linnaeus, Carolus, 87
Lleras, Lorenzo María, 16, 65, 280 n.54; on educational policy, 132–133, 293 n.43; as educator, 138, 179
Lleras Camargo, Alberto, 236
Lleras Restrepo, Carlos, 238
Lombana, Vicente, 16, 280 n.54, 293 n.45; on philanthropic societies, 65, 279 n.42
López, Gen. José Hilario, 53, 169, 173, 281 n.62; administration of, 125, 135–139, 181
Lozano, Jorge Tadeo, 94, 96–97, 286 n.22
Luaces, Ernesto L., 211

Mallarino, Manuel María, 154–155
Malo Blanco, Jesús, 160–161
Manrique C., Alejandro, 165
Mantilla, José María, 177
Manual training. See Industrial education
Manufacturing: in Antioquia, 191–192; attempts at, 26–27, 43–43, 62; in Bogotá, 191–192; in twentieth century, 233
Markham, R. Clements, 197
Márquez, José Ignacio de, 128–129, 144, 148, 297 n.12
Martínez, Rito Antonio, 177–178
Mathematics instruction: by Colegio Militar alumni, 182; in colonial period, 87, 89, 91, 94; 1830–1860, 105, 111, 126, 129, 137; in military training, 169–172; in normal schools, 202
Matís, Francisco J., 97, 103–104, 289 n.15
Mechanical training, 205–207. See also Industrial education

Mendicity, 57–60
Menocal, Aniceto, 211
Messia de la Zerda, Pedro, viceregal government of, 57
Meteorology, 199, 200
Michelsen Uribe, Carlos, 199–200
Military-polytechnical instruction, 96, 166–168, 171–173, 179–180; plans for, 96, 102, 112, 167–172, 177–180
Mineralogy instruction: before 1860, 101–102, 105, 106, 129–130, 138, 168; after 1860, 200–201
Mining economy, Antioquia: and technical development, 215
Mining schools, plans for, 101–103, 167–168, 200
Mining technology: improvements in, in Antioquia, 43, 92, 102, 106, 305 n.38; interest in, 92, 101–103, 167–168
Moderados, 56, 57. See also Neo-Bourbons
Montoya, Francisco (merchant), 228, 280 n.47
Montoya M., Francisco (science professor), 198
Moore, Tyrell, 158, 191, 305 n.38
Morales R., Enrique, 220, 305 n.33
Moreno y Escandón, Francisco Antonio, 66, 85–86, 88–89; university reform plan of, 88–89, 284 n.11
Mosquera, Gen. Tomás Cipriano de, 65, 281 n.64; and Colegio Militar, 169, 171, 173, 179; as disruptive politician, 230–231; first administration of, 65, 68, 124–135, 144, 169–176, 181, 209–210; policies of, favoring Colombian engineers, 144, 169, 209–210; and public works, 124–125, 144, 169, 173, 209–210; as supporter of science instruction, 124–125, 128; tensions of, with Radicals, 140, 185
Mosquera, Joaquín, 65
Mosquera, José María, 163
Mosquera, Manuel María, 126, 127
Murillo Toro, Manuel, 187, 282 n.75
Museum of natural history, Bogotá, 101–103

Musschenbroek, Peter van, 91
Mutis, José Celestino, 87–89, 91, 92, 93–94
Mutis, Sinforoso, 97–98, 286 n.21

National Academy, 64–65
National Federation of Coffee Growers, 233, 239
National market, development of, 232–233
National University, Bogotá, 194, 196, 198, 210, 236; creation of, 186, 193; and engineering specialization, 235
Nautical school, Cartagena, 169, 309 n.1
Neo-Bourbonism: decline of, 129–135, 192; and higher education, 99, 116–117
Neo-Bourbons: described, 12–17; goals of, 116–117
Nieto París, Rafael, 162, 223
Nollet, Jean-Antoine, 91, 105, 284 n.13
Normal schools, 193, 202–203, 205–206
Norton, William A., 156
Núñez, Rafael, 189, 206; administrations of, 179–180, 193, 205–206, 207
Núñez Conto, Juan Nepomuceno, 105

Obaldía, José de (vice-president), 178
Obando, Gen. José María, 231
Obregón, Francisco A., 290 n.20
Observatory, Bogotá, 68, 94, 97, 111, 135, 164, 196
Olavide, Pablo Antonio, 86
Ortega, Gen. José María, 171, 174, 310 n.18
Osorio, Alejandro, 130, 170, 280 n.54
Osorio, Benito, 105
Ospina, Pastor, 67, 151, 153–154, 159, 300 n.41
Ospina, Pedro Nel, 153, 159, 201, 225, 233, 238
Ospina, Sebastián, 153, 164, 303 n.19
Ospina, Tulio, 153, 201, 219
Ospina Barrientos, Santiago, 158
Ospina Pérez, Mariano, 225, 238
Ospina Rodríguez, Mariano, 13, 151,

178, 193, 219, 240–241, 280 nn.47 and 54; on education of sons, 149–151, 153, 156, 302–303 n.18; as educator, 101, 105, 114–116, 290 n.20; national educational policies of, 117–125, 129–130, 132–135, 230–231; program of, compared to contemporary United States institutions, 121–122, 295 n.68, 296 n.73
Otálora, José Eusebio, 205; administration of, 179–180

Papel Periódico de la Ciudad de Santa Fe, 58, 90
Paredes, Victoriano de, colegio of, Piedecuesta, 140
Parra, Aquileo, 282 n.75, 321 n.12
Parsons, Talcott, pattern variables of, 3
Pastrana Borrero, Misael, 238
Peña, Manuel H., 158, 161, 220, 305 n.37, 313 n.52
Pereira Gamba, Nicolás, 192, 197, 211
Philanthropic societies, 53, 56, 64–71; aimed at upper class, 75; decline of, 74; Liberal attitudes toward, 279 n.42; members of, 280 nn.47 and 54; in Panama, 67, 71, 75
Philosophy, modern, introduction of, 88–89, 90–91, 95, 97
Pineda, Col. Anselmo, 280 n.47; as proponent of industrial education in Panama, 67–68, 75
Pinzón, Cerbeleón, 105
Plata, Isidoro, 164
Plaza, José Antonio de, 96, 283 n.2
Political careers, absorption of elite by, 100
Political opportunities, as deterrent to development of technical elite, 99–101, 228
Pombo, Fidel, 307–308 nn.52 and 54
Pombo, José Ignacio, 111, 286 n.21, 292 n.34
Pombo, Lino de: aristocratic origins of, 291 n.33; family of, involved with useful knowledge, 97, 111, 174, 292 n.34, 307–308 n.54; as mathematics professor, 101, 105, 111–112, 292

n.39, 300 n.21; as neo-Bourbon, 13,
15–17, 111–113, 144, 230, 241; as
promoter of useful knowledge, 68,
101, 111–113, 125, 148, 280 n.54;
public posts of, 292 n.38; and public
works policy, 144; as shaper of
Colegio Militar, 168–173, 175, 177,
310 n.21
Pombo, Miguel, 97, 292 n.34
Ponce de León, Manuel, 182, 217–218
Poncet, Antoine, 69, 125, 170, 320 n.10
Population, of New Granada, 24
Porter, John A., 156
Posada, Father, 64
Practical orientation, 13; among
antioqueño engineers, 219; among
engineering faculty, Bogotá, 224–
225; in higher and secondary education, 240–241; neo-Bourbon desire
for, 228, 229; among parents in
Antioquia and Cundinamarca, 200;
among parents of Colombians studying abroad, 152–155, 159
Primary education, 49–50, 193, 240;
adult, 53; and social and economic
structures, 31–33
Proyectismo, 100
Public works: Colombian enterprise in,
210–212, 216, 224–226, 323–324
n.44; 1830–1870, 143–144, 169–170,
181–182; 1863–1900, 185, 187–191,
209–213; employment of Colombian
engineers in, 209–212, 218–220;
policy, 143–144, 169–170, 190–191;
in twentieth century, 232–235. *See
also* Canal del Dique; Railroad construction; Road construction
Purdue University, 157
Pureza de sangre, 34

Quijano, Dr. Manuel María, 103

Railroad construction: in Antioquia,
201, 215, 233; by Colegio Militar
alumni, 161, 166, 182; Colombian
enterprise in, 210, 211, 212, 216,
224–225; by Colombians trained
abroad, 161, 162, 165; debates over,

190, 211–212, 320–321 nn.11, 12,
and 13; 1870–1900, 186, 187, 188–
192, 216, 221–222; employment opportunities in, 145, 210–212, 217–
220; foreign interest in, 184, 210–
212, 216, 232–234, 313–314 n.53,
320 n.3; obstacles to, 10, 190–191;
priorities in, 190–191, 211–212,
320–321 nn.11, 12, and 13; retardation of, 188–191, 211–212; in
twentieth century, 232–233
Ramos, Abelardo, 195, 219, 220, 305
n.33
Rampon, Eugene, 125
Reed, Thomas, 76, 125, 170
Regional rivalry, 200–201, 203–205,
214–215
Rensselaer Polytechnic Institute, 122,
157, 211, 323 n.38; Colombians at,
156; compared to Ospina program,
296 n.73; Japanese at, 148; Latin
Americans at, 148–150, 160, 307
n.46
Restrepo, Carlos E., 238
Restrepo, José Felix: political roles,
96, 98; as propagator of modern
philosophy, 91, 94, 114–115, 285
n.16
Restrepo, José Manuel, 280 n.54,
311 n.35; contradictions between
career and doctrines of, 155, 230;
educational policies of, 108, 113, 288
n.6, 293 n.43; interest of, in industry
and industrial training, 15, 61; interest of, in science, 100, 108; neo-
Bourbon attitudes of, 61, 108, 113,
155, 230; in public office, 17, 108,
113, 155, 230, 293 n.43
Restrepo, Manuel, 155
Restrepo, Vicente, 159, 161
Revenues, national and provincial, 44,
189, 276 n.42, 314–315 n.9. *See also*
Fiscal resources, lack of
Reyes, Gen. Rafael, administration of,
232
Rivas, Medardo, 79
Rivero, Mariano, 101–102, 288 n.5
Road construction: by Colegio Militar

alumni, 166, 181–182; by Colombians trained abroad, 162, 164; 1830–1870, 45–46, 143–144, 181–182, 187–188; after 1870, 187–188, 211–212; by first Mosquera administration, 169–170, 181; in twentieth century, 233
Rodríguez, Juan N., 206
Rojas, Ezequiel, 130
Rojas Pinilla, Gen. Gustavo, 238
Romero, Fr. Francisco, 64
Rosario, Colegio Mayor de Nuestra Señora de, 13, 85, 88, 89, 135; scientific instruction in (colonial period), 87, 91, 94, 96; scientific instruction in (republican period), 105, 162, 182
Roulin, François Desiré, 101–103
Ruiz, Clemente, 92

St. John's College (Fordham University), 155, 159, 165
Salazar, José María, 95
Salesian Order, 207
Salgar, Fr. Felipe, 64
Samper, José María, 192–193, 282 n.75, 320 n.4
Samper, Miguel, 186
Samper, Santiago, 224
San Bartolomé, Colegio Real Mayor y Seminario de, 13, 85, 88, 91; scientific instruction in, 105, 182
Santa Librada, Colegio de, Cali, 118, 130, 132, 216, 297 n.14, 298 n.22; foreign science professors at, 119, 125–126, 129, 297 n.14
Santamaría, Eustacio, 158, 300 n.41
Santamaría, Nepomuceno, 300 n.41
Santamaría, Raimundo, 228, 280 n.47
Santander, Gen. Francisco de Paula, 16–17, 50, 147–148, 272 n.11; administration of, 52; on philanthropic societies, 65, 279 n.42; as proponent of Casa de Refugio, 58–62
Sanz de Santamaría, Carlos, 238
Sarrailh, Jean, 13
Savings banks, 70–71

School of Arts and Crafts, Antioquia, 215. *See also Escuelas de artes y oficios*
School of Domestic Service, 206
School of Engineering, National University, Bogotá, 179, 182, 193–196, 215. *See also* Escuela de Ingeniería Civil y Militar, Bogotá
School of Mines, Medellín, 215, 217. *See also* Escuela Nacional de Minas
Science, as instrument for social order, 83, 116
Science curricula: proposed by Caballero y Góngora, 90, 284 n.13; proposed by Lino de Pombo, 112, 171–172, 310 n.20; proposed by Moreno y Escandón, 88, 284 nn.9 and 13
Science instruction: in artisans' schools, 204; clerical resistance to, 86–91, 100, 287 n.2; in colonial period, 85–91, 94–95, 97; cost of, compared to that of traditional fields, 106–107, 118, 126–127; 1810–1845, 101–107, 110, 111, 167–168; 1850–1865, 135–140; 1865–1900, 193–196, 198–199, 200–201, 202, 204–205, 224; in Medellín, 105, 106–107, 137, 200–201, 204; in Mosquera administration (1845–1849), 125–129; in normal schools, 202–203; in private *colegios*, 137–138, 182, 299–300 n.41; programs for in colonial period, 88–91, 95; programs for, 1820–1850, 101–102, 108–109, 112–113, 117–121, 130, 293 n.45; programs for, 1851–1900, 177, 193, 198–199, 202–204, 311 n.36; in provincial *colegios*, 105–106, 125–126, 129, 130, 132; in United States compared, 121–122; in university in Cartagena, 105, 106; in university in Popayán, 105, 125, 126
Science professors, availability of: before 1850, 96–98, 100–105, 118–119, 125–126, 129; 1851–1890, 137, 162–163, 182–183, 198, 200–202; in United States compared, 288–289 n.10
—, salaries of, 118, 126–127, 291

n.26, 297 n.15, 313 n.49; compared
to those of other professors, 290–291
n.22; in United States compared,
288 n.10
Scientific community: absence of, 83,
95–98, 103–107, 162–163, 196, 200;
development of, before 1850, 92–98,
101–104; development of, 1851–
1900, 182–183, 196, 202, 213, 215,
219–225; in twentieth century,
233–237; in United States compared,
288–289 n.10
Scientific equipment, lack of, 107, 196,
198–199
Scientific and technical courses: lack of
student interest in, 107, 126, 139;
resistance to, 119–121, 126, 130, 132
Scientific study, economic irrelevance
of, 106, 122–123, 129–130
*Semanario de Agricultura y Artes
Dirigido a los Párrocos*, 63
*Semanario del Nuevo Reino de
Granada*, 63–64, 94–95, 97; distri-
bution of, 286–287 n.25
Sheffield Scientific School. *See* Yale
Scientific School
Shop culture, in England and English
America, 9
Shop training, 204–205. *See also* Indus-
trial education
Silliman, Benjamin, 156, 304 n.27
Social mobility, upward, 35
Social models, ambiguity of, 4, 228–229
Social stratification, 27–39
Social structure, as deterrent to tech-
nical development, 227
Social values: as deterrent to technical
development, 227; of Latin Ameri-
can upper class, 3; need for reform of,
33–34; in New Granada, 33–35
Sociedad Antioqueña de Ingenieros,
215
Sociedad Colombiana de Ingenieros,
157, 165, 195, 209, 213–214, 219–
221, 224–226, 234–235; membership
of, 213–215, 321–322 n.17
Sociedad de Agricultores Colombianos,
197

Sociedad de Artesanos, Bogotá, 72
Sociedad de Fomento Industrial, Car-
tagena, 67
Sociedad Democrática, 72
Sociedad de Naturalistas Neo-
Granadinos, 162
Sociedad de San Vicente de Paul, 206–
207
Sociedad Filantrópica: in Bogotá, 67;
in Panamá, 67, 71, 75; in Santander
region, 69, 71
Sociedad Patriótica de Amigos del Pais,
65
Sociedad Patriótica del Nuevo Reino de
Granada, 94
Society of Engineers, 216. *See also*
Sociedad Colombiana de Ingenieros
Spanish Pacification, effect on New
Granadan science, 97–98
Stevens Institute of Technology, 156,
157, 222, 323 n.38
Students abroad, social origins of, 152
Suárez, Marco Fidel, 234
Surveying, 143, 181–182, 210

Tanco, Carlos, 224
Technical dependency of Colombian
engineers, 223–224, 226
Technical development: economic
deterrents to, 11, 227; economic
incentives to, 229, 230; social structure and, 227; social values and, 227
Technical education: coercive
mechanisms in, 56–63; coercive
spirit in United States compared,
229; and conservatism, 17; and development, 11, 227; elite interest in,
15–16, 272 n.11, 305 n.35; as instrument for social order, 13, 49, 56–57,
83; and Liberals, 17–18, 73–74, 78–
79, 125, 132–140, 192–193
Technical innovations, Colombian,
characterized, 222–223
Technology, assimilation of, 208, 223,
227
Téllez, Carlos, 221
Temperance Society, Bogotá, 65
Totten, George M., 170

Trabajadores de tierra caliente, Los (Rivas), 79
Tracy, Henry, 170
Traditional professions, orientation toward, 120–121, 139
Transportation, coast to interior, 21, 24
Travel abroad, 15–16, 149. *See also* Foreign study
Triana, José G., 158, 162–163, 300 n.41
Trujillo, Gen. Julián, 197

Union College, 122
United States Military Academy, 156, 157, 323 n.38; Latin Americans at, 304 n.29; as model for Colegio Militar, 166–167, 173
Universidad Católica Bolivariana, Medellín, 236
Universidad del Cauca, Popayán, 236
Universidad de Santo Tomás, 85, 89
Universidad Republicana, Bogotá, 194
Universities, financial resources of, 117, 136–137, 294 nn.55 and 56, 308 n.56
University, Bucaramanga, 236
University, Cali, 236
University of Antioquia, 194
University of California, Berkeley, 156, 159; School of Mines at, as model for Escuela Nacional de Minas, 201
University of Lausanne, 159
University of the Andes, Bogotá, 240
University rectors, centralizing tendency of, 113, 293 n.43, 298 n.22
University revenues: in Bogotá, 294 n.56; in Cartagena, 294 n.55, 308 n.56
Uribe Uribe, Julián, 216, 322 n.23
Uricoechea, Ezequiel, 162, 300 n.41
Urrutia family, Popayán, 126, 296 n.4
Useful knowledge, Spanish Bourbon interest in, 86–87, 88–89, 92–93

Vagrancy, 57–60, 62, 274 n.19
Vagrancy laws, 62–63, 279 n.35; abandoned by Liberals, 73

Valencia, Guillermo León, 238
Valenzuela, Crisanto, 97
Valenzuela, Fr. Eloy, 64, 91, 97, 285 n.21
Value ambiguity, 3–5, 79, 225; among neo-Bourbons, 15–16, 116–117, 230; in twentieth-century Colombia, 241–242
Value orientations: achievement of, 34; ascriptive, 34; among Colombian elite, 128–129. *See also* Social values; Values, Colombian
Values, Colombian: efforts to reform, through foreign study, 151, 154; shift in, 241–242
Vargas, Dr. Antonio, 300 n.41
Vargas, Pedro Fermín de, 285–286 n.21
Vásquez, Uladislao, 164
Vélez, Alejandro, 272 n.11, 293 n.43
Vergara, Liborio, 297 n.14
Vergara y Caycedo, Felipe, 91
Veterinary medicine, instruction in, 196, 199
Villa, José María, 156, 205, 222

Wages, 29. *See also* Income levels
Wayland, Francis, 156
Wiesner, Jacob, 92
Wolff, Christian von, 284 n.9
Work ethic, efforts to inculcate: in lower class, 55–63, 73; in upper class, 4, 13–15, 33–34, 56, 75–79, 219

Yale College, 156, 159, 160, 162, 164, 304 n.27
Yale Scientific School, 122, 156, 157, 164, 304 n.27

Zaldúa, Francisco J., 16, 281 nn.62 and 64
Zawadsky, Stanislas, 125, 170, 310 n.15
Zea, Francisco Antonio, 91, 97, 101, 286 n.21